Xenotransplantation and Risk

Some developing biotechnologies challenge accepted legal and ethical norms because of the risks they pose. Xenotransplantation (cross-species transplantation) may prolong life but may also harm the xeno-recipient and the public due to its potential to transmit infectious diseases. These transboundary diseases emphasise the global nature of advances in health care and highlight the difficulties of identifying, monitoring and regulating such risks and thereby protecting individual and public health. Xenotransplantation raises questions about how uncertainty and risk are understood and accepted, and exposes tensions between private benefit and public health. Where public health is at risk, a precautionary approach informed by the harm principle supports prioritising the latter, but the issues raised by genetically engineered solid organ xenotransplants have not, as yet, been sufficiently discussed. This must occur prior to their clinical introduction because of the necessary changes to accepted norms which are needed to appropriately safeguard individual and public health.

SARA FOVARGUE is a senior lecturer in law at Lancaster University, where she specialises in health care law and ethics. Her main interests are clinical research involving human and non-human animals, risk and regulation with regard to developing biotechnologies and decision-making practices for vulnerable groups within health care law and practice.

Cambridge Law, Medicine and Ethics

This series of books was founded by Cambridge University Press with Alexander McCall Smith as its first editor in 2003. It focuses on the law's complex and troubled relationship with medicine across both the developed and the developing world. In the past twenty years, we have seen in many countries increasing resort to the courts by dissatisfied patients and a growing use of the courts to attempt to resolve intractable ethical dilemmas. At the same time, legislatures across the world have struggled to address the questions posed by both the successes and the failures of modern medicine, while international organisations such as the WHO and UNESCO now regularly address issues of medical law.

It follows that we would expect ethical and policy questions to be integral to the analysis of the legal issues discussed in this series. The series responds to the high profile of medical law in universities, in legal and medical practice, as well as in public and political affairs. We seek to reflect the evidence that many major health-related policy debates in the UK, Europe and the international community over the past two decades have involved a strong medical law dimension. Organ retention, embryonic stem cell research, physician assisted suicide and the allocation of resources to fund health care are but a few examples among many. The emphasis of this series is thus on matters of public concern and/or practical significance. We look for books that could make a difference to the development of medical law and enhance the role of medico-legal debate in policy circles. That is not to say that we lack interest in the important theoretical dimensions of the subject, but we aim to ensure that theoretical debate is grounded in the realities of how the law does and should interact with medicine and health care.

General Editors

Professor Margaret Brazier,
University of Manchester

Professor Graeme Laurie,
University of Edinburgh

Editorial Advisory Board

Professor Richard Ashcroft,
Queen Mary, University of London

Professor Martin Bobrow,
University of Cambridge

Dr Alexander Morgan Capron,
Director, Ethics and Health, World Health Organization, Geneva

Professor Jim Childress,
University of Virginia

Professor Ruth Chadwick,
Cardiff Law School

Dame Ruth Deech,
University of Oxford

Professor John Keown,
Georgetown University, Washington, DC

Dr Kathy Liddell,
University of Cambridge

Professor Alexander McCall Smith,
University of Edinburgh

Professor Dr Mónica Navarro-Michel,
University of Barcelona

Marcus Radetzki, Marian Radetzki, Niklas Juth
Genes and Insurance: Ethical, Legal and Economic Issues

Ruth Macklin
Double Standards in Medical Research in Developing Countries

Donna Dickenson
Property in the Body: Feminist Perspectives

Matti Häyry, Ruth Chadwick, Vilhjálmur Árnason, Gardar Árnason
The Ethics and Governance of Human Genetic Databases: European Perspectives

Ken Mason
The Troubled Pregnancy: Legal Wrongs and Rights in Reproduction

Daniel Sperling
Posthumous Interests: Legal and Ethical Perspectives

Keith Syrett
Law, Legitimacy and the Rationing of Health Care

Alastair Maclean
Autonomy, Informed Consent and the Law: A Relational Change

Heather Widdows, Caroline Mullen
The Governance of Genetic Information: Who Decides?

David Price
Human Tissue in Transplantation and Research

Matti Häyry
Rationality and the Genetic Challenge: Making People Better?

Mary Donnelly
Healthcare Decision-Making and the Law: Autonomy, Capacity and the Limits of Liberalism

Anne-Maree Farrell, David Price and Muireann Quigley
Organ Shortage: Ethics, Law and Pragmatism

Sara Fovargue
Xenotransplantation and Risk: Regulating a Developing Biotechnology

Xenotransplantation and Risk: Regulating a Developing Biotechnology

Sara Fovargue

CAMBRIDGE UNIVERSITY PRESS
Cambridge, New York, Melbourne, Madrid, Cape Town,
Singapore, São Paulo, Delhi, Tokyo, Mexico City

Cambridge University Press
The Edinburgh Building, Cambridge CB2 8RU, UK

Published in the United States of America by
Cambridge University Press, New York

www.cambridge.org
Information on this title: www.cambridge.org/9780521195768

© Sara Fovargue 2012

This publication is in copyright. Subject to statutory exception
and to the provisions of relevant collective licensing agreements,
no reproduction of any part may take place without
the written permission of Cambridge University Press.

First published 2012

Printed in the United Kingdom at the University Press, Cambridge

A catalogue record for this publication is available from the British Library

Library of Congress Cataloging-in-Publication Data

Fovargue, Sara, 1971–
  Xenotransplantation and risk : regulating a developing biotechnology / Sara Fovargue.
    p. cm. – (Cambridge law, medicine, and ethics ; 14)
  ISBN 978-0-521-19576-8 (Hardback)
  1. Xenografts. 2. Transplantation immunology. 3. Xenografts–Moral and ethical aspects. 4. Transplantation of organs, tissues, etc. I. Title. II. Series.
  QD188.8.F58 2012
  344.04′194–dc23
                                                            2011020298

ISBN 978-0-521-19576-8 Hardback

Cambridge University Press has no responsibility for the persistence or
accuracy of URLs for external or third-party internet websites referred to
in this publication, and does not guarantee that any content on such
websites is, or will remain, accurate or appropriate.

For Mia

Contents

Acknowledgements	*page* xiii

1 Introducing the issues — 1
What is xenotransplantation? — 1
Why focus on xenotransplantation? — 4
Themes — 5
  Risk — 5
  The public — 6
  Regulating risk — 7
  Challenges to legal and ethical norms — 9
  Public health and global concerns — 10
  Respecting individual and collective human rights — 11
Conclusion — 12

2 Dealing with risk — 14
The science — 16
  Immunological — 16
  Physiological — 17
  Microbiological — 18
Risk assessment: evaluating the risks — 19
  What could be transmitted? — 19
    Known infections — 19
    Unknown infections — 21
    Can xenotransplants transmit infections? — 21
Communicating and managing risks — 23
  Risk communication — 24
    Trust and confidence — 28
    (Dis)trust in practice – BSE in the UK — 29
    The fallout — 32
  Managing risks — 35
    Cost–benefit analysis — 36
    A precautionary approach — 37
    The harm principle — 39
    Precaution, harm and xenotransplantation — 40
Public health — 43
  Public health and xenotransplantation — 45
  Public involvement in the decision-making process — 47

x   Contents

	GM crops	49
	Gene therapy	51
	Xenotransplantation	51
	Involving the public in xenotransplant decisions	54
	Conclusion	57
3	**Regulating experimental procedures and medical research**	**61**
	Definitions	62
	Experimental procedures	62
	Medical research	64
	Genetically engineered solid organ clinical xenotransplants	65
	Regulatory schemes	70
	Experimental procedures	70
	The law	70
	Ethical guidance	76
	Xenotransplantation	78
	Regulating research	80
	The law	80
	Ethical guidance	81
	Xenotransplantation	83
	Selecting xenotransplant recipients	87
	Involving those with no other hope	88
	Xenotransplantation	90
	Offering experimental procedures	92
	The law	92
	Ethical guidance	93
	Xenotransplantation	93
	Offering medical research	94
	The law	94
	Ethical guidance	95
	Xenotransplantation	98
	Conclusion	99
4	**Regulatory responses to developing biotechnologies**	**103**
	Devising IVF national regulation	104
	Pre-clinical	104
	Post-clinical 1978–88	107
	Government-established committees	107
	Guidelines and reports from NGOs	108
	Statutory activity	109
	International activity	110
	Devising national gene therapy regulation	111
	Pre-clinical	111
	Post-clinical 1990–2000	113
	Government-established committees	113
	Guidelines and reports from NGOs	114
	Statutory activity	115
	International activity	115
	Emerging themes	117
	Devising national xenotransplant regulation	119

Contents   xi

Pre-clinical	119
Government-established committees	120
Guidelines and reports from NGOs	123
Statutory activity	124
International activity	125
Implementing the recommendations	127
National committees	128
New	128
Existing	132
Legislation	135
International regulation	137
Some problems with regulating developing biotechnologies	138
Global health and health tourism	138
Business, finance and 'the market'	141
Global regulation	143
Conclusion	144

5 Challenges to legal and ethical norms: first-party consent and third parties at risk   **148**

Consenting to being a xeno-recipient	150
Requirements of valid consent	154
Questions of competency	154
Can a xeno-recipient with no other hope be competent to consent to a clinical trial?	155
Competency status of those with no other hope	157
Voluntariness	159
Dual role	160
Obtaining consent	163
Informed decision-making	166
Who decides what should be disclosed?	167
What should be disclosed?	168
What should be disclosed to xeno-recipients?	172
Problems disclosing information	177
Changes to first-party consent for xenotransplantation	179
The nature of consent	179
The process	180
Third-party consent to xenotransplantation	183
Conclusion	185

6 Surveillance and monitoring: balancing public health and individual freedom   **189**

Pre-2000 proposed surveillance regimes	191
Local	192
Sampling and archiving	193
Xeno-recipients	193
Close contacts	195
Health workers	196
Additional requirements	197
Xeno-recipients	197
Procreation	198

Donation, post-mortems and tissue storage		200
Contacts		201
Health workers		202
National		203
International		204
Effective surveillance?		205
Post-2000 regimes		208
Consent, compliance and enforcement		211
Consent and non-compliance		212
Third parties		214
Withdrawing consent		216
Alternative methods of ensuring compliance		217
Contract law		218
Existing public health law		220
Existing criminal law		223
Introducing specific xenotransplantation legislation		226
Surveillance and human rights		228
Conclusion		233
7 Summary and concluding thoughts: looking to the future		237
Conclusion		245
Bibliography		247
Index		281

Acknowledgements

I am very fortunate to have been supported and encouraged by many friends and colleagues during the writing of this book. I am immensely grateful to all of them. In particular I would like to thank Hazel Biggs, Margot Brazier, Sharon Hinnigan, Barbara Mauthe, José Miola and Suzanne Ost. They know why and what they mean to me. I am especially grateful to Hazel and José for reading a draft of this book, and to José for his (painful) editing advice and patience. I would also like to thank Dave Archard, Wendy Doggett, Sue Eckstein, Bobbie Farsides, Jonathan Herring and David Price for their support. Research assistance has also been provided to me in various guises by Emma Cave, Catherine Deering, Tugba Dolan, Lorna Pimperton, Amy Salter and Tania Vazquez-Erosa. David Milman has been an incredibly supportive friend and Head of School, and I am grateful to Lancaster University for granting me study leave during 2010 which greatly assisted my completion of this book. Thanks also to Rodney Brazier, Nita Bright-Thomas, Claire Goli, Helen Higham, Jo Pinnock, Lisa Stoddart, and Frances Wareing for keeping me entertained and vaguely sane during this project. Janet Turnbull and Barbara Salter – thank you for keeping me going for nearly a decade. I cannot thank my family enough for helping and allowing me to find my way during some extraordinary times. My twin sister Bea, without whom I would not want to achieve anything, Gavin, Jack and Alex have provided much needed comfort and light relief. I hope I can repay my parents' continued encouragement, and I thank Ciaran for his inimitable support. Most of all I want to thank my amazing daughter Mia for incontrovertibly proving what is most important.

You have all helped me get here. Thank you.

1   Introducing the issues

A day rarely passes without a media report which suggests that 'miracle' cures for some diseases and conditions are imminent. This 'forward stampede' which advocates new (bio)technologies may distract attention from other, less technological, problems and solutions[1] and, to fulfil its promise, a developing biotechnology must move from pre-clinical to clinical trials. At this point, the relationships between science, ethics and law are brought into sharp focus. Xenotransplantation not only highlights these relationships but also the (ab)use of non-human animals. This is not my focus here; rather, I am concerned with whether and how xenotransplantation, a developing biotechnology which *may* benefit an individual but inherently risks harming others, can be accommodated within existing legal and ethical structures and conventions. What is at issue is how to appropriately reconcile private benefit with collective risk.[2] The risks of xenotransplantation are such that it necessarily challenges accepted legal and ethical norms and existing regulatory structures may thus be ill-equipped to deal with it, but insufficient attention has been paid to these challenges by policy-makers and regulators to date. English law is my base but I draw on legal and ethical material from other jurisdictions where appropriate to explore how, if at all, the problems I identify have been addressed elsewhere. My analysis and discussions are thus not dependent on a legal system similar to England's; my concerns and questions are relevant across the world because of the *global* nature of the issues and risks raised by this biotechnology.

What is xenotransplantation?

In England xenotransplantation is defined as 'any procedure that involves the transplantation, implantation, or infusion into a human recipient of

---

[1] F. Schumacher, *Small is Beautiful* (London: Vintage, 1973), p. 128.
[2] E.R. Gold and W.A. Adams, 'Reconciling Private Benefit and Public Risk in Biotechnology: Xenotransplantation as a Case Study in Consent' (2002) 10 *Health Law Journal* 31, 32.

either live tissues or organs retrieved from animals, or, human body fluids, cells, tissues or organs that have undergone *ex vivo* contact with live non-human animal cells, tissues or organs'.[3] Work on this biotechnology has been motivated by the consistent gap between the demand for and supply of human organs available for transplantation.[4] Pigs are currently the main focus as the source for these organs, and the hypothesis is that if pig organs are genetically engineered to minimise their rejection by humans, a never-ending supply of suitable organs, cells and tissues may be produced. The longest a human has survived with a non-human animal solid organ is nine months;[5] however, this chimpanzee kidney

---

[3] Department of Health (DH), *Xenotransplantation Guidance* (2006), p. 1 (at: www.dh.gov.uk/prod_consum_dh/groups/dh_digitalassets/@dh/@en/documents/digitalasset/dh_063074.pdf, accessed 16/03/11). Similarly, Australia – National Health and Medical Research Council (NHMRC), 'Animal to Human Transplantation Research (Xenotransplantation) – Definition: What is Animal to Human Transplantation' (2010) (at: www.nhmrc.gov.au/health_ethics/health/xeno.htm, accessed 16/03/11); Canada – Health Canada, Science & Research, 'Xenotransplantation' (2006) (at: www.hc-sc.gc.ca/sr-sr/biotech/about-apropos/xeno-eng.php, accessed 16/03/11); France – Comité Consultatif National d'Ethique pour les Sciences de la Vie et de la Santé (CCNE), *Opinion on Ethics and Xenotransplantation* (1999) No. 61, p. 2 (at: www.ccne-ethique.fr/docs/en/avis061.pdf, accessed 16/03/11); New Zealand – HRC (Health Research Council) Gene Technology Advisory Committee, *Guidelines for Preparation of Applications Involving Clinical Trials of Xenotransplantation in New Zealand* (2007), p. 3 (at: www.hrc.govt.nz/assets/pdfs/publications/Guidelines%20for%20Preparation%20of%20Applications%20Involving%20Clinical%20Trials%20of%20Xenotransplantation%20in%20NZ.pdf, accessed 16/03/11); Sweden – A Report by the Swedish Committee on Xenotransplantation, *From One Species to Another – Transplantation from Animals to Humans: Summary and Statutory Proposals* (Stockholm: Swedish Committee on Xenotransplantation, 1999) Swedish Government Official Report No. 1999: 120, Proposal for an act (2000: 000) for clinical trials on humans involving transfer of living biological material from animals (Xeno Licensing and Control Act), s. 1; Switzerland – Statement of Position of the SAMS (Swiss Academy of Medical Sciences), 'Medical–Ethical Principles of Xenotransplantation' (2001) 131 *Swiss Medical Weekly* 388, 389; US – US Department of Health and Human Services (DHHS), Food and Drug Administration (FDA), *PHS Guideline on Infectious Disease Issues in Xenotransplantation* (2001), p. 4 (at: www.fda.gov/downloads/BiologicsBloodVaccines/GuidanceComplianceRegulatoryInformation/Guidances/Xenotransplantation/UCM092858.pdf, accessed 16/03/11); Council of Europe, *Report on the State of the Art in the Field of Xenotransplantation*, CDBI/CDSP-XENO (2003) 1, p. 9, ch. 4 (at: www.coe.int/t/dg3/healthbioethic/activities/06_xenotransplantation_en/XENO(2003)1_SAR.pdf, accessed 16/03/11); World Health Organization (WHO), 'Xenotransplantation' (at: www.who.int/transplantation/xeno/en/, accessed 16/03/11).

[4] In the UK, e.g., 3,706 transplants were performed between 1 April 2009 and 31 March 2010 but at 31 March 2010 7,997 people were registered on the active transplant list, 2,545 were temporarily suspended from transplant lists, and 552 patients died waiting for a transplant: NHS Blood and Transplant, *Activity Report 2009–2010, Transplant Activity in the UK* (2010), pp. 1, 3–4 (at: www.uktransplant.org.uk/ukt/statistics/transplant_activity_report/transplant_activity_report.jsp, accessed 16/03/11).

[5] K. Reemtsma *et al.*, 'Renal Heterotransplantation in Man' (1964) 160 *Annals of Surgery* 384.

was not genetically engineered and the viability of a genetically engineered pig organ in a human is unknown. Clinical cellular xenotransplants have been performed,[6] but a clinical xenotransplant of a genetically engineered solid organ has yet to be reported. This is my focus.

If genetically engineered solid organ xenotransplants are able to prolong and maintain life the individual recipient will have benefited. Society will also benefit from their return to work and increased productivity, minimising ill health and disease, confidence in science and medicine may increase, and 'spin-offs' from the biotechnology may develop.[7] Xenotransplants may also be preferable to allotransplants (human-to-human transplants) by enabling operations to be timed for the patient's benefit and not when an organ becomes available, reducing time in hospital, minimising the need for immunosuppression, providing an unlimited source of organs, and circumventing the difficulties of obtaining consent for donation.[8] The initial immunological barriers to solid organ xenotransplantation *may* have been negotiated via the use of genetically engineered pigs, but other potential physiological and microbiological barriers have been identified and remain unaddressed, as discussed in Chapter 2.[9] Of particular concern is the risk of transmitting infectious diseases across the species barrier and from the xeno-recipient to her close contacts, relatives *and* the wider public, causing pandemics.[10] The risk of transmitting infectious diseases is widely acknowledged but there is no consensus on the nature, extent or degree of it. The diseases may be known, such as porcine endogenous retroviruses, and unknown; making it difficult to devise detection tests, respond to any infections, or monitor their existence and spread. Some diseases may be latent, with the length of this also unknown. Nevertheless, pre-clinical research into genetically engineered solid organ xenotransplantation continues,[11] even though other biotechnological advances, such as cloning and stem cells, have led the utility of this

---

[6] R.B. Elliott *et al.*, 'Live Encapsulated Porcine Islets from A Type 1 Diabetic Patient 9.5 Years after Xenotransplantation' (2007) 14 *Xenotransplantation* 157.
[7] P.D. Kumar, 'Xenotransplantation in the New Millennium: Moratorium or Cautious Experimentation?' (2000) 4 *Perspectives in Biology and Medicine* 562, 569.
[8] NHMRC, *Discussion Paper – Xenotransplantation: A Review of the Parameters, Risks and Benefits* (2009), pp. 20–21 (at: www.nhmrc.gov.au/_files_nhmrc/file/about/committeess/expert/gtrap/nhmrc_xeno_discussion_paper_website.pdf, accessed 16/03/11).
[9] G. Griffin and D. Muir, *Infection Risks in Xenotransplantation* (London: DH, 2001); J.M. Dobson, J.H. Dark, *The Physiology of Xenotransplantation* (London: DH, 2002).
[10] D. Butler, 'Last Chance to Stop and Think on Risks of Xenotransplants' (1998) 391 *Nature* 320.
[11] See reports in *Xenotransplantation* (at: www.wiley.com/bw/journal.asp?ref=0908–665X, accessed 16/03/11).

type of xenotransplantation to be questioned.[12] Despite these problems it has been suggested that a small number of clinical trials should be permitted in order to determine the nature and extent of these barriers and risks.[13]

Why focus on xenotransplantation?

I focus on xenotransplantation for two reasons; first, it is a developing biotechnology with profound inherent risks which go beyond the intended beneficiary. Performing an experimental procedure or embarking on clinical trials is always risky but when this involves a biotechnology which has the potential to prolong or save millions of lives with a market worth millions of dollars, the drive to clinically proceed may be irresistible. Indeed, '[t]he "technological imperative" to keep pushing back the barriers can place enormous strains on our legal and ethical institutions and frameworks of analysis. Yet the huge therapeutic potential requires us to embrace and confront these questions.'[14] In the light of this, I use xenotransplantation as an example to explore *how* risks can be regulated and discuss the importance of public involvement in decision-making. One question which must be publicly considered is whether some risks are too great to take, despite their potential to prolong or save life, because of the need to protect public health from serious infectious diseases with uncertain and unknown consequences.

Secondly, the nature and extent of these risks are such that existing legal and ethical frameworks may not offer sufficient protection to xeno-recipients and others. There has been a trend in many Western countries to base health care systems on concepts of individual autonomy and individual rights, but the implications of biotechnologies such as xenotransplantation support not only the calls for a rethinking of autonomy but also the suggestion that individual autonomy *cannot* be the central ethical principle in health care.[15] More particularly, '[x]enotransplantation

---

[12] United Kingdom Xenotransplantation Interim Regulatory Authority (UKXIRA), *Third Annual Report September 1999–November 2000* (London: DH, 2001), para. 6.19.

[13] A.S. Daar, 'Xenotransplantation: Three Questions to Advance the Discourse' (2000) *British Medical Journal* (at: www.bmj.com/content/320/7238/868/reply#bmj_el_7566, accessed 16/03/11).

[14] D. Price, *Legal and Ethical Aspects of Organ Transplantation* (Cambridge University Press, 2000), p. 2.

[15] N. Manson and O. O'Neill, *Rethinking Informed Consent in Bioethics* (Cambridge University Press, 2007); M. Brazier, 'Do No Harm – Do Patients Have Responsibilities Too?' (2006) 65 *Cambridge Law Journal* 397; A. Dawson and E. Garrard, 'In Defence of Moral Imperialism: Four Equal and Universal Prima Facie Principles' (2006) 32 *Journal of Medical Ethics* 200; O. O'Neill, *Autonomy and*

raises issues such as the protection of the interests of future generations, the prevention of harm, the acceptance of some harm for the achievement of a "higher good", or the supremacy of the freedom to choose (autonomy)'.[16] The risks of xenotransplantation highlight the fact that we are interconnected individuals who are related to, interdependent and reliant on others. Thus, health care systems which are premised on legal and ethical notions of individual autonomy alone may not be appropriate for xenotransplantation with its potential to harm the intended beneficiary *and* others. However, there is a tendency to assume that such developments *can* fit into existing regulatory structures, an assumption I challenge.

Before setting out the themes which underpin this book I want to make it clear that I am not arguing that xenotransplantation *is* a viable solution to overcoming the shortage of human organs available for transplantation. In fact I would suggest that the science has not advanced sufficiently to merit clinical trials, and that there are other less risky alternatives.[17] However, the fact that pre-clinical research continues, as do claims about the imminence of solid organ clinical trials,[18] necessitates that the legal and ethical implications, ramifications, and realities of clinical xenotransplants are analysed.

Themes

Risk

Risk, its nature, understanding of it, the possibility of explaining and then regulating it, is central to this book because much is still unknown and uncertain about xenotransplantation. In Chapter 2 I discuss the potential risks involved in the biotechnology and in Chapter 6 I explore some suggestions for managing, controlling and regulating them. One of the problems is that '[i]n the absence of hard data,

---

Trust in Bioethics (Cambridge University Press, 2002); D. Beyleveld and R. Brownsword, *Human Dignity in Bioethics and Biolaw* (Oxford University Press, 2001), ch. 2.

[16] Gold and Adams, 'Reconciling Private Benefit', 46.

[17] See, e.g., J.K. Mason and G.T. Laurie, *Mason & McCall Smith's Law and Medical Ethics* (8th edn, Oxford University Press, 2011), ch. 17; J. Herring, *Medical Law and Ethics* (Oxford University Press, 2010), ch. 8; E. Jackson, *Medical Law: Text, Cases and Materials* (Oxford University Press, 2010), ch. 11.

[18] E.g., R.N. Pierson *et al.*, 'Current Status of Xenotransplantation and Prospects for Clinical Application' (2009) 16 *Xenotransplantation* 263; D.K.C. Cooper *et al.*, 'Recent Advances in Pig-to-Human Organ and Cell Transplantation' (2008) 8 *Expert Opinion in Biological Therapeutics* 1.

attempts to assess risks and develop a rational policy are exercises in reasoned speculation',[19] and these questions need addressing:

> [h]ow can we appraise and predict such unknown health risks? What kind of balance ideally should be struck between our obligations to accept some risk to ourselves in order to benefit designated individuals or groups of individuals whose lives might be sustained through our actions, and our obligation to protect and foster the health of the community – locally, nationally, and internationally? And if a biomedical procedure with the characteristics of xenotransplantation is clinically initiated, with what kinds of precautions, surveillance, social controls, and regulations should it be surrounded?[20]

Where the risks are unidentifiable or latent until a biotechnology is clinically in use, effective risk management will be difficult if not impossible to attain. There may be ways to regulate risk, such as a moratorium or via the precautionary principle, but will these strategies appropriately safeguard public health while also offering the possibility of benefit to individuals in need? Xenotransplantation raises questions about acceptance and understanding of uncertainty and risk, personally and to others, questions which it may not be possible to address prior to its clinical introduction. We are not experienced in assessing risks and benefits which go beyond the individual; thus, 'the key question today is how to develop an ethics discourse adequately evaluating the balance between a low (or unknown) risk of occurrence of an adverse event against the enormous negative consequences should that event come to pass'.[21] These issues are explored in Chapters 2 and 5.

The public

The lack of knowledge about the risks of xenotransplantation may have an impact on public confidence in and an understanding of science, both of which are crucial because of these risks. British experiences of the Bovine Spongiform Encephalopathy (BSE) crisis and the introduction of genetically modified (GM) crops highlight the importance of such confidence, trust and understanding, and the risks of xenotransplantation are such that public consultation and engagement is

---

[19] L. Chapman, 'Speculation, Stringent Reasoning and Science' (1999) 77 *Bulletin of the World Health Organization* 68, 69.
[20] R.C. Fox and J.P. Swazey, *The Courage to Fail – A Social View of Organ Transplants and Dialysis* (New Brunswick, NJ: Transaction, 2002), pp. xviii–xix.
[21] A.S. Daar, 'Xenotransplantation – Science, Risk and International Regulatory Efforts', in T.A. Caulfield and B. William-Jones (eds.), *The Commercialization of Genetic Research – Ethical, Legal and Policy Issues* (New York, NY: Kluwer Academic, 1999), pp. 129, 130.

crucial. However, traditionally, only the consent of the individual recipient is required to an experimental procedure or to authorise a person's involvement in a clinical trial, rather than a more general 'community consent'. There is thus little space for wider considerations and discussions. However, the risks of xenotransplantation require public participation and involvement in decision-making processes as this is a novel biotechnology,[22] and genetically engineered solid organ xenotransplants should not be performed without this because '[t]he public must be able to make informed choices with regard to practices which could endanger the future of our species and the principle of human dignity'.[23] Yet the value of such consultation may be limited if public understanding of risk along with the means of expressing it are poor or similarly restricted. I discuss ways to address these points in Chapter 2.

Public consultations are becoming more common in England,[24] and while they can be criticised for limited publicity and appealing to respondents with vested interests, difficulties or concerns about such consultations should not be used as excuses not to engage in them. Experiences of and lessons from public consultations in other areas and jurisdictions must be drawn on to improve what will always be an imperfect exercise, and in Chapter 2 I discuss how public debate and consultation on biotechnologies can be encouraged, while acknowledging that this will not be straightforward given that where ethically sensitive topics are concerned consensus is unlikely. Nevertheless, the public need to be involved in the decision-making process surrounding xenotransplantation because they are, essentially, being *expected* to accept risks to themselves without specifically consenting to them. If some form of participatory decision-making is not possible, it is important to consider whether a biotechnology which inherently risks public health should be introduced.

Regulating risk

Having set out the risks involved in xenotransplantation and the importance of public involvement in decisions to accept such risks,

---

[22] J. Wilsdon and R. Willis, *See-through Science: Why Public Engagement Needs to Move Upstream* (London: Demos, 2004), p. 12.
[23] N. Lenoir, 'Biotechnology, Bioethics and Law: Europe's 21st Century Challenge' (2006) 69 *Modern Law Review* 1, 5.
[24] E.g., DH, 'Consultations' (at: www.dh.gov.uk/en/Consultations/Liveconsultations/index.htm, accessed 16/03/11); Human Fertilisation and Embryology Authority (HFEA), 'Consultations & Reviews of Policy' (at: www.hfea.gov.uk/122.html, accessed 16/03/11).

I explore how law regulates risk in two contexts. First, in Chapter 3 I consider how experimental procedures and medical research are defined and regulated, and discuss which category the first genetically engineered solid organ xenotransplant will fall into. This is important because while medical research in the form of clinical trials is now statutorily regulated in England,[25] regulation of the former is less clear. I consider whether the current regulatory regimes are appropriate in the light of the risks of xenotransplantation, and then discuss selecting the first recipients. This matters because the needs and demands of those who are desperately ill must be balanced with the wider demands of society; for health protection and medical advances. I explore whether the suggested first recipients (those with no other hope) will be adequately safeguarded when deciding to receive a xenotransplant under existing regulatory schemes. I also introduce some issues explored further in Chapter 5 regarding whether the principle of autonomy supports allowing people to sacrifice themselves in the (limited) hope of gaining some benefit to themselves, but with the more likely outcome of providing information for future generations. I question whether the extraordinary risks of xenotransplantation mean that individual autonomy *must* be legally limited with regard to this biotechnology. Essentially, can A's need for a xenotransplant outweigh B and C's need not to have their health and life jeopardised?

Secondly, in Chapter 4, I discuss how risk is regulated by considering the regulatory schemes which have been proposed and adopted for *in vitro* fertilisation (IVF), gene therapy and xenotransplantation. These biotechnologies have all stretched the limits of and, to some extent, changed or led to questions about the boundaries of science and what it is to be human. Thus, alongside a country's general regulatory framework on experimental procedures or medical research, a further layer of specific regulation has been considered or introduced for these developing biotechnologies. I explore how these schemes were devised and implemented, and highlight the problems of regulating *developing* biotechnologies. These regulatory issues are important because there is a concern that ethical discussions and debate occur too late in the regulatory process, when the move from laboratory to the hospital seems inevitable and unstoppable. Furthermore, where the risks of a biotechnology go beyond the individual, I suggest that public involvement in regulatory decision-making is essential and any regulatory body must encourage this.

---

[25] The Medicines for Human Use (Clinical Trials) Regulations 2004, SI 2004 No. 1031.

Challenges to legal and ethical norms

The risks of xenotransplantation require a reconsideration of general and specific regulatory schemes *and* challenge accepted legal and ethical norms, especially those premised on individual consent. The precedence given to autonomy in many Western countries has been questioned,[26] and some developing biotechnologies further highlight the difficulties with this legal and bioethical principle, particularly in prioritising it over other concepts. Xenotransplantation thus requires a review of the balance between the autonomy of the individual and community interests in public health. While '*intense individualism* – possible individualism to the exclusion of any real sense of community'[27] has been in evidence in areas such as euthanasia and reproductive technologies, 'respecting the rights of the individuals who make up a society, important as this is, is not always sufficient to protect the society itself. Sometimes, in carefully justified instances, to do so we must give priority to the needs of the community over the claims of individuals.'[28] Given the risks, xenotransplantation is a developing biotechnology where individual autonomy should not automatically rule; rather, a more communitarian and public health perspective is appropriate where 'the acceptability of an action is to be judged by the goodness or badness of its effect not on an individual *per se* but on persons as interdependent units of society'.[29] Thus, while the exercise of individual autonomy may lead to self-fulfilment, 'there is a social dimension to life which is potentially equally enriching. Autonomy must be qualified by the legitimate interests and expectations of others . . .'[30]

However, as discussed in Chapter 5, in many countries involvement in experimental procedures, medical research, and/or medical practice generally only require the consent of the individual concerned. I explore whether existing consent practices in England are legally and ethically sufficient and appropriate for xenotransplantation; consider the process of obtaining consent; and whether 'first-party' consent offers sufficient protection where a biotechnology exposes the recipient *and* others to risks. Consenting to a genetically engineered solid organ xenotransplant will involve two layers: (i) to the experimental procedure or clinical trial; and (ii) to the surveillance and monitoring regime, considered in Chapter 6, which is necessary because of the risks. This dual consent

---

[26] Above, n. 15.
[27] M.A. Sommerville, 'Searching for Ethics in a Secular Society', in *Ethics of Science and Technology, Explorations of the Frontiers of Science and Ethics* (Paris: UNESCO, 2006), p. 22, emphasis in original.
[28] *Ibid.*, p. 23.   [29] Mason and Laurie, *Mason & McCall Smith's*, p. 7.   [30] *Ibid.*, p. 8.

raises a number of questions including whether consent will be required from xeno-recipients *and* others such as their contacts and relatives, whether if the former but not the latter consent the recipient's involvement is prohibited, and whether the accepted right to withdraw from a clinical trial can remain in this context. Furthermore, first-party consent as currently conceived may not adequately safeguard and protect the third parties affected by the xenotransplant, particularly with regard to complying with the surveillance regime. Thus, obtaining 'third-party' consent from contacts, relatives and relevant health professionals to the post-xenotransplant surveillance regime also needs to be considered, and introducing this will set xenotransplantation further apart from other biotechnologies, medical research and treatments. However, the legal and ethical implications of xenotransplantation have not been seriously considered to date despite the fact that 'many of the proposals which are being considered by the policy making community are not consistent with current legal frameworks'.[31]

I thus suggest that 'a decision must be made within a given community as to whether to even allow the products of innovation to be applied'.[32] If it is not possible to implement a system for this, then the clinical introduction of xenotransplantation needs careful consideration; specifically, how should, or can, potentially competing interests be balanced? Is it a choice between individual autonomy, choice and independence, and public health, protection and societal benefit? Given the risks, might xenotransplantation be a biotechnology which people *should not* be able to consent to because while the potential benefit is to the individual, the risks are to society?

Public health and global concerns

Xenotransplantation highlights the global nature of advances in health, risk,[33] and some issues and problems with identifying and monitoring risks internationally. For example, if genetically engineered solid organ xenotransplants are prohibited in country V, will a patient be prevented from having the operation in country X or Y and, if so, how will this occur? If such xeno-tourism cannot be prevented, will it be possible to minimise the risks to the xeno-recipient and others? Some consulates hold records on their citizens who seek medical treatment overseas but as

---

[31] T.A. Caulfield, G.B. Robertson, 'Xenotransplantation: Consent, Public Health and Charter Issues' (2001) 5 *Medical Law International* 81, 82.
[32] Gold and Adams, 'Reconciling Private Benefit', 33.
[33] U. Beck, *Risk Society: Towards A New Modernity* (London: Sage, 1992).

the risks of xenotransplantation go beyond the recipient and are global in nature, in all the countries which have considered this biotechnology *specific* surveillance and monitoring schemes have been suggested and/or introduced.[34] In Chapter 6 I explore whether the schemes are or will be sufficient to control and monitor the known, unknown and unidentifiable risks posed by xenotransplantation. Of particular concern is xenotransplantation's global risk, risk which has been recognised by some regulators.[35] Problems with monitoring xeno-recipients have been noted, especially as '[f]requent and easy transit of individuals across national borders is a fact of modern life and ease of access to medical care anywhere around the globe has greatly increased the phenomenon of "medical tourism". Just as humans today travel more easily, microbes can spread, unhindered by borders.'[36] Effective surveillance and monitoring regimes must exist if a genetically engineered solid organ is xenotransplanted into a human, but (how) can a sufficient and adequate *global* regime be devised, implemented and enforced? Practically, is it possible to regulate and contain global risks and, if not, should clinical xenotransplants proceed?

Respecting individual and collective human rights

Some of the problems of regulating risks on a global level include the fact that '[b]ioethics, in our pluralistic society, means respect for others and being able to compromise even on sensitive issues'.[37] It is unclear whether this will be possible on a global scale where values, opinions, cultures, religions, faiths, and beliefs will undoubtedly compete and/or conflict. Nevertheless, '[t]he need to establish common values and benchmarks, as well as to promote ethical principles and standards to guide scientific progress and technological development ... is becoming increasingly acute, especially in developing countries that do not equally enjoy the benefits of scientific and technological advances'.[38] During the second half of the twentieth century there has been a trend in the Western world to protect human rights and civil liberties, and conventions

---

[34] E.g., Canada – Health Canada, *Proposed Canadian Standard for Xenotransplantation* (Ottawa: Health Canada, 1999); UK – UKXIRA, *Draft Report of the Infection Surveillance Steering Group of the UKXIRA* (London: DH, 1999); US – US DHHS, FDA, *PHS Guideline*.
[35] E.g., Australia – NHMRC, *Discussion Paper*, p. 18; UKXIRA, *Draft Report*.
[36] Organisation for Economic Co-operation and Development (OECD), *Xenotransplantation: International Policy Issues* (Paris: OECD, 1999), p. 43.
[37] Lenoir, 'Biotechnology', 1.
[38] H. ten Have, 'UNESCO and Ethics of Science and Technology', in *Ethics of Science and Technology*, p. 6.

and other documents have been introduced which set out 'common values and benchmarks'.[39] Alongside the practical questions of devising, implementing and enforcing effective surveillance and monitoring regimes, it is also important to consider the impact the proposed surveillance provisions will have on the lives of those involved in or affected by xenotransplantation. In Chapter 6 I thus explore the human rights and civil liberties implications of the proposed surveillance regimes, implications which have not been adequately explored so far. However, in calling for national and international surveillance schemes there appears to be some agreement, or at least recognition, that *some* encroachment on human rights is required. But, within an era where individual human rights are rightly protected, is this encroachment permissible and how can such surveillance regimes be legally and ethically accommodated? Xenotransplantation and its necessary surveillance regime thus raise questions about whether individuals who seek to benefit from an experimental procedure or clinical trial should also bear the burden of involvement in it, and accept that their rights must be curtailed to protect the wider public. If genetically engineered solid organ clinical xenotransplants are performed, does the recipient, her relatives and contacts have to accept such a regime 'for the greater good', and is this ethically acceptable and legally possible?

Again, it is imperative that the public are involved in discussing this because it is their rights at stake; as potential recipients, close contacts and relatives, health professionals or members of the public. If xenotransplantation is to clinically proceed, it is hard to envisage that anything other than a statutory-based surveillance regime will be sufficient to protect those involved; although whether such schemes can be globally regulated and enforced is debatable. Law may not be the ideal tool to regulate and control the risks posed by a developing biotechnology, if the decision is made to introduce such risks into society, law can, at the very least, be used to ensure that the interests and well-being of recipients and others are, as much as possible, safeguarded and considered.

Conclusion

I am concerned with the 'technological imperative',[40] the tendency to assume that if something can be done it should be, and the 'seductive

---

[39] *Ibid.*
[40] I. Kennedy, *Treat Me Right – Essays in Medical Law and Ethics* (Oxford University Press, 1988), p. 288.

sirens of medical progress'.[41] These might be appropriate in some situations but there are some developing biotechnologies which pose too great a risk to the recipient and others, such that fundamental questions need to be asked as to whether they should be clinically introduced. Indeed:

> [t]he belief that surrogate mothers and clonal babies are inevitable because science always moves forward ... represents a form of *laissez-faire* nonsense dismally reminiscent of the creed that American business if left to itself will solve everybody's problems. Just as the success of a corporate body in making money need not set the human condition ahead, neither does every scientific advance automatically make our lives 'meaningful'.[42]

While many may agree, the reality and implications of adopting this position makes it harder to implement. Who wants to be the one to tell those on the organ transplant waiting list that research on the developing biotechnology they have seen reported in the press has been halted because there *might* be risks to others? Despite these difficult discussions, there are some things which are 'inherently wrong – that is, wrong no matter how much good could come from doing it',[43] and xeno-transplantation may fall into this category *because* in possibly benefiting the individual xeno-recipient, the wider public is put at risk. Furthermore, '[t]he globalization of science, economics, and information all elevate transgenerational concerns beyond the domestic scale to an international one. Similarly, bioethics must move from the realm of individual concern to that of collective concern, and must ultimately be considered at a truly universal level.'[44] In the following chapters I highlight how genetically engineered solid organ xenotransplantation engages these concerns and how, if it is to clinically proceed, existing regulatory structures need revising to accommodate the challenges it poses to accepted legal and ethical norms.

---

[41] M.J. Hanson, 'The Seductive Sirens of Medical Progress – The Case of Xenotransplantation' (1995) *Hastings Center Report* 5.
[42] J.D. Watson, 'Moving Toward the Clonal Man' (1971) 227 *Atlantic Monthly* 50.
[43] Sommerville, 'Searching for Ethics', p. 25.
[44] B.M. Knoppers, 'Reflections: The Challenge of Biotechnology and Public Policy' (2000) 45 *McGill Law Journal* 559, 563, reference removed.

2 Dealing with risk

The concept of risk is central to my argument that xenotransplantation cannot necessarily or automatically be accommodated within existing legal and ethical norms. The consequences of clinical *genetically engineered* solid organ xenotransplants are events of the future as none have yet been performed. Their benefits *and* harms are uncertain. If such clinical xenotransplants prolong the recipient's life, then the benefit to them, their relatives and society is clear; spending on alternative treatments can be reduced, early deaths prevented, hospitalisations reduced, and recipients can enter or remain in employment. Xenotransplants would also eliminate consent issues raised by human donation, provide an unlimited source of organs, enable operations to be performed at the optimum time, and recipients may require reduced levels of immunosuppression compared to allotransplants.[1] However, in xenotransplanting these organs into humans, infectious diseases may be transmitted to the recipient, their close contacts *and* the public. This possibility is widely acknowledged but there is no consensus on its nature or extent, nor can it be quantified without clinical experience. When the risks of a biotechnology may significantly impact on the health of individuals *and* society they should not be ignored; particularly where its nature and extent could be severe. Such risks are outside most of our experiences as they are largely unknown and unidentifiable, their extent unclear, possibly latent, and not confined or confinable to the xeno-recipient or one country. Xenotransplantation is thus an example of Beck's global and invisible risks of the risk society.[2]

An overview of the science and risks of xenotransplantation set the foundations for this book, and I consider risk assessment (evaluation, communication and management) of unclear and unknown risks. Here, public understanding of and confidence in science[3] is crucial and

---

[1] NHMRC, *Discussion Paper*, pp. 20–21.   [2] Beck, *Risk Society*.
[3] I mean the public needs to understand scientific matters and not as a shorthand for scientific outreach activities to the public: House of Lords Select Committee on Science and Technology, *Science and Society*, Third Report (London: House of Lords, 2000), para. 3.1.

experiences with BSE, a cross-species disease, and GM crops, another developing biotechnology, are explored to see whether wider lessons can be learned from how these risks were communicated and managed. The risks of xenotransplantation also need to be considered in the context of the chronic shortage of human organs available for transplantation,[4] and the pre-clinical and clinical results achieved to date. A pig heart has survived for 57 days, a liver for 8 and a kidney for 90 days in orthotopic life-supporting xenotransplants to non-human primates.[5] Humans have survived for 9 months with a chimpanzee's kidney, 20 days with a baboon's heart and 70 days following a baboon's liver xenotransplant.[6] But no solid organ non-human animal-to-human xenotransplant has been reported since 1993[7] and a genetically engineered solid organ is yet to be xenotransplanted into a human. It is thus questionable *how* those involved in clinical xenotransplants and the public can be advised about and protected from such risks. Effective risk management may be complicated by these unknowns, but a precautionary approach to risk, informed by Mill's harm principle, is required to safeguard public health. Issues of public health are particularly important where there is a disjunction between the potential individual beneficiary and those who may bear the burdens of a biotechnology. Xenotransplantation engages three aspects of interest in public health: that of 'the public' as a whole, the individuals who comprise the public, and the advancement of medicine. When regulating and managing xenotransplantation risks these interests should, as far as possible, be accommodated and the response proportionate given the possible benefits and risks.[8] The public are crucial constituents of the decision-making process in determining

---

[4] E.g., Australia and New Zealand (at: www.anzdata.org.au, accessed 16/03/11); UK (at: www.uktransplant.org.uk/ukt/statistics/transplant_activity_report/transplant_activity_report.jsp, accessed 16/03/11; US: www.ustransplant.org, last accessed 16/03/11; www.unos.org, accessed 16/03/11).

[5] C.G.A. McGregor *et al.*, 'Preclinical Orthotopic Cardiac Xenotransplantation' (2009) 28 *Xenotransplantation* S224; J.B. Cabezuelo *et al.*, 'Assessment of Renal Function during the Postoperative Period Following Liver Xenotransplantation from Transgenic Pig to Baboon' (2002) 34 *Transplantation Proceedings* 321; N. Baldan *et al.*, 'Ureteral Stenosis in HDAF Pig-to-Primate Renal Xenotransplantation: A Phenomenon Related to Immunological Events?' (2004) 4 *American Journal of Transplantation* 475.

[6] K. Reemtsma *et al.*, 'Renal Heterotransplantation'; L.L. Bailey, S.L. Nehlsen-Cannarella, W. Concepcion, J.B. Jolley, 'Baboon-to-Human Cardiac Xenotransplantation in a Neonate' (1985) 254 *Journal of the American Medical Association* 3321; T.E. Starzl *et al.*, 'Baboon-to-Human Liver Transplantation' (1993) 341 *The Lancet* 65.

[7] A human may have received a pig heart in India in 1996 but no results have been published (K.S. Jayaraman, 'Pig Heart Transplant Surgeon Held in Jail' (1997) 385 *Nature* 378).

[8] Strategy Unit, Cabinet Office, *Risk: Improving Government's Capability to Handle Risk and Uncertainty: Full Report – A Source Document* (London: Cabinet Office, 2002), p. 91.

this *because of* the risks they may be exposed to.[9] Public participation in this process is thus necessary but if appropriate mechanisms are not (or cannot be) introduced, clinical xenotransplants should not proceed because without such it *may* directly benefit a limited few but jeopardise the health of more.

The science

Pigs are now mainly used as the source of xeno-organs because of, *inter alia*, their availability in large numbers, and the similarity in organ size and functions to human organs.[10] The biological differences between the species may mean the risks of transmitting infections are lower, and pigs can be bred and raised in specific pathogen-free environments, further minimising these risks. For a genetically engineered solid organ xenotransplant to support human life three barriers must be addressed: immunological, physiological and microbiological.

Immunological

When any organ is transplanted the recipient's immune system will recognise it as 'foreign' and try to reject it. Three types of rejection must be overcome for all transplants: hyperacute (HAR), acute and chronic.[11] HAR begins almost as soon as the new organ is perfused with the recipient's blood and it causes rapid loss of graft function within about twenty-four hours. The degree of the immune response is affected by the genetic difference between the organ and recipient, and in allotransplants HAR is managed by tissue typing, blood group testing and immunosuppressants. More than this is required for xenotransplants because of the increased genetic disparity between the organ source and recipient. Trials between pigs genetically engineered without both copies of the gene involved in HAR and non-human primates indicate that using such pigs may help to control HAR.[12] If HAR is avoided, acute rejection in the form of acute cellular rejection or humoral

---

[9] The importance of involving the public in science, research and policy decisions has been recognised by the UK's Medical Research Council (MRC): MRC, 'Science & Society, Introduction' (at: www.mrc.ac.uk/Sciencesociety/index.htm, accessed 16/03/11).

[10] J.M. Dobson and J.H. Dark, *The Physiology of Xenotransplantation* (London: DH, 2002), ch. 1.

[11] P. Malhotra *et al.*, 'Immunology of Transplant Rejection' (2009) (at: http://emedicine.medscape.com/article/432209-overview, accessed 16/03/11).

[12] A. Shimizu *et al.*, 'Thrombotic Microangiopathy Associated with Humoral Rejection of Cardiac Xenografts from Alpha 1,3-Galactosyltransferase Gene-Knockout Pigs in Baboons' (2008) 172 *American Journal of Pathology* 1471.

rejection may occur and destroy the organ within six months of the transplant. Pre-clinical results indicate it may be possible to delay the latter,[13] but information on the former is scarce although it appears to resemble the cellular rejection process in allotransplants.[14] Acute rejection is managed in allotransplantation via immunosuppressants but for xenotransplants larger doses may be required resulting in 'clinically unacceptable complication rates'.[15] The anti-pig cellular response may thus be the major challenge to clinical xenotransplantation.[16] There is also limited information on chronic rejection which may occur months or years post-transplant. Its process is poorly understood for allotransplants but as post-allotransplant survival increases so does the incidence of chronic rejection.[17] This is likely to be replicated with xenotransplants but is currently unproven because of the limited pre-clinical post-xenotransplant survival times. It is similarly unknown whether immunosuppressive therapies will be useful for xenotransplants in this context, but inducing immunologic tolerance in xeno-recipients may help to prevent chronic rejection.[18]

Physiological

If the immunological barriers are overcome, the effects of the physiological differences between pig and human solid organs are largely unknown because of limited clinical experiences. Results of pre-clinical research are such that it remains contested whether the physiologic demands of the human xeno-recipient will be met by a pig heart or kidney.[19] Although humans are biped and pigs quadruped it appears that pig hearts will be able to pump blood upwards to the brain and thus may be able to support the life of a human, but '[i]t is not unreasonable to propose that postural effects may have ultimately contributed to the eventual demise of the experimental animals. Only long-term survival of

---

[13] *Ibid.*
[14] D.K.C. Cooper *et al.*, 'Report of the Xenotransplantation Advisory Committee of the International Society for Heart and Lung Transplantation: The Present Status of Xenotransplantation and Its Potential Role in the Treatment of End-Stage Cardiac and Pulmonary Diseases' (2000) 19 *Journal of Heart and Lung Transplantation* 1125, 1128, 1130.
[15] N. Perico *et al.*, 'Xenotransplantation in the 21st Century' (2002) 20 *Blood Purification* 45, 47.
[16] S. Le Bas-Bernardet and G. Blancho, 'Current Cellular Immunological Hurdles in Pig-to-Primate Xenotransplantation' (2009) 21 *Transplant Immunology* 60, 63.
[17] D.K.C. Cooper *et al.*, 'Will the Pig Solve the Transplantation Backlog?' (2002) 53 *Annual Review of Medicine* 133, 140.
[18] *Ibid.*, pp. 141–142.   [19] Dobson and Dark, *Physiology*, ch. 6.

xenotransplanted animals will allow the full effects of a change in posture to be determined.'[20] It is also unclear whether a pig liver will adequately function inside a human because few pig liver to non-human primate xenotransplants have occurred, survival times are low, and there have been limited opportunities to analyse the physiological functions of xenotransplanted livers.[21] There are differences between the number of products of pig and human livers, and the former may not be able to fulfil the functions required of it.[22] Some of the physiological differences may not substantially affect the organ's function, but it is not known *which* differences may be important for solid organ xenotransplants or the well-being of the xeno-recipient and this 'will only be able to be examined in the clinical setting'.[23] A key remaining, currently unanswerable, issue is whether the pig's lifespan of ten–twenty years will affect its organs' ability to support a human's longer lifespan.

Microbiological

The preceding barriers are concerned with the source pig or individual xeno-recipient, and although there is a microbiological risk of transmitting infectious diseases following an allotransplant these are predominantly limited to the recipient.[24] The microbiological barrier to xenotransplantation is different; in performing a xenotransplant from a genetically engineered pig to a human infectious diseases *may* be transmitted to the recipient, her close contacts *and* the public. In allowing an individual to (possibly) benefit from a xenotransplant, the wider community may be put at risk and, '[a]s the HIV/AIDS pandemic demonstrates, persistent latent infections may result in person-to-person transmission for many years before clinical disease develops in the index case, thereby allowing an emerging infectious agent to become established in the susceptible population before it is recognized'.[25] The *possibility* of transmission is a crucial issue but there is a lack of information about what may be transferred and detection methods are necessarily limited. The unknown nature and possibly wide-ranging extent of these risks set xenotransplantation apart from other biotechnologies. Although post-*allotransplant* infection is common because of

---

[20] *Ibid.*, para. 4.4. [21] *Ibid.*, para. 5.6.5. [22] *Ibid.*, ch. 5, Annex 2, Table 2.
[23] G.A. Levy *et al.*, 'The Present Status of Xenotransplantation' (2001) 33 *Transplantation Proceedings* 3050, 3052.
[24] A.-L. Millard and N.J. Mueller, 'Critical Issues Related to Porcine Xenograft Exposure to Human Viruses: Lessons from Allotransplantation' (2010) 15 *Current Opinion in Organ Transplantation* 230.
[25] US DHHS, *PHS Guideline*, para. 1.3.

the immunosuppressants, post-xenotransplant infection may be *increased* by the extra levels of immunosuppression needed, imported pig novel pathogens, bypassing the usual host defences, and the consequences of genetically engineering the pigs.[26] The risk of infection is acknowledged but as no genetically engineered pig to human solid organ xenotransplants have occurred it is impossible to quantify their nature or magnitude. Nevertheless, surveillance regimes have been proposed for xeno-recipients, their contacts and relevant health professionals,[27] and their existence and content indicate that xenotransplantation risks are not taken lightly.

Risk assessment: evaluating the risks

What could be transmitted?

Known infections

Some of the known pig infection risks, including bacteria, parasites and viral pathogens, may be removed or reduced by early weaning, selective breeding and breeding the pigs in specific pathogen-free environments.[28] Since the 1990s when it was discovered that porcine endogenous retroviruses (PERVs) could infect human cells *in vitro* and, under certain circumstances, actively infect human cells so that they can replicate and spread to other cells in the human, this retrovirus has been of most concern.[29] PERVs are present in all breeds of pig and it is unclear whether they can be removed via genetic engineering or a vaccine utilised, as there are multiple copies of it in each pig genome.[30] Retroviruses inject themselves into human cells and reverse transcribe RNA into DNA which is then inserted into a cell's genes and into its chromosomes.[31] If a retrovirus inserts itself into germline cells, the host's

---

[26] G. Mattiuzzo *et al.*, 'Strategies to Enhance the Safety Profile of Xenotransplantation: Minimizing the Risk of Viral Zoonoses' (2008) 13 *Current Opinion in Organ Transplantation* 184; C.A. Wilson, 'Porcine Endogenous Retroviruses and Xenotransplantation' (2008) 65 *Cellular and Molecular Life Sciences* 3399.

[27] See Chapter 6.

[28] D. Louz *et al.*, 'Reappraisal of Biosafety Risks Posed by PERVs in Xenotransplantation' (2008) 18 *Reviews in Medical Virology* 53.

[29] E.g., V. Specke *et al.*, 'Productive Infection of Human Primary Cells and Cell Lines with Porcine Endogenous Retroviruses' (2001) 285 *Virology* 177; C. Patience *et al.*, 'Infection of Human Cells by Endogenous Retrovirus of Pigs' (1997) 3 *Nature Medicine* 282.

[30] J. Ramsoondar *et al.*, 'Production of Transgenic Pigs that Express Porcine Endogenous Retrovirus Small Interfering RNAs' (2009) 16 *Xenotransplantation* 164; U. Fiebig *et al.*, 'Neutralizing Antibodies against Conserved Domains of p15E of Porcine Endogenous Retroviruses: Basis for a Vaccine for Xenotransplantation?' (2003) 307 *Virology* 406.

[31] Mattiuzzo *et al.*, 'Strategies to Enhance'.

offspring will carry it; and when a retrovirus inserts itself into a cell's chromosomes it blocks infection by other retroviruses and any offspring is resistant to those viruses. Species have successfully incorporated these viral DNA into their chromosomes and created resistance, but if those cells are transplanted into another species there is no resistance and the virus can develop and infect the new host. Retroviruses can be passed down to offspring over successive generations without causing harm but may be lethal if transferred cross-species.[32] With PERVs the pig itself will be protected but if pig cells are xenotransplanted into a human she is not protected from that virus and can be infected. Retroviruses can also recombine with viruses from the new host species possibly 'generat[ing] viruses with novel mechanisms of virulence'.[33]

Retroviruses *may* induce immunodeficiencies, neurodegeneration and cancers of the blood system, leukaemia and lymphoma.[34] The viruses which cause AIDS in humans resulted from retroviral cross-species transmissions from non-human primates,[35] and '[e]vidence from naturally occurring retroviral zoonosis and cross-species infections by animal retroviruses ... provides a basis for reasoned speculation on the risk posed by PERVs. In a worst case scenario xenograft-related PERV transmission would be the starting point of a new viral disease resulting in a public health problem.'[36] The nature, existence and ability of PERVs to cause disease, and the means of detecting them, remain under investigation but examples of cross-species infection transmission include swine flu, Ebola, influenza and new-variant Creutzfeldt–Jacob disease (vCJD).[37] Indeed, the majority of emerging infectious diseases have been caused by zoonotic pathogens with a non-human animal cause.[38] Non-human animal retroviruses have adapted and spread within the human population and there is 'mounting evidence that ... [Human T cell Lymphotropic Virus] and HIV entered the human population through multiple interspecies transmission events, from non-human primates'.[39] Lists of RNA and DNA viruses which may pose an

---

[32] *Ibid.*
[33] C. Moran, 'Xenotransplantation: Benefits, Risks and Relevance of Reproductive Technology' (2008) *Theriogenology* 1269, 1271.
[34] Mattiuzzo *et al.*, 'Strategies to Enhance'; B. Dieckhoff *et al.*, 'Knockdown of Porcine Endogenous Retroviruses (PERV) Expression by PERV-Specific shRNA in Transgenic Pigs' (2008) 15 *Xenotransplantation* 36.
[35] Dieckhoff *et al.*, 'Knockdown'.   [36] Louz *et al.*, 'Reappraisal of Biosafety Risks', 60.
[37] D.A. Muir and G. Griffin, *Infection Risks in Xenotransplantation* (London: DH, 2001), ch. 2.
[38] K.E. Jones *et al.*, 'Global Trends in Emerging Infectious Diseases' (2008) 451 *Nature* 990.
[39] Muir and Griffin, *Infection Risks*, p. 38.

infection risk to xeno-recipients have been compiled,[40] but xenotransplant infection risks can only reliably be determined by clinical trials. Three key issues are hard to determine without such trials: the effect of PERVs, its consequences and the magnitude of risk. Nevertheless, experience with other retroviruses suggests that more than flu-like symptoms are likely and that genetically engineered solid organ xenotransplants *could* introduce a lethal infectious disease. It is unclear whether there is a small risk to many or a high risk to a few, but 'the risk of PERV infection following [xenotransplantation] will never be zero'.[41]

Unknown infections

Whatever the uncertainties around PERVs, 'the greatest remaining risk comes from non-PERV unknown viruses that may be non-pathogenic in source animals but could adapt and become pathogenic in immunosuppressed humans'.[42] These could be newly recognised viruses which have been around for a long time undetected or genuinely just emerged viruses, perhaps due to a variation of existing organisms.[43] Examples include the Nipah virus and swine hepatitis E virus, and there are '[c]ertain porcine viruses [which] may have the potential, if given the opportunity, to infect new host species ... through a process of adaptation, even though human infection has, as yet, never been observed'.[44] Emerging infectious diseases have recently been identified in allotransplants,[45] and there are organisms which are known to infect pigs but which do not occur in the UK, for example, otherwise than via rare imported cases.[46] Thus, while pigs may be bred free from specific organisms, 'newly emerging or unrecognised organisms, as well as those that cannot be eliminated ... continue to pose a potential threat'.[47]

Can xenotransplants transmit infections?

In vitro studies have indicated that PERVs have the *potential* to transfer from imported tissue to the human host, that human cells are susceptible

---

[40] *Ibid.*
[41] C. Patience *et al.*, 'Porcine Endogenous Retrovirus – Advances, Issues and Solutions' (2002) 9 *Xenotransplantation* 373, 373.
[42] M. Sykes, '2007 IXA Presidential Address: Progress toward an Ideal Source Animal: Opportunities and Challenges in a Changing World' (2008) 15 *Xenotransplantation* 7, 10.
[43] Muir and Griffin, *Infection Risks*, p. 102.   [44] *Ibid.*, p. 104.
[45] L. Scobie and Y. Takeuchi, 'Porcine Endogenous Retrovirus and Other Viruses in Xenotransplantation' (2009) 14 *Current Opinion in Organ Transplantation* 175.
[46] Muir and Griffin, *Infection Risks*, pp. 105–108.   [47] *Ibid.*, p. 118.

to PERV infection, and PERVs from a xenotransplant *might* be able to infect living human recipients.[48] Evidence from *in vivo* studies is limited but, as yet, there is *no* evidence that PERVs have been transmitted to living human recipients of pig cells or tissues.[49] These studies have been criticised for the recipient's limited exposure time to pig cells and tissues, not being long-term studies of immunosuppressed recipients, and not involving solid organs.[50] It is thus not known if genetically engineered cell and solid organ xenotransplants present the same risks and 'we have no data on infectivity ... or latency of PERV agents in either man or immunosuppressed man: indeed there are no clinical data indicating how such agents would affect a patient ... we know nothing of the ecological dynamics of PERV in relation to other porcine viruses or human endogenous retroviruses and other human infections'.[51] Nevertheless, some have suggested that although PERVs may infect human cells *in vivo* and *in vitro*, they may have limited *clinical* effect.[52] Attempts to assess the risks of PERVs are further complicated by the fact that it is contested whether the results of pre-clinical trials can be extrapolated to the clinical situation as the value of the pig to non-human primate model here is unclear.[53] While specific screening methods obviously do not exist for unknown pathogens, 'modern technology ... allow[s] the screening for certain types of viruses, even if the virus has not yet been characterized'.[54] However, detection may be hindered by latent infections, so the risks could be unidentifiable for some time, perhaps generations, and by then any infection could have spread (undetected) widely. Indeed, 'we have no way of predicting when a virus may manifest itself. The expression of a virus could occur after only a few or perhaps thousands of xenotransplants have been performed. Almost certainly, we

---

[48] Patience *et al.*, 'Infection of Human Cells'; P. Le Tissier *et al.*, 'Two Sets of Human-Tropic Pig Retrovirus' (1997) 389 *Nature* 681.
[49] E.g., G. Di Nicuolo *et al.*, 'Long-Term Absence of Porcine Endogenous Infection in Chronically Immunosuppressed Patients after Treatment with the Porcine Cell-Based Academic Medical Center Bioartificial Liver' (2010) 17 *Xenotransplantation* 431; R.B. Elliott *et al.*, 'No Evidence of Infection with Porcine Endogenous Retrovirus in Recipients of Encapsulated Porcine Islet Xenografts' (2000) 9 *Cell Transplantation* 895; K. Paradis *et al.*, 'Search for Cross Species Transmission of Porcine Endogenous Retrovirus in Patients Treated with Living Pig Tissue' (1999) 285 *Science* 1236.
[50] E.g., Louz *et al.*, 'Reappraisal of Biosafety'; R.A. Weiss, 'Xenografts and Retroviruses' (1999) 285 *Science* 1221.
[51] C. Michie, 'Xenotransplantation: Endogenous Pig Retroviruses and the Precautionary Principle' (2001) 7 *Trends in Molecular Medicine* 62, 63.
[52] E.g., L.E. Chapman and E.T. Bloom, 'Clinical Xenotransplantation' (2001) 285 *Journal of the American Medical Association* 2304.
[53] Louz *et al.*, 'Reappraisal of Biosafety'.
[54] Health Canada, *Report of the Xenotransplantation Surveillance Workshop – Infection Control Database and Sample Archiving* (2001) 27S1 *Canada Communicable Disease Report*.

would have to perform xenotransplantation on humans to ascertain this risk. And only if a patient became infected would we be able to begin estimating the risk.'[55] Nevertheless, it was suggested at the 2007 Congress of the International Xenotransplantation Association (IXA) that there was a consensus that as long as there was 'appropriate monitoring' PERVs should not prevent xenotransplantation moving ahead clinically.[56] Such monitoring may not be possible[57] and, of course, the issues raised by unknown pathogens remain. Furthermore, while there is a consensus that there *is* a risk of infectious disease transmission, there is disagreement on its extent, and the lack of clinical information means 'it is impossible to make accurate predictions concerning the relative risks of infection ... as well as their likely disease manifestations'.[58]

Communicating and managing risks

The benefits and risks of xenotransplantation are largely unknown but when we talk of 'benefit' most people understand the concept; gain, advantage, help. What about 'risk'? Risk is a social construct,[59] is not static[60] and describes an undesirable consequence that *might* occur (it is *possible*), but the occurrence of that consequence is *not certain*.[61] Risk involves the probability and magnitude of harm,[62] and can be classified by concepts such as justifiability, acceptability, seriousness, avoidability.[63] There is an intrinsic and inherent element of uncertainty with risk because while knowing the probability of a possible outcome makes it a more *concrete* risk, it is still uncertain whether that risk will *actually* occur and, if it does, all of its consequences. Decision-making in risk situations can thus be categorised as being (i) under known outcomes and probabilities, (ii) under uncertainty, where outcomes are known but not probabilities, or (iii) under ignorance, where neither

---

[55] F.H. Bach et al., 'Ethical and Legal Issues in Technology: Xenotransplantation' (2001) 27 *American Journal of Law and Medicine* 283, 286.
[56] C.G. Groth, 'Editorial – Looking Back, Heading Forward' (2008) 15 *Xenotransplantation* 1, 1.
[57] See Chapter 6. [58] Muir and Griffin, *Infection Risks*, p. 118.
[59] Beck, *Risk Society*.
[60] M. McKee and R. Coker, 'Trust, Terrorism and Public Health' (2009) 31 *Journal of Public Health* 462, 464.
[61] S.O. Hansson, 'Philosophical Perspectives on Risk' (2004) 8 *Techné* 10.
[62] A. Edwards and G. Elwyn, 'Understanding Risk and Lessons for Clinical Risk Communication about Treatment Preferences' (2001) 10 (suppl. 1) *Quality in Health Care* i9, i9.
[63] K.C. Calman, 'Cancer: Science and Society and the Communication of Risk' (1996) 313 *British Medical Journal* 799, 801.

outcomes nor probabilities are known.[64] Clinical xenotransplants fall within (iii) and create an environment of *'manufactured risk'*;[65] risk which is created by scientific and biotechnological advances and of which we have no prior experience to help calculate the probability of negative consequences occurring. It is an example of the changing nature of risk; change which has occurred because of the 'greater connectedness of the world'.[66] Risk assessment is thus essential to evaluate the dangers, communicate information and develop appropriate means of controlling and managing them.

Risk communication

Technological risks have specific characteristics; they are scientifically uncertain, behaviourally uncertain as the nature and extent of them may depend on human behaviour, a better understanding of them may not be gained by more research, and the acceptability of the risk(s) depends on the cultural context.[67] The nature of biotechnological risks are such that the public need to be informed of them and involved in the decision-making process as situations of uncertainty sit uncomfortably in health systems predicated on evidence-based medicine. The UK government has acknowledged the importance of communicating risk to the public,[68] but 'understanding technoscientific innovations is a complex business'[69] and involves bodies which might be in conflict; social and political institutions and organisations, the media, public, and decision-makers.[70] Such communication aims to provide information to educate people, enable them to make informed decisions about whether potential hazards are acceptable, and decide whether to take action to mitigate risk(s). It has a number of elements but is complicated where available 'facts' are lacking, there are conflicting interpretations of any facts, and differing levels of risk acceptance and acceptability exist. Some level of

---

[64] A. Stirling, *On Science and Precaution in the Management of Technological Risk. Volume I: A Synthesis of Case Studies* (Seville: European Commission Institute for Prospective Technological Studies, 1999) EUR 19056 EN, pp. 40–41.
[65] A. Giddens, 'Risk and Responsibility' (1999) 62 *Modern Law Review* 1, 4, emphasis in original.
[66] Strategy Unit, *Risk*, para. 1.6.
[67] E. Fisher, *Risk Regulation and Administrative Constitutionalism* (Oxford: Hart, 2007), p. 8.
[68] E.g., Strategy Unit, *Risk*.
[69] M. Michael and N. Brown, 'The Meat of the Matter: Grasping and Judging Xenotransplantation' (2004) 13 *Public Understanding of Science* 379, 380.
[70] D. Miller and S. Macintyre, 'Risk Communication: The Relationships between the Media, Public Beliefs and Policy-Making', in P. Bennett and K. Calman (eds.), *Risk Communication and Public Health* (Oxford University Press, 2001), p. 229.

uncertainty may be accepted by and acceptable to members of the public, but the extent of it with xenotransplantation will be outside most people's experience. Scientific uncertainty must thus be explained in a meaningful and understandable way, and care taken with the language used. Presenting information in different formats is essential and it should be framed 'in as fair and balanced a way as reasonably possible, set in the context where appropriate of everyday risks with which the consumer is familiar'.[71] The importance of framing risk statements is widely acknowledged,[72] but '[i]n the absence of data [on xenotransplantation], it is difficult to develop a meaningful dialogue regarding the potential risks to the recipient or to the community at large'.[73]

Some have suggested that the public *cannot* understand scientific and risk information because of a lack of basic science education and knowledge, and it was necessary to correct this; the 'deficit' approach to public understanding of science.[74] Here, if the public 'understood' science they would view it and any risks as scientists do, and approve of or sympathise with science's goals. The public's reaction to risk is thus based on *misunderstanding* information. Others have, however, argued that there *is* 'understanding and reacting to information in a different, but no less valid, way'.[75] People's perceptions and attitudes to risk are likely to be influenced by whether the risk is controllable, individual, increasing, voluntary, new or globally catastrophic, and not just uni-dimensional statistics which are often set out in tables and used by experts.[76] Indeed, 'riskiness' means more to people than 'expected number of fatalities':[77]

[c]alculating the probability of danger (i.e. the risk) concentrates on what is physically 'out there' in man's intervention in the natural world. What is *acceptable* depends on the uncertainty that is 'in here', within a person's mind. Going from 'out there' to 'in here' requires a connection between the dangers of technology and people's perceptions of them. Consequently, it is

---

[71] Edwards and Elwyn, 'Understanding Risk', i12.
[72] E.g., *ibid*; P. Bennett, 'Understanding Responses to Risk: Some Basic Findings', in Bennett and Calman, *Risk Communication*, p. 3.
[73] J. Fishman, 'Infection and Xenotransplantation: Developing Strategies to Minimize Risk', in J. Fishman, D. Sachs and R. Shaikh (eds.), *Xenotransplantation: Scientific Frontiers and Public Policy* (New York, NY: New York Academy of Sciences, 1998), pp. 52, 62.
[74] T. Bubela *et al.*, 'Science Communication Reconsidered' (2009) 27 *Nature Biotechnology* 514.
[75] E. Green *et al.*, 'Public and Professional Perceptions of Environmental and Health Risks', in Bennett and Calman, *Risk Communication*, p. 51.
[76] DH, *Communicating about Risks to Public Health: Pointers to Good Practice* (London: DH, 1997), p. 5.
[77] P. Slovic, 'Perception of Risk' (1987) 236 *Science* 280, 285.

never enough to assume that the science of risk is only about objective, external danger. It is also about attitudes of mind.[78]

Additionally, whereas individuals are likely to perceive risk in terms of their own lives and experiences, professionals may describe or evaluate risk in different ways;[79] so what 'experts' or regulators perceive to be an acceptable risk may be deemed otherwise by potential xeno-recipients and the public. Given this, '[t]he gap between technical, scientific analyses of risk and public perceptions must be acknowledged and addressed for risk communication to be successful'.[80]

The way science and risk are portrayed in the media may also influence the public's perception of risk, and at the start of the 2000s a UK pressure group, Sense About Sense, was established to 'respond to the misrepresentation of science and scientific evidence on issues that matter to society'.[81] Communicating risk is complicated by the beliefs and perspectives of the relevant parties, misunderstandings or ignorance of these positions, and 'everyone ... is prone to bias in the use of information, particularly when it comes to processing probabilities'.[82] Not everyone understands probability, people may manage information in such a way as to give misleading results, and availability bias (if we can easily recall examples of events they are perceived to be more frequent), confirmation bias (when we have a view we shape new evidence to that view), overconfidence (we are generally overly confident in judging our probability of being correct), and difficulties of combining separate probabilities in one scenario must all be addressed.[83] An individual's perception of risk will change as new information is obtained and previous experiences and perceptions, underlying assumptions, critical incidents, and conscious thoughts and imagery are elements of this 'dynamic process'.[84] Additionally:

> the 'general public' itself is not homogenous but highly differentiated in terms of attitudes towards risk; people actively seek out information, and also receive

---

[78] R.J. Maxwell, 'The British Government's Handling of Risk: Some Reflections on the BSE/CJD Crisis', in Bennett and Calman, *Risk Communication*, pp. 95, 103, emphasis in original.

[79] I. Oliver and D. Lewis, 'Public Trust is Necessary to Protect the Population from Threats to Public Health' (2009) 31 *Journal of Public Health* 468; K. Glanz and H. Yang, 'Communicating about Risk of Infectious Diseases' (1996) 275 *Journal of the American Medical Association* 253.

[80] Glanz and Yang, 'Communicating about Risk', 254.

[81] Sense About Science (at: www.senseaboutscience.org.uk/index.php, accessed 16/03/11).

[82] Bennett, 'Understanding Responses', p. 4.   [83] *Ibid.*

[84] I.H. Langford *et al.*, 'Public Reactions to Risk: Social Structures, Images of Science and the Role of Trust', in Bennett and Calman, *Risk Communication*, pp. 33, 39.

information and interpretations from other sources significant to them such as family and friends; 'non-experts' can be shown to hold valid local knowledge about aspects of the risk management process ... which will sometimes be overlooked by scientists and other experts; and the sources, transmitters, and receivers are embedded in their own very different cultures, which will have a bearing upon how they interpret the meaning of hazards and 'risk'.[85]

Nevertheless, communicating with, and not at, people is important to help establish trust, may show why there are concerns about particular risks, and aid in developing a broader view of the issue under consideration.[86] In particular, 'the public needs to understand more about the nature of science, and the real differences of opinion which may occur during the often unstructured process of discovery',[87] and groups such as Sense About Science may assist here.[88] With xenotransplantation, it *cannot* categorically be stated whether infectious diseases *will* be transmitted post-xenotransplant although there is 'no evidence of risk *so far*' rather than 'no evidence' of risk or 'no risk at all'.[89] These are important but subtle distinctions. Denying the risks of xenotransplantation is inappropriate because '[i]f the recognition of a risk is denied on the basis of an "unclear" state of information, this means that the necessary counteractions are neglected and *the danger grows*. By turning up the scientific standard of accuracy, the circle of recognized risks justifying action is *minimized*, and consequently, *scientific license is implicitly granted for the multiplication of risks*.'[90] The epistemic uncertainty must be explained; we do not *definitely* know what will happen if a genetically engineered solid organ is xenotransplanted into a human. The public in general and potential xeno-recipients in particular will have to make decisions under ignorance as little is known about the outcomes of xenotransplantation, or their certainty. Most people will have some experience of making decisions about their health under uncertainty but doing so under ignorance is less common. As the risks cannot be predicted or calculated, and expert knowledge may be insufficient, irrelevant and unable to assess or avoid the risks, negotiation ('a multiple engagement of diverse forms of knowledge and experience') is required

---

[85] N. Pidgeon *et al.*, 'Public Health Communication and the Social Amplification of Risks: Present Knowledge and Future Prospects', in Bennett and Calman, *Risk Communication*, pp. 65, 66–67.
[86] P. Bennett *et al.*, 'Risk Communication as a Decision Process', in Bennett and Calman, *Risk Communication*, pp. 207, 212–213.
[87] Calman, 'Cancer', 800–801.   [88] Above, n. 81.
[89] D. Fisk, 'Perception of Risk – Is the Public Probably Right?', p. 133; I.E. Taylor, 'Political Risk Culture: Not Just A Communication Failure', p. 152 both in Bennett and Calman, *Risk Communication*.
[90] Beck, *Risk Society*, p. 62, emphasis in original.

to deal with uncertainty 'where trust is generated through open dialogue'.[91] Such negotiation will help 'build ... relationships that can tolerate conflicting views and differences of opinion, so that politicians and experts can say what they do and do not know, while individuals and groups can question and legitimately contest and contribute to political decisions'.[92] It is particularly necessary where there is uncertainty; as are clarity, openness about what we know and 'a realistic appraisal of the evidence at our disposal'.[93] This requires public involvement and participation in decision-making, especially where the risks are not limited to the individual *possible* beneficiary. For this negotiation to be effective there must be trust and confidence in those communicating the information, and effective communication and negotiation will enhance public confidence and trust in xenotransplantation and in those regulating it.

Trust and confidence
Recent experiences with risk messages in the UK with regard to BSE and GM crops, for example, emphasise the importance of trust in the person conveying the information and how hard it is to re-establish once it is lost. *Who* says something as well as *what* is being said matters, and if the public does not trust a source then '*any* message from [it] will often be disregarded, no matter how well intentioned and well delivered'.[94] While it is hard to generate trust, secrecy, only acting under pressure, message delivery, consistency and objectivity may be relevant;[95] but 'each new public health crisis tends to put a new strain on the government's credibility. Trust is in danger of spiralling into decline.'[96] For trust to exist there must be confidence in being able to *rely* on the knowledge, expertise and ability of an individual or organisation, and trust in the companies and scientists using gene technology, for example, appears to affect the perception of its risks and benefits.[97] Trust takes time to build, is based on a clear record of competence and credibility, and is likely to be stronger where institutions are clear about their objectives and values, decisions are evidence based, open and transparent, public concerns and values are taken into account in the decision-making process, sufficient

---

[91] A. Coote and J. Franklin, 'Negotiating Risks to Public Health – Models for Participation', in Bennett and Calman, *Risk Communication*, pp. 183, 187.
[92] *Ibid.*   [93] *Ibid.*, p. 189.
[94] Bennett, 'Understanding Responses', p. 4, emphasis in original.
[95] *Ibid.*, p. 5; DH, *Communicating about Risks*, p. 3.
[96] Coote and Franklin, 'Negotiating Risks', p. 185.
[97] M. Siegrist, 'The Influence of Trust and Perceptions of Risks and Benefits on the Acceptance of Gene Technology' (2000) 20 *Risk Analysis* 195, 196, 201.

information is provided so individuals can make balanced judgements, and 'mistakes are quickly acknowledged and acted on'.[98] It 'requires mechanisms to be in place for *listening to* potential audiences',[99] and can be encouraged by openness, dialogue, clear regulation and an acknowledgement that there *are* limits to experts' knowledge.

Experts and other risk communicators are not, however, value free or immune to influence, and they are often making *judgements*. It has been suggested that independent *regulatory* agencies accountable to government should 'provide a backdrop of reliable information for the public',[100] but because of the potential for conflicts of interest it is more appropriate for independent *advisory* agencies to take this role. Such agencies are important because if the public do not otherwise have access to information on risk they will have to rely on intermediaries such as government officials, campaigners or the media who may have their own agendas and 'distort the "facts" to further their own cause, making it difficult for the layperson to conceptualise risk in the face of conflicting perspectives'.[101] When confidence and trust are established, the public are more likely to accept and understand that 'public health policy may need to be adapted over time as knowledge increases'[102] and that change is part of responsible decision-making. Without such, fear, panic and inappropriate public responses may result, and distrust in institutions and science increase.[103] Indeed, one of the seven key messages from the public debate on GM crops, discussed below, was that there was 'a strong and wide degree of suspicion about the motives, intentions and behaviour of those taking decisions about GM – especially government and multi-national companies'.[104]

(Dis)trust in practice – BSE in the UK

The UK's BSE crisis of the 1980s and 1990s is a good example of the importance of risk communication and the rise in distrust in risk advice.[105] In November 1986 BSE was identified by a government

---

[98] Strategy Unit, *Risk*, para. 5.7, references removed.
[99] Bennett *et al.*, 'Risk Communication', p. 212, emphasis in original.
[100] Langford *et al.*, 'Public Reactions', p. 48.
[101] D. Lupton, 'Risk as Moral Danger: The Social and Political Functions of Risk Discourse in Public Health' (1993) 23 *International Journal of Health Services* 425, 431, reference removed.
[102] Oliver and Lewis, 'Public Trust', p. 468.
[103] Strategy Unit, *Risk*, paras. 3.22–3.33, 5.10–5.11.
[104] DTI, *GM Nation? The Findings of the Public Debate* (London: DTI, 2003), p. 7.
[105] E.g., P. van Zwanenberg and E. Millstone, *BSE: Risk, Science, and Governance* (Oxford University Press, 2005); D. Powell and W. Leiss, *Mad Cows and Mother's Milk: The Perils of Poor Risk Communication* (Quebec: McGill-Queen's University Press, 1997).

laboratory, the minister of agriculture informed of it in June 1987, and in December research suggested ruminant-derived meat and bone meal might be a cause.[106] The chief medical officer (CMO) was informed of BSE and advice sought on the risk to humans in March 1988, and health ministers informed and an expert advisory committee (the Southwood Committee) established in April 1988. On 13 May footage of a 'mad cow' was broadcast, and in the June the first agricultural and regulatory provisions designed to address BSE were introduced, with almost twenty statutory instruments produced between then and 1996. In January 1989 the BBC broadcast a television programme on BSE, and the Southwood Committee's report of February 1989 concluded that on '*present evidence*, it is ... *most unlikely* that BSE will have any implications for human health' but '*if our assessments of these likelihoods are incorrect, the implications would be extremely serious*'.[107] A new expert committee was subsequently established (the Spongiform Encephalopathy Advisory Committee (SEAC)), and reported to the government in June 1989. On July 19 the BBC rescreened its January BSE programme, and the European Union introduced agricultural restrictions on cows, with at least eight European Commission decisions and two regulations made up to 1996. In January 1990 the UK's Ministry of Agriculture, Fisheries and Food (MAFF) stated that 'independent experts have concluded that BSE is *most unlikely to have any implications for human health*'.[108] On 15 May John Gummer, the Minister for MAFF, said '*British beef is perfectly safe to eat*',[109] with a similar reassurance issued by the CMO on 16 May, and on 20 May the parliamentary secretary at MAFF was reported as saying that BSE was '*a very remote risk to human health*'.[110] During May 1990 John Gummer publicly fed beefburgers to his daughter, and the National CJD Surveillance Unit was set up to monitor Creutzfeldt–Jakob disease (CJD) and identify any changes in its pattern which might be due to

---

[106] This summary is based on Lord Phillips *et al.*, *The BSE Inquiry: Report: Evidence and Supporting Papers of the Inquiry into the Emergence and Identification of Bovine Spongiform Encephalopathy (BSE) and variant Creutzfeldt–Jakob Disease (CJD) and the Action Taken in Response to it up to 20 March 1996* (London: Stationery Office, 2000), vol. 16, ch. 1; Maxwell, 'The British', pp. 97–98, Table 7.1.
[107] MAFF, DH, *Report of the Working Party on Bovine Spongiform Encephalopathy* (London: MAFF/DH, 1989), para. 9.2, emphasis supplied.
[108] MAFF, *Government Action on BSE*, news release FF 1/90, 9 January 1990 (London: MAFF, 1990), as cited in van Zwanenberg and Millstone, *BSE*, p. 103, emphasis supplied.
[109] Phillips *et al.*, *BSE Inquiry*, vol. 16, ch. 1, p. 13, emphasis supplied.
[110] S. Rule, 'Fatal cow illness stirs British fear', *New York Times*, 20 May 1990, emphasis supplied.

BSE.[111] On 24 July 1990 the SEAC chair publicly wrote to the CMO that '*any risk as a result of eating beef products is minute. Thus we believe that there is no scientific reason for not eating British beef and that it can be eaten by everyone.*'[112] On 27 March 1991 the first case of BSE in a calf born following the ruminant feed ban was identified, and on 11 March 1993 the CMO again reassured the public that beef was safe to eat. In September confirmed cases of BSE in Britain reached 100,000.

The first known human victim of new-variant CJD died (aged 18) on 21 May 1995, and in August the CJD Surveillance Unit identified the second case of suspected new-variant CJD, later confirmed, in another young person. A high incidence of CJD in farmers was noted, including three confirmed cases in dairy farmers who had BSE in their herd, and in October the SEAC issued a press release about suspected CJD in a cattle farmer and published a statement on CJD in adolescents. Two letters were also published in *The Lancet* on CJD in a 16-year-old and an 18-year-old.[113] In November 1995 two more people died of new-variant CJD. On 8 March 1996 the CJD Surveillance Unit informed the SEAC of a possible new form of CJD; first known as new-variant CJD and now as vCJD. On 20 March 1996 the secretary of state for health announced to Parliament that the Unit had identified a new disease pattern, there were ten cases of vCJD, and a possible link with BSE. The CMO wrote to all doctors about vCJD on 1 July, and in October a paper in *Nature* reported that the biochemical characteristics of vCJD were closer to BSE than standard CJD.[114] Ten people died from vCJD during 1996. On 22 December 1997 the BSE Inquiry was announced and set up on 12 January 1998 'to establish and review the history of the emergence and identification of BSE and new variant CJD in the United Kingdom, and of the action taken in response to it up to 20 March 1996; to reach conclusions on the adequacy of that response, taking into account the state of knowledge at the time'.[115] Its report, published in 2000, noted issues with the government's handling of risk and communicating it to the public,[116] and recommendations included clearer lines of

---

[111] National CJD Surveillance Unit, 'CJD Funding Unit' (at: www.cjd.ed.ac.uk/funding.htm, accessed 16/03/11).
[112] MAFF in House of Commons, *Agriculture and Health Committees*, as cited in Maxwell, 'The British', p. 97, Table 7.1, emphasis supplied.
[113] T.C. Britton *et al.*, 'Sporadic Creutzfeldt–Jakob Disease in a 16-year-old in the UK' (1995) 346 *The Lancet* 1155; D. Bateman *et al.*, 'Sporadic Creutzfeldt–Jakob Disease in a 18-year-old in the UK' (1995) 346 *The Lancet* 1155.
[114] J. Collinge *et al.*, 'Molecular Analysis of Prion Strain Variation and the Aetiology of "New Variant" CJD' (1996) 383 *Nature* 685.
[115] Phillips *et al.*, *BSE Inquiry*, vol. 1, Executive Summary, p. xvii.
[116] *Ibid.*, pp. xx–xxiv.

accountability for risk management decisions and more open communication with the public about risks.[117]

The fallout

The BSE crisis drew attention to issues such as the use of expert committees to determine risk and regulation,[118] the time lag between the identification of BSE in non-human and then human animals,[119] uncertainty about the possibility of diseases crossing the species barrier,[120] and the doubt which surrounded, and still surrounds, the link between BSE and vCJD.[121] The 1990 declaration that the risk to humans of eating British beef was '*minute*'[122] might have been an appropriate *scientific* description, but transmission *was* possible although the probability was unknown. What this meant and the inherent uncertainty was not clearly communicated and the Southwood Committee '[w]hilst ... [drawing] attention to the uncertainties that existed ... did not and do not consider that the highlighting of numerous "potential" risks was then or is now desirable especially when such potential risks are based on speculation rather than scientific knowledge'.[123] It was worried about being alarmist and increasing public anxiety,[124] and members of the government admitted that protecting the beef industry was also a concern.[125] This approach and other government actions and statements led many to conclude there was 'no risk', rather than there being 'no *evidence* of risk so far'. Importantly, the magnitude of the risk for those who have contracted vCJD cannot be described as 'minute' as it includes significant psychiatric and neurological symptoms, is progressive, incurable and terminal; with 'treatments' limited to reducing symptoms.[126]

---

[117] *Ibid.*, ch. 14, paras. 1275, 1290–1300.
[118] Fisher, *Risk Regulation*, ch. 2; Lord Phillips, 'Lessons from the BSE Inquiry' (2001) 17 *FST Journal* 3, 4–5.
[119] MAFF, DH, *Report of the Working Party*, para. 5.3.1.
[120] *Ibid.*, para. 5.3.5; van Zwanenberg and Millstone, *BSE*, ch. 4.
[121] van Zwanenberg and Millstone, *BSE*, pp. 75–77; National CJD Surveillance Unit, 'The Different Types of CJD – Variant CJD' (2002) (at: www.cjd.ed.ac.uk/cjdtype.htm#variant, accessed 16/03/11).
[122] Above, n. 112, emphasis supplied.
[123] Southwood Working Party, 'Witness Statement No. 1D' (1999), para. 9 in Phillips *et al.*, *BSE Inquiry*, as cited in van Zwanenberg and Millstone, *BSE*, p. 113.
[124] Phillips *et al.*, *BSE Inquiry*, vol. 1, ch. 13, paras. 1178–1179, 1189, ch. 14, para. 1294; van Zwanenberg and Millstone, *BSE*, pp. 103–113.
[125] W. Waldegrave, The BSE Inquiry/statement 299, as cited in M. O'Brien, 'Have Lessons Been Learned from the UK Bovine Spongiform Encephalopathy (BSE) Epidemic?' (2000) 29 *International Journal of Epidemiology* 730.
[126] National CJD Surveillance Unit, 'Creutzfeldt–Jakob Disease: Clinical Features – Variant CJD' (2003) (at: www.cjd.ed.ac.uk/clinfeat.htm#variant, accessed 16/03/11).

BSE had a significant impact on those who contracted vCJD and their families, and on the economy, the interaction of science and policy, how policies and decisions are made, and how risk is communicated to and perceived by the public. It showed the fallibility of stating or implying that policy decisions were science based where that science was incomplete and uncertain, and that while scientists and others might deem a low risk to be acceptable others may not; especially where the consequences if the risk materialises are grave and irreversible. Questions were raised as to where protecting the public sits in expert risk assessments,[127] and BSE reminded the public that experts can be wrong and that probabilities, hopes and certainties should not be confused. It made it clear that the public *did* want information about uncertainty rather than rash reassurances of (unproven) safety, and that 'earlier engagement between citizens and experts might have led to more comprehensive and better characterization of risks, as well as diversified and realistic policy responses'.[128] The public was told or, at least, *heard* that British beef was safe when it appears not to have been.[129] When the government's and scientists' seemingly unconditional statements that British beef was safe were proved wrong, trust in science, scientific experts and science-based policy decisions was eroded, as was the government's credibility as a source of expertise.[130] The uncertainties surrounding BSE were such that the 'scientifically uninformed public was almost as well positioned as the experts to make sensible decisions about how to avoid the ill-defined and poorly characterized risk of BSE'.[131] In 2000 the House of Lords declared that following the BSE saga there was a 'crisis of confidence' and trust in scientific advice to the government,[132] aided by an increase in the 'consumer citizen' and a decrease in the role of the 'expert' because of the availability of information.[133] Indeed, following numerous food scares, 'a breach of trust ... now yawns between citizens and

---

[127] J. Murphy-Lawless, 'The Impact of BSE and FMD on Ethics and Democratic Process' (2004) 17 *Journal of Agricultural and Environmental Ethics* 385, 396.

[128] S. Jasanoff, 'Civilization and Madness: The Great BSE Scare of 1996' (1997) 6 *Public Understanding of Science* 221, 230. Similarly, the public GM debate highlighted that there *was* a desire to know more about GM and for a 'corpus of agreed "facts", accepted by all organisations and interests' to be produced (DTI, *GM Nation?*, p. 7).

[129] See National CJD Surveillance Unit, 'CJD Figures' (2011) (at: www.cjd.ed.ac.uk/figures.htm, accessed 16/03/11).

[130] van Zwanenberg and Millstone, *Risk*, p. 2.   [131] Jasanoff, 'Civilization', 229.

[132] House of Lords, *Science and Society*, Report Summary, paras. 1, 7, Main Report, paras. 1.1, 2.2, 2.36.

[133] L. Frewer and B. Salter, 'Public Attitudes, Scientific Advice and the Politics of Regulatory Policy: The Case of BSE' (2002) 29 *Science and Public Policy* 137, 138.

government'; particularly as 'the modern state, with its regulatory machinery, appears to be less able to provide safeguards for its citizens'.[134]

The BSE crisis exemplified the fact that some policy questions are 'trans-scientific'; they 'hang on the answers to questions which can be asked of science and yet *which cannot be answered by science*'.[135] Here science can only say 'don't know' and policy-makers cannot rely on it to do more. The fact that science does not and cannot have all the answers needs to be widely disseminated, and decisions must be based on other factors. One way to bolster trust in those providing risk messages is by encouraging transparency, openness and involving the public in risk decisions, 'a participatory communication process, rather than the "top-down" approach that has been used in the past'.[136] Not doing so may lead to 'public perceptions that the "real risks" are being "hidden" because they are unacceptable to the public, further compromising trust in those responsible for risk regulation.'[137] If risks are not appropriately communicated, partial information may be released or leaked, and risk information vacuums created which are filled by others such as the media, interest groups or intuitive fears.[138] If these are created, risk amplification may develop and '[r]isk communication failures can initiate a cascade of events that exacerbate risk controversies and render risk issues difficult to manage'.[139] The media had an important role in informing the public of the development of BSE in cows and then the possible link between BSE and vCJD in humans. It communicated government and scientists 'official lines' but also helped encourage a sense, for some, that the 'real risks' were being 'hidden' and so contributed to (understandable) public anxiety. Similarly, with the more recent severe acute respiratory syndrome (SARS) epidemic in the early 2000s, the 'antagonistic nature of the media's relationship with the government [in Hong Kong] led to accusations of inaction and cover up, increasing fear in the community and having a direct impact on the economy'.[140] As the media and its reach ever expands, its importance in developing or undermining trust and confidence in risk communication cannot be

---

[134] Murphy-Lawless, 'Impact of BSE', 390.
[135] A.M. Weinberg, 'Science and Trans-science' (1972) 10 *Minerva* 209, 209, emphasis in original.
[136] L.J. Frewer, 'Public Risk Perceptions and Risk Communication', in Bennett and Calman, *Risk Communication*, pp. 20, 26.
[137] *Ibid.*, p. 30.   [138] Powell and Leiss, *Mad Cows*, p. 31.
[139] *Ibid.*, p. 214. Also N. Pidgeon *et al.*, *The Social Amplification of Risk* (Cambridge University Press, 2003).
[140] S. Griffiths and J. Lau, 'The Influence of SARS on Perceptions of Risk and Reality' (2009) 31 *Journal of Public Health* 466, 466.

overemphasised. Indeed, reports on infections such as SARS and avian flu have familiarised the public with the possibility of infectious diseases being transmitted inter- and intra-species, and increased awareness of the evidence and uncertainty surrounding these diseases. Most people access some form of news media daily but trusting the media to convey complex and uncertain scientific information is risky, as the professions have different conventions, cultures and motivations. Scientists might, for example, be more interested in discrete facts about a particular phenomenon and not its broader implications, while journalists need 'news', something 'big', with impact; preferably something with which readers, viewers or listeners can personally identify.[141] Nevertheless, the media remain an essential part of the risk communication process but should not be the sole source of information for the public. The UK government has accepted that it has a central role in this process but has acknowledged that this has become more difficult as information sources have increased, public expectations changed, and a number of events, including BSE, have affected trust and confidence in the government.[142]

Managing risks

The BSE saga highlighted some of the problems in understanding and communicating uncertainty to the public, the consequences of issuing no risk statements which are later proved wrong, different perceptions of risk with regard to probability and magnitude, the importance of trust in the communicator to keep the public 'onside', and the role of the media. Xenotransplantation raises similar issues and lessons from BSE must be learned; indeed, 'the likelihood of further loss of life as a result of vCJD should serve as a constant reminder of both the complex nature of risk control, and the possible causes and consequences of regulatory failure'.[143] Xenotransplantation also requires risks which extend beyond the intended beneficiary to be managed, and this poses additional problems. In managing risks to the public the UK's Strategy Unit suggested the government would follow five principles: be 'open and transparent about its understanding of the nature of risks to the public and about the process it is following in handling them'; 'seek wide

---

[141] Bubela *et al.*, 'Science Communication', 516; House of Lords, *Science and Society*, ch. 7.
[142] House of Lords, *Science and Society*, Report Summary, paras. 1, 7, Main Report, paras. 1.1, 2. 2, 2.36; Strategy Unit, *Risk*, paras. 3.22–3.28, ch. 5, esp. paras. 5.5–5.8.
[143] G. Little, 'BSE and the Regulation of Risk' (2001) 64 *Modern Law Review* 730, 756.

involvement of those affected by risks in the decision process'; 'act proportionately in dealing with risks to the public, and will take a precautionary approach where necessary'; 'seek to base decisions on all relevant evidence'; and 'seek to allocate responsibility for managing risks to those best placed to control them'.[144] How then should the risks of xenotransplantation be appropriately managed?

Cost–benefit analysis

In health care generally and particularly with clinical trials, risks are often managed by applying cost–benefit analysis. In this utilitarian approach the risks and benefits of a procedure are weighed and if the latter outweighs the former it is justified to proceed. One form of such analysis is the logic of lesser harms; an intervention is appropriate if the risks it poses are lower than the risks of the condition which it is intended to treat or prevent.[145] It 'requires the probability of net benefit. But risk to subjects can be balanced by the expectation of a contribution to the greater social good.'[146] For cost–benefit analysis generally to work the risks and benefits must, to some extent, be quantifiable; they must fall within categories (i) and (ii), situations of known outcomes or known probabilities.[147] Where probabilities are not known at all and decisions are being made under ignorance, category (iii), it is unclear how cost–benefit analysis can apply because of the lack of knowledge of benefits and harms. Even in situations (i) and (ii), cost–benefit analysis is not straightforward because, for example, it is unclear what ratio of risk to benefit justifies proceeding, what outcomes should be considered when making these calculations, how different outcomes should be weighed, and whether potential recipients' perceptions of risks and benefits should be considered. It can also be difficult to interpret the relevant (usually uncertain) scientific evidence, and 'such evidence is open to multiple interpretations, and researchers often disagree in their assessments'.[148]

The UK's Nuffield Council on Bioethics recognised the limitations of cost–benefit analysis, particularly in situations of ignorance, and noted that '[s]ince the possible consequences of developing xenotransplantation are potentially very serious, it is hardly wise to use a method of risk analysis that cannot address such consequences until they start to be seen'.[149] To apply cost–benefit analysis to xenotransplantation some of

---

[144] Strategy Unit, *Risk*, p. 91.
[145] S.A. Halpern, *Lesser Harms: The Morality of Risk in Medical Research* (University of Chicago Press, 2006), p. 4.
[146] *Ibid.*, p. 5.   [147] Above, n. 64.   [148] Halpern, *Lesser Harms*, p. 8.
[149] Nuffield Council on Bioethics, *Animal-to-Human Transplants – The Ethics of Xenotransplantation* (London: Nuffield Council on Bioethics, 1996), para. 6.20.

the uncertainty would need to be eradicated and pre-clinical research might help with this; but their efficacy and risks can only really be determined by allowing their *clinical* use. If the risks were limited to the potential beneficiary, this might be acceptable but where *public* health is in danger this approach is inappropriate.

A precautionary approach
The precautionary principle, often used in environmental policy, essentially holds that 'where there are threats of serious and irreversible damage, lack of full scientific certainty shall not be used as a reason for postponing cost-effective measures to prevent environmental degradation'.[150] It is 'a risk management policy applied in circumstances with a high degree of scientific uncertainty, reflecting the need to take action for a potentially serious risk without awaiting the results of scientific research'.[151] There is no agreed definition of the principle and its legal status is unclear,[152] but it is generally agreed that it is more appropriate to talk of a precautionary *approach*.[153] Such an approach is dynamic and commonly includes anticipating risk and harm, uncertainty, lack of evidence, acting in advance of established risks to minimise not necessarily eradicate risk, public participation in decision-making, and protecting existing and future generations.[154] It recognises that 'the damaging effects of human activities may become irreversible *before* the scientific community can agree the precise nature and scope of their impact'.[155] It favours preventing false negatives, helping to avoid disease and possibly harmful exposures, and respecting autonomy by allowing

---

[150] United Nations Rio Declaration on Environment and Development 1992, Principle 15.
[151] WHO, *Electromagnetic Fields and Public Health Cautionary Policies* (2000) (at: www.who.int/docstore/peh-emf/publications/facts_press/EMF-Precaution.htm, accessed 16/03/11).
[152] For Europe, see Fisher, *Risk Regulation*, ch. 6; more generally, United Nations Educational, Scientific and Cultural Organization (UNESCO), World Commission on the Ethics of Scientific Knowledge and Technology, *The Precautionary Principle* (2005), section 2.2 (at: http://unesdoc.unesco.org/images/0013/001395/139578e.pdf, accessed 16/03/11).
[153] E.g. House of Commons Science and Technology Committee, *Scientific Advice, Risk and Evidence Based Policy Making Seventh Report of Session 2005–6*, vol. I (London: Stationery Office, 2006), HC 900-I, para. 166; C.F. Cranor, 'Learning from the Law to Address Uncertainty in the Precautionary Principle' (2001) 7 *Science and Engineering Ethics* 313.
[154] E.g. M. Feintuck, 'Precautionary Maybe, But What's the Principle? The Precautionary Principle, the Regulation of Risk, and the Public Domain' (2005) 32 *Journal of Law and Society* 371; R.L. Keeney and D. von Winterfeldt, 'Appraising the Precautionary Principle – A Decision Analysis Perspective' (2001) 4 *Journal of Risk Research* 191.
[155] J. Holder and S. Elworthy, 'The BSE Crisis: A Study of the Precautionary Principle and the Politics of Science in Law', in H. Reece (ed.), *Law and Science: Current Legal Issues*, vol. 1 (Oxford University Press, 1998), pp. 129, 131, emphasis supplied.

people to choose the risks they want to bear.[156] Harms which may result from human actions should be avoided or diminished but these do not have to be certain outcomes; rather, 'it is sufficient that they be *scientifically plausible*'.[157] A precautionary approach recognises intrinsic and extrinsic links to the to-be-managed activity, and presumes a flexible legal approach which is open and adjustable.[158] It is not a formula and applying it requires 'a judgement that takes into account the particular circumstances of the problem to be addressed'.[159] Under this approach risky activities can be regulated, constrained or prohibited, even though the risks are scientifically uncertain, directed at community interests, and may harm individuals, the public *and* future generations.[160] It has an 'intimate, though often implicit, connection with collective, democratic interests and the public domain, which it may serve to reassert in the face of increasingly dominant private interests'.[161]

Adopting a precautionary approach does not automatically result in a moratorium, a choice between action and inaction, or allowing and blaming; rather it involves a process of *'learning through experimentations'* and *acting while doubting*'[162] and focuses on appropriate responses to developments which may harm human health, for example.[163] It '[tempers] the permissive approach through the taking into account of risks which are uncertain. This permits a sound decision to be made based on adequate risk assessment.'[164] Where there are recognised harms to human health but their extent is unknown, the person proposing the action has the burden of disproving risks;[165] they do not have to show there are no risks but must proactively seek to determine their

---

[156] D. Jamieson, 'The Precautionary Principle and Electric and Magnetic Fields' (2001) 91 *American Journal of Public Health* 1355, 1357.
[157] K. Steele, 'The Precautionary Principle: A New Approach to Public Decision-Making' (2006) 5 *Law, Probability and Risk* 19, 19, emphasis supplied.
[158] L. Boisson de Chazournes, 'New Technologies, the Precautionary Principle, and Public Participation', in T. Murphy (ed.), *New Technology and Human Rights* (Oxford University Press, 2009), pp. 161, 165.
[159] Nuffield Council on Bioethics, *Public Health: Ethical Issues* (London: Nuffield Council on Bioethics, 2007), para. 3.19.
[160] E. Soule, 'Assessing the Precautionary Principle' (2000) 14 *Public Affairs Quarterly* 309; Steele, 'Precautionary Principle', 24.
[161] Feintuck, 'Precautionary Maybe', 372.
[162] J. Dratwa, 'Taking Risks with the Precautionary Principle: Food (and the Environment) for Thought at the European Commission' (2002) 4 *Journal of Environmental Policy and Planning* 197, 207, emphasis in original.
[163] Nuffield Council, *Animal-to-Human*, para. 6.22.
[164] Nuffield Council, *Public Health*, p. 180.
[165] Commission of the European Communities, *Communication from the Commission on the Precautionary Principle* COM(2000) 1 Final, para. 6.4.

nature and magnitude.[166] The European Commission has stated that measures based on a precautionary approach should be proportional, non-discriminatory, consistent, based on an examination of the potential costs and benefits of acting or not, subject to review and able to assign responsibility for producing scientific evidence.[167] A precautionary approach has, however, been criticised for being ill-defined, absolutist, 'anti-science', marginalising science, and deterring progress and development.[168] Nevertheless, if the risks are plausible and the precautionary measures adopted reasonable, these criticisms will not manifest and are unfounded.[169] A precautionary approach is identifiable in the European response to the BSE crisis where action was taken *prior* to a scientifically established link between BSE and vCJD,[170] and was stated to be the basis of the UK government's response to the public debate on GM crops, discussed below.[171] The approach expands Mill's harm principle so that it encompasses public goods and possible harm to future generations.[172]

The harm principle

Under Mill's harm principle an individual's liberty can *only* be limited through law or moral coercion *if* the individual's behaviour causes harm to others.[173] Harm includes acts which are 'injurious to others' and '[e]ncroachment of their rights; infliction on them of any loss or damage not justified by his own rights' are provided as examples.[174] The British Better Regulation Commission endorsed this principle stating that 'all policy-making should start with a simple principle: "*When informed adults choose voluntarily to expose themselves to a risk and/or take responsibility for managing that risk and their behaviour does not harm others, the government should not intervene*".'[175] Mill's principle applies to 'definite

---

[166] R. Andorno, 'The Precautionary Principle: A New Legal Standard for a Technological Age' (2004) 1 *Journal of International Biotechnology Law* 11, 19.
[167] Commission, *Communication*, pp. 3–4, para. 6.3.
[168] P. Sandin *et al.*, 'Five Charges Against the Precautionary Principle' (2002) 5 *Journal of Risk Research* 287; T. O'Riordan and A. Jordan, 'The Precautionary Principle in Contemporary Environmental Politics' (1995) 4 *Environmental Values* 191.
[169] D.B. Resnik, 'Is the Precautionary Principle Unscientific?' (2003) 34 *Studies in History and Philosophy of Biological and Biomedical Sciences* 329.
[170] Department for Environment, Food and Rural Affairs (DEFRA) *et al.*, *The GM Dialogue: Government Response* (London: DEFRA, 2004), p. 3.
[171] *Ibid.* and p. 5.   [172] Steele, 'Precautionary Principle', 24.
[173] J.S. Mill, 'On Liberty', in *On Liberty and Other Essays* (Oxford University Press, 2008), pp. 13–14, 83–84.
[174] *Ibid.*, p. 87.
[175] Better Regulation Commission (BRC), *Risk, Responsibility and Regulation – Whose Risk Is It Anyway?* (London: BRC, 2006), p. 31, emphasis in original.

damage, or a definite risk of damage',[176] but extending it to a *risk* of harm may distort or exaggerate the principle,[177] and as it is difficult to *definitely* ascertain that conduct poses no significant risk of future harm it may be too easy to formulate arguments based on harm, so the principle collapses in on itself.[178] It is thus important to take care when using harm claims to ensure that the principle remains sufficiently defined. Developing the harm principle, Feinberg contends that there are two notions of harm: as a setback to an interest and as a wrong. Interests are 'things in which one has a stake' and are central to an individual's well-being,[179] and harm in the first sense occurs when an individual's behaviour *prevents* another's interest leaving it 'in a worse condition than it would otherwise have been in had the invasion not occurred at all'.[180] Harm as a wrong occurs when an individual's 'indefensible (unjustifiable and inexcusable) conduct violates the other's right'[181] or she treats another unjustly. Only harms which fit into both categories justify legally prohibiting conduct. Although the harm principle is often read as being concerned with *individual* autonomy it *can* operate for *public* health,[182] and it would detract from Mill's utilitarian outlook if it could not function to allow collective interests to be considered and utility maximised.[183]

Precaution, harm and xenotransplantation

Xenotransplantation poses risks of harm but their nature and severity are unclear. All first-in-human trials necessarily involve risk which is one reason why they are regulated in most countries, and an example of a precautionary approach in practice. The Council of Europe considered this approach for xenotransplants and said it should mean that the risks are 'minimal and controllable' and that although there could be 'no absolute guarantees', in the light of pre-clinical research and following 'internationally accepted standards', it must be 'highly probable that

---

[176] Mill, *On Liberty*, p. 91.
[177] N. Persak, *Criminalising Harmful Conduct: The Harm Principle, Its Limits and Continental Counterparts* (New York, NY: Springer-Verlag, 2007), pp. 44–45.
[178] B.E. Harcourt, 'The Collapse of the Harm Principle' (1999) 90 *Journal of Criminal Law and Criminology* 109; A. von Hirsch, 'Extending the Harm Principle: "Remote" Harms and Fair Imputation', in A.P. Simester and A.T.H. Smith (eds.), *Harm and Culpability* (Oxford: Clarendon Press, 1996), pp. 259, 260.
[179] J. Feinberg, *The Moral Limits of the Criminal Law: Harm to Others, Volume One* (New York, NY: Oxford University Press, 1984), p. 34.
[180] *Ibid.* [181] *Ibid.*
[182] J. Coggon, 'Harmful Rights-Doing? The Perceived Problem of Liberal Paradigms and Public Health' (2008) 34 *Journal of Medical Ethics* 798, 799.
[183] *Utilitarianism*, in Mill, *On Liberty*; also, *On Liberty*, p. 15.

there is *no* risk involved'.[184] Given the need to 'gain and maintain' public confidence, clinical xenotransplants should thus only occur when there is 'a high level assurance about safety'.[185] The UK's Nuffield Council also recommended adopting a precautionary approach involving collating information on the risks, establishing an advisory committee, and monitoring xeno-recipients.[186] This was, to some extent, adopted by the establishment of the United Kingdom Xenotransplantation Interim Regulatory Authority (UKXIRA) in 1997 which produced draft guidance on surveillance recommending monitoring of xeno-recipients and others.[187] Similarly, 'deliberative precaution' which 'instructs to take account of all relevant knowledge in circumstances of scientific uncertainty and ignorance'[188] may be appropriate for xenotransplantation because of the uncertainty and 'potentially irreversible (health) risks to future generations'.[189]

Where risks go beyond the individual and may endanger the public a precautionary approach along with the harm principle is appropriate to effectively manage those risks. A more proactive response to xenotransplantation is thus needed; an approach which involves asking whether it is needed in the first place, if it is, then how much harm can be avoided while achieving its goals, and whether there are alternatives which avoid harm.[190] Regulatory measures which address and minimise the risks are required and if this is not possible then, as has occurred with other developing (bio)technologies,[191] a moratorium on clinical xenotransplants is appropriate. The latter initially occurred in some countries but, as Chapter 4 shows, there is now a sense that the risks *can* be otherwise effectively managed even though this is contestable. Where private benefit and public risk are at issue and the beneficiary and risk bearers different, clinical application is premature unless and until the risks move into category (i) or (ii).[192] The disjunction of benefit and risk

---

[184] Council of Europe, *Report on the State*, para. 7.5.4, emphasis supplied. [185] *Ibid.*
[186] Nuffield Council, *Animal-to-Human*, ch. 6, esp. paras. 6.38, 6.41.
[187] See Chapters 4 and 6.
[188] H. Somsen, 'Cloning Trojan Horses: Precautionary Regulation of Reproductive Technologies', in R. Brownsword, K. Yeung (eds.), *Regulating Technologies: Legal Futures, Regulatory Frames and Technological Fixes* (Oxford: Hart, 2008), pp. 221, 228–229.
[189] *Ibid.*, p. 241.
[190] D. Kriebel and J. Tickner, 'Reenergizing Public Health Through Precaution' (2001) 91 *American Journal of Public Health* 1351, 1352.
[191] E.g. Halpern, *Lesser Harms*; R.C. Fox and J.P. Swazey, *The Courage to Fail: A Social \View of Organ Transplants and Dialysis* (New Jersey, NJ: Transaction, 2002); D.B. Dutton, *Worse than the Disease: Pitfalls of Medical Progress* (New York, NY: Cambridge University Press, 1988).
[192] Above, n. 64.

is important because it is an accepted legal principle that the person who benefits should bear any loss, 'the polluter pays principle', but xenotransplantation challenges this norm and necessitates a different risk management strategy. Where the effects of waiting for the risks to materialise may be catastrophic, a precautionary approach combined with the harm principle supports *anticipatory* state action to protect others.[193]

Clinical xenotransplants could cause harm in both of Feinberg's senses; by setting back an individual's interests, if the risk of an infectious disease materialises and the individual's health is thereby threatened and, unless everyone at risk of harm consents to it, as a wrong by violating others' right to consent. Using the harm principle in circumstances of uncertainty is not unproblematic as it is easier to apply it where the harm is concrete and ascertainable but, in another context, the UK's House of Lords has held that the lack of concrete or easily measurable potential harm to 'vulnerable' individuals did not prevent that harm outweighing a person's personal autonomy.[194] The harm principle recognises that harm can be caused for a legitimate reason,[195] but (possibly) preserving a xeno-recipient's life is not sufficient because ensuring the health of the public outweighs the benefit of saving one person's life. Although investigators and the xeno-recipient are acting to preserve life and do not intend to harm others, they are arguably reckless in proceeding, given that foreseeable risk of harm and legal accountability for this may follow.[196] Once a clinical xenotransplant is performed it is impossible to guarantee that public health is not at risk and the danger of disease transfer and a pandemic moves from the theoretical to the real; and if the risks actualise, it will be too late. Interest in public health is thus a powerful reason for state interference in advance and could support prohibiting clinical xenotransplants. This may be appropriate because of the risks of this biotechnology, but combining a precautionary approach with the harm principle does not necessarily lead to this outcome. Rather, the type of state intervention is context specific and there will be cases where state intervention is not justified, even though an individual's action has caused harm.[197] For xenotransplants, Mill's harm principle is liberty limiting and when combined with a precautionary approach supports giving precedence to *public* health.

---

[193] S. Fovargue and S. Ost, 'When Should Precaution Prevail? Interests in (Public) Health and the Risk of Harm: The Xenotransplantation Example' (2010) 18 *Medical Law Review* 302.
[194] *R (Pretty)* v. *DPP* [2002] 1 UKHL 61.   [195] Mill, *On Liberty*, p. 104.
[196] M. Brazier and J. Harris, 'Public Health and Private Lives' (1996) 4 *Medical Law Review* 171; Mill, *On Liberty*, p. 90.
[197] Mill, *On Liberty*, p. 104.

Public health

The historical legal and ethical focus on the individual in health care has started to subtly shift towards consideration of theories, ethics and issues of public health,[198] perhaps because of infectious diseases scares, bio-terrorist threats and increases in global travel and migration. Public health measures draw attention to the appropriate relationship between the state and the individuals within it, the duties individuals have to each other, and xenotransplantation engages three particular aspects of interest in public health; first, the health of the public. Public health 'emphasises *collective responsibility* for health, its protection and disease prevention';[199] is concerned with the good of the public but is not necessarily incompatible with the good of the individual;[200] and is 'both an intrinsic and an instrumental value for society ... a good in itself and for what it enables society to do'.[201] Public health measures are essentially based on communitarian and utilitarian theories,[202] and to facilitate public health, laws may permit the state to take preventive, sometimes coercive, action in *society's* interest.[203] Determining the appropriate level of state intervention to protect public health is not easy because if the measures are 'broadly drafted and strictly enforced' infection transmission and public support may be reduced,[204] and the acceptability of such interventions may be linked to the trust the public has in the body implementing the action.[205] Public health laws and measures thus highlight a tension between private and public rights. The European Court of Human Rights has confirmed that public health powers *can* comply with Article 5 of the European Convention on Human Rights (ECHR), the right to liberty and security,[206] but without

---

[198] E.g. publication of the journal *Public Health Ethics* by Oxford University Press since 2008 (at: http://phe.oxfordjournals.org, accessed 16/03/11); Nuffield Council, *Public Health*; A. Dawson and M. Verweij (eds.) *Ethics, Prevention and Public Health* (Oxford University Press, 2007).
[199] UK – Faculty of Public Health, 'The Faculty's Public Health Approach' (at: www.fph.org.uk/what_is_public_health, accessed 16/03/11, emphasis supplied).
[200] Coggon, 'Harmful Rights-Doing?'.
[201] J.F. Childress and R.G Bernheim, 'Beyond the Liberal and Communitarian Impasse: A Framework and Vision for Public Health' (2003) 55 *Florida Law Review* 1191, 1194.
[202] *Ibid*.
[203] Or individuals working within the UK's health system: e.g. General Medical Council (GMC), *Confidentiality* (London: GMC, 2009), paras. 8, 36–56; *W* v. *Egdell* [1990] Ch. 359.
[204] M.A. Rothstein, 'Are Traditional Public Health Strategies Consistent with Contemporary American Values?' (2004) 77 *Temple Law Review* 175, 176.
[205] *Ibid.*, p. 177.
[206] *Enhorn* v. *Sweden* (2005) 41 EHHR 30, European Court of Human Rights, discussed further in Chapter 6.

legislative guidance on assessing and measuring risk, using public health powers when risks cannot be scientifically proven *might* contravene the Article.[207] This is important because public health measures are often directed towards reducing or eliminating *risks* of harm and are concerned with '*probable* rather than certain *benefits*'.[208]

The state, secondly, has an interest in the health of the *individuals* in society. In the UK this has translated into establishing the National Health Service to provide appropriate health care to those in need in a timely manner. International conventions and charters have set out 'rights' to health, language which suggests that states may be accountable and have obligations if these are violated,[209] and an individual's 'right' to health may be evolving in the UK under Article 2 of the ECHR and Human Rights Act 1998.[210] If so, this must be a qualified and not an absolute right, 'a right to health care of a certain level',[211] just as other rights, such as personal autonomy via a right to bodily integrity under Article 8 of the Convention,[212] are not absolute. There are thus situations where, for example, the need to protect the rights of vulnerable others can take precedence over personal autonomy;[213] so although individual interests in health and personal autonomy and rights are legally and ethically recognised, they can be offset by other public and private interests. Finally, there is an interest in advancing medicine for public and individual health purposes; particularly that which might prolong or save lives. It is part of the human psyche to want to develop and move forward, and the 'seductive sirens of medical progress'[214] can be hard to ignore. However, just because something can technically be done, it does not mean it should be,[215] and some 'advances' may pose such risks that their continued development and introduction should be questioned. Halting advances may have undesirable consequences for those hoping to benefit from them, but 'the new science

---

[207] R. Martin, 'The Exercise of Public Health Powers in Cases of Infectious Disease: Human Rights Implications: *Enhorn* v. *Sweden*, European Court of Human Rights: [2005] ECHR 56529/00' (2006) 14 *Medical Law Review* 132, 141.
[208] J. Coggon, 'Public Health, Responsibility and English Law: Are There Such Things as No Smoke without Ire or Needless Clean Needles?' (2009) 17 *Medical Law Review* 127, 135 n. 54, emphasis supplied.
[209] E.g. Article 25 Universal Declaration of Human Rights of 1948; Articles 11 and 13 European Social Charter of 1961; L.O. Gostin, *Public Health Law: Power, Duty, Restraint* (2nd edn, Berkeley, CA: University of California Press, 2008), p. 278.
[210] E.g. *Osman* v. *UK* (1998) 29 EHRR 245.   [211] O'Neill, *Autonomy and Trust*, p. 79.
[212] E.g. *R (on the application of Burke)* v. *GMC* [2005] EWCA Civ. 1003.
[213] E.g. *Pretty* v. *UK* [2002] 2 FLR 45, European Court of Human Rights.
[214] Hanson, 'Seductive Sirens', 5.
[215] I. Kennedy, *Treat Me Right – Essays in Medical Law and Ethics* (Oxford: Clarendon Press, 1988), ch. 14.

Public health   45

has moved us from chance to choice in many matters ... With choice comes the responsibility to use that choice ethically. Doing so requires two kinds of courage: the courage to go forward with the new science and technology when it is morally and ethically acceptable to do so, and the courage to exercise restraint when it is morally and ethically required.'[216] Xenotransplantation requires such courage because of the conflict between public health, individual health and advancing medicine.

Public health and xenotransplantation

Clinical xenotransplants can be seen as a risk and benefit to public health. The need to protect public and individual health from the former could require the state to prohibit xenotransplants, and not doing so could mean the state was knowingly permitting the public to be exposed to serious, unquantifiable and possibly uncontrollable risks. Everyone is at risk of a pandemic following a clinical xenotransplant and experiences with swine flu and SARS, for example, suggest that public disorder and the collapse of infrastructures may result.[217] Without minimising the harm suffered by those requiring a (xeno)transplant, the insufficient number of human organs available for transplantation has a more limited impact on public health. The harm suffered by those individuals is different in magnitude as it is the health of a limited number and not society's capacity to function that is in jeopardy. Thus, the risks of clinical xenotransplants outweigh the harm caused by the ill health of a limited few. On the other hand, by encouraging xenotransplantation the state would be promoting individual and public health by (if successful) prolonging or saving life, minimising suffering and ill health within the community, and enabling resources to be released for other treatments. The interest in advancing medical knowledge and progress would also be served. There may thus be more advantages of proceeding with clinical xenotransplants. Nevertheless, there is a precedent for prohibiting a developing biotechnology which *may* risk the health of others: reproductive cloning. This biotechnology might have benefited public health as an infertility 'treatment' and satisfied an individual's interest in having a biologically related child, but it is unlawful in the UK.[218] One reason

---

[216] Sommerville, 'Searching for Ethics', p. 29.
[217] E.g. WHO, Global Alert and Response (GAR), 'Pandemic (H1N1)' (2009) (at: www.who.int/csr/disease/swineflu/en, accessed 16/03/11); WHO, GAR, 'Severe Acute Respiratory Syndrome (SARS)' (2004) (at: www.who.int/csr/sars/en, accessed 16/03/11).
[218] Initially s. 1 Reproductive Cloning Act 2001, now s. 3 Human Fertilisation and Embryology Act 2008.

46   Dealing with risk

for this is the potential harm to the clone via birth defects; the probability of which is unclear but could be severe in nature.[219] Despite the uncertainty, prohibiting reproductive cloning was deemed an appropriate regulatory response as the benefits of it were also unclear. This holds true for xenotransplantation. When considering an individual's interest in health and interest in public health, the likelihood of a positive outcome for the xeno-recipient's health *is* as relevant as the risks. While preventing clinical xenotransplants *would* set back the interests of the recipient by depriving her of a chance of prolonging her life, pre-clinical results do not suggest that an individual's health *would* be so enhanced.

Nonetheless, such a prohibition could be viewed as infringing xeno-recipients' autonomy by breaching the negative obligation of individual autonomy not to constrain the autonomous actions of others,[220] but *is* consenting to a xenotransplant an affirmative expression of individual autonomy? It will not be easy to fulfil the positive obligation of autonomy, involving disclosing information to enable autonomous decision-making,[221] because of the limited evidence which exists on the affect of receiving a genetically engineered solid organ xenotransplant. Furthermore, consenting to a xenotransplant will lead to such severe infringements of the recipient's personal autonomy in the future, including lifelong surveillance and having to refrain from having children,[222] that it is questionable whether an informed decision can be made about as-of-yet unexperienced liberty-limiting measures.[223] Although English law does not require an individual to have experienced treatments and health care options in order to give an informed refusal to them,[224] the situation here is different. A xeno-recipient is consenting to a medical intervention which will lead to unexperienced potentially severe restrictions on liberty, the extent of which are unknown and will depend on the as-yet-unknown consequences of having a xenotransplant. Even taking into account individual interests and autonomy, clinical xenotransplants place more at stake as the health of the recipient, contacts and public might be adversely affected. If prohibiting xenotransplantation on the basis of risk is questionable, then so too is clinically proceeding on the

---

[219] K.L. Macintosh, *Illegal Beings: Human Clones and the Law* (New York, NY: Cambridge University Press, 2005), Part One.
[220] T.L. Beauchamp and J.F. Childress, *Principles of Biomedical Ethics* (6th edn, New York, NY: Oxford University Press, 2009), p. 104.
[221] Ibid.   [222] See Chapter 6.   [223] See Chapter 5.
[224] E.g. *B v. NHS Hospital Trust* [2002] EWHC 429, but note *Re E (A Minor) (Wardship: Medical Treatment)* [1993] 1 FLR 386, where it was held that an adolescent could not understand the nature of his impending death.

basis of unproven benefit. And where there are risks to the public, the public must be involved in the decision-making process on whether to clinically proceed.

Public involvement in the decision-making process

Public involvement in decision-making about developing biotechnologies is essential as '[s]cience should not be expected to have sole responsibility for the future of [new developments in science]; there is a responsibility to society to involve all citizens in decisions to the extent that this is possible'.[225] The UK government has recognised the importance of consultation, provided information on possible methods of participation, and noted the difference between consulting the public to obtain their opinion and consulting experts of a certain community to obtain technical advice or feedback.[226] There are, however, concerns about public participation, including that it is part of the largely discredited deficit model of science.[227] A formal example of public participation is the Swiss system of direct democracy whereby if 100,000 signatures are collected within eighteen months an 'initiative' can be submitted and must be debated by the national parliament and government.[228] The initiative can be supported, rejected or counter-proposed, and a referendum on the initiative has to be held within five years of its being submitted. Public deliberation 'actively engages the public ... as partner and full participant in public health. It assumes and communicates that individual community members can be trusted to think and act collectively and voluntarily when threatened',[229] and can be viewed as 'the social equivalent of informed consent'.[230] Ideally it would occur at an early stage of a (bio)technology's developmental process as research and development priorities are determined because '[i]f the public is not conscious or involved at early stages there is a risk of a strong reaction later if the outcomes of research or its applications are presented and found to be at odds with the values or expectations of stakeholder groups and publics'.[231] Timing is important because

---

[225] R. Jackson et al., 'Strengths of Public Dialogue on Science-Related Issues' (2005) 8 Critical Review of International Social and Political Philosophy 349, 350.
[226] House of Commons, Scientific Advice, paras. 133–145.
[227] M. Michael and N. Brown, 'Scientific Citizenships: Self-Representations of Xenotransplantation's Public' (2005) 14 Science as Culture 39, 51.
[228] Switzerland.com, 'Direct Democracy: The People Decide' (at: www.swissworld.org/dvd_rom/direct_democracy_2005/index.html, accessed 16/03/11).
[229] Childress and Bernheim, 'Beyond the Liberal', 1215.
[230] Peter Healey as cited in House of Lords, Science and Society, para. 5.2.
[231] Jackson et al., 'Strengths of Public', 353.

'upstream' debate when new areas are emerging 'enables society to discuss and clarify the public value of science',[232] and permits certain questions to be asked: 'Why this technology? Why not another? Who needs it? Who is controlling it? Who benefits from it? Can they be trusted? What will it mean for me and my family? Will it improve the environment? What will it mean for people in the developing world?'[233] If engagement has not occurred at an early stage, this does not prevent later consultation, but it may be of a different nature and type. For example, small-scale deliberation might be appropriate at earlier stages where there is uncertainty[234] and mass participation methods where more is known of the applications and consequences.[235] Public engagement does not have to be a 'one-off' event, and where there is a significant lapse between the initial discussion and possible clinical application of a biotechnology, for example, the public should be consulted again and involved in the decision-making process as to whether to proceed.

Deliberative decision-making can improve the quality of decisions 'by opening it up to scrutiny through a dialogue in which ideas are interplayed and flaws in reasoning exposed'.[236] It is particularly important when a precautionary approach is adopted because without established facts it provides the basis for decisions in situations of ignorance, and as risk and uncertainty are socially constructed the public should debate them.[237] Different types of knowledge can be introduced, their reliability challenged, and when a precautionary approach engages the public potential problems may be anticipated before clinical application. Involving the public in framing and interpreting precaution should thus be 'just one more process through which complex decisions can be made – a process which may help to bring us a few steps closer to see-through science'.[238] However, a precautionary approach 'requires . . . a degree of

---

[232] J. Wilsdon et al., *The Public Value of Science: Or How to Ensure that Science Really Matters* (London: Demos, 2005), p. 29.
[233] Wilsdon and Willis, *See-Through Science*, p. 28.
[234] E.g. E. Grießler et al., *Final Report – Increasing Public Involvement in Debates on Ethical Questions of Xenotransplantation* (Vienna: Institute for Advanced Studies, 2004), p. 11; Science and Technology Policy Research Unit, Environment and Science Research Unit, Policy Studies Institute, 'Deliberative Mapping: Briefing 5 Using the Multi-Criteria Mapping Technique' (2004) (at: www.deliberative-mapping.org/papers/f-briefing-5.pdf, accessed 16/03/11).
[235] Jackson et al., 'Strengths of Public', 353, 356.
[236] E. Fisher and R. Harding, 'The Precautionary Principle: Towards a Deliberative, Transdisciplinary Problem-Solving Process', in R. Harding and E. Fisher (eds.), *Perspectives on the Precautionary Principle* (New South Wales: Federation Press, 1999), pp. 292, 293.
[237] *Ibid.*, p. 292; Boisson de Chazournes, 'New Technologies', pp. 178–181, 190.
[238] Wilsdon and Willis, *See-Through Science*, p. 54.

honesty around issues of uncertainty and hazard that has not always been forthcoming from business or from government', and this may not sit well '[i]n the age of "political spin"'.[239] Public consultation exercises are becoming more common in the UK and have been held on, for example, GM crops, gene therapy and xenotransplantation. These are considered here, along with the official post-consultation analysis of the process(es) used in the former two exercises.

GM crops

There was public disquiet in the mid-1990s when the first GM food was sold in the UK and the EU permitted the import and use of GM soya beans for human consumption as there was a sense that these foods had appeared without debate, there was distrust of the company involved, and widespread media debate on the dangers of GM foods.[240] The Nuffield Council published a report on GM crops in 1999[241] and the Agriculture and Environment Biotechnology Commission recommended that public debate and/or 'consent' was sought to such crops and food.[242] During 2003 and 2004 the government instigated 'GM Dialogue'[243] with three elements: public debate, a review of the science and a study into the overall costs and benefits associated with growing GM crops.[244] The public were involved in framing the issues for debate for the former, via nine discussion workshops held across the UK during November 2002,[245] and the debate, *GM Nation?*, was launched in June 2003

---

[239] D. Fischbacher-Smith and K. Calman, 'A Precautionary Tale: The Role of the Precautionary Principle in Policy-Making for Public Health', in P. Bennett, K. Calman, S. Curtis and D. Fischbacher-Smith (eds.), *Risk Communication and Public Health* (2nd edn, Oxford University Press, 2010), pp. 202–206, 209.
[240] BBC News, 'Genetically-modified Q&A' (1999) (at: http://news.bbc.co.uk/1/hi/special_report/1999/02/99/food_under_the_microscope/280868.stm, accessed 16/03/11); BBC Home, 'On this Day 5 February 1996' (at: http://news.bbc.co.uk/onthisday/hi/dates/stories/february/5/newsid_4647000/4647390.stm, accessed 16/03/11); House of Lords, *Science and Society*, Appendix 5.
[241] Nuffield Council on Bioethics, *Genetically Modified Crops: The Ethical and Social Issues* (London: Nuffield Council on Bioethics, 1999).
[242] Agriculture and Environment Biotechnology Commission (AEBC) *Crops on Trial – A Report by the AEBC* (London: AEBC, 2001), para. 40.
[243] DEFRA, 'GM Dialogue' (at: http://webarchive.nationalarchives.gov.uk/20081023141438/www.defra.gov.uk/environment/gm/crops/debate/index.htm, accessed 16/03/11).
[244] The GM Science Review Panel, *GM Science Review: First Report* (London: Department of Trade and Industry (DTI), 2003); GM Science Review Panel, *GM Science Review: Second Report* (London: DTI, 2004); Strategy Unit, *Field Work: Weighing Up the Costs and Benefits of GM Crops* (London: Cabinet Office, 2003), respectively. The public could also contribute to the science review: GM Science, *GM Science Review: First Report*, para. 2.2.
[245] DTI, *GM Nation?*, pp. 14–18.

comprising regional and local meetings involving an invited audience, open public meetings, and was overseen by an independent steering board.[246] A 'toolkit' was produced including a video, CD-ROM and workbook with a feedback form for individuals' views,[247] and over 1,000 people attended the six regional meetings and 675 local meetings were organised.[248] The website had 2.9 million hits and 1,200 letters or emails were received.[249] Public debate was 'welcomed and valued' by the public,[250] and although it was 'an innovative attempt at public engagement, and may come to be seen as marking a sea change in the government's approach to science and technology' it has been criticised for its timing, limited funding and failure to engage those not already involved in GM issues.[251]

After the public debate and the publication of the findings, the Department for Environment, Food and Rural Affairs (DEFRA) published a report on the consultation process.[252] It noted the need for public debate to be sufficiently funded with a reasonable and realistic timetable for it to occur, the importance of publicity, consideration of the appropriateness of an independent steering board, the importance of a project manager to coordinate the debate and act as a reference point for the board, and the need for independent evaluation.[253] The public's involvement in framing the issues for debate was important, the relationship between public engagement and policy-making should be clearly explained prior to the debate,[254] and attributed information should be provided.[255] The combination of invited and open meetings was useful, but at an early stage different ways of engaging people should be considered as large public meetings may not suit all.[256] DEFRA concluded that 'the multi-strand approach [public debate, science review, costs and benefits study] has been extremely valuable and ... is worth considering as a model for the future'.[257] It has been suggested that '[a]s a consequence ... policy-makers in the UK are now more sensitive to the need to encourage open and informed public discussion at earlier stages and to encourage scientists themselves to be aware of this need to consider issues and implications, including with the public'.[258]

---

[246] For more information, see *ibid.*, paras. 1–28.   [247] *Ibid.*, paras. 20–21, 104.
[248] *Ibid.*, paras. 24–25, 82.   [249] *Ibid.*, paras. 26–27, 95.   [250] *Ibid.*, p. 7.
[251] Wilsdon and Willis, *See-Through Science*, p. 37.
[252] DEFRA, *The GM Public Debate: Lessons Learned from the Process* (London: DEFRA, 2004).
[253] *Ibid.*, paras.7–20, 25–28.
[254] On how this debate would influence policy, see DEFRA *et al.*, *The GM Dialogue: Government Response* (London: DEFRA, 2004).
[255] DEFRA, *GM Public*, paras. 6, 21–22.   [256] *Ibid.*, paras. 23–24.
[257] *Ibid.*, para. 30.   [258] Jackson *et al.*, 'Strengths of Public', 355–356.

Gene therapy

Consultations on other developing biotechnologies have usually involved the publication of a short discussion document with responses requested to set questions,[259] but a different approach was adopted in a 1999 study on gene therapy.[260] Adults were interviewed face to face (696 in total), sent a copy of a specially written magazine on aspects of gene therapy, interviewed by telephone (under 500), and then invited to a series of 22 day-long group events near to where they lived. A video was shown at these events followed by a moderated discussion. Non-attendees were sent the video and all 696 were reinterviewed by telephone, with some of the non-attendees at the meeting interviewed about why they did not participate. Six months later all those who had seen the video were interviewed to see if their views had changed (under 400); ten months after the first interview.[261] A separate report was published on the methods and processes used, concluding that 'it is hard to get people's attention' and 'gene therapy was not a topic that many participants were particularly interested in'.[262] As to increasing interest in the area, providing information (magazine or video) was not 'brilliantly successful', but there was a more positive reaction to participation and interaction via meetings as the issues were too complex for simple 'yes' or 'no' responses.[263] Providing information in different formats was welcomed, although '[s]ending out information ... seems likely to make a big impression if it is part of a longer-term campaign or is timed to coincide with a period of sustained media coverage'.[264]

Xenotransplantation

Public consultation on xenotransplantation occurred in the UK in 1995 when the Nuffield Council contacted 130 organisations and an advertisement was placed in some national newspapers.[265] The majority of respondees were organisations or individuals affiliated to organisations, with only five submissions from individuals writing in their private capacity.[266] In 1996, over 200 interested organisations were contacted

---

[259] E.g. HFEA, 'Consultations & Reviews of Policy' (at: www.hfea.gov.uk/122.html, accessed 16/03/11); Human Genetics Commission (HGC), 'Consultations' (at: www.hgc.gov.uk/Client/library_category.asp?CategoryId=3, accessed 16/03/11).
[260] Wellcome Trust, *What Do People Think about Gene Therapy?* (London: Wellcome Trust, 2005).
[261] Wellcome Trust, *Information and Attitudes: Consulting the Public about Biomedical Science* (London: Wellcome Trust, 2005), p. 9.
[262] *Ibid.* [263] *Ibid.*, pp. 9–10. [264] *Ibid.*, p. 11.
[265] Nuffield Council, *Animal-to-Human*, Annex A. [266] *Ibid.*, Annex D.

52   Dealing with risk

prior to the publication of the UK's DH report on xenotransplantation, and there was an advertising campaign in the UK's national and specialist press.[267] There were 333 responses received, almost half from private individuals, and 500 postcards were sent as part of an anti-xenotransplantation campaign. No other xeno-consultations have been launched since 1996 and, while in operation, the UKXIRA did little to encourage participatory decision-making with public involvement limited to attendance at annual public meetings in London and reading annual reports. There were unexplained delays in publishing some of these,[268] and while consultation exercises were launched on, for example, the surveillance regime and the biosecurity of the non-human animals, these were not widely publicised but relied on interested parties checking the website for details.[269] UKXIRA's website did not provide easily accessible summaries of the key issues; rather, these were contained within reports which could be downloaded from the site, so a member of the public might have to sift through many pages to obtain the information required. The UKXIRA also appeared reluctant to publish material critical of it or the biotechnology and it did not publish a commissioned report on the legal and ethical issues of xenotransplantation and did not explain this decision.[270]

These experiences contrast with more recent public consultation exercises in Canada and Australia but, notably, Canadian federal government rules mandate public consultation so it has a more central role in policy formation.[271] Indeed, when recommendations are proposed and discussed with the relevant minister, Health Canada officials have

[267] DH, *Animal Tissue*, Annex B, Appendix C.
[268] The Annual Report for December 2000–November 2001 was due to be published in October 2002 but was not published until December 2002. The fifth and final *annual* report for January 2002–September 2003, covering a twenty-one-month period, was published in February 2004 (at: www.dh.gov.uk/ab/Archive/UKXIRA/DH_087899, accessed 16/03/11).
[269] UKXIRA, *Draft Report* (advertised on the UKXIRA website on 4 August 1999 and required comments by 15 October 1999); UKXIRA, *Draft Guidance Notes on Biosecurity Considerations in Relation to Xenotransplantation* (London: DH, 1999) (sent to those requesting a copy of the consultation paper with an undated letter that requested comments by 10 December 1999).
[270] For criticism of this, see M. Townsend, 'Doubts on pig organ transplants ignored', *The Observer*, 29 June 2003. The UKXIRA website lists *The Law and Ethics of Xenotransplantation – Bibliography and Abstracts of Key Articles* as a publication and the collection of material ceased in September 2002 (at: www.dh.gov.uk/prod_consum_dh/groups/dh_digitalassets/@dh/@ab/documents/digitalasset/dh_087885.pdf, accessed 16/03/11). The report was eventually published as S.A.M. McLean and L. Williamson, *Xenotransplantation Law and Ethics* (Aldershot: Ashgate, 2005).
[271] Treasury Board of Canada Secretariat, 'Cabinet Directive on Streamlining Regulation' (at: www.tbs-sct.gc.ca/ri-qr/directive/directive01-eng.asp, accessed 16/03/11).

to show how the outcomes have been influenced and shaped by public input.[272] Canadian debates on xenotransplantation began during 1997, primarily involving experts and other interested parties and not the public per se.[273] In 2000 Health Canada published a proposed plan for public involvement in xenotransplantation aiming to ensure that 'there [was] as broad a representation of public perspectives as possible to develop policy on xenotransplantation'.[274] This took place during 2001, involving citizen forums (107 panellists in 6 cities),[275] telephone surveys (1,519 interviews of over-18-year-olds), posted surveys to stakeholder groups (3,700 sent and 216 returned), a survey on a website (367), and informal feedback via letters and emails.[276] National and regional media coverage was sought, and the Canadian Public Health Association carried out the consultation and set the framework for it, along with the Public Advisory Group which oversaw the process.[277] In Australia the NHMRC published two public xeno-consultation documents in 2002 and 2003,[278] with the first announced via a press release and advertisements for comments placed in national and local

---

[272] Health Canada, 'Public Involvement' (2010) (at: www.hc-sc.gc.ca/ahc-asc/public-consult/index-eng.php, accessed 16/03/11).

[273] In Sweden views on xenotransplantation were sought from the public and patients awaiting a transplant, Committee members attended conferences, and involved research groups and regulators were consulted (Swedish Committee, *From One Species*, p. 7).

[274] Health Canada, 'Proposal for a Public Involvement Plan for Xenotransplantation', p. 3 in Health Canada, *Report from the Planning Workshop: Public Involvement on Xenotransplantation – Government Conference Centre, April 10–11 2000, Ottawa, Ontario* (2000) (at: www.hc-sc.gc.ca/dhp-mps/alt_formats/hpfb-dgpsa/pdf/brgtherap/awsreport-rapportvif-eng.pdf, accessed 16/03/11).

[275] Including education prior to the meeting and discussions. These were found to be '[t]he most effective model for consulting the public' on this subject and were recommended for future use in consultations on 'complex and not well understood policy issues' (Canadian Public Health Association (CPHA), *Animal-to-Human Transplantation: Should Canada Proceed? A Public Consultation on Xenotransplantation* (Ontario: CPHA, 2001), p. v).

[276] *Ibid.*, pp. 11–12. For evaluations of the process see, e.g., E.F. Einsiedel, 'Assessing a Controversial Medical Technology: Canadian Public Consultations on Xenotransplantation' (2002) 11 *Public Understanding of Science* 315; E.F. Einsiedel and H. Ross, 'Animal Spare Parts? A Canadian Public Consultation on Xenotransplantation' (2002) 8 *Science and Engineering Ethics* 579.

[277] CPHA, *Animal-to-Human*, pp. 2–4.

[278] NHMRC Xenotransplantation Working Party (XWP), *Draft Guidelines and Discussion Paper on Xenotransplantation – Public Consultation 2002* (2002) (at: www.nhmrc.gov.au/_files_nhmrc/file/about/committees/expert/gtrap/xeno.pdf, accessed 16/03/11); NHMRC, XWP, *Animal-to-Human Transplantation Research: How Should Australia Proceed? Response to the 2002 Public Consultation on Draft Guidelines and Discussion Paper on Xenotransplantation – Public Consultation 2003–04* (2003) (at: www.nhmrc.gov.au/_files_nhmrc/file/publications/synopses/e55.pdf, accessed 16/03/11).

54   Dealing with risk

newspapers. There were 97 written submissions received, public meetings held in Sydney, Melbourne and Perth, and 'targeted meetings' in Perth and Adelaide, with 116 participants in total.[279] The Xenotransplantation Working Party concluded that this consultation had 'promoted a high level of community engagement' and provided valuable information on the public's views.[280] However, as the respondents were not representative of all interest groups and only solid organs were covered, the public were consulted again as a response to the issues raised during the first exercise and a community guide on xenotransplantation was also published.[281] These were advertised in newspapers and on a website, and responses invited. A public relations company was used to increase awareness of the debate, and public meetings were held during February 2004 in all state and territory capital cities. These meetings were attended by 377 people, 343 written submissions were received from individuals and organisations, along with an email petition of 435 people.[282]

Involving the public in xenotransplant decisions

The need for public involvement in decision-making about xenotransplantation and other forms of 'technoscience'[283] has been widely mooted,[284] and the IXA has recognised the importance of public support for xenotransplantation and that a way to facilitate this is via discussion.[285] Public involvement is imperative where there is a dislocation between the

---

[279] NHMRC, XWP, *Animal-to-Human Transplantation (Xenotransplantation): Final Report and Advice to the National Health and Medical Research Council* (Canberra: NHMRC, 2004), p. 2, Appendix B.
[280] *Ibid.*
[281] *Ibid.*, p. 3; NHMRC, XWP, *Animal-to-Human Transplantation Research: A Guide for the Community – Public Consultation on Xenotransplantation 2003/4* (2003) (at: www.nhmrc.gov.au/_files_nhmrc/file/publications/synopses/e54.pdf, accessed 16/03/11).
[282] NHMRC, XWP, *Animal-to-Human Transplantation: Final Report*, pp. 3–4, Annex B. On the effectiveness of these consultations, see P.S. Cook, 'What Constitutes Adequate Public Consultation? Xenotransplantation Proceeds in Australia' (2011) 8 *Bioethical Inquiry* 67.
[283] M. Tallacchini, 'Community and Public Participation in the Risk Assessment of Experimental Clinical Trials' (2007) 14 *Xenotransplantation* 356, 356.
[284] E.g. Australia – NHMRC, *Discussion Paper*, p. 19; Canada – Health Canada, *Proposed Canadian Standard*, p. 4; UK – DH, *Xenotransplantation*, p. 2; US – US DHHS, FDA, Center for Biologics Evaluation and Research (CBER), *Guidance for Industry: Source Animal, Product, Preclinical and Clinical Issues Concerning the Use of Xenotransplantation Products in Humans – Final Guidance* (2003) (at: www.fda.gov/downloads/BiologicsBloodVaccines/GuidanceComplianceRegulatoryInformation/Guidances/Xenotransplantation/ucm092707.pdf, accessed 16/03/11).
[285] Sykes, '2007 IXA Presidential Address', 11.

benefits and risks of a biotechnology, and '[w]here there is much uncertainty about alternative courses of action, it is risky for experts to decide without input from affected communities'.[286] The experiences of public consultation in the UK and elsewhere should be drawn on but consideration must be given to the appropriate methodology as, for example, it has been suggested that such consultation might not be possible in the US because of scientists' concerns with the Canadian methodology.[287] This should not be allowed to be fatal; rather, scientists should be involved in discussions on the appropriate methodology so as to explore, and address, their concerns. Although there are limited empirical results on participation processes, there are some broadly accepted 'rules of thumb'; the organization conducting it must be committed to it, a needs assessment is a critical part of planning for stakeholder participation, participants must be well informed about the issues on which they are to comment in order for them to be meaningful, and the success of the process will depend on how it has been designed, planned and implemented and other external factors.[288]

Wilsdon and Willis's suggestions for a 'Nano Nation?'[289] debate could be adapted for a 'Xeno Nation?' debate, with it made clear from the outset *how* the outcomes of debate will influence policy and decision-making.[290] This does not mean governments are bound by the results but that 'a detailed rationale for ignoring informed public opinion'[291] should be provided and 'policy proposals [should be] both reasonable and supported with reasons'.[292] This is important because 'sometimes an engaged public might reach collective decisions that go against the self-interests of scientists'[293] and the public might use the same material as regulators or experts but draw different conclusions. Secondly, the debate should be deliberative, allow the public to form their own views by discussing with others via a number of means, and as 'the development of opportunities for public participation in public health is a complex and variable process',[294] a combination of opinion polls,

---

[286] Kriebel and Tickner, 'Reenergizing Public Health', 1353.
[287] K.M. Allspaw, 'Engaging the Public in the Regulation of Xenotransplantation: Would the Canadian Model of Public Consultation Be Effective in the US?' (2004) 13 *Public Understanding of Science* 417.
[288] V.M. Bier, 'On the State of the Art: Risk Communication to the Public' (2001) 71 *Reliability Engineering and System Safety* 139, 146–147.
[289] Wilsdon and Willis, *See-Through Science*, pp. 57–59.   [290] *Ibid.*, p. 16.
[291] F. Furger and F. Fukuyama, 'A Proposal for Modernizing the Regulation of Human Biotechnologies' (2007) 37 *Hastings Center Report* 16, 19.
[292] L.M. Fleck, 'Can We Trust "Democratic Deliberation"?' (2007) 37 *Hastings Center Report* 22, 23.
[293] Bubela *et al.*, 'Science Communication', 515.
[294] Green *et al.*, 'Public and Professional', p. 60.

surveys, deliberative polls, focus groups, consensus conferences, public meetings, citizens' panels, citizens' forums, *cafés scientifiques*, deliberative mapping, citizens' juries, referenda, citizen advisory committees should be employed.[295] This is necessary because 'serious efforts at public engagement are likely to employ a mixed strategy – the various methods of addressing the public are not mutually exclusive',[296] and each method has its advantages and disadvantages and, for example, place different weight on the involvement of the public, how participants are asked for feedback, how much feedback influences final decisions, and the timing of consultation.[297] A 'Xeno Nation?' debate should influence further research on the biotechnology, should not be a one-off event, and inform the UK's position at European and international levels.

The UK's *GM Nation?* debate and xeno-consultation in Canada show it *is* possible to interest and engage the public in seemingly complex and complicated scientific issues which may have an impact on them, provided information is supplied in an accessible format. The sponsor of the exercise may, however, affect the response rate and, in the light of the trust issues noted above, an organisation independent from the government should oversee the xenotransplant debate. Public xeno-deliberation should not seek to achieve consensus or manage discontent but to uncover, explore and, if possible, address concerns of the public.[298] Even though this deliberation will now take place at a later stage of the biotechnology's development, the public should still determine the frames of the debate and there must be 'as much public access to [experts'] knowledge and their deliberations, and wide public debate about what they say: their ideas, their evidence and their interpretations'.[299] Information must be accessible, understandable, authoritative and balanced so that all views are represented;[300] although it may be harder to develop a meaningful dialogue with the public because of the limited information available on xenotransplantation. Importantly, 'the focus of these deliberative exercises should be an honest effort at relationship- and trust-building rather than persuasion, with mechanisms for actively incorporating the input of lay participants into decision-making'.[301] Involvement in the

---

[295] For explanations, see www.peopleandparticipation.net, accessed 16/03/11; House of Lords, *Science and Society*, ch. 5.
[296] Wellcome Trust, *Information and Attitudes*, p. 11.
[297] Bubela *et al.*, 'Science Communication', 515.
[298] Furger and Fukuyama, 'A Proposal', 19.
[299] Coote and Franklin, 'Negotiating Risks', p. 188.
[300] Bach *et al.*, 'Ethical and Legal Issues', 288.
[301] Bubela *et al.*, 'Science Communication', 517, references removed.

decision-making process may translate into greater confidence and trust in xenotransplant regulators and the government,[302] and deliberation should include a broad and diverse range of people representative of their local communities.

Conclusion

While it appears that some of the immunological barriers to xenotransplantation have been overcome, the physiological barriers have not yet been addressed and it is unclear whether a xenotransplant will be able to support the life of a human. All transplantation poses infection risks to the recipient, but xenotransplantation may also unleash unknown and unidentifiable diseases into the population. PERVs *may* pose little risk to the xeno-recipient and/or others but an accurate assessment of the risk cannot occur until genetically engineered pig solid organs are xenotransplanted into humans, and the latency of some diseases and limited diagnostic tools may delay an accurate risk assessment. Nevertheless, although clinical trials may be the only means of assessing the risks and testing the efficacy of xenotransplantation itself, a precautionary approach is required because '[t]here exists a virtual risk that is impossible to measure. The histories of lentiviruses and prions have taught us about the untameable distances between the laboratory, the spread of infectious diseases and public health. These same errors cannot be made again.'[303] To protect and support public health and enhance voluntary action with the required surveillance regimes, public cooperation is essential and effective communication about infection risks and public participation in decision-making are important components of this.[304] Gostin suggests that measures taken to protect public health should be based on significant risks, not just 'speculative, theoretical, or remote' ones and in order to assess the level of risk account should be taken of the nature and duration of the risk, the probability of the harm occurring, and the severity of this harm.[305] However, in situations of uncertainty a precautionary approach informed by the harm principle is preferable 'when people face a potentially catastrophic risk

---

[302] Childress and Bernheim, 'Beyond the Liberal', 1219; D. Coles, 'The Identification and Management of Risk: Opening Up the Process', in Bennett and Calman, *Risk Communication*, pp. 195, 203.
[303] Michie, 'Xenotransplantation', 63.
[304] Childress and Bernheim, 'Beyond the Liberal'; Glanz and Yang, 'Communicating about Risk', 253.
[305] Gostin, *Public Health Law*, p. 57.

to which probabilities *cannot* be assigned'.[306] This may result in a moratorium as there *are* alternatives to xenotransplantation, and risk avoidance supports not creating these risks in the first place. While not suggesting that all risks of new biotechnologies are excluded, xenotransplantation is different because of the nature and magnitude of the risks and the fact that 'we are in a position *now* to annul foreseeable adverse consequences and thus have a particular moral responsibility to do so'.[307] A precautionary approach requires involving the public in decision-making *because of* the lack of established facts, the social construction of concepts such as risk, uncertainty and threat, and the need for the quality and reliability of different forms of knowledge to be introduced and challenged.[308] Applying a precautionary approach via a deliberative process enables the quality of the decision to be scrutinised, helps to ensure that a decision made in situations of scientific uncertainty has a democratic basis,[309] and to engender trust.[310]

To be effective, decision-making systems should be transparent and open, helping to develop a 'credible decision-making process' which will further inspire confidence and trust in decisions.[311] It is debatable whether the UKXIRA did this but the risks of xenotransplantation necessitate a societal, *global*, decision as to whether the benefit an individual may obtain outweighs the burdens the public may have to bear.[312] Indeed, '[t]he associated social stakes are so extensive that it is difficult to see how technical experts acting as proxy on society's behalf can address them adequately'.[313] At national levels the public need to be involved in *meaningful* dialogue on xenotransplantation because '[s]cience should not be expected to have sole responsibility for the future of [new developments in science]; there is a responsibility to society to involve all citizens in decisions to the extent that this is possible'.[314] Such consultation should enable 'creative and democratic

---

[306] C.R. Sunstein, *Laws of Fear: Beyond the Precautionary Principle* (Cambridge University Press, 2005), p. 225, emphasis supplied.
[307] A. Ravelingien, 'Xenotransplantation and the Harm Principle: Factoring Out Foreseen Risk' (2007) 16 *Journal of Evolution and Technology* 127, 135, emphasis in original.
[308] Fisher and Harding, 'Precautionary Principle', pp. 292–293.
[309] On this, see C. Mullen, D. Hughes and P. Vincent-Jones, 'The Democratic Potential of Public Participation: Healthcare Governance in England' (2011) 20 *Social and Legal Studies* 21.
[310] Fisher and Harding, 'Precautionary Principle', p. 293.
[311] Swedish Committee, *From One Species*, p. 14.
[312] F.H. Bach *et al.*, 'Uncertainty in Xenotransplantation: Individual Benefit versus Collective Risk' (1998) 4 *Nature Medicine* 141.
[313] I. Welsh and R. Evans, 'Xenotransplantation, Risk, Regulation and Surveillance: Social and Technological Dimensions of Change' (1999) 18 *New Genetics and Society* 197, 212.
[314] Jackson *et al.*, 'Strengths of Public', 350.

thinking to work alongside traditional mechanisms of decision-making',[315] with the method(s) adopted matching the purpose; informing and empowering the public and, ultimately, aimed at making 'better' decisions.[316] This may not be easy but it is important to remember why it is necessary; if clinical xenotransplants are performed the public will be *unknowingly* required to accept risks. Given that the public, in the UK particularly, has experience of not agreeing to but being subjected to risks it is vital that lessons are learned from the BSE and new vCJD tragedies. These events diminished public trust in 'apparently absolute, quantified risk assessments',[317] in the government as a credible source of expertise, and 'specific institutional failures in providing protection from technological risks'[318] have increased this distrust. Xenotransplantation is an exemplar of the fact that risks from 'contemporary techniques have implications across time and space'[319] and:

> when what we do transcends science and when it impinges on the public, we have no choice but to welcome the public – even encourage the public – to participate in the debate. Scientists have no monopoly on wisdom where this kind of trans-science is involved: they will have to accommodate to the will of the public and its representatives. The republic of trans-science, bordering as it does on both the political republic and the republic of science, can be neither as pure as the latter nor as undisciplined as the former. The most science can do is to inject some intellectual discipline into the republic of trans-science; politics in an open society will surely keep it democratic.[320]

Experiences in the UK of engaging the public are developing and must continue because 'overall experience suggests that policies and decisions made in collaboration with stakeholders tend to be more effective and durable'.[321] If they are communicated with clearly, the public *can* be trusted to reach sensible conclusions, can identify 'self-serving and partisan special pleading', may take its time to reach a conclusion but this is no bad thing.[322] Public consultations on xenotransplantation should be held in every country considering its application because if it clinically proceeds a few may benefit but many may suffer, and it

---

[315] Coote and Franklin 'Negotiating Risks', p. 193.   [316] *Ibid.*, p. 192.
[317] Welsh and Evans, 'Xenotransplantation', 202.
[318] Tallacchini, 'Community and Public Participation', 356.
[319] Welsh and Evans, 'Xenotransplantation', 202.
[320] Weinberg, 'Science and Trans-science', 222.
[321] Green *et al.*, 'Public and Professional', p. 60.
[322] M.H. Johnson, 'Regulating the Science and Therapeutic Application of Human Embryo Research: Managing the Tension between Biomedical Creativity and Public Concern', in J.R. Spence and A. du Bois-Pedain (eds.), *Freedom and Responsibility in Reproductive Choice* (Oxford: Hart, 2006), pp. 91, 106.

is unacceptable to expect the public to bear risks they have had no opportunity to debate. If, after public consultation, it is decided that clinical xenotransplantation is acceptable, then it is important to consider how it is regulated, and I address these issues in the following two chapters.

3 Regulating experimental procedures and medical research

Involving humans in experimental procedures or medical research involves possible benefit and risk, and in regulating such activities three interests are usually involved: the recipient's, the professional's, and advancing medicine and science. With xenotransplantation the public interest is also engaged. When regulating any biotechnology these interests must be recognised and regulation usually takes two forms: the general regulatory framework applying to any experimental procedure and medical research, and any additional systems governing specific biotechnologies. The latter is considered in Chapter 4; here I explore how experimental procedures and medical research are defined, regulated and into which category genetically engineered solid organ xenotransplants fall. The regulatory schemes in England are used as an example of the problems which may be encountered when trying to regulate a developing biotechnology. I also draw on Australian, Canadian, New Zealand and the US schemes where relevant, and consider whether the current regimes are appropriate given the risks of xenotransplantation. To what extent is xenotransplantation on the general 'regulatory radar'?[1]

Knowing how an activity is classified is important as this affects the regulatory scheme to be followed and how and which recipients can be selected.[2] I explore the legal provisions and ethical guidance on selecting recipients, and whether these offer appropriate parameters for experimenters/researchers and potential recipients. Can and should a competent, desperately or terminally ill patient with little or 'no other hope' be able to receive the first genetically engineered solid organ xenotransplant, as has been suggested?[3] The risk is that desperately ill

---

[1] A.S. Ahmed, 'The Last Twist of the Knife: Encouraging the Regulation of Innovative Surgical Procedures' (2005) 105 *Columbia Law Review* 1529, 1539.
[2] S. Fovargue, '"Oh Pick Me, Pick Me": Selecting Participants for Xenotransplant Clinical Trials' (2007) 15 *Medical Law Review* 176.
[3] E.g. S. Welin and M.S. Sandrin, 'Some Ethical Problems in Xenotransplantation: Introductory Remarks at Ethics Workshop' (2006) 13 *Xenotransplantation* 500;

patients with no other hope will be used as research tools because of their understandable willingness to rely on remote chances of benefit. I consider the protection offered to potential xeno-recipients, and introduce some of the issues explored further in Chapter 5 relating to the principle of autonomy. Should people be allowed to sacrifice themselves in the (limited) hope of gaining some benefit for themselves, but with the more likely outcome being providing information for future generations, especially when the risks go beyond the potential beneficiary? *Who* receives a genetically engineered solid organ xenotransplant is important as there is a consensus that the risks necessitate recipients, and others, to agree to and comply with surveillance regimes,[4] and if recipients are unable or unwilling to comply with these requirements public health may be jeopardised.

Definitions

There is only a statutory regime for medical research in the form of clinical trials in the UK;[5] so the level of protection afforded to recipients of experimental procedures may differ. But it is not easy to distinguish between the two because 'the experiment-to-therapy process is neither a simple, linear progression, totally conscious, entirely logical and rational, nor altogether biomedically determined',[6] and professionals performing an experimental procedure may be doing the same things with the same intentions as those undertaking research but without the research regulatory framework.[7] Nevertheless, the distinction must be made because of the consequences of falling within a particular category.

Experimental procedures

I use 'experimental procedure' to cover what can be called experimental medicine, therapy, practices or treatments, or innovative or novel medicine,

---

Z. Ibrahim *et al.*, 'Which Patients First? Planning the First Clinical Trial of Xenotransplantation: A Case for Cardiac Bridging' (2005) 12 *Xenotransplantation* 168. S. Welin, 'Starting Clinical Trials of Xenotransplantation – Reflections on the Early Phase' (2000) 26 *Journal of Medical Ethics* 231.

[4] See Chapter 6.
[5] Medicines for Human Use (Clinical Trials) Regulations 2004, SI 2004 No. 1031, as amended by Medicines for Human Use (Clinical Trials) Amendment Regulations 2006, SI 2006 No. 1928, Medicines for Human Use (Clinical Trials) Amendment (No. 2) Regulations 2006, S.I. 2006 No. 2984, Medicines for Human Use (Clinical Trials) and Blood Safety and Quality (Amendment) Regulations 2008, SI 2008 No. 941.
[6] Fox and Swazey, *Courage*, p. 305; also, ch. 3.
[7] I. Kennedy, A. Grubb, *Medical Law* (3rd edn, London: Butterworths, 2000), p. 1686.

therapy, procedures, practices or treatments.[8] I do not use 'treatment' or 'therapy' as these suggest the procedure *has* been *shown* to benefit the recipient[9] and, as a treatment, it will fall within the doctor's clinical judgement whether to provide it; a discretion the courts are reluctant to interfere with. Additionally, doctors may provide different levels of information if they are acting in a treatment and not research situation, and risk and benefit issues may be viewed differently.[10] Furthermore, 'labelling a procedure only as therapy tends to evade prospective independent evaluation, regulation and on-going monitoring'.[11]

The New Zealand Ministry of Health deems 'innovative practice' to involve 'the provision of a clinical intervention (diagnostic, therapeutic or prophylactic), be it a therapeutic drug, medical device or clinical procedure, that is untested, unproven or not in common use and therefore poses its own unique set of characteristics and issues'.[12] Its goal is to 'provide some immediate treatment in relation to an individual consumer or consumer group concerned, or to create new efficiencies in practices that will benefit consumers on a more general basis'.[13] Performing it 'may be considered to be a planned deviation from current accepted practice of a New Zealand body of health professionals involving an untested or unproven clinical intervention intended to be used on an ongoing basis'.[14] These are useful definitions of an *experimental procedure* because here it is not known what will happen the first time it is used in or on a human; it will be 'novel and unvalidated', with often no more than a chance or hope that it will succeed.[15] It will generally be used in or on a *specific* patient as a last resort; the only remaining option to stop their health further deteriorating.[16] Using an experimental procedure will not be as part of a formal research project, otherwise it would be termed research. By using such a procedure, the doctor/experimenter is conducting

---

[8] For debates on these terms, see, e.g., D. Price, 'Remodelling the Regulation of Postmodern Innovation in Medicine' (2005) 1 *International Journal of Law in Context* 121; N. King, 'Experimental Treatment: Oxymoron or Aspiration?' (1995) 25 *Hastings Center* Report 6.
[9] S. McLean, 'Gene Therapy – Cure or Challenge?', in M. Freeman, A. Lewis (eds.), *Law and Medicine: Current Legal Issues*, vol. 3 (Oxford University Press, 2000), p. 205.
[10] See Chapter 5.   [11] Price, 'Remodelling', p. 130.
[12] Ministry of Health (MH), *Operational Standard for Ethics Committees* (Wellington: MH, 2006), para. 116; also, paras. 117–135.
[13] *Ibid.*, para. 118.   [14] *Ibid.*, para. 121; also, p. 101.
[15] Royal College of Physicians (RCP), *Guidelines on the Practice of Ethics Committees in Medical Research with Human Participants* (London: RCP, 2007), para. 3.5.
[16] Jackson, *Medical Law*, p. 441.

'an investigation in humans ... to test the validity and importance of new discoveries and treatments'.[17] As such it 'precedes and informs the development of late phase clinical medicine' and the aim is to 'demonstrate proof-of-concept evidence' of new discoveries and treatments.[18] An experiment involves 'a more speculative, ad hoc approach to an *individual* subject' and can be adapted in the light of a subject's response to it.[19]

The UK's Royal College of Physicians (RCP) states that in 'innovative medical practice' the doctor's *only* aim is to benefit *that* patient,[20] but the doctor surely has mixed motives when performing an experimental procedure; to do the best for and benefit that patient *and* to ensure the scientific value of their work for future use. If so, 'innovative medical therapies' *should* be treated as research 'whenever data are gathered to develop new medical information and for publication'.[21] As experimental procedures are directed at an *individual* and occur outside a research project, the recipient remains a patient, under the care of a doctor and within the standard doctor–patient relationship.[22] Their health and welfare *should* thus be the doctor's *primary* concern.[23]

Medical research

The focus on the individual patient in experimental procedures contrasts with medical research which 'attempt[s] to derive generalisable new knowledge by addressing clearly defined questions with systematic and rigorous methods'.[24] It has a more collective gaze and care is needed so

---

[17] UKCRC Experimental Medicine Resources, 'Frequently Asked Questions' (at: www.ukcrcexpmed.org.uk/aboutus/Pages/faqs.aspx#ans1, accessed 22/03/11).
[18] MRC, 'Experimental Medicine' (at: www.mrc.ac.uk/Ourresearch/ResearchInitiatives/ExperimentalMedicine/index.htm, accessed 22/03/11).
[19] Mason and Laurie, *Mason & McCall Smith's*, pp. 612–613, emphasis supplied.
[20] RCP, *Guidelines*, para. 3.4.
[21] L. Snyder and C. Leffler, for the Ethics and Human Rights Committee, American College of Physicians, 'Position Paper – Ethics Manual Fifth Edition' (2005) 142 *Annals of Internal Medicine* 560, 577.
[22] Mason and Laurie, *Mason & McCall Smith's*, p. 613.
[23] Snyder and Leffler, 'Position Paper', 577.
[24] UK – DH, *Research Governance Framework for Health and Social Care* (2nd edn, London: DH, 2005), para. 1.10; Canada – Canadian Institutes of Health Research, Natural Sciences and Engineering Research Council of Canada, Social Sciences and Humanities Research Council of Canada, *TCPS2 – Tri-Council Policy Statement: Ethical Conduct for Research Involving Humans* (2010), Article 2.1 (at: www.pre.ethics.gc.ca/pdf/eng/tcps2/TCPS_2_FINAL_Web.pdf, accessed 22/03/11); New Zealand – MH, *Operational Standard*, p. 104; US – 45 CFR 46 (DHHS, Code of Federal Regulations Title 45 Public Welfare, Part 46 Protection of Human Subjects, 2009), § 46.102.

that the patient does not become objectified.[25] Medical research includes observational and psychological research, and clinical trials,[26] and can be therapeutic or non-therapeutic. In the former, patients hope to *directly* benefit from involvement, and the investigator has the dual intention of obtaining information for future use *and* benefiting the patient-participant. Non-therapeutic research involves healthy volunteers and aims to test procedures and gain knowledge *for the future*. It may not be easy to distinguish between these categories,[27] and the distinction is somewhat discredited,[28] but in both the investigator is *outside* the traditional doctor–patient relationship as the patient's doctor is not usually involved in the research. Again, though, the distinction must be made as long as different regulatory frameworks apply and there are important distinctions concerning the benefits and harm participants can be exposed to.

Genetically engineered solid organ clinical xenotransplants

When a genetically engineered solid organ is xenotransplanted into a human for the first time the question is *what* will happen. The *hope* will be that the recipient's health and life expectancy will improve, but what follows or for how long the effects and/or side effects will last cannot be known. These xenotransplants will necessarily involve 'relatively – or entirely – untried treatment applied to an individual with little more scientific basis other than expediency';[29] it will thus be an experimental procedure and its experimental nature has been recognised by others.[30] This is partly supported by the UK's Nuffield Council on Bioethics which recognised that 'early recipients are being used as experimental subjects for the development of the technology'.[31] However, it also

---

[25] J. Katz, 'Human Experimentation and Human Rights' (1993) 38 *Saint Louis University Law Journal* 7, 15–16.
[26] RCP, *Guidelines*, ch. 3.   [27] Jackson, *Medical Law*, pp. 443–444.
[28] H. Biggs, *Healthcare Research Ethics and Law: Regulation, Review and Responsibility* (London: Routledge-Cavendish, 2010), p. 7.
[29] Mason and Laurie, *Mason & McCall Smith's*, p. 627.
[30] E.g. WMA, *World Medical Association Statement on Human Organ Donation and Transplantation*, Section I, adopted by the 52nd WMA General Assembly in Edinburgh, Scotland during October 2000, revised by the WMA General Assembly, Pilanesberg, South Africa, October 2006; Australia – NHMRC, XWP, *Animal-to-Human Transplantation: Final Report*, para. 3.6; Canada – Health Canada, *Proposed Canadian Standard*, p. 4; France – CCNE, *Opinion on Ethics*, p. 7; Netherlands – Health Council of the Netherlands, Committee on Xenotransplantation, *Xenotransplantation* (Rijswijk: Health Council of the Netherlands, 1998), No. 1998/01E, p. 27.
[31] Nuffield Council, *Animal-to-Human*, para. 1.21.

stated that '[p]rocedures, which are experimental but offer the chance of genuine treatment for the patients, are termed therapeutic research', and it implies that xenotransplantation falls within this category.[32] The Council of Europe seems similarly confused using the phrases 'experimental nature', 'innovative treatment' and 'medical experimental research' in two consecutive sentences to describe initial xenotransplants.[33] But it would not be correct to describe the first clinical genetically engineered solid organ xenotransplants as research because while it is known that xenotransplants can technically be performed, and in the early 1960s a woman survived for nine months with a non-genetically engineered chimpanzee kidney,[34] it is not known *how* a genetically engineered solid organ will function inside a human nor whether infections, and their nature and type, will be transmitted. Limited survival times have been achieved in pre-clinical life-supporting solid organ xenotransplants from genetically engineered pigs to non-human primates, but it is questionable whether human recipients will benefit from such a xenotransplant because of the significant remaining immunological, physiological and microbiological hurdles. The first genetically engineered solid organ clinical xenotransplants, as with the first allotransplants and non-genetically engineered xenotransplants,[35] should thus properly be classified as experimental procedures.

It is difficult to categorise subsequent genetically engineered solid organ xenotransplants, but in the light of the nature of xenotransplantation and pre-clinical results, more than the *first* clinical solid organ xenotransplant should be deemed experimental procedures. It is, however, hard to put a figure on how many should be performed before this classification changes and the classification will depend on the outcome of the first xenotransplants. At some point subsequent xenotransplants could be deemed research because once the first ones have been performed, the results published and analysed, the answers to some of the unknowns may be clearer and a research programme may thus be developed. It has been suggested that subsequent xenotransplants as clinical trials should be therapeutic with 'a reasonable chance of success',[36]

---

[32] *Ibid.*, para. 7.6; also para. 7.7. Similarly, DH, *Animal Tissue*, para. 7.5.
[33] Council of Europe, *Report on the State*, para. 7.5.2. [34] See Chapter 2.
[35] E.g. Butler-Sloss P. in *Simms v. Simms and another*; *PA v. JA and another* [2002] EWHC 2734, para. 48; Bailey *et al.*, 'Baboon-to-Human'; J.B. Dossetor, 'Innovative Treatment Versus Clinical Research: An Ethics Issue in Transplantation' (1990) 22 *Transplantation Proceedings* 966.
[36] UK – Nuffield Council, *Animal-to-Human*, para. 7.7; also,7.6; DH, *Animal Tissue*, paras. 7.5–7.6. Similarly, Australia – NHMRC, XWP, *Guidelines for Clinical Animal-to-Human*

and it 'thought possible' for the patient to benefit.[37] This is problematic. In the early stages of clinical research the distinction between therapeutic and non-therapeutic xenotransplants will not be clear-cut because of the existing uncertainties and the results of the first experimental xenotransplant will need to be analysed. If the results are similar to those achieved pre-clinically, a not unreasonable surmise, it is hard to argue that any subsequent xenotransplant would be *therapeutic* research and benefit the recipient. *Any* intervention in a sick person can be viewed as therapeutic,[38] and if a xenotransplant is a person's only chance of prolonging their life how could it not be of benefit to give them the *possibility* of a few more days, weeks, or months? The World Health Organization (WHO) has reinforced the idea of benefit,[39] but there is no requirement that this must relate to *individual* recipients. Indeed, the recipient may be realistic about her chances of survival and her primary reason for receiving a xeno-organ may be to help others in her situation and not to prolong her own life; this being a bonus. Nevertheless, where there is tension between the individual's interests and public health, the likelihood of a positive outcome for *that* recipient's health is relevant, and this is a problem for xeno-recipients as the risks and benefits are uncertain.

The English High Court explored issues of risk and benefit in *Simms* v. *Simms*.[40] A declaration was sought that it would be lawful to provide pentosan polysulphate (PPS) to two probable variant CJD sufferers, in their best interests as they were unable to make that decision for themselves, when it was not licensed for that purpose. One witness stated that better results were *likely* the earlier PPS was provided, but it was 'difficult' to say whether the research showed 'the *possibility* of a good effect' on humans in an advanced stage of vCJD, as these patients were.

Transplantation (Xenotransplantation) Research – DRAFT for NHMRC Consideration (2004) Guidelines 3, 5, accompanying NHMRC, *Animal-to-Human Transplantation*; Council of Europe, Recommendation Rec(2003)10 of the Committee of Ministers to Member States on Xenotransplantation and Explanatory Memorandum, Adopted by the Committee of Ministers on 19 June 2003 at the 844th meeting of the Minister's Deputies, Article 5 (1); New Zealand – HRC, *Guidelines for Preparation*, p. 5; Sweden – Swedish Committee, *From One Species*, s. 5 of the Proposal for an Ordinance (32000:000) on clinical trials on humans involving the transfer of living biological material from animals (Xeno Licensing and Control Ordinance).

[37] DH, *Animal Tissue*, para. 7.5.
[38] G.J. Annas, 'The Changing Landscape of Human Experimentation: Nuremberg, Helsinki and Beyond' (1992) 2 *Health Matrix* 119.
[39] 'First WHO Global Consultation on Regulatory Requirements for Xenotransplantation Clinical Trials, Changsha, China, 19–21 November 2008' (2009) 16 *Xenotransplantation* 61, Principle 5.
[40] [2002] EWHC 2734.

68   Regulating experimental procedures and research

Rather, '[i]t would be very difficult to have better outcomes from terminal stage patients'.[41] Another agreed that PPS might not work in humans or against CJD, that limited data were available, and based on non-human animal research.[42] He was prepared to try it because 'it *may* ... [limit] the deterioration of the patient's condition', and 'the only proper place for the study of CJD is in CJD patients. Whilst it would be a considerable leap to a new disease and a new species if the PPS treatment were carried out on humans, such a leap had to be made at some time.'[43] This was despite the possibility that there might be no adverse but no beneficial effect.[44]

The third witness thought there was 'a *rational* basis for coming to the conclusion that the proposed treatment did provide the *possibility* of a positive effect on the progress of the disease and a prolongation of life for each patient'.[45] However, when the case was heard it was 'not possible ... to have scientific proof of the efficacy of the proposed treatment' because the research had only involved non-human animals, but it was 'highly probable' that the progression from normal to abnormal prions was similar in human and non-human animals.[46] Furthermore, it could not, however, be said with certainty what the disease mechanism was nor whether PPS would affect it; but there was a duty not to cause undue suffering to a patient and 'unless there was *no prospect whatsoever* of success, the balance was affected by the progressive and fatal nature of the CJD disease. Whilst there was no scientific basis and no evidence of efficacy and safety, he would ... administer it.'[47] There was '*some* chance of benefit' and he would give the PPS treatment on the families' understanding that this was 'a very *theoretical* chance'.[48] The final expert stated that '[f]rom a scientific perspective ... the *likely* benefits of the treatment are *speculative* and there are *clearly significant* risks', but these should be balanced against the 'firmly held and informed' views of the families.[49] Uncertainty over the benefits of PPS was emphasised, and whereas the other experts concluded that providing PPS was in JS and JA's best interests, he said it was not. Nevertheless, he 'could not say that there would be no potential benefit',[50] but he was concerned about the method of providing PPS.[51]

Dame Butler-Sloss P. subsequently interpreted the meaning of benefit widely: 'the concept of "benefit" to a patient suffering from vCJD ...

---

[41] *Ibid.*, para. 20, emphasis supplied.
[42] *Ibid.*, para. 22.
[43] *Ibid.*, para. 22, emphasis supplied.
[44] *Ibid.*, para. 30.
[45] *Ibid.*, para. 31, emphasis supplied.
[46] *Ibid.*
[47] *Ibid.*, para. 33, emphasis supplied.
[48] *Ibid.*, para. 32, emphasis supplied.
[49] *Ibid.*, para. 36, emphasis supplied.
[50] *Ibid.*, para. 38.
[51] *Ibid.*, para. 40; also paras. 53–54.

encompass[es] an improvement from the present state of illness, or a continuation of the existing state of illness without deterioration for a longer period than might otherwise have occurred, or the prolongation of life for a longer period than might otherwise have occurred'.[52] For xeno-recipients with no other hope, the *chance* of extending their life *must* be viewed as of benefit to them, but their health status makes it imperative that those seeking to conduct the trial approach the concept of benefit with caution and do not overstate its likelihood,[53] because '[w]hile a patient may grasp at a 1:1000 chance of improvement, it is quite another thing for a doctor to reasonably describe such an intervention as therapeutic'.[54] In England defining benefit is not a solely medical judgement,[55] and King's definition is useful: '[a] reasonable chance of direct benefit exists when a reasonable person under all the circumstances would consider the nature, magnitude, and likelihood of direct benefit sufficient to reasonably choose to participate in research in anticipation of the benefit'.[56] A variation of this 'reasonable chance' test is in evidence in the Court of Appeal decision in *Pearce v. United Bristol Healthcare Trust* where Lord Woolf used a 'reasonable patient' test to determine what risks should be disclosed with regard to medical treatment.[57] Given the difficulties of defining benefit and problems with communicating its meaning, King's test is an appropriate tool for the former and legal support for its adoption is important.

As the results of the first genetically engineered solid organ xeno-transplants may not be known for years, because of latent infections, it is difficult to say that individual subsequent xeno-recipients have the chance to benefit. *That* person's involvement may enable *others* to benefit, but that is not the point of therapeutic research and without more subsequent xenotransplants must be *non*-therapeutic research. As such, 'whether ... people [can] indeed validly consent to the harm of involvement in them (irrespective of any potential benefits) is a question worth posing',[58] and I address this in Chapter 5. Furthermore, *Simms* highlights the blurred line between doctors researching on their patients

---

[52] *Ibid.*, para. 57.   [53] See Chapter 5.
[54] W.M. Kong, 'The Regulation of Gene Therapy Research in Competent Adult Patients, Today and Tomorrow: Implications of EU Directive 2001/20/EC' (2004) 12 *Medical Law Review* 164, 168.
[55] E.g. *Re S (Sterilisation: Patient's Best Interests)* [2000] 2 FLR 389, CA; *Re F (Mental Patient: Sterilisation)* [1990] 2 AC 1, HL.
[56] N. King, 'Defining and Describing Benefit Appropriately in Clinical Trials' (2000) 28 *Journal of Law, Medicine and Ethics* 332, 336.
[57] [1999] PIQR 53, 59, supporting Lord Browne-Wilkinson's judgment in *Bolitho v. City and Hackney HA* [1997] 4 All ER 771, HL. See Chapter 5.
[58] McLean and Williamson, *Xenotransplantation*, p. 92.

and doing their best for them, and the difficulties of applying the legally important distinctions between experimental procedures and medical research, and therapeutic and non-therapeutic research. Thus, a similar regulatory framework should apply to experimental procedures and medical research,[59] and the Bristol Inquiry Report proposed that newly constituted ethics committees competent to consider applications to 'undertake new and hitherto untried invasive clinical procedures' should be convened.[60] This recommendation has not been adopted. In contrast, in the US Belmont Report it was stated that '[r]adically new [experimental] procedures ... should ... be made the object of formal research at an early stage in order to determine whether they are safe and effective'.[61] This may be appropriate for some experimental procedures and in order to simplify an overly complicated area, similar regimes should regulate both medical research and experimental procedures.

Regulatory schemes

Experimental procedures

The law

The distinctions between experimental procedures and medical research may not be clear but are important because different regulatory schemes apply depending on the classification. Two English cases have considered whether a court can sanction an experimental procedure as a 'one-off', outside an approved research protocol; *R* v. *Cambridge HA, ex parte B* [62] and *Simms*.[63] In the former, it was held that it was appropriate to term a treatment experimental where its first stage had an estimated 10–20 per cent chance of success and the second stage, with the same chance of success, did not have 'a well-tried track record of success. It was ... at the frontier of medical science'.[64] This was regardless of the fact that there were practitioners who supported providing the treatment because 'there was a worthwhile chance of success'.[65] The court should determine the lawfulness of the health authority's decision not to provide

---

[59] Similarly, Price, 'Remodelling'; Kennedy and Grubb, *Medical Law*, p. 1686.
[60] DH, *Learning from Bristol: The Report of the Public Inquiry into Children's Heart Surgery at the Bristol Royal Infirmary 1984–1995* (London: Stationery Office, 2001) Cm. 5207(I), paras. 100–101.
[61] The National Commission for the Protection of Human Subjects of Biomedical and Behavioural Research, *Ethical Principles and Guidelines for the Protection of Human Subjects of Research* (1979), Section AA (at: http://ohsr.od.nih.gov/guidelines/belmont.html, accessed 22/03/11).
[62] [1995] 2 All ER 129, CA.   [63] [2002] EWHC 2734.
[64] Above, n. 62, p. 137 *per* Sir Thomas Bingham MR; also, p. 133.   [65] *Ibid.*, p. 136.

treatment but not judge the treatment's likely effectiveness or the clinical judgements expressed.[66] In *Simms* it was said that providing PPS to the patients when it was not licensed for vCJD was 'untried *treatment*',[67] 'pioneering *treatment*',[68] even though pre-clinical research had not been validated.[69] When this case was heard there were no recognised effective drugs to prolong life or halt the neurological deterioration, but non-human animal research indicated that PPS inhibited abnormal prion proteins in scrapie cases and a way of introducing PPS directly to the brain had been devised. Nevertheless, the effect of PPS on humans at an advanced stage of vCJD, as these patients were, was unknown. Three of the four experts were in favour of providing it and Dame Butler-Sloss P. said that '[a]lthough this *cannot* be a research project, there would be an opportunity to learn, for the first time, the possible effect of PPS on patients with vCJD and to have the opportunity to compare it with the treatment about to be given to patients in Japan'.[70] Where there was an application to the court for treatment to be provided, four questions had to be answered: does the patient have capacity?[71] Does the treatment come within the *Bolam* test? Is it in the patient's best interests to have it? And, if questions two and three are positively answered, is the NHS capable of providing it?[72]

It was uncontested that the patients lacked capacity and the final question is not relevant here, but the second and third questions require consideration. Dame Butler-Sloss P. said it was 'in one sense unclear' whether PPS came within the *Bolam* test because it was untried and the Japanese research was being peer reviewed, but was currently unvalidated.[73] It could thus not be said to be treatment which a responsible body of medical practitioners could endorse. However, the *Bolam* test[74] 'ought not to be allowed to inhibit medical progress' and 'if one waited for the "*Bolam* test" to be complied with to its fullest extent, no innovative work ... would ever be attempted'.[75] There was 'evidence from responsible medical opinion which does not reject the research' and 'there is a responsible body of relevant professional opinion which supports this innovative treatment', subject to the seriousness of the risks

---

[66] *Ibid.* [67] *Simms*, para. 48, emphasis supplied.
[68] *Ibid.*, paras. 57, 61, emphasis supplied. [69] *Ibid.*, para. 48.
[70] *Ibid.*, para. 72, emphasis supplied.
[71] Now determined by the Mental Capacity Act (MCA) 2005. [72] *Simms*, para. 46.
[73] *Ibid.*, para. 48.
[74] 'A doctor is not guilty of negligence if he has acted in accordance with a practice accepted as proper by a responsible body of medical men skilled in that particular art': *Bolam* v. *Friern Hospital Management Committee* [1957] 2 All ER 118, 121 *per* McNair J.
[75] *Simms*, para. 48.

involved and the degree of benefit that might be achieved.[76] On the risks, the operations were routine and the patients would be subject to the same risks of surgery and general anaesthesia as non-vCJD patients, and a 5 per cent risk of haemorrhage did not 'fall outside the bounds of responsible surgical and medical treatment so as to become an unacceptable risk'.[77] Whether it was reasonable to take those risks with these patients falls within considerations of best interests,[78] and while the benefits of PPS were 'less tangible and more difficult to assess'[79] and there could be no obvious benefit or no benefit at all, an 'expansive and pragmatic construction'[80] to the concept of benefit was adopted.[81] As the research suggested that the earlier the treatment was provided the greater the chance for benefit, there was no alternative treatment, and the disease was 'progressive and fatal', it was 'reasonable to consider experimental treatment with unknown benefits and risks, but without significant risks of increased suffering to the patient, in cases where there is some chance of benefit to the patient'.[82] Dame Butler-Sloss concluded that 'it [could not] be said that in principle this is treatment which is clearly futile or that it would not, in suitable cases, be proper to give the PPS treatment to those suffering from prion disease, and I am therefore satisfied that the proposed PPS treatment complies with the "*Bolam* test"'.[83]

The court had to assess best interests 'in the widest possible way to include the medical and non-medical benefits and disadvantages, the broader welfare issues of the two patients, their abilities, their future with or without treatment, the views of the families, and the impact of refusal of their applications'.[84] For the patients the chance of improvement was 'slight but not non-existent', and the families should see it as 'unlikely but not impossible, since no one knows the outcome'.[85] Furthermore:

[a] reduced enjoyment of life even at quite a low level is to be respected and protected ... even the prospect of a slightly longer life is a benefit worth having ... There is sufficient possibility of unquantifiable benefit ... to find that it would be in their best interests to have ... the treatment subject to an assessment of the risks. There is no alternative treatment.[86]

Additionally, 'if there is a possibility of continuation of a life which has value to the patient and the patient is bound to die sooner rather than

---

[76] *Ibid.*, paras. 48, 51, respectively.   [77] *Ibid.*, para. 56.   [78] *Ibid.*
[79] *Ibid.*, para. 57.
[80] J. Laing, 'Incompetent Patients, Experimental Treatment and the "*Bolam* Test" – *JS* v. *An NHS Trust; JA* v. *An NHS Trust*' (2003) 11 *Medical Law Review* 237, 240.
[81] Above, n. 52.   [82] *Simms*, para. 57.   [83] *Ibid.*, para. 58.   [84] *Ibid.*, para. 60.
[85] *Ibid.*, para. 61.   [86] *Ibid.*

later without the treatment, *these two young people have very little to lose* in the treatment going ahead ... it is a *reasonable risk* to take on their behalf'.[87]

The precedent value of *Simms* is unclear,[88] but it appears that an experimental *treatment* may be offered in England provided it is appropriate in the clinician's judgement to do so, and the law appears to support this *outside* the clinical trials framework. Research ethics committees (RECs) are not required to review experimental procedures; rather, practitioners who want to perform a 'new interventional procedure' *outside* an REC-approved trial[89] should seek approval from their NHS Trust's Clinical Governance Committee (CGC), and the CGC chair should notify the Interventional Procedures Programme at the National Institute for Health and Clinical Excellence (NICE) if the procedure is not already listed by NICE.[90] An 'interventional procedure' is 'one used for diagnosis or treatment that involves incision, puncture, entry into a body cavity, electromagnetic or acoustic energy',[91] and it should be considered new 'if a doctor no longer in a training post is using it for the first time in his or her NHS clinical practice'.[92] If there is NICE guidance on the procedure, the CGC should consider whether the proposed use of the procedure complies with it, before approving that use.[93] If there is no guidance, the CGC should only approve using the procedure if: (i) the doctor has met externally set training standards; (ii) the patients are aware, among other things, of the procedure's special status and lack of use; and (iii) the proposed arrangements for clinical audit are sound and will record data on clinical outcomes that can be used to review its continued use.[94] If there are no other treatment options the new procedure *can* be used 'in a clinical emergency so as not to place a patient at serious risk'.[95] If this occurs, the doctor must inform the CGC within 72 hours and the Committee then considers whether to approve future use of the procedure by applying the above procedure.

Under this regulatory framework each NHS Trust's CGC has a key role because if there is no NICE guidance and the three conditions are fulfilled, it can approve the use of a new interventional procedure. Even if there is guidance, the CGC does not have to comply with

---

[87] *Ibid.*, para. 62, emphasis supplied.
[88] Mason and Laurie, *Mason & McCall Smith's*, p. 628.
[89] HSC 2003/011, *The Interventional Procedures Programme: Working with the National Institute for Clinical Excellence to Promote Safe Clinical Innovation*, paras. 2, 12.
[90] *Ibid.*, paras. 1, 7. See further, para. 4   [91] *Ibid.*, para. 15.   [92] *Ibid.*, para. 16.
[93] *Ibid.*, para. 7.   [94] *Ibid.*, para. 8.   [95] *Ibid.*, para. 10.

it, but merely 'consider' whether the proposed use complies with it. CGCs 'work to improve and assure the quality of clinical services for patients'[96] and each NHS Board has a CGC which is responsible to the Board,[97] is chaired by a non-executive director, and the non-executive chair of the Audit Committee, a non-executive director, employee director, medical director and nursing director sit on it.[98] It is thus debatable whether CGC members will have the expertise to decide whether a new interventional procedure should be used, with or without NICE guidance and, in contrast to the situation in New Zealand,[99] there is no requirement for *ethical* review of new interventional procedures. Furthermore, NICE guidance and Health Service Circulars are not legally binding and although health professionals are expected to take the former 'fully into account' when exercising their clinical judgement, it 'does not override the individual responsibility of health professionals to make appropriate decisions according to the circumstances of the individual patient in consultation with the patient'.[100] Indeed, even if a procedure is not recommended or is only recommended in certain situations, this does not mean its use is otherwise prohibited; rather, '[i]f, having considered that guidance, a health professional considers that the treatment or procedure would be the appropriate option in a given case, there is no legal bar on the professional recommending the treatment or on the NHS funding it'.[101] In any legal dispute NICE guidance will carry 'great weight as it is arrived at by considering the best available evidence and expert professional advice', but it should only be followed if it is a doctor's clinical judgement that it is in the patient's best interests to do so.[102] Departing from the guidance does not necessarily mean the doctor is negligent as 'a reasoned and reasonable decision to reject the guidance in an individual case, together with a good record, made at the time, may be acceptable'.[103]

---

[96] DH, *Xenotransplantation*, p. 6.
[97] NHS Scotland, 'Clinical Governance Committee' (2007) (at: www.clinicalgovernance.scot.nhs.uk/section1/govcommittee.asp, accessed 22/03/11).
[98] NHS 24, 'Clinical Governance Committee, Terms of Reference' (2007), para. 2.1.1 (at: www.nhs24.com/content/mediaassets/doc/CLINICAL%20GOVERNANCE%20COMMITTEE%20-%20Terms%20of%20Reference.pdf, accessed 22/03/11).
[99] MH, *Operational Standard*, para. 1.
[100] NICE, *The Legal Implications of NICE Guidance* (2004), p. 3 (at: www.nice.org.uk/niceMedia/pdf/Legal_context_nice_guidance.pdf, accessed 22/03/11).
[101] *Ibid.* [102] *Ibid.*, p. 4.
[103] Dr Paul Colbrook, medico-legal adviser at the Medical Defence Union, *Doctor* magazine special report, March 2002, as cited in *ibid.*

A doctor/experimenter may thus rely on her clinical judgement to justify her decision to offer a particular patient an experimental procedure, but consideration should be given to whether the *Bolam* test would support her decision as the procedure is experimental and it is unlikely that there will be a responsible body of medical opinion to support its use. This was not viewed as a non-negotiable obstacle in *Simms* and 'where the patient's condition is very serious and the standard treatment is ineffective, a doctor will be justified in taking greater risks in an attempt to provide some effective treatment'.[104] In *Hunter* v. *Hanley*[105] deviation from ordinary medical practice was not necessarily evidence of nor amounted to negligence,[106] as a substantial deviation from standard practice may be 'warranted by the particular circumstances'.[107] If this occurred and the patient wanted to establish negligence, she would have to prove that: (i) there was a 'usual and normal practice'; (ii) the doctor had not adopted it; and (iii) the doctor's actions were such that 'no professional man of ordinary skill would have taken if he had been acting with ordinary care'.[108] The court is essentially considering 'whether the deviation from established practice was a reasonable course of conduct for the patient at hand',[109] and the decision in *Bolitho*[110] could support the argument that in all the circumstances of the case the doctor's decision to use an experimental procedure on a particular patient was logical.[111] A court will consider each case on its facts and merits when deciding if it was reasonable to use that procedure, and may be more 'lenient' where the alternatives are serious harm or death.[112] Nevertheless, a patient should not be exposed to excessive risk and there should be some effort to scientifically validate the procedure or technique.[113] Finally, the exception from the process granted to new interventional procedures performed in 'clinical emergencies' is important as this term is not defined, and it appears that a doctor/experimenter can use a new procedure and declare after the fact that there was such an emergency, perhaps supported by the health status of the patient; terminally ill with no other hope and at serious risk of death.

---

[104] M. Jones, *Medical Negligence* (4th edn, London: Sweet & Maxwell, 2008), para. 3-057.
[105] (1955) SLT 213 (Scotland).
[106] Also, England – *Waters* v. *West Sussex Health Authority* [1995] 6 Med. LR 362; *Wilsher* v. *Essex Area Health Authority* [1987] QB 730, CA; Scotland – *Landau* v. *Werner* (1961) 105 SJ 257, CA; Canada – *Zimmer* v. *Ringrose* (1981) DLR (3d) 215, CA.
[107] Above, n. 105, p. 217. [108] *Ibid*.
[109] Mason and Laurie, *Mason & McCall Smith's*, p. 627, reference removed.
[110] [1997] 4 All ER 771, HL.
[111] Mason and Laurie, *Mason & McCall Smith's*, pp. 143–144, 627–628.
[112] E.g. *Simms*, though not *ex parte B*. [113] *Hepworth* v. *Kerr* [1995] 6 Med. LR 139.

Ethical guidance

Unless it is assumed that ethical guidance on research also applies to experimental procedures, there is little specific ethical guidance on the latter. If the former is applicable, then, amongst other things, a protocol should exist, be ethically reviewed, and REC approval obtained prior to a procedure being performed, as discussed below.[114] Of the provisions directed to experimental procedures the Declaration of Helsinki states:

> [i]n the *treatment* of a patient, where *proven interventions do not exist or have been ineffective*, the physician, after seeking expert advice, with informed consent from the patient or a legally authorized representative, may use an *unproven intervention* if in the *physician's judgement* it offers *hope* of saving life, re-establishing health or alleviating suffering. *Where possible*, this intervention should be made the object of research, designed to evaluate its safety and efficacy. In all cases, new information should be recorded and, where appropriate, made publicly available.[115]

Thus, new interventions *can* be ethically performed *outside* a research project where the doctor *hopes* that the patient will benefit. Many could argue their work falls within this vague and wide-ranging justification for providing experimental procedures, and there is no indication as to how, or whether, the doctor/experimenter's judgement is assessed or monitored otherwise than via the advice of unspecified 'experts'. Other relevant Declaration principles should presumably be followed, but the situation of those considering accepting an experimental procedure (no other hope) is not specifically addressed.[116] Notably, REC approval is not required for the use of such 'treatments' despite the likely health status of the patients. The Council for International Organizations of Medical Sciences (CIOMS) and WHO Guidelines contain similar provisions and state that '"compassionate use"' of 'drugs or other therapies not yet licensed for general availability' to 'patients with incurable diseases or serious, potentially disabling or life-threatening diseases' should 'not properly [be] regarded as research' but contributes to 'ongoing research into the safety and efficacy of the interventions used'.[117] Such use is said to be compatible with the Declaration of Helsinki.

---

[114] E.g. Council for International Organizations of Medical Sciences (CIOMS) and WHO, *International Ethical Guidelines for Biomedical Research Involving Human Subjects* (Geneva: CIOMS, 2002), Guidelines 2, 3.

[115] WMA, *Declaration of Helsinki, Ethical Principles for Medical Research Involving Human Subjects* adopted by the 18th WMA, Helsinki, Finland, June 1964, as amended in 2008, C35, emphasis supplied.

[116] Annas, 'The Changing Landscape'.

[117] CIOMS and WHO, *International Ethical*, Commentary on Guideline 13.

Under HSC 2003/011 new interventional procedures do not have to be ethically reviewed in England and experimental procedures are also not covered by Australian or Canadian ethical research guidelines.[118] In contrast, in New Zealand innovative practice *and* research must be ethically reviewed.[119] Not every deviation from 'accepted practice' must be ethically reviewed, but if it is a 'planned deviation ... intended to be used on an ongoing basis', then a review is required.[120] Professional judgement, preferably involving consulting experts, will determine whether something is an innovative practice, a specific protocol is required and the REC must be satisfied of the information available for a patient to make an informed decision, that the purpose is to treat a condition of a particular patient or group, that there are 'appropriate safeguards' for independent clinical assessment so that if necessary the patients can change to standard treatment instead, and there are 'appropriate evaluative mechanisms' to assess the effectiveness of the practice.[121] Relevant information to be considered by the REC is also set out.[122]

The UK's GMC guidance on research does not apply to 'innovative treatments designed to benefit individual patients',[123] but its guidance on consent and confidentiality does.[124] Patients must be given the information they 'want or need' on whether what is proposed 'is part of a research programme or is an innovative treatment designed specifically for their benefit', and should be told 'how the proposed treatment differs from the usual methods, why it is being offered, and if there are any additional risks or uncertainties'.[125] The RCP also cautions doctors/experimenters to be prepared to justify 'innovative therapy both ethically and scientifically' if challenged, and any extension of an experimental interventional procedure into 'wider use or general application' should then be seen as research.[126] There is, however, little sense that providing an experimental procedure to those with no other hope raises particular ethical problems, but being in this position inevitably places the potential recipient in a different position to others, and this needs acknowledging.[127]

---

[118] Australia – NHMRC, Australian Research Council, Australian Vice-Chancellor's Committee, *National Statement on Ethical Conduct in Human Research* (Canberra: Australian Government, 2007), p. 7; Canada – Canadian Institutes *et al.*, *TCPS2*, Article 2.1, Application.
[119] MH, *Operational Standard*, para. 1.   [120] *Ibid.*, paras. 120–121, 123.
[121] *Ibid.*, paras. 125, 132, 134.   [122] *Ibid.*, para. 135.
[123] GMC, *Good Practice in Research* (London: GMC, 2010), para. 4.
[124] GMC, *Consent: Patients and Doctors Making Decisions Together* (London: GMC, 2008); GMC, *Confidentiality*.
[125] GMC, *Consent*, para. 9(f); also, GMC, *Consent to Research* (London: GMC, 2010).
[126] RCP, *Guidelines*, paras. 3.5, 3.7.   [127] See Chapter 5.

Xenotransplantation

The Council of Europe appears to agree that clinical xenotransplants *can* be performed outside the research context but has recommended that this is not authorised unless conditions are met concerning the infection risks to others, and therapeutic benefit has been established.[128] The Explanatory Report on the Recommendation states that performance outside of research should only occur once xenotransplantation becomes a 'validated clinical intervention',[129] and that '[t]o begin with, it must be emphasised that xenotransplantation procedures, taking into account their nature, is still largely experimental, are destined to take place *mainly* within the framework of biomedical research'.[130] Additionally, '[a]s long as xenotransplantation remains experimental, last resort procedures should not be considered as possible exceptions to the requirements applicable to clinical research'.[131] The majority of countries that have considered the issue also require clinical xenotransplants to be performed *within* a research protocol.[132] In contrast, in England as the first genetically engineered solid organ xenotransplants will be experimental procedures, xeno-recipients and the public are essentially reliant on the professionalism and conscience of the doctor/experimenter to follow a regulatory scheme with which they are not legally obliged to comply. Given the risks of xenotransplantation and the research community's concern about its reputation after the events in Bristol and Liverpool,[133] it may be that 'it is most unlikely in the current climate that the practical application of xenotransplantation would be tested in anything other than the context of clinical trials (research)'.[134]

---

[128] Council of Europe, Recommendation Rec(2003)10, Article 5 (2).
[129] Steering Committee on Bioethics (CDBI), European Health Committee (CDSP), *Explanatory Report to Recommendation Rec(2003)10 of the Committee of Ministers to member states on xenotransplantation* CDBI/INF (2003) 12, para.12; also, paras. 10–16.
[130] *Ibid.*, para. 10, emphasis supplied.   [131] *Ibid.*, para. 14.
[132] E.g. Australia – NHMRC, XWP, *Animal-to-Human Transplantation: Final Report*, p. viii; NHMRC, NHMRC, XWP, *Guidelines for Clinical*, Guideline 1, accompanying NHMRC, XWP, *Animal-to-Human Transplantation: Final Report*; Canada – Health Canada, *Proposed Canadian Standard*, Section E, p. 28; New Zealand – HRC, *Guidelines on Preparation*, p. 1; Spain – 'Recommendations for the Regulation of Xeno Activities in Spain – Extracted from the Report of the Xenotransplantation Commission of the National Transplant Commission' (1998) 18 suppl. 7 *Nefrologia* 35; Sweden – Swedish Committee, *From One Species*, p. 15; US – US DHHS, FDA, *PHS Guideline*, para. 2.3.
[133] *Learning from Bristol*; *The Royal Liverpool Children's Inquiry Report* (London: Stationery Office, 2001); R. Smith, 'All Changed, Changed Utterly' (1998) 316 *British Medical Journal* 1917.
[134] McLean and Williamson, *Xenotransplantation*, p. 197.

But it does not *have* to be so. Indeed, although the UKXIRA's guidance stated that 'any intervention involving xenotransplantation should be classified as research',[135] it appears that a xenotransplant *can* legally be performed outside of a research project in England under either the common law as experimental *treatment* (*Simms*) or HSC 2003/011 as a new interventional procedure, with no REC approval.

Since 2006 the UK's DH has recommended that '*all* xenotransplant procedures are carried out with a research protocol approved by a research ethics committee';[136] but the guidance outlines three ways in which a clinical xenotransplant can be performed.[137] Clinical xenotransplantation can be performed as '*experimental medicine*', where 'a clinician offer[s] a particular course of *treatment* tailored to a particular patient's needs, either a brand new treatment or a new use of a drug or product licensed for use in other ways'.[138] When considering offering such medicine, doctors/experimenters are 'required' to follow the procedure in HSC 2003/011, and those wanting to provide '*experimental treatment*' outside of research 'are encouraged to take public health issues and long-term health surveillance of patients into account'.[139] Given the risks, it is surprising that xenotransplants can be legally performed as 'treatment' outside the research context; further supporting my argument that experimental procedures and medical research should be similarly regulated, particularly with regard to ethical review. Without such, the protection afforded to xeno-recipients and the public is questionable, particularly given the 'hazy' role of CGCs in the approval process.[140] The ability of CGCs to consider xenotransplant experimental procedures is debatable, and 'local ad hoc decision-making [is] unsuited to practices whose consequences could be national – even international'.[141]

---

[135] UKXIRA, *Guidance on Making Proposals to Conduct Xenotransplantation on Human Subjects* (London: DH, 1998), para. 5.3.
[136] DH, *Xenotransplantation*, p. 2, emphasis supplied.
[137] The others are discussed at pp. 83–5, below.
[138] DH, *Xenotransplantation*, p. 3, emphasis supplied.   [139] *Ibid.*, pp. 3–4.
[140] S. McLean and L. Williamson, 'The Demise of UKXIRA and the Regulation of Solid-Organ Xenotransplantation in the UK' (2007) 33 *Journal of Medical Ethics* 373, 373.
[141] *Ibid.*, p. 374.

Regulating research[142]

The law

Clinical trials[143] of 'medicinal products'[144] are statutorily regulated in the UK by the Medicines for Human Use (Clinical Trials) Regulations 2004. No distinction is drawn between therapeutic and non-therapeutic trials. A favourable opinion is required from an REC,[145] and the Medicines and Healthcare products Regulatory Agency (MHRA) must authorise the trial before it begins.[146] A timetable is provided for obtaining the opinion and authorisation,[147] and each trial must have an identified sponsor who is responsible for its initiation, management and conduct,[148] and it should be conducted in accordance with good clinical practice.[149] Trials should be 'scientifically sound and guided by ethical principles in all their aspects', and the Declaration of Helsinki's principles complied with.[150] Prior to its start, the 'foreseeable risks and inconveniences' have to be weighed against the 'anticipated benefit' for the 'individual trial subject and other present and future patients', with the benefit justifying the risk, and the REC and MHRA must conclude that 'the anticipated therapeutic and public health benefits justify the risks'.[151] Compliance must be 'permanently monitored' for the trial to continue, there are specific requirements for investigators and sponsors, and enforcement powers including infringement notices and criminal sanctions.[152]

---

[142] Research regulation in the UK was reviewed in 2010 and recommendations, including a new Health Research Agency to 'rationalise the regulation and governance of all health research' and revision of the EU Clinical Trials Directive, were published in January 2011: Academy of Medical Sciences, *A New Pathway for the Regulation and Governance of Health Research* (London: Academy of Sciences, 2011), pp. 4–6.

[143] 'any investigation in human subjects, other than a non-interventional trial intended (a) to discover or verify the clinical ... effects of one or more medicinal products, or (b) to identify any adverse reactions to one or more such products ... with the object of ascertaining the safety and efficacy of those products' (2004 Regulations, Reg. 2 (1)).

[144] '(a) a medicinal product within the meaning given by Article 1 of Directive 2001/83/EC, or (b) any product which is not a medicinal product within the meaning given by Article 1 of Directive 2001/83/EC, but which is a medicinal product within the meaning given by section 130 of the [Medicines] Act [1968]' (*ibid.*).

[145] *Ibid.*, Reg. 12(3)(a).   [146] *Ibid.*, Reg. 12(3)(b).
[147] *Ibid.*, Regs. 15(10), 18–20, respectively.   [148] *Ibid.*, Reg. 3.
[149] *Ibid.*, Reg. 28; also, Regs. 29–31A, Sched. 1.   [150] *Ibid.*, Sched. 1, Part 2, paras. 3, 6.
[151] *Ibid.*, paras. 10, 12.
[152] *Ibid.*, Sched. 1, Part 2, para. 12, Regs. 33 (1), 47–52, Sched. 9, respectively.

Regulatory schemes 81

Ethical guidance

It is inherent within many international and national ethical guidelines[153] that medical research and participating in it is important, but participants may need protection from, among other things, unnecessary risks,[154] being used merely as a means to an end,[155] and participation should be premised on informed consent.[156] Research should be conducted within a protocol,[157] by appropriately qualified personnel,[158] which has been reviewed and approved by an REC.[159] Some guidelines also address the specific issues raised by therapeutic and non-therapeutic research, and

---

[153] The UK's GMC guidance can be described as professional ethical guidance because while it may primarily be viewed as concerned with professional standards, it is based on ethical principles and concerns.

[154] WMA, *Declaration*, B18, 20–21; CIOMS and WHO, *International Ethical*, Guideline 8; International Conference on Harmonisation of Technical Requirements for Registration of Pharmaceuticals for Human Use, *ICH Harmonised Tripartite Guideline – Guideline for Good Clinical Practice E6(R1)* (1996), para. 2 (at: www.ich.org/fileadmin/Public_Web_Site/ICH_Products/Guidelines/Efficacy/E6_R1/Step4/E6_R1__Guideline.pdf, accessed 22/03/11); Australia – NHMRC et al., *National Statement*, paras. 1.6–1.9, Section 2.1; Canada – Canadian Institutes et al., *TCPS2*, chs. 1, 2B; New Zealand – MH, *Operational Standard*, paras. 52–57; UK – GMC, *Good Practice*, paras. 9, 15–20; MRC, *MRC Guidelines for Good Clinical Practice in Clinical Trials* (London: MRC, 1998), para. 2.2; US – National Commission, *Ethical Principles*, 'Ethical Principles & Guidelines', Sections B2, C2.

[155] WMA, *Declaration*, A3, A4, A6; International Conference, *ICH Harmonised*, para. 2.3; Australia – NHMRC et al., *National Statement*, Section 1; Canada – Canadian Institutes et al., *TCPS2*, ch. 1; UK – GMC, *Good Practice*, para. 8; MRC, *MRC Guidelines*, para. 2.3; US – American Medical Association (AMA), *Opinion 2.07 – Clinical Investigation* (1998), para. (5)(a) (at: www.ama-assn.org/ama/pub/physician-resources/medical-ethics/code-medical-ethics/opinion207.shtml, accessed 22/03/11).

[156] WMA, *Declaration*, B24–29; CIOMS and WHO, *International Ethical*, Guidelines 4–6, 9, 15; International Conference, *ICH Harmonised*, para. 2.9; Australia – NHMRC et al., *National Statement*, Section 2.2; Canada – Canadian Institutes et al., *TCPS2*, ch. 3; New Zealand – MH, *Operational Standard*, paras. 29–41; HRC, *Guidelines on Ethics in Health Research* (2002) revised 2005, paras. 3.1, 4.3, 4.5 (at: www.hrc.govt.nz/assets/pdfs/publications/Ethics%20Guidelines%20July%202006.pdf, accessed 22/03/11); UK – GMC, *Good Practice*, paras. 28–30; GMC, *Consent to Research*; MRC, *MRC Guidelines*, para. 2.9; US – AMA, *Opinion 2.07*, paras. (4), 5(b); National Commission, *Ethical Principles*, C1.

[157] WMA, *Declaration*, B14; CIOMS and WHO, *International Ethical*, Comment on Guideline 1, Appendix 1; International Conference, *ICH Harmonised*, para. 2.5, section 6; Australia – NHMRC, *National Statement*, para. 1.1(b); UK – GMC, *Good Practice*, para. 7; MRC, *MRC Guidelines*, para. 2.5; US – AMA, *Opinion 2.07*, para. (1).

[158] WMA, *Declaration*, B16; CIOMS and WHO, *International Ethical*, Commentary on Guideline 1; International Conference, *ICH Harmonised*, paras. 2.7–2.8; Australia – NHMRC et al., *National Statement*, para. 1.1(e); UK – GMC, *Good Practice*, para. 13; MRC, *MRC Guidelines*, paras. 2.7–2.8; US – AMA, *Opinion 8.0315*, para. (1).

[159] WMA, *Declaration*, B15; CIOMS and WHO, *International Ethical*, Guidelines 2–3; International Conference, *ICH Harmonised*, para. 2.6, section 3; Australia – NHMRC, *National Statement*, Section 5; Canada – Canadian Institutes et al., *TCPS2*, chs. 2, 6; New Zealand – MH, *Operational Standard*, para. 97; HRC, *Guidelines on Ethics*, section 2; UK – GMC, *Good Practice*, para. 7; RCP, *Guidelines*; MRC, *MRC Guidelines*,

82   Regulating experimental procedures and research

the Declaration of Helsinki contains five additional principles for 'medical research combined with medical care'.[160] These include the principle that such research should occur only 'to the extent that [it] is justified by its potential preventive, diagnostic or therapeutic value', and if there are 'good reasons' to believe that participation 'will not adversely affect the health of the patients who serve as research subjects'.[161] The 'benefits, risks and effectiveness' of the 'new intervention' should be tested against the best current proven intervention if there is one,[162] and the patient/participant should be told which aspects of her care relate to the research.[163] There are similar provisions in the CIOMS and WHO guidelines; the risks 'must be justified in relation to the expected benefits to the individual subject',[164] and under the UK's GMC guidance 'foreseeable risks' should be kept 'as low as possible'.[165] Non-therapeutic research, under the CIOMS and WHO guidelines, must be justified 'in relation to the expected benefits to society (generalizable knowledge). The risks ... must be reasonable in relation to the importance of the knowledge to be gained.'[166] The ICH guidelines state that such research should be performed on competent individuals who are informed that they will not benefit from it,[167] but those without capacity may only be involved if certain conditions are fulfilled, including consent from a 'legally acceptable representative', 'the foreseeable risks to the subjects are low',[168] 'the negative impact on [their] well-being is minimized and low', and an REC has expressly approved their inclusion.[169] Unless there is a justifiable exception, participants without capacity should have the disease or condition which the research is aimed at ameliorating.[170]

Unusually, the UK's 2004 Clinical Trials Regulations enshrine the 1996 Declaration of Helsinki's principles into law.[171] Importantly, under

---

para. 2.6; US – AMA, *Opinion 8.0315 – Managing Conflicts of Interest in the Conduct of Clinical Trials* (2001), paras. (1)–(2) (at: www.ama-assn.org/ama/pub/physician-resources/medical-ethics/code-medical-ethics/opinion80315.shtml, accessed 22/03/11); also, WHO, *Operational Guidelines for Ethics Committees that Review Biomedical Research* (Geneva: WHO, 2000), TDR/PRD/ETHICS/2000.1.

[160] WMA, *Declaration*, C31–35.   [161] *Ibid.*, C31.   [162] *Ibid.*, C32.   [163] *Ibid.*, C33.
[164] CIOMS and WHO, *International Ethical*, Guideline 8. Similarly, UK – GMC, *Good Practice*, para. 9.
[165] GMC, *Good Practice*, para. 9.
[166] CIOMS and WHO, *International Ethical*, Guideline 8.
[167] International Conference, *ICH Harmonised*, paras. 4.8.13, 4.8.10(h), respectively.
[168] Also, UK – GMC, *Good Practice*, para. 9, such risks should be 'minimal'.
[169] International Conference, *ICH Harmonised*, para. 4.8.14; also, WMA, *Declaration*, B27–29; CIOMS and WHO, *International Ethical*, Guidelines 15, 9.
[170] International Conference, *ICH Harmonised*, para. 4.8.14; CIOMS and WHO, *International Ethical*, Guideline 15.
[171] Sched. 1, Part 1, para. 2, 2004 Regulations.

this version patients *cannot* be involved in non-therapeutic research as such participants should be volunteers,[172] and therapeutic research need only be 'justified by its potential diagnostic or therapeutic value to the patient'.[173] The 1996 principles are thus more restrictive for non-therapeutic and less restrictive for therapeutic research than the 2008 version discussed above. As the 2004 Regulations have been amended, it is disappointing that the differences between the versions have not been addressed and the protection offered to potential investigators and participants clarified.

Xenotransplantation
The UK's DH 2006 xenotransplantation guidance states that:

> the potential of xenotransplantation [should be explored] in a cautious, stepwise fashion. *It is extremely important to carry out a xenotransplant procedure in a controlled research context.* Clearly, the well-being of the individuals concerned, and the safety of the public in general, must be foremost in the consideration of any proposal to undertake a xenotransplantation procedure. No xenotransplantation procedures involving humans will be allowed to take place unless the approving body is fully satisfied that the evidence put forward is sufficient to justify the particular procedure proposed.[174]

There are now three ways in which a clinical xenotransplant can be legally performed in the UK: (i) as experimental medicine;[175] (ii) in a clinical trial; and (iii) as research involving NHS patients but not within the 2004 Regulations. Providing these options places the UK *outside* the WHO's principles under which xenotransplants are presumed to be performed as clinical trials,[176] but the Council of Europe has also indicated that clinical xenotransplants can be performed outside the research context.[177] In relation to (ii), a clinical trial of a 'xenogeneic medicinal product' performed under the 2004 Regulations requires approval from the MHRA and ethical review by a recognised REC.[178] If the xenotransplant is genetically modified, the Gene Therapy Advisory Committee (GTAC) must ethically approve it; otherwise, the National Research Ethics Service (NRES)[179] will ensure the proposal

---

[172] WMA, *Declaration of Helsinki, Recommendations Guiding Physicians in Biomedical Research in Biomedical Research Involving Human Subjects* adopted by the 18th WMA, Helsinki, Finland, June 1964, as amended in 1996, Section III. 2.
[173] *Ibid.*, Section II. 6.   [174] DH, *Xenotransplantation*, p. 2, emphasis supplied.
[175] Above, p. 79.   [176] 'First WHO', Principles 5, 6.
[177] Council of Europe, Recommendation Rec(2003)10, Article 5 (1).
[178] 2004 Regulations, Reg. 12(3).
[179] NRES's future is under review, DH, *Liberating the NHS: Report of the Arm's Length Bodies Review* (London: DH, 2010), and the Academy of Sciences has proposed that a new National Research Governance Service is included within the new Health

84 Regulating experimental procedures and research

is ethically reviewed.[180] For (iii), xenotransplant research involving NHS patients outside the 2004 Regulations, ethical review is still required by the GTAC for genetically modified cellular xenotransplants and NRES will organise the ethical review of non-genetically modified cellular xenotransplants and all solid organ xenotransplants.[181] An REC must thus ethically approve the xenotransplant proposal under (ii) and (iii), and if under the former the MHRA must also authorise it. It is thus important to determine whether a genetically engineered solid organ xenotransplant falls within the 2004 Regulations.

With regard to (ii), in the 2004 Regulations a medicinal product is either that which is so defined in Article 1 of Directive 2001/83/EC or in section 30 of the Medicines Act 1968.[182] Under Article 1 a xenogeneic medicinal product is 'any procedure that involves the transplantation, implantation or infusion into a human recipient of either live tissues or organs retrieved from animals, *or*, human body fluids, cells, tissues or organs that have undergone *ex vivo* contact with live non-human animal cells, tissues or organs'.[183] Genetically engineered solid organs *appear* to fall within this definition but this is not clear,[184] and it has been suggested that the removed organs need to be manipulated *ex vivo* and the definition above 'is not a definition of "xeno-transplantation medicinal product"'.[185] However, the emphasised 'or' indicates that *ex vivo* manipulation is one of two options and the DH has stated that this *is* a definition of a xenogeneic medicinal product.[186] The Directive itself also suggests this as the definition appears directly under the heading 'Specific Statement on Xeno-transplantation Medicinal Products'.[187] Furthermore, according to the RCP 'xenotransplantation is now fully embedded in UK regulations on medicinal products' with any clinical trial of a xenogeneic product to be approved by a recognised REC.[188] Finally, Lord Warner stated that 'EU legislation on medicinal products

Research Agency (HRA) with NRES a 'key component' of this (Academy of Medical Sciences, *A New Pathway*, p. 86, ch. 9).
[180] DH, *Xenotransplantation*, pp. 2–3.   [181] *Ibid.*, p. 3.
[182] 2004 Regulations, Reg. 2(1).
[183] Directive 2003/63/EC of 25 June 2003 amending Directive 2001/83/EC of the European Parliament and of the Council on the Community Code Relating to Medicinal Products for Human Use, Annex 1, Part IV, para. 4, emphasis supplied.
[184] E.g. D. Beyleveld *et al.*, 'The Regulation of Hybrids and Chimeras in the UK', in J. Taupitz and M. Weschka (eds.), *Chimbrids: Chimeras and Hybrids in Comparative European and International Research: Scientific, Ethical, Philosophical and Legal Aspects* (Berlin: Springer, 2009), pp. 645, 649–650; DH, *Animal Tissue*, paras. 8.50–8.58.
[185] S. Pattinson, *Medical Law and Ethics* (2nd edn, London: Sweet & Maxwell, 2009), p. 501.
[186] DH, *Xenotransplantation*, p. 3.
[187] Directive 200EC, Ann/63/EC, Annex 1, Part IV, para. 4.
[188] RCP, *Guidelines*, para. 8.76.

(Commission Directive 2003/63/EU) and the Clinical Trials Regulations (2004) make specific provision for xenotransplantation proposals'.[189]

Nevertheless, if genetically engineered solid organs do not fall within the definition, they *may* come under section 130 of the Medicines Act 1968 where a medicinal product is 'any substance or article ... which is manufactured, sold, supplied, imported or exported for use wholly or mainly ... (a) use by being administered to one or more human beings for a medicinal purpose'. Such a purpose includes '(a) treating or preventing disease ... (e) otherwise preventing or interfering with the normal operation of a physiological function, whether permanently or temporarily, and whether by way of terminating, reducing or postponing, or increasing or accelerating, the operation of that function or in any other way'. In the DH's 1996 report it was suggested that the 1968 Act appears to apply to xenotransplantation but that the intention and purpose of the Act should be taken into account and as xenotransplantation was not 'in the minds of the legislators', the Act does not apply.[190] This could be argued about any post-statute advances but precedent suggests that a court adjudicating such a matter would adopt a purposive approach to statutory interpretation, particularly without other more relevant legislation.[191] Adopting a different approach could necessitate constant amendments to statutes, the introduction of new legislation, or bringing cases to determine the applicability of the original Acts.

Regardless, it *does* matter whether genetically engineered non-human animal solid organs fall within this definition because of the consequences which follow. Unfortunately, the UK's MHRA has not clarified this as without a protocol they could not comment on whether such an organ would be a medicinal product within the 2004 Regulations.[192] It *may* thus be that genetically engineered solid organs are medicinal products within the ambit of the 2004 Regulations and, if so, a clinical trial would have to comply with the provisions of the Regulations, noted above. If the

---

[189] Lord Warner, Hansard, HL Written Statements, vol. 687, col. WS181 12 December 2006 (at: www.publications.parliament.uk/pa/ld200607/ldhansrd/text/61212-wms0001.htm, accessed 22/03/11).
[190] DH, *Animal Tissue*, para. 8.59; also, 8.60–8.62.
[191] E.g. *R v. Secretary of State for Health, ex parte Quintavalle* [2003] UKHL 13; *Royal College of Nursing v. DHSS* [1981] 1 All ER 545, HL.
[192] Personal communication with the Medicines Healthcare products Regulatory Agency (MHRA) dated 13 May 2010, on file with author. Further correspondence on 28 May 2010 indicated that the Clinical Trials Helpline were to 'consult further with colleagues in the Agency' but no further communication has been received. The MHRA guidance note also does not answer this query: MHRA, *A Guide to What Is A Medicinal Product* (London: MHRA, 2007) MHRA Guidance Note No. 8.

clinical trial involves medicinal products with 'special characteristics'[193] there is a different authorisation procedure, and xenogeneic cell therapies have a different timetable for ethics committee approval.[194] For ethical review, the GTAC is *only* responsible for clinical trials or research involving genetically modified non-human cells and *not* solid organs.[195] Non-specialist RECs will consider the latter. In distinguishing between cells and solid organs in this way, the DH guidance differs from the definition used in the Human Tissue Act 2004[196] and is an inappropriate alteration to the previous regulatory scheme. By publishing xeno-specific guidance the DH implies that this biotechnology raises issues which require a particular regulatory regime, but by then adopting existing regulatory structures it is suggesting these issues *can* be appreciated, understood or managed by existing non-specialist bodies. The DH has said that 'UKXIRA was set up as an interim body and a number of standing (statutory and advisory) bodies adequately cover the issues',[197] but this is debatable and the new system sits awkwardly with the previous scheme under which any xenotransplant clinical trial application had to be approved by a specialist body or bodies, an REC *and* the secretary of state.[198] It is unclear why between 1997 and 2006 all forms of xenotransplantation were worthy of a three- or four-stage approval process, whereas since 2006 only cellular xenotransplantation merits the particular attention of a specialist body. The distinction in the regulatory schemes between the different types of xenotransplant requires explanation and clarification because it is not known whether one type of xenotransplant is more 'risky' than another due to, for example, differences in conduct, exposure and duration. The incorporation of xenotransplantation into existing regulatory schemes may be indicative of the trend in regulating health care in England and Wales to reduce the number of regulatory and/or advisory bodies,[199] but given the risks involved this is not appropriate in this context.

---

[193] They have an 'active ingredient' that is a biological product of, or contains biological components of, human or non-human animal origin (2004 Regulations, Reg. 20(1)(a)(ii)).
[194] *Ibid.*, Reg. 15 (4).   [195] DH, *Xenotransplantation*, p. 5.
[196] Section 53 'relevant material' for the purposes of the Act is defined as 'material, other than gametes, which consists of or includes human cells'. Tissues, cells *and* solid organs would thus fall within this definition.
[197] Personal communication with DH dated 9 August 2007, on file with author.
[198] UKXIRA, *Guidance*, paras. 2.5–2.6, 4.5; HSC 1998/126 *Clinical Procedures Involving Xenotransplantation*, paras. 7, 9, 11.
[199] E.g. DH, *Liberating the NHS*, pp. 13, 18–21, 37–38.

Additionally, problems with RECs are well documented[200] and a non-specialist REC may not have the sufficient skills to consider applications for genetically engineered solid organ xenotransplants because of the particular issues they raise. Local RECs' 'expertise in xenotransplantation has yet to be established',[201] and they are used to dealing with certain types of proposals and 'traditional' consent issues; not those involving third parties or surveillance.[202] The wisdom of allowing them to take local decisions where the consequences to public health may be widespread is thus debatable,[203] and although when considering a solid organ xenotransplant proposal the REC can 'seek further specialist advice',[204] it is not obvious who would or could provide this given that the UKXIRA, the initial specialist regulatory and advisory body, no longer exists. By abolishing the UKXIRA, the central recommendations of the DH and Nuffield Council reports on xenotransplantation have now been disregarded,[205] and in doing so 'the new guidance seems to weaken rather than strengthen the controls available to protect the public'.[206] However, as RECs in England and Wales are fairly risk averse, delegating this responsibility to them may effectively prevent the clinical application of genetically engineered solid organ xenotransplants.

Selecting xenotransplant recipients

The regulatory scheme under which a xenotransplant is performed affects those to whom it can be offered. Those conducting experimental procedures and clinical trials are central in the selection process because of their experience, the confidential or commercially sensitive information they hold, and their professional vested interest in its performance. Where what is proposed involves risks beyond the recipient and it is unknown what will subsequently happen to them or others, the role of doctors and/or investigators in selecting recipients must be examined to ensure that those at risk are appropriately protected. Can and should those with no other hope be able to receive an experimental procedure or participate in a clinical trial – particularly one involving a genetically engineered solid organ xenotransplant?

---

[200] E.g., E. Angell *et al.*, 'Consistency in Decision Making by Research Ethics Committees: A Controlled Comparison' (2006) 32 *Journal of Medical Ethics* 662; DH, *Report of the Ad Hoc Advisory Group on the Operation of NHS Research Ethics Committees* (London: DH, 2005), Section 3.
[201] McLean and Williamson, 'Demise', 373.   [202] See Chapters 5 and 6.
[203] McLean and Williamson, 'Demise', 375.   [204] DH, *Xenotransplantation*, p. 3.
[205] DH, *Animal Tissue*, ch. 9; Nuffield Council, *Animal-to-Human*, para. 10.31.
[206] McLean and Williamson, 'Demise', 373.

Involving those with no other hope

For those with no other hope, distinctions between experimental procedures, therapeutic and non-therapeutic research are largely irrelevant. Indeed, some with limited treatment choices have, understandably, sought to characterise initial experiments or trials *as treatment* because they represent their only hope of survival or an improved quality of life. Here, rather than participation in an experiment or trial being 'an unqualified sacrifice' it is viewed as 'a potentially risky opportunity',[207] and HIV and AIDS have highlighted how 'high quality clinical care and responsible research [are on] a continuum rather than a dichotomy'.[208] Patients, their families and health interest groups often lobby for access to experimental procedures or drugs in development to be provided *as treatments*,[209] but this may raise safety issues and minimise the number of trial participants available, thereby undermining the clinical trial process.[210] These changes in behaviour coupled with easier access to medical information may also result in a 'combination of eager researchers and desperate relatives [who] may obscure the fact that the patient's condition is best addressed with conservative, rather than aggressive therapy'.[211] This is of especial concern with xenotransplantation because of the risks. Involvement in experimental procedures or trials can, however, benefit participants by uncovering previously unknown abnormalities.[212] It can also benefit them in unexpected and indirect ways; they may be given special considerations, be more involved in their treatment, be given more technical information about their health status and 'treatment', and the shared 'awareness of impending death' may increase the relationship between them and their medical team.[213]

---

[207] M. Fox, 'Research Bodies: Feminist Perspectives on Clinical Research', in S. Sheldon, M. Thomson (eds.), *Feminist Perspectives on Health Care Law* (London: Cavendish, 1998), pp. 115, 123.

[208] M. Fox, 'Clinical Research and Patients: The Legal Perspective', in J. Tingle and A. Cribb (eds.), *Nursing Law and Ethics* (2nd edn, Oxford: Blackwell Science, 2002), pp. 252, 253, reference removed.

[209] E.g., V. Hughes, 'When Patients March In' (2010) 28 *Nature Biotechnology* 1145; *Simms*, paras. 32, 36, 64.

[210] M. Chahal, 'Off-Trial Access to Experimental Cancer Agents for the Terminally Ill: Balancing the Needs of Individuals and Society' (2010) 36 *Journal of Medical Ethics* 367.

[211] J.A. Harrington, 'Deciding Best Interests: Medical Progress, Clinical Judgment and the "Good Family"' [2003] 3 *Web Journal of Current Legal Issues*.

[212] N.M. Orme *et al.*, 'Incidental Findings in Imaging Research: Evaluating Incidence, Benefit, and Burden' (2010) 170 *Archives of Internal Medicine* 1525.

[213] Fox and Swazey, *Courage*, p. 105.

Selecting xenotransplant recipients 89

Discussion of selection for experimental procedures or clinical trials is limited[214] but important because in some situations 'patients are participating in societally sponsored, potential[ly] harmful, physically invasive procedures'.[215] Issues of autonomy, beneficence and justice are raised and the motivations for and outcomes of research must be analysed to ensure that a proposal to participate is 'decent',[216] particularly where the recipient has no other hope. Involving such patients has largely been assumed to be unproblematic perhaps because if they are competent they can refuse life saving treatment.[217] However, even if there appears to be a compelling societal interest for conducting the experimental procedure or research, justice may limit the harms to which a person can be subjected because the requests we make 'reflect how we as a society value individuals and what we consider to be fair and reasonable burdens'.[218] It must thus be considered whether it is 'fair' to ask those with a specific health status to consent to an experimental procedure or research, especially where it is only likely to benefit others. At issue is whether those with no other hope should be involved in procedures or trials where they may be viewed as 'esteemed and heroic companions in a perilous but promising group endeavour that makes "front-line" kindred of all participants'.[219]

Those with no other hope were involved in initial allotransplants and non-genetically engineered xenotransplants,[220] and the team involved in the first cardiac allotransplants commented that 'heroic operations are not infrequently performed on the terminally ill patient in the desperate hope, but remote chance, that life can be prolonged'.[221] More recently it has been suggested that stem cell therapies and experimental cancer drugs should and can be tested on the terminally ill, and the English High Court has sanctioned experimental 'treatment' on a patient in a persistent vegetative state (PVS).[222] Nevertheless, 'research in all

---

[214] Exceptions include W.M. Kong, 'Legitimate Requests and Indecent Proposals: Matters of Justice in the Ethical Assessment of Phase I Trials Involving Competent Patients' (2005) 31 *Journal of Medical Ethics* 205; D.C. Addicott, 'Regulating Research on the Terminally Ill: A Proposal for Heightened Safeguards' (1999) 15 *Journal of Contemporary Health Law and Policy* 479.
[215] Kong, 'Legitimate Requests', 206.   [216] *Ibid.*, 207.
[217] *Re T* (Adult: Refusal of Treatment) [1992] 4 All ER 649, CA.
[218] Kong, 'Legitimate Requests', 207.   [219] Fox and Swazey, *Courage*, p. 105.
[220] J.D. Hardy and C.M. Chavez, 'The First Heart Transplant in Man – Developmental Animal Investigations with Analysis of the 1964 Case in the Light of Current Clinical Experience' (1968) 22 *American Journal of Cardiology* 772; Reemtsma *et al.*, 'Renal Heterotransplantation'.
[221] J.D. Hardy *et al.*, 'Heart Transplantation in Man' (1964) 188 *Journal of the American Medical Association* 1132, 1135.
[222] Chahal, 'Off-Trial Access'; *B NHS Trust* v. *J* [2006] EWHC 3152, respectively.

cultural settings should manifest a bottom line of respect for those who are approached as research subjects. We should not use the lower status of grievously sick persons as a means toward the ends of our personal and scientific pursuits.'[223] The risks of xenotransplantation take the ethics 'out of the realm of individual consent and into the realm of *justice*, raising questions about the extent to which it is permissible for an individual to impose risks on others for his own benefit'.[224]

Xenotransplantation

It has been suggested that those with no other hope should be involved in early xenotransplants,[225] with the US Department of Health and Human Services (DHHS) adding the proviso that they have '*potential for a clinically significant improvement with increased quality of life following the procedure*' and their ability to comply with monitoring is considered.[226] Others have recommended that patients who are 'moribund or so terminally ill that they would not benefit' should not be involved, but those with 'end-stage cardiac or pulmonary disease may represent ideal candidates when no other therapy will support life'.[227] Alternatively, there are two categories of first recipients: those with no other hope and nothing to lose, and those with another option so receiving a xenotransplant will not harm them as there is a 'back-up' if something goes wrong.[228] Going further, initial xeno-recipients could be in a PVS.[229] If the first xeno-recipient is someone with no other hope, then she is likely to know of her terminal condition, be willing to receive it aware that it may not help her but that the results may benefit others. In so acting she is displaying 'heroic altruism'; 'sacrificing' herself for the benefit of future generations.[230] She will thus not fall within the usual therapeutic research category by hoping to *directly* benefit, nor will she

---

[223] H.Y. Vanderpool, 'Informed Consent in Clinical Research' (2007) 14 *Xenotransplantation* 353, 354.
[224] J. Hughes, 'Xenografting: Ethical Issues' (1998) 24 *Journal of Medical Ethics* 18, 21, emphasis in original.
[225] Above, n. 3; also, 'First WHO', p. 63, Recommendation 3; Council of Europe, Recommendation Rec(2003)10, Article 12; Switzerland – Statement of Position, 'Medical–Ethical Principles', p. 391.
[226] US DHHS *et al.*, *Guidance for Industry: Source Animal*, Section VIII D, emphasis supplied.
[227] Cooper *et al.*, 'Report of the Xenotransplantation', 1137–1138.
[228] D.K.C. Cooper and R.P. Lanza, *Xeno – The Promise of Transplanting Animal Organs into Humans* (New York, NY: Oxford University Press 2000), pp. 179–187.
[229] A. Ravelingien *et al.*, 'Proceeding with Clinical Trials of Animal to Human Organ Transplantation: A Way Out of the Dilemma' (2004) 30 *Journal of Medical Ethics* 92.
[230] Hughes, 'Xenografting', 20.

be a healthy volunteer in non-therapeutic research. Rather, she will be considering receiving a xenotransplant which is untested on humans *because of* the lack or failure of alternatives.

The unenviable position of such recipients was recognised by the Nuffield Council which acknowledged that progress is sometimes made at the 'expense' of those who first receive a new procedure, drug or treatment, and that '[i]n some cases, it has been cruel to offer a possible life-saving procedure that resulted in a long drawn-out painful death, instead of a relatively peaceful end. The offer of such a procedure in itself puts pressure on patients to accept – and may distort judgement.'[231] Nevertheless, those who want to contribute to medical research should be permitted to do so, provided there are 'adequate safeguards' to ensure that consent is 'free and properly informed'.[232] Individual choice is thus respected and as long as those with no other hope are competent, informed of their situation and the proposed procedure or trial, their consent can be 'cast as one of the ultimate expressions of personal autonomy' and is legally and ethically acceptable *provided* 'the threat of harm is only at the individual level'.[233] However, their capacity to consent is *not* certain *because of* their health status and the situation they are in,[234] but it is understandable why they would want the chance to say yes to such developments.

But, just as coerced participation in experimental procedures or clinical trials is abusive, so too is not being given the opportunity to be involved in these activities, and 'policies designed to protect vulnerable individuals may inadvertently create barriers to the development of therapies essential to combat their diseases'.[235] It may be discriminatory not to allow those with no other hope the *chance* to benefit *themselves* by receiving a xenotransplant, and it is preferable to let people determine their own best interests and decide whether to be involved because although they might misunderstand their own interests and act against them, *they* are more likely to best understand their own interests. Indeed, it is 'more respectful of research subjects for us to assume that this is the case unless there are powerful reasons for not so doing'.[236] However, while it is reasonable to presume that most people will not consent to things which are against their own or public interests 'clinical trial

---

[231] Nuffield Council, *Animal-to-Human*, para. 7.7; also, para. 7.4.   [232] *Ibid.*, para. 7.5.
[233] Mason and Laurie, *Mason & McCall Smith's*, p. 615.   [234] See Chapter 5.
[235] R.J. Levine, 'The Impact of HIV Infection on Society's Perception of Clinical Trials' (1994) 4 *Kennedy Institute of Ethics Journal* 93, 95.
[236] J. Harris, 'Research on Human Subjects, Exploitation and Global Principles of Ethics', in M. Freeman and A.D.E. Lewis (eds.), *Law and Medicine: Current Legal Issues*, vol. 3 (Oxford University Press, 2000), pp. 379, 389, reference removed.

subjects, by virtue of their vulnerability, their ignorance of the nature of a clinical trial, and the diverse influences acting on the investigator, are ill-equipped to defend their own interests'.[237] It is thus questionable whether those with no other hope are able to act in their *and* our best interests, and the risks to public health *are* a 'powerful reason' for exploring whether this is so for xenotransplantation.[238] This does not necessarily mean that those with no other hope cannot be involved in experimental procedures or research; rather that their involvement needs careful consideration, public discussion and additional protection may be required *because of* their health status. The experiences of Baby Fae and other early allotransplant and non-genetically engineered xenotransplant recipients support this conclusion.[239]

Offering experimental procedures

The law

There is no English judicial dicta on who can receive experimental *procedures* and limited authority on recipients of experimental *treatments*, but in *Simms* Dame Butler-Sloss P. held that a 'patient who is not able to consent to pioneering treatment ought not to be deprived of the chance in circumstances where he would have been likely to consent if he had been competent'.[240] It thus appears that regardless of capacity 'pioneering treatments' can be offered. For those without capacity, if there is no application to the court, the doctor must adhere to the *Bolam* test and act in the best interests of the patient, which 'encompasses medical, emotional and all other welfare issues'.[241] Where there is an application to the court, the judge decides what is in the patient's best interests and four questions need to be answered.[242] Thus, unless a declaration is sought for patients without capacity, the doctor determines their participation; they also decide whether to offer participation to those with capacity. The doctor/experimenter will also determine who receives a new interventional procedure, noting, it is hoped, that 'medical experiments ... on human beings [are] morally justified only in extreme

---

[237] D.S. Shimm and R.G. Spece, 'An Introduction to Conflicts of Interest in Clinical Research', in R.G. Spece *et al.*, *Conflicts of Interest in Clinical Practice and Research* (Oxford University Press, 1996), pp. 361, 362.
[238] See Chapter 5.
[239] G.J. Annas, 'Baby Fae: The "Anything Goes" School of Human Experimentation' (1985) *Hastings Center Report* 15.
[240] [2002] EWHC 2734, para. 57.
[241] *Ibid.*, para. 42; *Re A* [2000] 1 FCR 193, 200, CA *per* Butler-Sloss P., respectively.
[242] Above, n. 72. Best interests is now governed by section 4 MCA 2005.

conditions'.[243] Where there is no NICE guidance on a new interventional procedure, the CGC should only approve its use if three conditions are satisfied.[244] Recipients should be made aware of certain information about the procedure,[245] but capacity issues are not specifically addressed.

Ethical guidance

There is no specific UK ethical guidance on selecting recipients for experimental procedures, but the Declaration of Helsinki requires that informed consent is provided by recipients or their legal representative.[246] Although phrased in terms of research, CIOMS and WHO Guideline 13 states that '[s]pecial justification is required for inviting vulnerable individuals to serve as research subjects and, if they are selected, the means of protecting their rights and welfare must be strictly applied'. 'Vulnerable' individuals include 'patients with incurable disease' and '[p]atients who have serious, potentially disabling or life-threatening diseases are highly vulnerable'.[247] When selecting participants, care should be taken to ensure that the benefits and burdens are equitably distributed and excluding groups or communities who might benefit from participation must be justified.[248] Furthermore, '[m]embers of vulnerable groups . . . have the same entitlement to access to the benefits of investigational interventions that show promise of therapeutic benefit as persons not considered vulnerable, particularly when no superior or equivalent approaches to therapy are available';[249] thus, those with no other hope should have the opportunity to benefit from involvement, with consent provided by them or their legal representative.[250] As the chance to benefit is offered to these groups in the research context and the compassionate use of drugs or therapies for vulnerable groups with no other hope is also endorsed,[251] it appears that experimental procedures can be ethically offered under these Guidelines, including to those with no other hope, as long as the recipient or their legal representative (if the recipient lacks capacity) consent to its use.

Xenotransplantation

As the first genetically engineered solid organ xenotransplants were deemed to be therapeutic research by the UKXIRA and in the two UK

---

[243] Mason and Laurie, *Mason & McCall Smith's*, p. 627.   [244] Above, n. 94.
[245] HSC 2003/011, para. 8.   [246] WMA, *Declaration* (2008), C35.
[247] CIOMS and WHO, *International Ethical*, Commentary on Guideline 13.
[248] *Ibid.*, Guideline 12.   [249] *Ibid.*, Commentary on Guideline 12.
[250] *Ibid.*, Guideline 4.   [251] *Ibid.*, Commentary on Guideline 13.

reports on the biotechnology,[252] questions raised by involving patients in experimental procedures were not directly addressed then or subsequently. It is thus reasonable to assume that the first recipients of xeno-experimental procedures can be with or without capacity as long as they or their legal representatives consent. The Council of Europe's report and Recommendation appear to support this,[253] but clarification is needed, especially as clinical xenotransplants can be performed in the UK as 'experimental medicine'.[254] Discussions elsewhere on selecting candidates for this experimental procedure are limited, presumably because clinical xenotransplants are only to be performed within a research protocol.[255]

Offering medical research

The law

Under the UK's 2004 Regulations participants should not be recruited to a clinical trial unless a favourable opinion has been received from an REC,[256] the trial protocol should 'provide for the definition of inclusion and exclusion of subjects participating in a clinical trial, monitoring and publication policy', and participants must give their informed consent to involvement following an interview with the investigator or member of the team.[257] No further guidance on who can be offered the chance to participate is provided, so the common law on consent to treatment seemingly applies.[258] Those with capacity can consent to therapeutic and non-therapeutic research, provided it does not amount to actual bodily harm,[259] and if asked to account for including a particular person in a trial, the investigator will presumably rely on the *Bolam* and best interests' tests. For those without capacity, the general principles in the 2004 Regulations apply along with eleven conditions and four additional principles,[260] and the research *must* be therapeutic.[261] If the research does not fall within the 2004 Regulations the Mental Capacity Act 2005 regulates the involvement of those without capacity.[262] 'Intrusive

---

[252] UKXIRA, *Guidance*, para. 4.3; Nuffield Council, *Animal-to-Human*, para. 7.6; DH, *Animal Tissue*, para. 7.5.
[253] Council of Europe, *State of the Art*, para. 7.5.2; Council of Europe, Recommendation Rec(2003) 10, Articles 5, 16, 19.
[254] DH, *Xenotransplantation*, p. 3.
[255] Above, n. 132.   [256] 2004 Regulations, Regs. 12(2), 12(3)(a).
[257] *Ibid.*, Sched. 1 Part 3, paras. 3, 1; also, paras. 2, 4–5.   [258] See Chapter 5.
[259] *R* v. *Brown* [1993] 2 All ER 75, HL.
[260] 2004 Regulations, Sched. 1 Part 5, paras. 1–15.   [261] *Ibid.*, Sched. 1 Part 5, para. 9.
[262] Section 30 (3) MCA 2005, as amended.

research'[263] involving such an adult is illegal unless it is carried out as part of an approved research project,[264] and sections 32 and 33 of the 2005 Act must be complied with.[265] Adults without capacity can be involved in therapeutic or non-therapeutic research which falls under the 2005 Act.[266]

Ethical guidance

There is a consensus in ethical guidance on involving people in medical research that 'informed consent' is required from those with capacity, preferably evidenced by written consent.[267] For adults without capacity, consent is required from their legal representative,[268] and there is some agreement that such adults should only be involved in therapeutic research or research which will 'promote the health of the population represented by the potential subject'.[269] The Declaration of Helsinki notes that some research populations are 'particularly vulnerable and need special protection', including those who might be 'vulnerable to coercion or undue influence'.[270] Those seeking to benefit from therapeutic research could fall within these categories but specially protecting the 'vulnerable' is not directly addressed in the Declaration, apart from the provisions relating to those without capacity. In contrast, the CIOMS

---

[263] Research which would be unlawful if it was carried out on a person with capacity but without their consent (s. 30(2) MCA 2005).
[264] In England the project has to be approved by an REC recognised by the secretary of state for that purpose (Mental Capacity Act 2005 (Appropriate Body) (England) Regulations 2006, SI 2006/2810).
[265] Consulting someone about the adult's involvement in the research, and dealing with objections from the person without capacity, including their desire to withdraw from the research, respectively.
[266] Section 31 (5) MCA 2005.
[267] WMA, *Declaration* (2008), B24, 26; CIOMS and WHO, *International Ethical, Guidelines* 4–6 and their Commentaries; International Conference, *ICH Harmonised*, paras. 1.28, 2.9, 4.8; Australia – NHMRC *et al.*, *National Statement*, paras. 2.2.1–2.2.7; Canada – Canadian Institutes *et al.*, *TCPS2*, ch. 3; New Zealand – MH, *Operational Standard*, paras. 29–41; HRC, *Guidelines on Ethics*, para. 3.1; UK – GMC, *Good Practice*, para. 28; GMC, *Consent*; RCP, *Guidelines*, paras. 2.38, 5.21–5.30; MRC, *MRC Guidelines*, paras. 2.9, 3.1.10, 5.4; US – AMA, *Opinion 2.07*, paras. (4)(b), 5(b).
[268] WMA, *Declaration* (2008), B27; CIOMS and WHO, *International Ethical*, Guideline 4; International Conference, *ICH Harmonised*, para. 4.8.2; Australia – NHMRC *et al.*, *National Statement*, para. 2.2.12; Canada – Canadian Institutes *et al.*, *TCPS2*, Article 3.9; New Zealand – MH, *Operational Standard*, para. 32; HRC, *Guidelines on Ethics*, para. 3.1; UK – GMC, *Good Practice*, para. 28; US – AMA, *Opinion 2.07*, paras. (4)(b), (5)(b).
[269] WMA, *Declaration* (2008), B27; also, B28–29; CIOMS and WHO, *International Ethical*, Guideline 9; International Conference, *ICH Harmonised*, para. 4.8.14; Canada – Canadian Institutes *et al.*, *TCPS2*, Article 4.6; UK – GMC, *Consent*, paras. 25–26.
[270] WMA, *Declaration* (2008), A9.

and WHO guidelines contain provisions for involving vulnerable persons and patients in research,[271] including those with incurable or life-threatening diseases, with their participation needing 'special justification'.[272] The benefits and burdens of research should be equitably distributed and excluding groups or communities who might benefit from participation justified.[273] Furthermore, under the ICH GCP guidelines, ethics committees should pay 'special attention' to involving 'vulnerable subjects',[274] including 'patients with incurable diseases'.[275]

There is little UK or US ethical guidance on selecting the terminally ill or those with no other hope for involvement in research,[276] and the GMC's section on 'vulnerable adults', including those with learning difficulties, mental illness or living in care homes, is not relevant here.[277] The RCP guidelines address research on 'patients at the end of life'[278] and note that such research participants might 'grasp at any therapeutic possibility', be in a 'particularly close' relationship with professionals and so find it hard to refuse a request to participate, that issues of consent may be raised because of their disease or the effects of drugs, and family members may want to be involved in any decision to participate.[279] It may be difficult to balance risk and benefit and research and care roles but '[t]hese difficulties should not prevent such research. RECs should review such proposals sympathetically including innovative methods of consent, such as the use of advance directives'.[280] In contrast, the Australian research guidelines note that '[i]n "first-time-in-humans" research projects, risks are uncertain, and recruitment into the study should therefore be gradual and monitored with special care',[281] and a particular chapter deals with 'people highly dependent on medical care who may be unable to give consent'.[282] Included in this are the terminally ill and research involving them must be reviewed by a Human REC, and can be approved where it is likely to lead to 'increased understanding about, or improvements in, the care of this population', the risks are justified by the benefits to the participants or, if they have capacity, they accept any risks and these are justified by the benefits.[283]

---

[271] Above, nn. 248–252.   [272] CIOMS and WHO, *International Ethical*, Guideline 13.
[273] *Ibid.*, Guideline 12; also, Australia – NHMRC *et al.*, *National Statement*, para. 1.4; Canada – Canadian Institutes *et al.*, *TCPS2*, ch. 4; New Zealand – MH, *Operational Standard*, paras. 73–76.
[274] International Conference, *ICH Harmonised*, para. 3.1.1.   [275] *Ibid.*, para. 1.6.1.
[276] In the US the vulnerability of the 'very sick' was noted in National Commission, *Ethical Principles*, C3.
[277] GMC, *Consent*, para. 21.   [278] RCP, *Guidelines*, paras. 8.64–8.69.
[279] *Ibid.*, para. 8.66.   [280] *Ibid.*, paras. 8.67–8.68.
[281] NHMRC *et al.*, *National Statement*, para. 3.3.7.   [282] *Ibid.*, ch. 4.4.
[283] *Ibid.*, para. 4.4.1.

Consent to involvement can be provided by participants or their legal representative, and if the investigator is also the doctor, then it should be considered whether another person should obtain consent.[284] The terminally ill are also considered in the New Zealand Standard which acknowledges their vulnerability and the need for additional protection against undue influence and coercion, because their competence may be affected or they may believe that some 'treatment' is better than no treatment.[285] Of particular concern is proposed research which 'is likely to present more than minimal risk', but competent terminally ill patients should not automatically be excluded from research.[286] RECs must consider when to exclude such participants and when to provide those with no other alternatives the chance to benefit from 'experimental interventions'.[287] They should 'give careful attention' to involving terminally ill participants, consider whether special procedures are needed to protect them, and be satisfied that 'the nature, magnitude, and probability of the risks and benefits of the research have been identified as clearly and as accurately as possible'.[288] The consent process requires particular attention, RECs should consider whether there is other information which might be relevant to the decision-making process, and whether the participant's doctor should be other than the investigator.[289]

The central role of RECs in approving research protocols, including endorsing the criteria for selecting participants, is acknowledged in international and national ethical guidance.[290] Depending on the guidance being observed, trial protocols should include information on the recruitment advertisements, and inclusion and exclusion criteria.[291] Responsibility for selection criteria and procedures thus rests with investigators and RECs, and, according to the CIOMS and WHO, the Declaration of Helsinki does not preclude 'well-informed volunteers, capable of fully appreciating risks and benefits of an investigation, from participating in research for altruistic reasons'.[292] In contrast, the Australian and New Zealand guidance make it clear that involving those with no other hope in research is the exception.

---

[284] *Ibid.*, paras. 4.4.9–4.4.10, 4.4.12.
[285] MH, *Operational Standard*, Appendix 5, paras. 326, 330.
[286] *Ibid.*, Appendix 5, paras. 329, 330.   [287] *Ibid.*, Appendix 5, para. 327.
[288] *Ibid.*, Appendix 5, para. 334.   [289] *Ibid.*, Appendix 5, paras. 334–336.
[290] WMA, *Declaration* (2008), para. B15; CIOMS and WHO, *International Ethical*, Guideline 2, Appendix 1; International Conference, *ICH Harmonised*, para. 2.6, section 6; Australia – NHMRC *et al.*, *National Statement*, Section 5; Canada – Canadian Institutes *et al.*, *TCPS2*, Article 2.1, ch. 6; New Zealand – MH, *Operational Standard*, ch. 6; UK – GMC, *Good Practice*, para. 7; MRC, *MRC Guidelines*, para. 2.6.
[291] E.g. CIOMS and WHO, *International Ethical*, Appendix 1; International Conference, *ICH Harmonised*, paras. 3.1.2, 6.5.1–6.5.2.
[292] CIOMS and WHO, *International Ethical*, Commentary on Guideline 8.

Xenotransplantation

If xenotransplantation is performed as a clinical trial under the UK's 2004 Regulations those with capacity can be involved if they consent to it but, for those without capacity, *only* if it is deemed to be *therapeutic* research. For a clinical xenotransplant performed under a research protocol not within the 2004 Regulations, *all* adults can be involved *whether or not* the procedure is deemed therapeutic. In permitting adults without capacity to receive a non-therapeutic xenotransplant, the UK's DH 2006 guidance departs from the recommendations of the two UK reports on the biotechnology, the UKXIRA, and other countries.[293] It also appears to differ from the Council of Europe,[294] but the Council also recommended that those without capacity could '[e]xceptionally' be a recipient, provided there was no other alternative to save their life, clinical research indicated it '*might*' be life saving, it is expected to be therapeutic and their legal representative consents.[295] In contrast, the WHO requires 'a high expectation of benefit' *and* competent recipients as they must 'understand the risks and consequences of the procedure, including the need for compliance with life-long follow up and ... are motivated to modify their behavior accordingly'.[296]

Despite the UK's unusual position, the 2006 guidance offers nothing more on selecting recipients but previous UKXIRA guidance required investigators to describe the number of recipients, their medical indications, possible alternatives, and the 'rationale' for patient selection,[297] including an assessment of the likelihood of their compliance with the proposed surveillance regime.[298] There was no specific consideration of those with no other hope, perhaps because if only those with capacity were to be involved, then this decision was within the sphere of personal decision-making. The UKXIRA's policy and guidance documents have

---

[293] UK – UKXIRA, *Guidance*, paras. 4.3, 7.21; Nuffield Council, *Animal-to-Human*, paras. 7.6, 7.25–7.26; DH, *Animal Tissue*, paras. 7.5, 7.7; Australia – NHMRC, XWP, *Guidelines for Clinical*, Guidelines 3, 5, 7, accompanying NHMRC, XWP, *Animal-to-Human Transplantation: Final Report*; New Zealand – HRC, *Guidelines on Preparation*, paras. 2, 8; Sweden – Swedish Committee, *From One Species*, s. 5 of the Proposal for an Ordinance; Switzerland – Statement of Position, 'Medical–Ethical Principles', p. 391.
[294] Council of Europe, Recommendation Rec(2003)10, Article 12; CDBI and CDSP, *Explanatory Report*, para. 13.
[295] Council of Europe, Recommendation Rec(2003)10, Article 19 (2), emphasis supplied.
[296] 'First WHO', Principle 5, p. 63, Recommendation 3.
[297] Similarly, Australia – NHMRC, XWP, *Guidelines for Clinical*, Guideline 5, accompanying NHMRC, XWP, *Animal-to-Human Transplantation: Final Report*; New Zealand – HRC, *Guidelines on Preparation*, p. 5.
[298] UKXIRA, *Guidance*, para. 7.15; UKXIRA, *Draft Report*, para. A5.7.

no legal status but remain 'helpful guidance to researchers';[299] thus, selection decisions will be made by the relevant investigator and reviewed by the REC. In contrast, by requiring 'written, free and informed consent' from patients there is an implication that in Canada only those with capacity can be involved.[300] It was recognised that xenotransplantation raises selection issues including involving those without capacity and those who are dying, that it raises issues 'of ethical gravity and merit not only local ethical review, but national review',[301] and the Tri-Council policy statement on research ethics was referred to.[302] The latter does not specifically consider the position of those with no other hope, and selection issues are not otherwise addressed in the *Standard*. The now defunct US Secretary's Advisory Committee on Xenotransplantation (SACX) also ruled out involving those without capacity unless doing so would restore their capacity,[303] but clinical xenotransplants do not have to be therapeutic.[304] Elsewhere, although the Swedish Committee stated that 'children and other vulnerable groups' (undefined) will only be able to participate in clinical trials 'in rare exceptional cases and [their] participation in the initial trials is excluded',[305] the position of those with no other hope is not otherwise considered.

Conclusion

The different regulatory regimes for experimental procedures and medical research necessitate a consideration of *how* a particular biotechnology is classified, because of the different rules on participation. It is not always easy to determine into which category a developing procedure falls and, in reality, experimentation, research and treatment are part of the same spectrum, despite law's requirement for a clear dichotomy. The difficulty in distinguishing between these activities is exacerbated by the frequent conflation of terms such as 'medical practice', 'medical research', 'experimental procedures' and 'experimental treatment'. The

---

[299] Personal communication with DH dated 9 August 2007, on file with author.
[300] Health Canada, *Proposed Canadian Standard*, pp. 6–7, 30; also, Netherlands – Health Council, *Xenotransplantation*, p. 43.
[301] Health Canada, *Proposed Canadian Standard*, p. 5.
[302] Now Canadian Institutes *et al.*, *TCPS2*.
[303] US DHHS, Secretary's Advisory Committee on Xenotransplantation (SACX), *Informed Consent in Clinical Research Involving Xenotransplantation – Draft* (2004), pp. v, 26–27 (at: www.scribd.com/doc/1111353/National-Institutes-of-Health-IC-draft-030905, accessed 22/03/11).
[304] US DHHS *et al.*, *Guidance for Industry: Source Animal*, Section VIII J2c.
[305] Swedish Committee, *From One Species*, p. 17.

paucity of ethical guidance and limited regulation of experimental procedures in the UK makes it questionable whether those involved in such are currently appropriately protected, even though they will be asked to participate in activities which carry risks. To adequately protect those involved, similar regulatory schemes should apply to experimental procedures and medical research as '[w]ith seriously ill patients, because of the higher risks which it seems justifiable to take, research can join more closely with innovative treatment to the point where the two merge, perhaps indistinguishably'.[306] It is vital to question whether the balance for risks and benefits *should* be drawn at different places for different practices, or whether experimental procedures *should* be subject to legally mandated ethical review as these procedures have 'historically been introduced in haphazard and unregulated fashion into medical practice without independent "objective" assessment of their value, based on the largely unencumbered discretion of medical practitioners'.[307] In the context of transplantation the WHO states that 'experimental procedures require protocols, including ethics review, that are different and more rigorous than those for standard medical procedures',[308] and this must be true where the risks go beyond the individual. RECs should scrutinise patient selection decisions for experimental procedures to minimise the possibility that those with no other hope are not taken advantage of. That xenotransplantation can currently be performed in the UK as 'experimental medicine' without such review is alarming. When it is performed as research, RECs have an important role but their efficacy in reviewing research is debatable, as is whether existing *general* UK RECs are able to consider xenotransplant protocols where the individual may benefit but others bear the risks. The ability of Institutional Review Boards (IRBs) in the US to protect 'first-of-their-kind organ transplants' has similarly been questioned and it has been suggested that IRBs are 'way over their heads in this type of surgical innovation' as '[h]omogeneous IRBs without experience in transplant innovation are no match for surgical "pioneers"'.[309] The abolition of the UKXIRA in 2006 is thus curious and the reintroduction of a specialist xenotransplantation regulatory body imperative.

Initial xeno-recipients are likely to have no other hope and may be actively lobbying for the procedure, thus increasing the pressure that

---

[306] S. Guest, 'Compensation for Subjects of Medical Research: The Moral Rights of Patients and the Power of Research Ethics Committees' (1997) 23 *Journal of Medical Ethics* 181, 182.
[307] Price, 'Remodelling', p. 122.
[308] WMA, *World Medical Association Statement on Human Organ*, Section I33.
[309] Annas, 'Baby Fae', 16.

general RECs and investigators may be under. Involving those with no other hope in experimental procedures and research thus requires specific legal regulation and ethical guidance to protect those who may grasp at any possible chance of assistance. The limited international guidance on research involving the terminally ill may be because it would have 'little practical relevance' for them as 'the terminal diagnosis itself determines both what researchers and physicians deem "reasonable", and what the subjects (patients) themselves find acceptable – even desirable'.[310] But such is required for all potential experimental procedure or research participants, regardless of their health status. At present, deciding and applying the selection criteria approved within a trial's protocol essentially remains with those with vested interests and the most to gain or lose in proceeding: the individual investigator. The doctor as gatekeeper is not limited to the research setting and while they may have the greatest understanding of the benefits and risks of the procedure, they may also be too close to it to be able to consider whether to offer it to a particular individual. Indeed, '[p]atients who seek novel therapy through science can share a strong enthusiasm for research with the industry sponsors and medical investigators who endorse it. Yet if risk estimation can influence perceptions of risk acceptability, then there is at least an apparent [conflict of interest] in allowing those who endorse the research to be the sole arbiters of its estimated risks.'[311] There will be an understandable desire to see a procedure on which they have been working put into practice but, in the light of personal, professional and financial pressures, will they be able to appropriately deal with these issues? Doctors and/or investigators *may* be competent to make these decisions but it should not automatically be assumed that they are. Indeed, 'clinician gatekeeping' may violate respect for autonomy, beneficence and justice by enabling individual or groups of patients to be denied access to trials for reasons other than the eligibility criteria.[312]

The limited ethical and legal guidance on offering and selecting patients to receive experimental procedures means that reliance is placed on the professional clinical judgement of individual doctors/experimenters. The terminally ill are especially vulnerable to 'coercion and inattentive or unethical researchers' because of their diagnosis, the psychological and physiological implications of it, the 'coercive effect

---

[310] Annas, 'The Changing Landscape', 126.
[311] D.R. Waring and T. Lemmens, 'Integrating Values in Risk Analysis of Biomedical Research: The Case for Regulatory and Law Reform', in Law Commission of Canada (ed.), *Law and Risk* (Vancouver: UBC Press, 2005), p. 182.
[312] K. Sharkey *et al.*, 'Clinician Gate-Keeping in Clinical Research Is Not Ethically Defensible: An Analysis' (2010) 36 *Journal of Medical Ethics* 363.

of hospitalization', the effect on their decision-making capacity, and therapeutic misconceptions.[313] While others may have similar responses, the terminally ill are an identifiable and defined group who may be more easily accessed by investigators *because of* their health status. It is thus crucial that they are appropriately protected so that when they participate they do so as freely, voluntarily and with the same information as participants without their health status. Where experimental procedures are proposed, the potential participant should be supported by an independent advocate,[314] experimenters psychologically trained for working with the terminally ill, and such procedures should only be performed if it is intended to benefit *that* patient.[315]

Where a developing biotechnology may expose public health to risks which may lie dormant for years, it is not appropriate for the clinical judgement of doctors and/or investigators on offering and selecting suitable recipients of experimental procedures to be so central. More direct regulation is required to 'protect patients' safety' and support the introduction of new interventional procedures,[316] but it is questionable whether the UK's regulatory scheme for introducing these procedures and the status of NICE's guidance ensure that the aims of protecting patients' safety, supporting doctors and other clinicians, and managing clinical innovation 'responsibly', are or can be achieved.[317] In the light of this, and the risks, it is vital that a specific xenotransplant regulatory regime is appropriately robust. In Chapter 4, I explore how the regulatory regimes for IVF, gene therapy and xenotransplantation have developed, and consider the efficacy of the specific xeno-regimes proposed and implemented to date.

---

[313] Addicott, 'Regulating Research', 524, 501; further, 496–505.
[314] See Chapter 5.   [315] Addicott, 'Regulating Research', 524.
[316] NICE, 'About Interventional Procedures' (at: www.nice.org.uk/aboutnice/whatwedo/aboutinterventionalprocedures/about_interventional_procedures.jsp, accessed 22/03/11).
[317] HSC 2003/011, para. 3.

4 Regulatory responses to developing biotechnologies

Along with any general provisions on experimental procedures or medical research, specific regimes to regulate a particular developing biotechnology are often introduced. This occurred with IVF, gene therapy and xenotransplantation, for example, and I chart here the regulatory landscape, history and development of these schemes, and highlight how they were devised *as* these biotechnologies were scientifically developing. Regulatory theory per se is not my concern, nor is the ethics of these biotechnologies, and I am not claiming that these are directly comparable; rather, I explore the regulatory responses to these advances because they raise similar issues with regard to questions of harm, risk and safety, and what it means to be human. One key difference is that unlike the former biotechnologies, no clinical genetically engineered solid organ xenotransplant has yet occurred. There is thus an opportunity to reflect on the experiences of regulating IVF and gene therapy and learn lessons from how their regulatory schemes were developed and implemented. I focus on how those schemes evolved prior to, at the time of, and in the decade post-clinical introduction; for IVF from 1978 to 1988 and gene therapy from 1990 to 2000. This is not a comprehensive comparative account of how IVF and gene therapy were regulated; rather, I identify *trends* in regulatory approaches. For xenotransplantation, I explore regulatory responses from the 1990s when (unfulfilled) claims were made that clinical solid organ xenotransplants were imminent,[1] and trace the development of solid organ xenotransplant regulation to date.

One of my aims is to consider whether there is a way of determining how to regulate a developing biotechnology which 'best ... balance[s] the needs of doctors and scientists with the concerns of the public at large so as to maximise beneficial outcomes for society as a whole'.[2] This

---

[1] E.g. L. Rogers, 'A heartbeat from history', *Sunday Times*, 29 September 1996; C. Arthur, 'Transplant patients to get organs from pigs', *The Independent*, 13 September 1995.
[2] M.H. Johnson, 'The Art of Regulation and the Regulation of ART: The Impact of Regulation on Research and Clinical Practice' (2002) 9 *Journal of Law and Medicine* 399, 404.

is important because existing legal frameworks have demonstrated four problems with regard to genetic science:

[t]hey can't seem to adapt to evolving science, and indeed the adaptive/reactive model is itself problematic; regulation has been introduced on an ad hoc basis focusing on a rather arbitrary selection of issues and creating different regulatory bodies to oversee connected areas of scientific research; the regulation is essentially technology-led; and the regulatory frameworks do not reflect any single ethical theory.[3]

The recent review of UK regulatory bodies and the proposed single research regulator may be a response to these problems,[4] and I explore the extent to which these four problems are evident in IVF, gene therapy and xenotransplant regulation. Of particular concern is that scientific advances 'frequently outstrip policy change. Policy change is usually reactive, developed only after the technology is widespread.'[5] It has been suggested that in the UK bodies with a proactive remit were being established 'to seek out ethical issues and encourage discussion before they become pressing and urgent',[6] and the accuracy of this and whether public engagement has occurred for this biotechnology is considered. The global context in which all biotechnologies are now developed and 'marketed' must be recognised because '[t]he biological metamorphosis is a global one; reassurance of insulation and isolation is something which genetics, fundamentally, will not permit – it almost prohibits it'.[7] I thus describe the international regulation of these three biotechnologies and consider whether it is possible to establish such regulation for xenotransplantation.

Devising IVF national regulation

Pre-clinical

The basis of IVF science and research can be traced back to the 1950s,[8] but it was not until 1969 that the first successful laboratory fertilisation of a human egg by human sperm was reported,[9] and in 1970 it was

---

[3] S. Halliday, D.L. Steinberg, 'The Regulated Gene: New Legal Dilemmas' (2004) 12 *Medical Law Review* 2, 13.
[4] DH, *Liberating the NHS*.
[5] R.M. Cook-Deegan, 'Human Gene Therapy and Congress' (1990) 1 *Human Gene Therapy* 163, 164.
[6] J. Montgomery, *Health Care Law* (2nd edn, Oxford University Press, 2002), p. 485.
[7] D. Morgan, *Issues in Medical Law and Ethics* (London: Cavendish, 2001), p. 185.
[8] J. Gunning and V. English, *Human In Vitro Fertilisation – A Case Study in the Regulation of Medical Innovation* (Aldershot: Dartmouth, 1993), pp. 2–3.
[9] R.G. Edwards et al., 'Early Stages of Fertilization *In Vitro* of Human Oocytes Matured *In Vitro*' (1969) 221 *Nature* 632.

announced that human embryos could be grown *in vitro* up to at least the blastocyst stage.[10] At this time there was no separate regulatory structure for IVF research proposals and so existing schemes were used for this developing biotechnology. For example, in 1971 a clinical research proposal which included transferring embryos to patients was submitted to the UK's MRC which was rejected, partly because of ethical concerns.[11] So, as the science was developing it was recognised that IVF raised ethical, legal and safety issues which required discussion and, possibly, regulation, with this primarily led by scientists and investigators engaged in the area.[12] Indeed, in 1971 Edwards and Sharpe suggested that 'perhaps what is needed is not heavy handed public statute, or rule-making committees, or the conscience of individual doctors but a simple organization easily approached and consulted to advise and assist biologists and others to reach their own decisions'.[13] Statutory regulation was deemed inappropriate as too restrictive and inflexible and 'may be a continuing menace to those engaged in later work that is quite acceptable to the community'.[14] Similarly, in the US Watson cautioned that human embryology was 'a matter too important to be left solely in the hands of the scientific and medical communities'.[15]

Official bodies were considering the issues raised by IVF in the US and UK during the 1970s, and the UK's MRC set up a working group on IVF and embryo transfer in 1975. This concluded that there were no legal or ethical objections to transferring an IVF egg into a woman's uterus, no objections to obtaining eggs for research purposes, but the importance of consent was emphasised.[16] A draft report was produced but not acted upon. In contrast, in the US assisted reproductive technologies (ARTs) were subject to more formal scrutiny and in 1973 the then Department of Health, Education and Welfare (DHEW) began to discuss and draft regulations on IVF and embryo transfer.[17] In 1974 the US Congress applied a temporary moratorium on federally funded

---

[10] R.G. Edwards *et al.*, 'Fertilization and Cleavage *In Vitro* of Preovulator Human Oocytes' (1970) 227 *Nature* 1307.

[11] Gunning and English, *Human In Vitro*, pp. 4–6.

[12] E.g. *ibid.*, chs. 1, 2; Ethics Advisory Board, Department of Health, Education and Welfare (DHEW), *Reports and Conclusions: HEW Support Involving Human In Vitro Fertilization and Embryo Transfer* (1979), pp. 11–13 (at: http://bioethics.georgetown.edu/pcbe/reports/past_commissions/HEW_IVF_report.pdf, accessed 23/03/11).

[13] R.G. Edwards and D.J. Sharpe, 'Social Values and Research in Human Embryology' (1971) 231 *Nature* 87, 90.

[14] *Ibid.*, 89. [15] J.D. Watson, 'Moving Toward'.

[16] Gunning and English, *Human in Vitro*, p. 10.

[17] US DHEW, 'Protection of Human Subjects, Policies and Procedures', 16 November 1973, 38 *Federal Register* 31738, p. 31743.

clinical research on embryos and embryonic tissue, including IVF, until national guidelines were introduced,[18] and a National Commission for the Protection of Human Subjects of Biomedical and Behavioral Research was established.[19] This was to identify the basic ethical principles that underpin research involving humans, including foetuses and embryos, and develop guidelines to ensure that research was conducted in accordance with those principles.[20] In 1975 it published a report on foetal research which recommended establishing a national ethics advisory board to approve specific types of research involving foetuses.[21] In 1975 the DHEW also published regulations on IVF and embryo transfer under which approval from a national Ethical Advisory Board (EAB) must be obtained before embryo research, and some other types of research, could be federally funded.[22] The regulations were not activated until 1977 when an application for research funding was received and the EAB was appointed.[23] The Board reviewed the research proposal, referred it back to the National Institutes of Health (NIH), and during 1978 eleven public hearings were held on the ethical, legal and social issues surrounding IVF and embryo transfer generally.[24]

In 1978 Louise Brown, the world's first 'test-tube' baby, was born in England. At this point ARTs were unregulated worldwide as regulations on IVF only existed in the US but had not been activated. Louise's birth may have caught regulators and society unaware with the science advancing more quickly than anticipated, but regulatory activity increased following her birth and as the number of births from ARTs increased. Three approaches are identifiable within this activity: governments requesting new or existing committees to explore the issues raised by ARTs; developing guidelines or publishing reports from non-governmental organisations (NGOs); or moving directly to legislation. In the ten years following Louise's birth, most countries adopted a combination of these approaches when regulating ARTs.

---

[18] D.C. Wertz, 'Embryo and Stem Cell Research in the United States: History and Politics' (2002) 9 *Gene Therapy* 674.
[19] National Research Act 1974.
[20] NIH, 'Regulations and Ethical Guidelines' (at: http://ohsr.od.nih.gov/guidelines/belmont.html, accessed 22/03/11).
[21] The National Commission for the Protection of Human Subjects of Biomedical and Behavioral Research, *Research on the Fetus: Report and Recommendations* (1975), pp. 74–75 (at: http://bioethics.georgetown.edu/pcbe/reports/past_commissions/research_fetus.pdf, accessed 25/03/11).
[22] US DHEW, 'Protection of Human Subjects: Fetuses, Pregnant Women and In Vitro Fertilization', 8 August 1975, 40 *Federal Register* 33526.
[23] Ethics Advisory Board, *Reports and Conclusions*, p. 15.
[24] Gunning and English, *Human In Vitro*, p. 18.

Post-clinical 1978–88

Government-established committees

Although the first IVF baby was born in England, '[p]olitically in the UK human *in vitro* fertilization was seen as rather a hot potato ... the British Government did not hasten into action',[25] and it was not until June 1982 that the government established a specific committee to consider the social, ethical and legal implications of developments in ARTs. In contrast, in Australia governmental regulatory activity occurred earlier when in 1979 the State of Victoria Committee of Inquiry on IVF was set up. Reporting in 1984, a statutory authority was recommended by the Waller Committee to regulate IVF[26] and the Standing Review and Advisory Committee, with an advisory and regulatory remit, was introduced by the world's first legislation on assisted conception; the State of Victoria's Infertility (Medical Procedures) Act 1984. Other Australian states subsequently instituted specific committees to consider the implications of ARTs.[27] In the UK in 1984 the Warnock Committee's report was published and recommended that a statutory licensing authority was convened to regulate IVF and embryo research.[28] The report provoked much debate and a voluntary licensing system was in place until 1991 when the Human Fertilisation and Embryology Act 1990 came into force.[29] This established the statutory IVF and embryo research regulatory authority; the Human Fertilisation and Embryology Authority. Special committees on ARTs were also convened by other European governments during the 1980s, with many recommending legislation and a specific regulatory body on IVF was subsequently established in Spain.[30] Existing committees were employed to consider ARTs in France and the Netherlands, both acknowledging the need for regulation,[31] and in Canada reports were

---

[25] *Ibid.*, p. 27.
[26] The Committee to Consider Social, Ethical and Legal Issues Arising from In Vitro Fertilization, *Report on the Disposition of Embryos Produced by In Vitro Fertilization* (Melbourne: Parliament of the State of Victoria, 1984).
[27] E.g. Tasmania – *Committee to Investigate Artificial Conception and Related Matters* (Hobart: Director-General of Health Services, 1985); South Australia – *Report of the Working Party on In Vitro Fertilization and Artificial Insemination by Donor* (Adelaide: South Australian Health Commission, 1984).
[28] Department of Health and Social Security, *Report of the Committee of Inquiry into Human Fertilisation and Embryology* (London: HMSO, 1984), Cmnd 9314.
[29] Gunning and English, *Human In Vitro*, pp. 41–45, chs. 4, 6.
[30] E.g. Austria, Spain, Sweden, West Germany (Gunning and English, *Human In Vitro*, ch. 9).
[31] France – CCNE, *Opinion on Research and Use of In-Vitro Human Embryos for Scientific and Medical Purposes. Report* (1986) No. 8 (at: www.ccne-ethique.fr/docs/en/avis008.pdf, accessed 25/03/11); CCNE, *Opinion on Ethical Problems Arising out of Assisted Reproductive Techniques. Report* (1984) No. 3 (at: www.ccne-ethique.fr/docs/en/avis003.

first produced by existing public bodies,[32] before a royal commission was appointed in 1989, reporting in 1993.[33]

Guidelines and reports from NGOs

As the Waller Committee was sitting the Australian NHMRC produced a statement and guidelines on IVF in the early 1980s, requiring institutional ethics committee approval of clinical and research IVF,[34] and the Family Law Council also published a report on IVF.[35] In contrast, *prior* to the establishment of the UK's Warnock Committee the MRC, continuing its work pre-Louise's birth, set up an advisory group on the ethics of IVF in March 1979.[36] This recognised that IVF use was likely to increase and that treatment should be safe and successful, so units offering it should be publicly scrutinised and records kept of pregnancies established following embryo transfer and attempts to do so. Five recommendations were made to the MRC, including establishing a confidential register of embryo transfers and pregnancies, and reconvening in five years to re-examine the issues raised by IVF and embryo transfer, meeting earlier if the MRC wanted ethical advice on a specific proposal. In 1981 the MRC approved IVF research and the group was reconvened early to review the policy on IVF research and embryo transfer, and it produced guidelines on the biotechnology.[37] At the same time, the UK's Royal College of Obstetricians and Gynaecologists (RCOG) requested

---

pdf, accessed 25/03/11); the Netherlands – Health Council of the Netherlands, *Heredity: Science and Society – On the Possibilities and Limits of Genetic Testing and Gene Therapy* (The Hague: Health Council of the Netherlands, 1989), Health Council of the Netherlands, *Artificial Procreation* (The Hague: Health Council of the Netherlands, 1986).

[32] E.g. Law Reform Commission of Canada, *Biomedical Experimentation Involving Human Subjects*, Working Paper 61 (Ottawa: Law Reform Commission of Canada, 1989); Ontario Law Reform Commission, *Report on Human Artificial Reproduction and Related Matters* (Ontario: Ministry of the Attorney-General, 1985), vols. 1–2.

[33] Royal Commission on New Reproductive Technologies, *Proceed with Care: Final Report of the Royal Commission on New Reproductive Technologies* (Ottawa: Ministry of Supply and Services, 1993).

[34] NHMRC, *Ethics in Medical Research Involving the Human Fetus and Human Fetal Tissue* (Canberra: Australian Government Publishing Service, 1983); NHMRC, 'Ethics in Medical Research', *Report of the NHMRC Working Party on Ethics in Medical Research* (Canberra: Australian Government Publishing Service, 1982).

[35] Family Law Council, *Creating Children: A Uniform Approach to the Law and Practice of Reproductive Technology in Australia* (Canberra: Australian Government Publishing Service, 1985).

[36] Gunning and English, *Human in Vitro*, pp. 15–17.

[37] MRC, 'Statement on Research Related to Human Fertilization and Embryology' (1982) 285 *British Medical Journal* 1480. See Gunning and English, *Human In Vitro*, pp. 22–25.

its Ethics Committee to produce guidance on IVF and a report was published in 1983.[38] Legislation was recommended but 'it would be impossible and undesirable to establish legislation to govern techniques of IVF and ER [embryo replacement]',[39] a statutory body should be established to advise the relevant Secretaries of State, and research on early embryos was deemed an ethical not legal concern.[40] The British Medical Association (BMA) also set up a working party on IVF in 1982 which reported in 1983 and accepted that IVF and gamete donation were ethical, emphasised informed consent, and recommended IVF registers.[41] In 1984 a report on human procreation was also published by the UK's Council for Science and Society,[42] and a code of practice was agreed by Italian university hospitals and recommendations on IVF made by a group of gynaecologists and researchers, in the absence of formal regulation.[43] In 1986 professional guidelines on IVF were also issued by the American Fertility Society.[44]

Statutory activity

The US was one of the first countries to regulate IVF prior to its clinical use, and the 1975 regulations required the approval of the EAB before a research project involving embryos could be federally funded.[45] In 1979 the EAB published a report on the ethical, legal and social issues surrounding IVF and embryo transfer generally which concluded that it was ethical to perform human IVF and embryo transfer if certain conditions were fulfilled.[46] The Board approved federal funds for a research proposal involving IVF and embryo transfer up to fourteen days' post-conception provided the donors were married, but the Secretary of HEW did not implement these recommendations,[47] even though the

---

[38] Royal College of Obstetricians and Gynaecologists (RCOG), *Report of the RCOG Ethics Committee On In Vitro Fertilization and Embryo Replacement or Transfer* (London: RCOG, 1983). See Gunning and English, *Human In Vitro*, pp. 27–30.
[39] Cited in Gunning and English, *Human In Vitro*, p. 30.   [40] *Ibid.*, pp. 29–30.
[41] British Medical Association (BMA) Working Group on In Vitro Fertilization, 'Interim Report on Human In Vitro Fertilization and Embryo Replacement and Transfer' (1983) 286 *British Medical Journal* 1594.
[42] Working Party of Council for Science and Society, *Human Procreation: Ethical Aspects of the New Techniques* (Oxford University Press, 1984).
[43] Gunning and English, *Human In Vitro*, p. 155.
[44] American Fertility Society, 'Ethical Considerations of the New Reproductive Technologies' (1986) 46 suppl. 1 *Fertility and Sterility* 1S.
[45] Above, n. 22.
[46] Ethics Advisory Board, *Reports and Conclusions*. See Gunning and English, *Human In Vitro*, pp. 18–22.
[47] Gunning and English, *Human In Vitro*, pp. 19–22.

President's Commission for the Study of Ethical Problems in Medicine and Biomedical and Behavioral Research (the President's Commission) endorsed them.[48] In 1980 the Board's charter ended.[49] Formal regulation of IVF thus existed from a fairly early stage in its scientific development, with formal reports produced *after* the 1975 regulations; however, IVF was not the subject of federal law in the US during the 1980s, although some States introduced legislation referring to it.[50] Other European countries followed the UK's, and Australia's, legislative approach including the Netherlands, Norway, Spain, Sweden and Switzerland.[51]

International activity

Alongside the discussions and regulatory activities in individual countries, ARTs were also on the European agenda,[52] and in 1986 the Parliamentary Assembly published a Recommendation on using human embryos and foetuses in research, but this was not adopted.[53] Internationally, the World Congress on IVF, for example, noted the need for legislation particularly with regard to parental status, storing gametes and embryos, and the legal status of embryos.[54] It recommended establishing an international ethical authority to 'provide a forum that establishes the ethical, scientific, and clinical framework for the further pursuance of work on *in vitro* fertilization'.[55] The global aspects of ARTs were thus recognised, as was the fact that 'many new procedures, such as embryo typing, the use of fetal cells in therapeutic procedures, and genetic engineering, are rapidly emerging, and will demand constant vigilance'.[56]

---

[48] *Ibid.*, p. 22. [49] *Ibid.* [50] *Ibid.*, ch. 9.
[51] *Ibid.*; R.G. Lee and D. Morgan, *Human Fertilisation and Embryology – Regulating the Reproductive Revolution* (Oxford: Blackstone Press, 2001), ch. 11.
[52] E.g. Standing Committee of European Doctors, *Recommendations on the Ethical Problems Concerning Artificial Insemination* (1985) (at: http://cpme.dyndns.org:591/adopted/cp%201985_93.pdf, accessed 25/03/11); European Medical Research Councils (EMRC), 'Recommendations on Human In Vitro Fertilization and Embryo Transfer' (1983) 322 *The Lancet* 1187.
[53] Parliamentary Assembly of the Council of Europe, Recommendation 1046 (1986) on the Use of Human Embryos and Foetuses for Diagnostic, Therapeutic, Scientific, Industrial and Commercial Purposes.
[54] International Advisory Board of the III World Congress on In Vitro Fertilisation and Embryo Transfer, 'Helsinki Statement on Human In Vitro Fertilization' (1985) 442 *Annals of New York Academy of Sciences* 571, paras. 4–7, 9.
[55] *Ibid.*, para. 11. [56] *Ibid.*

Devising national gene therapy regulation

Pre-clinical

As with IVF, pre-clinical research on gene therapy occurred during the 1960s and 1970s,[57] and the US was at the forefront of regulatory action, encouraging ethical debate on this developing biotechnology. In contrast to the essentially dormant 1975 DHEW regulations on IVF, a regulatory body was established while the science of gene therapy was still in its infancy, and in 1974 the US NIH created a Recombinant DNA Advisory Committee (RAC) to review all gene therapy protocols in conjunction with the Food and Drug Administration (FDA).[58] In 1975 the National Academy of Science held a conference on gene therapy,[59] and in 1976 the NIH published guidelines on recombinant DNA research.[60] In 1980 it was reported that an investigator from an American university had used gene therapy in humans in Italy and Israel without the approval of his IRB,[61] and this study was subsequently criticised and prompted further regulatory action and discussions on gene therapy.[62] Following representations from a number of religious denominations in 1980, the President's Commission was asked to explore the ethical and social aspects of genetic engineering and it reported in 1982.[63] It recommended that gene therapy research continued and that the RAC expanded its remit to include reviewing the ethical and social implications of gene therapy.[64] A report on gene therapy was published by the US House of Representatives in 1982 and by the US Office of Technology Assessment (OTA) in 1984.[65]

---

[57] J.M. Rainsbury, 'Biotechnology on the RAC – FDA/NIH Regulation of Human Gene Therapy' (2000) 55 *Food and Drug Law Journal* 575, 575–576.
[58] National Institutes of Health (NIH), Office of Biotechnology Activities (OBA), 'About RAC DNA Advisory Committee' (at: http://oba.od.nih.gov/rdna_rac/rac_about.html, accessed 25/03/11).
[59] P. Berg *et al.*, 'Summary Statement of the Asilomar Conference on Recombinant DNA Molecules' (1975) 72 *Proceedings of the National Academy of Science* 1981.
[60] US DHEW, NIH, 'Recombinant DNA Research: Guidelines', 7 July 1976, 41 *Federal Register* 27902.
[61] T. Friedmann, 'A Brief History of Gene Therapy' (1992) 2 *Nature Genetics* 93, 94–5.
[62] *Ibid.*
[63] President's Commission for the Study of Ethical Problems in Medicine and Biomedical and Behavioral Research, *Splicing Life: The Social and Ethical Issues of Genetic Engineering with Human Beings* (Washington, DC: President's Commission for the Study of Ethical Problems in Medicine and Biomedical and Behavioral Research, 1982).
[64] *Ibid.*, pp. 2–5.
[65] US House of Representatives, *Hearings on Human Genetic Engineering Before the Subcommittee on Investigations and Oversight of the Committee on Science and Technology*, 97th Congress 2nd session, No. 170 (Washington, DC: Government Printing Office,

In 1984 the FDA announced that it intended to regulate recombinant DNA-derived products,[66] and the RAC created the Human Gene Therapy Working Group (later renamed the Human Gene Therapy Subcommittee) to regulate gene therapy in humans.[67] In 1986 the Group's list of questions to be answered in applications seeking approval for gene therapy clinical trials was published,[68] and it reviewed and approved the first human gene-marking study, a gene transfer rather than gene therapy experiment.[69] The OTA published another paper on gene therapy in 1987, and the American Medical Association an opinion in 1988.[70] Gene therapy was the subject of ethical discussion during the 1980s,[71] and there was regulatory activity elsewhere with a report published by the Australian NHMRC in 1987,[72] and also in West Germany (the Commission was established in 1984).[73] The Health Council of the Netherlands was asked to consider gene therapy in 1988, reporting in 1989,[74] and in the UK some of the ethical issues raised were explored in the 1989 Glover report on new reproductive technologies to the European Commission,[75] and the government convened a specific committee on it in 1989.[76]

1982); US Congress, Office of Technology Assessment (OTA), *Human Gene Therapy – A Background Paper* (Washington, DC: OTA, 1984).

[66] Office of Science and Technology, 'Proposal for a Coordinated Framework for Regulation of Biotechnology', 31 December 1984, 49 *Federal Register* 50856.

[67] Rainsbury, 'Biotechnology on the RAC', 580–581.

[68] Human Gene Therapy Subcommittee, NIH Recombinant DNA Advisory Committee, 'Points to Consider in the Design and Submission of Protocols for the Transfer of Recombinant DNA into the Genome of Human Subjects' (1986) 11 *Recombinant DNA Research* 119.

[69] L. Roberts, 'Human Gene Therapy Test' (1988) 241 *Science* 419.

[70] US Congress, OTA, *New Developments in Biotechnology, Volume 2: Background Paper: Public Perceptions of Biotechnology* (Washington, DC: OTA, 1987); AMA, Council on Ethical and Judicial Affairs, *Opinions of the Council on Ethical and Judicial Affairs: Gene Therapy and Surrogate Mothers*, Report E (1–88) (Chicago, IL: AMA, 1988).

[71] E.g. G. Fowler et al., 'Germ-Line Gene Therapy and the Clinical Ethics of Medical Genetics' (1989) 10 *Theoretical Medicine* 151; J.C. Fletcher, 'Moral Problems and Ethical Issues n Prospective Human Gene Therapy' (1983) 69 *Virginia Law Review* 515; W.F. Anderson and J.C. Fletcher, 'Gene Therapy in Humans: When Is It Ethical to Begin?' (1980) 303 *New England Journal of Medicine* 1293.

[72] NHMRC, *Ethical Aspects of Research on Human Gene Therapy: Report to the NHMRC by the Medical Ethics Committee of NHMRC* (Canberra: Australian Government Publishing Service, 1987).

[73] Enquête Commission, 'An Extract from Prospects and Risks of Gene Technology: The Report of the Enquête Commission to the Bundestag of the Federal Republic of Germany' (1988) 2 *Bioethics* 254.

[74] Health Council of the Netherlands, *Heredity: Science and Society*.

[75] J. Glover, *Ethics of New Reproductive Technologies: The Glover Report to the European Commission – Studies in Biomedical Policy* (DeKalb, IL: Northern Illinois Press, 1989).

[76] DH, *Report of the Committee on the Ethics of Gene Therapy* Cm. 1788 (London: HMSO, 1992).

In September 1990 the first human gene therapy clinical trial began in the US.[77] Thus, as with IVF, US regulation of gene therapy pre-dated its clinical use and ran alongside its scientific development and ethical and public discussions of it. As regulations were in place significantly prior to an application to conduct a gene therapy clinical trial, this was 'an odd case of a bureaucratic panel outpacing the technology it was charged with regulating'.[78] Thus, and in contrast to the clinical use of IVF, when gene therapy was first clinically performed, the US investigators had to comply with the RAC's requirements. Gene therapy is thus an example of *anticipatory* regulatory action where 'the regulatory apparatus has long been in place and has waited for the technology to catch up'.[79] Formal regulation of gene therapy was not universal in 1990 and some countries were, again, slower than others to commence regulatory activity following its clinical use. Nevertheless, the methods of producing the regulatory schemes are reminiscent of those in evidence with IVF.

Post-clinical 1990–2000

Government-established committees

The UK government set up the Clothier Committee on gene therapy in 1989 but it only reported in 1992 after the biotechnology had been clinically used.[80] A national supervisory committee was recommended to consider and advise on specific protocols, and the non-statutory Gene Therapy Advisory Committee (GTAC) was established in 1993,[81] with guidance on gene therapy research on humans published in 1994.[82] In other European countries existing committees explored the issues,[83] and

---

[77] R.M. Blaese *et al.*, 'T Lymphocyte-Directed Gene Therapy for ADA Deficiency SCID: Initial Trial Results after 4 Years' (1995) 270 *Science* 475.
[78] Rainsbury, 'Biotechnology on the RAC', 581.
[79] Cook-Deegan, 'Human Gene Therapy', 164. [80] Above, n. 76.
[81] Gene Therapy Advisory Committee (GTAC), *First Annual Report November 1993–December 1994* (London: DH, 1995), p. 2.
[82] GTAC, *Guidance on Making Proposals to Conduct Gene Therapy Research on Human Subjects* (London: DH, 1994). Revised in 1999: GTAC, *Seventh Annual Report January 2000–December 2000* (London: DH, 2001), Part 2, section 1.
[83] E.g. France – CCNE, *Opinion on Gene Therapy* (1990) No. 22 (at: www.ccne-ethique.fr/docs/en/avis022.pdf, accessed 25/03/11); Italy – National Bioethics Committee, *Gene Therapy* (1991) (at: www.palazzochigi.it/bioetica/eng/opinions.html, accessed 25/03/11); Netherlands – Health Council of the Netherlands, Committee on Gene Therapy, *Gene Therapy* (Rijswijk: Health Council of the Netherlands, 1997) Publication no. 1997/12E; Sweden – Ministry of Health and Social Affairs, *Swedish Act Concerning the Use of Gene Technology on Human Beings and Experiments with Fertilised Ova* (Stockholm: The Ministry, 1991).

legislation was commonly recommended; primarily via existing general biomedical statutes or amendments to them.[84] In some of these countries, and in Australia,[85] a specific commission or body was also established to advise on clinical trials, or new regulatory bodies introduced, to work alongside existing advisory bodies or ethics committees.[86] There was thus a sense that gene therapy *was* different to existing biotechnologies, but not sufficiently so as to require specific regulatory regimes or legislation as with IVF. It could fit more easily into existing schemes.

Guidelines and reports from NGOs

In Canada regulatory activity was first instituted by the Medical Research Council which produced specific guidelines on gene therapy in 1990, and clinical trials also had to comply with the Tri-Council Policy Statement on Research.[87] Similarly, the NHMRC took the lead in Australia and its 1987 report, noted above, was updated in 1995.[88] Its 1992 statement on gene therapy was replaced by specific guidelines in 1999.[89] Human genetic research in Australia also had to comply with the NHMRC's general national statement on research,[90] and trials had to be approved by the newly established Gene and Related Therapies Research Advisory Panel (GTRAP),[91] and a number of existing regulatory bodies.[92] Specific guidelines on gene therapy were

---

[84] O. Cohen-Haguenauer et al., 'Opinion Paper on the Current Status of the Regulation of Gene Therapy in Europe' (2002) 13 *Human Gene Therapy* 2085.

[85] Gene and Related Therapies Research Advisory Panel (GTRAP): R.J.A. Trent, 'Oversight and Monitoring of Clinical Research with Gene Therapy in Australia' (2005) 182 *Medical Journal of Australia* 441.

[86] E.g. Austria, Belgium, Germany, Switzerland (Cohen-Haguenauer et al., 'Opinion Paper'); K. Cichutek and I. Krämer, 'Gene Therapy in Germany and in Europe: Regulatory Issues' (1997) 2 *Quality Assurance Journal* 141; O. Cohen-Haguenauer, 'Overview of Regulation of Gene Therapy in Europe: A Current Statement Including Reference to US Regulation' (1995) 6 *Human Gene Therapy* 773; France – CCNE, *Opinion on the Use of Somatic Gene Therapy Procedures. Report* (1993) No. 36 (at: www.ccne-ethique.fr/docs/en/avis036.pdf, accessed 25/03/11); CCNE, *Opinion on Gene Therapy*.

[87] Medical Research Council of Canada, *Guidelines for Research on Somatic Cell Gene Therapy in Humans* (Ottawa: Minister of Supply and Services, 1990); now see Canadian Institutes et al., *TCPS2*.

[88] NHMRC, *Human Gene Therapy and Related Procedures: An Information Paper to Assist in the Consideration of Ethical Aspects of Human Gene Therapy* (Canberra: Australian Government Publishing Service, 1995), rescinded in 2000.

[89] NHMRC, *Guidelines for Ethical Review of Research Proposals for Human Somatic Cell Gene Therapy and Related Therapies* (Canberra: NHMRC, 1999), revoked in 2008.

[90] NHMRC et al., *National Statement*.   [91] Above n. 85.

[92] NHMRC, *Guidelines for Ethical Review*, p. 8.

also introduced in Japan in 1995,[93] and other NGOs produced reports on the biotechnology during the 1990s.[94]

Statutory activity

Post-1990 further statutory regulatory activity occurred in the US,[95] and an overview of the supervision of human gene therapy in the US was conducted and a Gene Therapy Clinical Trial Monitoring Plan and random inspections of trials introduced following the death of Jesse Gelsinger in a gene therapy trial in 1999.[96] France, Germany and the Netherlands, for example, also preferred statutory regulation by either adopting or adapting existing general biomedical laws, or introducing specific laws.[97] In Austria a general law was utilised prior to a specific law on gene therapy being introduced, as well as a new advisory commission.[98]

International activity

The development of gene therapy prompted European debates and discussions and as early as 1982 the Council of Europe's Parliamentary Assembly adopted a recommendation on genetic engineering which recognised the possible benefits and risks of gene therapy.[99] In 1989 a resolution on the ethical and legal problems of genetic engineering,

---

[93] Director-General's Notice, Pharmaceutical Affairs Bureau, Ministry for Health and Welfare, *Guidance for Quality and Safety Assurance in Drugs for Gene Therapy* (Tokyo: Ministry for Health and Welfare, 1995).

[94] E.g. The Catholic Bishops' Joint Committee on Bioethical Issues, *Genetic Intervention on Human Subjects: The Report of a Working Party of the Catholic Bishops' Joint Committee on Bioethical Issues* (London: Catholic Bishops' Joint Committee, 1996); Council for Responsible Genetics, 'Position Paper on Human Germ Line Manipulation Presented by Council for Responsible Genetics, Human Genetics Committee Fall, 1992' (1993) 4 *Human Gene Therapy* 35; Catholic Health Association of the United States, Research Group on Ethical Issues in Early Human Development and Genetics, *Human Genetics: Ethical Issues in Genetic Testing, Counseling, and Therapy* (St Louis, MO: Catholic Health Association of the United States, 1990).

[95] E.g. US DHHS, FDA, CBER, *Guidance for Industry: Guidance for Human Somatic Cell Therapy and Gene Therapy* (1998) (at: www.fda.gov/downloads/BiologicsBloodVaccines/GuidanceComplianceRegulatoryInformation/Guidances/CellularandGeneTherapy/ucm081670.pdf, accessed 25/03/11).

[96] US DHHS, NIH, OBA, 'Recombinant DNA Research: Actions Under the NIH Guidelines' 19 November 2001, 66 *Federal Register* 57970; US DHHS, 'New Initiatives to Protect Participants in Gene Therapy Trials' (2000) (at: http://archive.hhs.gov/news/press/2000pres/20000307A.html, accessed 25/03/11); O. Obasogie, 'Ten Years Later: Jesse Gelsinger's Death and Human Subjects Protection' (2010) *Bioethics Forum* (at: www.thehastingscenter.org/Bioethicsforum/Post.aspx?id=4034&blogid=140, accessed 25/03/11).

[97] Cohen-Haguenauer *et al.*, 'Opinion Paper'. [98] *Ibid.*

[99] Parliamentary Assembly of the Council of Europe, Recommendation 934 (1982) on Genetic Engineering.

including somatic gene therapy, was adopted by the European Parliament,[100] and a guidance note on the biotechnology was published by the European Agency for the Evaluation of Medicinal Products in 1994.[101] A further draft was produced in 1998,[102] and the European Commission and European Medical Research Councils were also interested in the area.[103] Internationally, a number of religious bodies published reports on genetic therapy during the 1980s,[104] and international bodies also produced reports during this time and in the 1990s.[105] This early recognition of the transnational dimension of gene therapy resulted in a UNESCO declaration on the human genome but the value of this, in a regulatory sense, is limited because of its legal status.[106] Nevertheless, its existence indicates that the international scientific, legal and ethical aspects of gene therapy were widely recognised. Similarly, within Europe, conventions, decisions, resolutions, and directives from the European Parliament and Council are important but necessarily limited in their global reach.[107]

---

[100] European Parliament, Resolution on the Ethical and Legal Problems of Genetic Engineering 1989.

[101] European Agency for the Evaluation of Medicinal Products (EMEA), *Gene Therapy Product Quality Aspects in the Production of Vectors and Genetically Modified Somatic Cells* (1994) (at: www.ema.europa.eu/docs/en_GB/document_library/Scientific_guideline/2009/09/WC500003449.pdf, accessed 25/03/11).

[102] EMEA, Committee for Proprietary Medicinal Products (CPMP) Safety Working Party and Biotechnology Working Party, *Safety Studies for Gene Therapy Products – Annex to Note for Guidance on Gene Therapy Quality Aspects in the Production of Vectors and Genetically Modified Somatic Cells*, CPMP/SWP/112/98 draft (London: EMEA, 1998).

[103] E.g. Opinion of the Group of Advisers on the Ethical Implications of Biotechnology to the European Commission, *The Ethical Implications of Gene Therapy* (1994) No. 4: (at: http://ec.europa.eu/european_group_ethics/docs/opinion4_en.pdf, accessed 25/03/11); EMRC, 'Gene Therapy in Man: Recommendations of European Medical Research Councils' (1988) 2 *The Lancet* 1271.

[104] E.g. World Council of Churches, Subunit on Church and Society, *Biotechnology: Its Challenges to the Churches and the World* (Geneva: The Council, 1989); National Council of Churches, Panel on Bioethical Concerns, *Genetic Engineering: Social and Ethical Consequences* (New York, NY: Pilgrim Press, 1984); World Council of Churches, Subunit on Church and Society, *Manipulating Life: Ethical Issues in Genetic Engineering* (Geneva: The Council, 1982).

[105] E.g. UNESCO, *Report on Human Gene Therapy* (1998) (at: www.eubios.info/UNESCO/ibc1994.pdf, accessed 25/03/11); CIOMS, The Declaration of Inuyama, adopted by the *XXIVth Round Table Conference of CIOMS on Genetics, Ethics and Human Values: Human Genome Mapping, Genetic Screening and Gene Therapy* (Tokyo, 22–7 July 1990); WMA, *WMA Statement on Genetic Counseling and Genetic Engineering*, adopted by the 39th World Medical Assembly, Madrid, Spain, October 1987, rescinded at the WMA General Assembly, Santiago 2005.

[106] E.g. UNESCO, Universal Declaration on the Human Genome and Human Rights, Paris 1997.

[107] E.g. Convention for the Protection of Human Rights and Dignity of the Human Being with regard to the Application of Biology and Medicine: Convention on Human Rights

Emerging themes

The regulatory picture pre- and post-clinical use of IVF and gene therapy was fragmented with countries at very different stages in addressing those biotechnologies and in developing appropriate regulatory regimes. Three approaches to devising regulation are identifiable: using new and existing committees; guidelines or reports from NGOs; and a direct move to regulation. With both biotechnologies, while legal, ethical and regulatory discussions occurred as the science was developing, by the time each biotechnology was first clinically used in humans the regulatory framework was minimal, even in the country in which IVF or gene therapy was first used. This may seem logical, for how can a biotechnology be discussed or effectively regulated at a very early stage in its development? But the time lag means that when it leaves the laboratory it is effectively unregulated. While the US was an exception to this for gene therapy, this trend has, to some extent, subsequently been in evidence in the UK in relation to cloning and stem cell research,[108] and the intracytoplasmic sperm injection (ICSI) technique was clinically used without an experimental phase *despite* the existence of regulation on IVF.[109] The protection offered to those involved in these early clinical activities is thus questionable, and as the science advances there is a game of regulatory 'catch-up'.

Furthermore, the time lag between the science developing and regulatory activity may result in the public believing that they have been presented with a *fait accompli*; if the science has 'been done', can it be argued that a biotechnology should not be provided to those in need? This is particularly important where in benefiting the potential recipient the biotechnology may put public health at risk. On the other hand, a time lag may be necessary and important because of a desire not to act too soon and prevent scientific and medical advances by regulating at a time when relevant scientific and other knowledge is minimal or lacking. Inappropriate or ineffective regulation could thereby be introduced, and

---

and Biomedicine, ETS No. 164 (1997); Council Decision 94/913/EC of December 15 1994 adopting a specific programme of research and technological development, including demonstration, in the field of biomedicine and health (1994–8); Directive 98/44/EC of the European Parliament and of the Council of 6 July 1998 on the Legal Protection of Biotechnological Inventions.

[108] S. Halliday, 'A Comparative Approach to the Regulation of Human Embryonic Stem Cell Research in Europe' (2004) 12 *Medical Law Review* 40; A. Plomer, 'Beyond the HFE Act? The Regulation of Stem Cell Research in the UK' (2002) 10 *Medical Law Review* 132.

[109] P.G. Peters, *How Safe is Safe Enough? Obligations to the Children of Reproductive Technology* (New York, NY: Oxford University Press, 2004), p. 2, ch. 14.

118   Regulatory responses to developing biotechnologies

an example of this may be the Australian State of Victoria's Infertility (Medical Procedures Act) 1984 which, it has been suggested, 'exemplifies the mistake of rushing to legislate too quickly on an issue which is complicated medically, scientifically and ethically and which is poorly understood by those outside the field'.[110] The Act was passed six years after Louise Brown's birth and did not define 'embryo' or 'cloning', and apparently permitted research on embryos *in vitro* which then *had to be* implanted into a woman.[111] The UK's initial reluctance to formally regulate IVF and the preference for extensive consultation and discussion with those working in the field could be criticised, particularly the six-year delay from the publication of the Warnock Committee's report and passing the 1990 Act, but its subsequent longevity[112] supports the argument that 'wise government does not always legislate at the first opportunity'.[113] Although there are undoubted benefits in not rushing to legislatively regulate, at the time both IVF and gene therapy were first clinically used they were minimally regulated, despite numerous pre-clinical discussions on both biotechnologies. Such discussions are commendable but can raise their own problems and, in relation to IVF, it has been noted that in the UK '[b]y the end of 1983 ... a number of bodies had begun to issue recommendations or guidelines, not all entirely consistent. More than ten years after the first successful attempt to fertilize a human egg in vitro and five years after the birth of the first IVF child little had really been resolved on the ethical and legal fronts.'[114]

An immediate legislative response to a developing biotechnology is not necessarily appropriate but there is a danger of allowing regulatory lacunae, particularly where such a biotechnology has the potential to harm the recipient *and* others. At the very least, the relevant regulatory authorities must ensure that those seeking to clinically use a developing biotechnology comply with the general regulatory regime for either experimental procedures or medical research. This may not always be easy to do when it is not clear *what* a developing biotechnology is, in a regulatory sense.[115] But more than this may be required and it should not be assumed that general experimental procedures and/or research provisions are sufficient for all, or any, developing biotechnologies because of the particular legal and ethical issues they may engage. Some

---

[110] Gunning and English, *Human In Vitro*, p. 36.
[111] *Ibid.*, p. 34, ch. 3. The 1984 Act was subsequently amended by the Infertility (Medical Procedures) Amendments Act 1987.
[112] The Human Fertilisation and Embryology Act 1990 was not substantially amended until the Human Fertilisation and Embryology Act 2008.
[113] Lee and Morgan, *Human Fertilisation and Embryology*, p. 13.
[114] Gunning and English, *Human In Vitro*, p. 31.   [115] See Chapter 3.

countries have adopted this approach with regard to gene therapy by regulating it within existing general biomedical research laws and/or guidelines. However, where a developing biotechnology may harm more than the recipient, its clinical use should be prohibited until it has been considered whether a specific regulatory regime designed to address these issues is required. To what extent has this occurred for xenotransplantation?

Devising national xenotransplant regulation

Pre-clinical[116]

Xenotransplants have been recorded since the early 1900s with the research initially occurring in parallel with that on allotransplantation.[117] The 1960s was a key period for both forms of transplantation with one patient surviving for nine months with a chimpanzee kidney and the first heart allotransplant reported in 1967.[118] Notably, the need for specific regulatory systems were not considered prior to their clinical use. This was also the case when a baboon's heart was xenotransplanted into 14-day-old Baby Fae in the US in 1984.[119] As allotransplants became more successful in prolonging life, interest in xenotransplants declined but the subsequent demand-and-supply gap for human organs and advances in genetic engineering and immunosuppressive drugs led to a refocus on xenotransplantation in the 1990s. During that decade there were unfulfilled predictions of impending clinical solid organ xenotransplants.[120] However, in the first half of the 1990s, a pig kidney was temporarily connected to the circulatory system outside the body of a dialysis patient, an advisory committee of the FDA recommended that a patient with AIDS was permitted to receive a baboon bone marrow

---

[116] For a summary of the regulatory and/or administrative arrangements as of 1 April 2000, see Council of Europe, *Report on the State*, pp. 79–80; also, McLean and Williamson, *Xenotransplantation*, ch. 5.

[117] E.g. J.D. Haller and M.M. Cerruti, 'Heart Transplantation in Man: Compilation of Cases – January 1 1964 to October 23 1968' (1968) 22 *American Journal of Cardiology* 840, Table 1; E. Ullman, 'Tissue and Organ Transplantation' (1914) 60 *Annals of Surgery* 195.

[118] Reemtsma *et al.*, 'Renal Heterotransplantation'; C.N. Barnard, 'A Human Cardiac Transplant: An Interim Report of a Successful Operation Performed at the Groote Schuur Hospital, Cape Town' (1967) 41 *South African Medical Journal* 1271.

[119] Bailey *et al.*, 'Baboon-to-Human', discussed in, e.g., A.L. Caplan, 'Ethical Issues Raised by Research Involving Xenografts' (1985) 254 *Journal of the American Medical Association* 3339; G.J. Annas, 'Baby Fae'.

[120] E.g. D. Dickson, 'Pig Heart Transplant "Breakthrough" Stirs Debate Over Timing of Trials' (1995) 377 *Nature* 185; N. Moran, 'Pig-to-Human Heart Transplant Slated to Begin in 1996' (1995) 1 *Nature Medicine* 987; R. Nowak, 'Xenotransplants Set to Resume' (1994) 266 *Science* 1148.

xenotransplant, ten diabetics received pig embryo insulin producing cells, extracorporeal pig liver perfusions were used on four critically ill patients, and a baboon's liver was xenotransplanted into a man.[121] Some of these were performed within existing clinical trial ethical review systems but the protection afforded the recipients is uncertain, as is the extent to which public health issues were discussed and/or addressed. The minimal regulation on xenotransplants at this time is worrying, and is a reason why it is important to explore how genetically engineered solid organ xenotransplants are and should be regulated. Because of the risks, regulatory systems need to be established *before* the science leaps ahead and I now trace the history of xenotransplant regulation to determine if the three approaches to devising biotechnology regulation are in evidence here. As clinical genetically engineered solid organ xenotransplants have not yet been performed I describe the regulatory schemes in place for xenotransplantation up to March 2011, prior to its clinical use.

Government-established committees
Regulatory activity on xenotransplantation began in earnest from the mid-1990s, perhaps because of the scientific advances and announcements of imminent clinical trials. In the UK a specific committee was, again, established by the DH to consider the biotechnology in 1995,[122] and Sweden and Norway followed suit in 1997 and 2000, respectively.[123] The Swedish and UK committees called for a new statutory xenotransplant *regulatory* body, and the former also recommended new legislation.[124] Both committees attempted to consult the public, but the methods used and successes of these ventures are questionable.[125] In contrast, in Norway the public were consulted after the working party's report was published and forty-seven written

---

[121] Swedish Committee, *From One Species*, p. 5; E. Pennisi, 'FDA Panel OKs Baboon Marrow Transplant' (1995) 269 *Science* 293; C.G. Groth *et al.*, 'Transplantation of Porcine Fetal Pancreas to Diabetic Patients' (1994) 344 *The Lancet* 1402; R.S. Chari *et al.*, 'Brief Report: Treatment of Hepatic Failure with Ex Vivo Pig-Liver Perfusion Followed by Liver Transplantation' (1994) 331 *New England Journal of Medicine* 234; Starzl *et al.*, 'Baboon-to-Human'.
[122] DH, *Animal Tissue*.
[123] Norway – Working Group on Xenotransplantation, *Xenotransplantation: Medical Use of Live Cells, Tissues and Organs from Animals* (Oslo: Ministry of Health, 2001) NOU 2001, 18; I.L. Gjørv, 'Political Considerations of Controversial Medical Issues: Xenotransplantation and Society. A Presentation of the Work of the Norwegian National Working Group on Xenotransplantation' (2004) 45 (suppl. 1) *Acta Veterinaria Scandinavica* S53; Sweden – Swedish Committee, *From One Species*.
[124] Sweden – Swedish Committee, *From One Species*, pp. 15–16, 20–31, 34–41; UK – DH, *Animal Tissue*, paras. 6.9, 8.74, ch. 9.
[125] See Chapter 2.

Devising national xenotransplant regulation 121

statements were received, the majority in favour of the party's conclusions.[126] These included instituting an *advisory* board to supervise the international development of xenotransplant, offer advice to the government on the actions required, comment on all xenotransplant clinical trial applications and its use as medical treatment, and develop regulations on, for example, the mandatory surveillance of a recipient's health.[127] There was an 'urgent need' for a xenotransplantation act to regulate clinical research and treatment in this area, and a xenotransplant central register and xenobiobank were required.[128] In 1999, prior to the working party, the government placed a moratorium on any medical treatment of humans using biological material from non-human animals until 1 January 2003, and the working party concluded that this should cease on that date.[129] Following the report's publication and public consultation, there was governmental discussion as to how to proceed and it was decided to wait for action from the European Parliament; thus, 'the politicians ... adopt[ed] an awaiting attitude, whereas the scientists are quietly carrying on with their business'.[130]

Existing committees or new subcommittees of them considered xenotransplantation in France, Germany, the Netherlands, Spain and Switzerland from the mid-1990s.[131] Regulation was recommended in France, Germany, Spain and Switzerland via existing laws with amendments where necessary, whereas new legislation was recommended by the Health Council of the Netherlands.[132] In Canada, an expert working group recommended that a specific subcommittee develop a xenotransplantation standard,[133] and that a new xenotransplantation *advisory* body was established.[134] In 1999 the *Standard* was produced,[135] and the Expert

---

[126] Gjørv, 'Political Considerations', 55.   [127] *Ibid.*, 55–56.
[128] *Ibid.*, 56.   [129] *Ibid.*, 53, 55.   [130] *Ibid.*, 56.
[131] OECD, 'Regulatory Developments in Xenotransplantation in France' (at: www.oecd. org/document/29/0,3343,en_2649_34537_1887773_1_1_1_1,00.html, accessed 25/03/11); CCNE, *Opinion on Ethics and Xenotransplantation*; OECD, 'Regulatory Developments in Xenotransplantation in Germany' (at: www.oecd.org/document/62/0,3343,en_ 2649_34537_1887806_1_1_1_1,00.html, accessed 25/03/11); Health Council, *Xenotransplantation*; Spain – 'Recommendations for the Regulation'; Swiss Science Council, *Xenotransplantation – Tested on Heart and Kidneys – Short version of the TA study of Xenotransplantation* (1998), p. 10 (at: www.ta-swiss.ch/incms_files/filebrowser/ 1998_TA30A_KF_xenotransplantation_e.pdf, accessed 25/03/11).
[132] CCNE, *Opinion on Ethics and Xenotransplantation*, pp. 10, 12; Germany – OECD, 'Regulatory Developments'; Spain – 'Recommendations for the Regulation'; Swiss Science Council, *Xenotransplantation*, pp. 12–13; Health Council, *Xenotransplantation*, pp. 10–12, 37–45, 47, respectively.
[133] Health Canada, Therapeutic Products Programme (TPP), *Report of the National Forum on Xenotransplantation: Clinical, Ethical, and Regulatory Issues November 6–8, 1997* (Ottawa: Health Canada, 1998), p. i.
[134] *Ibid.*, p. 3.   [135] Health Canada, *Proposed Canadian Standard*.

Advisory Committee on Xenograft Regulation was established to provide the Biologics and Genetic Therapies Directorate with 'timely advice on our medical, scientific, ethical and communication issues related to the regulation of xenografts'.[136] The *Standard* 'strongly' recommended that a national review board was established to receive all xenotransplant clinical trial referrals from local research ethics boards and provide a 'complete assessment of safety and ethical issues'.[137] There have also been public consultation on xenotransplants in Canada since the late 1990s,[138] and the CPHA conducted these across Canada in the early 2000s.[139] In the resulting report it was recommended that xenotransplantation involving humans should not proceed until 'critical issues' were first resolved, and 'stringent and transparent' legislation and regulations to cover xenotransplant clinical trials developed.[140]

In New Zealand the Royal Commission on Genetic Modification, established in 2000, recommended that ethical guidelines for xenotransplants involving genetic modification were developed.[141] In 2001 the Ministry of Health received a xenotransplant clinical trial application, refused on safety grounds,[142] and the Toi de Taiao (Bioethics Council) produced a discussion document on xenotransplantation in January 2005,[143] public consultation occurred until May,[144] and the Toi de Taiao called for a new statutory body and new legislation to regulate xenotransplantation.[145]

---

[136] Health Canada, 'Expert Advisory Committee on Xenograft Regulation' (2009) (at: www.hc-sc.gc.ca/dhp-mps/brgtherap/activit/com/eacx-ccerx/index-eng.php, accessed 25/03/11). Its last recorded meeting was 26 June 2002.

[137] Health Canada, *Proposed Canadian Standard*, p. 9.

[138] E.g. Health Canada, *Report from the Planning*; Health Canada, TPP, *Survey on Human Organ Donation and Xenotransplantation* (1999) (at: www.hc-sc.gc.ca/dhp-mps/alt_formats/hpfb-dgpsa/pdf/brgtherap/xeno_survey-enquete-eng.pdf, accessed 25/03/11).

[139] See Chapter 2.

[140] CPHA, *Animal-to-Human Transplantation*, pp. v–vi.

[141] Royal Commission, *Report of the Royal Commission on Genetic Modification* (2002), pp. 255–257 (at: www.mfe.govt.nz/publications/organisms/royal-commission-gm/, accessed 25/03/11).

[142] Toi te Taiao, Bioethics Council, *The Cultural, Spiritual and Ethical Aspects of Xenotransplantation: Animal-to-Human Transplantation – A Discussion Document* (Wellington: New Zealand, 2005), p. 38.

[143] *Ibid.* [144] *Ibid.*, p. 7.

[145] Toi te Taiao, Bioethics Council, *The Cultural, Spiritual and Ethical Aspects of Xenotransplantation: Animal-to-Human Transplantation – Final Report* (Wellington: New Zealand, 2005), Recommendations 2–5, p. 35.

Guidelines and reports from NGOs

Many NGOs were interested in xenotransplantation during the 1990s and, for example, the Ethics Committee of the Transplantation Society produced a position paper in 1993,[146] and the US Institute of Medicine held a conference in 1995 and recommended that a new xenotransplantation *advisory* body be established.[147] In 1995 the UK's independent Nuffield Council of Bioethics, which sat at the same time as the DH's committee, also instituted public and professional consultation and called for a new xenotransplantation *regulatory* body.[148] The Transplantation Society of Australia and New Zealand reached the same conclusion in its 1998 report,[149] and reports were also published by pressure groups,[150] the New York Academy of Sciences,[151] and the US Council on Ethical and Judicial Affairs.[152] In 2001 the Pontifical Academy for Life stated that 'a substantial convergence of international legislation' on xenotransplantation was desirable with 'genuine co-ordination at different levels'.[153] The Xenotransplantation Advisory Committee of the International Society for Heart and Lung Transplantation also recommended that national not local regulation should be the 'minimal form of

---

[146] Ethics Committee of the Transplantation Society, 'Human Xenotransplantation – Position Paper' (1993) 1 *Transplantation Society Bulletin* 8.

[147] Committee on Xenograft Transplantation: Ethical Issues and Public Policy, Division of Health Sciences Policy, Division of Health Care Services, Institute of Medicine, *Xenotransplantation – Science, Ethics and Public Policy* (Washington, DC: National Academy Press, 1996), pp. 3–4.

[148] Nuffield Council, *Animal-to-Human*, paras. 6.38–6.42, 7.8, 10.31–10.32, 10.47, 6.41, 7.8, 10.32. On their public consultation see Chapter 2.

[149] Transplantation Society of Australia and New Zealand, *Xenotransplantation Ad Hoc Working Party* (1998), Principal Recommendation 6.1.

[150] E.g. G. Langley and J. D'silva, *Animal Organs in Humans – Uncalculated Risks & Unanswered Questions* (1998) (at: www.ciwf.org.uk/includes/documents/cm_docs/2008/a/animal_organs_in_humans_1998.pdf, accessed 25/03/11); A Report by the Medical Research Modernization Committee, *Of Pigs, Primates and Plagues: A Layperson's Guide to the Problems with Animal-to-Human Organ Transplants* (1997) (at: www.crt-online.org/mrmc.html, accessed 25/03/11); S. Beddard and D. Lyons, *The Science and Ethics of Xenotransplantation* (Sheffield: Uncaged Campaigns, 1997).

[151] J. Fishman et al., *Xenotransplantation: Scientific Frontiers and Public Policy* (New York, NY: New York Academy of Sciences, 1998).

[152] AMA, *Opinion 2.169 The Ethical Implications of Xenotransplantation* (2001) (at: www.ama-assn.org/ama/pub/physician-resources/medical-ethics/opinion2169.shtml, accessed 25/03/11); AMA, *Report of the Council on Ethical and Judicial Affairs: The Ethical Implications of Xenotransplantation* (2000) CEJA Report 4-I-00 (at: www.ama-assn.org/ama1/pub/upload/mm/code-medical-ethics/2169a.pdf, accessed 25/03/11).

[153] Pontifical Academy for Life, *Prospects for Xenotransplantation – Scientific Aspects and Ethical Considerations* (2001), para. 21 (at: www.vatican.va/roman_curia/pontifical_academies/acdlife/documents/rc_pa_acdlife_doc_20010926_xenotrapianti_en.html, accessed 25/03/11).

control', including the power to prevent or halt trials, with 'every effort ... made to establish international coordination to ensure a uniform system of regulation'.[154] Existing bodies should use current rules to regulate xenotransplantation with national or international authorities regulating compulsory infectious disease monitoring, and '[i]nternational oversight ... ensur[ing] that no duplication of effort occurs'.[155]

Draft guidelines were published by the Ethics Committee of the Transplantation Society in 1993,[156] and the Australian Health Ethics Committee considered xenotransplant guidelines towards the end of the 1990s.[157] In 2002 an NHMRC working party published a discussion paper and guidelines calling for a new statutory body and new legislation to regulate xenotransplantation.[158] A response paper and guide for the community on xenotransplantation were produced following public consultation,[159] and the final report recommended that solid organ clinical trials should not occur, a national animal-to-human transplantation committee be set up to oversee the biotechnology, the therapeutic goods legislation amended and revised to support this scheme, and ten guidelines adopted.[160] The latter were not endorsed nor were all of the recommendations supported by the NHMRC, but it was agreed that no xenotransplant clinical trials would occur in Australia for five years.[161]

Statutory activity
In the US there was an early move to formal regulation and the FDA first published a document on xenotransplantation in 1991 and this was revised in 1993,[162] which was timely as the Center for Biologics Evaluation Research (CBER) at the FDA received its first investigational new

---

[154] Cooper *et al.*, 'Report of the Xenotransplantation', 1142.   [155] *Ibid.*
[156] Ethics Committee of the Transplantation Society, 'The Transplantation Society and Xenotransplantation (Draft Guidelines)' (1997) 6 *Transplantation Society Bulletin* 11.
[157] NHMRC, *The Strategic Program for the 1997–1999 Triennium* (at: www.nhmrc.gov.au/publications/strtplan/strt4.htm, accessed 25/03/11).
[158] NHMRC, XWP, *Draft Guidelines and Discussion Paper*, pp. xix, xliii–xlvi, chs. 9, 11.
[159] NHMRC, XWP, *Animal-to-Human Transplantation Research: How Should Australia Proceed?*; NHMRC, XWP, *Animal-to-Human Transplantation Research: A Guide for the Community*. See Chapter 2.
[160] NHMRC, XWP, *Animal-to-Human Transplantation: Final Report*, pp. vii–ix, 5, 30, ch. 5; NHMRC, XWP, *Guidelines for Clinical Animal-to-Human Transplantation (Xenotransplantation) Research DRAFT for NHMRC Consideration* (2004) accompanying *ibid.*
[161] NHMRC, 'NHMRC Statement on Xenotransplantation' (2009) (at: www.nhmrc.gov.au/media/noticeboard/notice09/091210-xenotransplantation.htm, accessed 25/03/11).
[162] 'Points to Consider for Human Cell and Gene Therapy Products' (1991), cited in E.T. Bloom, 'Xenotransplantation: Regulatory Challenges' (2001) 12 *Current Opinion in Biotechnology* 312; US DHHS, FDA, 'Application of Current Statutory Authorities

Devising national xenotransplant regulation 125

drug application for a xenotransplant product in 1994.[163] Draft guidelines on infectious diseases and xenotransplantation were published by the US Department for Health and Human Services (DHHS) in 1996,[164] and other guidance documents aimed at the sponsors of clinical trials and concerned with public health risks of xenotransplantation were subsequently published.[165] The 1996 draft guidelines were revised and approved by the government in 2001,[166] and further final guidance for industry produced in 2003.[167] Additionally, following the receipt by the New Zealand Ministry of Health of a xenotransplant clinical trial application,[168] existing legislation was amended to cover xenotransplantation in 2002.[169]

International activity

The WHO, World Health Assembly (WHA), and Organization for Economic Co-operation and Development (OECD) have all held conferences, workshops, and published reports and guidelines on xenotransplantation.[170] Participants at the OECD and New York Academy of

---

to Human Somatic Cell Therapy Products and Gene Therapy Products', 14 October 1993, 58 *Federal Register* 53248, respectively.
[163] S.L. Smith, 'Xenotransplantation Action Plan: US Food and Drug Administration Approach to the Regulation of Xenotransplantation' (2000) 1 *Medscape Transplantation*.
[164] US DHHS, Public Health Service, 'Draft Public Health Service (PHS) Guideline on Infectious Disease Issues in Xenotransplantation', 23 September 1996, 61 *Federal Register* 49920.
[165] US DHHS, FDA, CBER, *Guidance for Industry: Precautionary Measures to Reduce the Possible Risk of Transmission of Zoonoses by Blood and Blood Products from Xenotransplantation Product Recipients and Their intimate Contacts – Draft Guidance* (2002) (at: www.fda.gov/downloads/ BiologicsBloodVaccines/GuidanceComplianceRegulatoryInformation/Guidances/Blood/ ucm080375.pdf, accessed 23/03/11); US DHHS, FDA, CBER, *Guidance for Industry – Public Health Issues Posed by the Use of Nonhuman Primate Xenografts in Humans* (1999) (at: www.fda.gov/downloads/BiologicsBloodVaccines/GuidanceComplianceRegulatory Information/Guidances/Xenotransplantation/ucm092866.pdf, accessed 23/03/11).
[166] US DHHS, FDA, *PHS Guideline*.
[167] US DHSS *et al.*, *Guidance for Industry: Source Animal*.
[168] Toi te Taiao, *Cultural, Spiritual and Ethical*, p. 38.   [169] *Ibid.*, p. 6.
[170] E.g. WMA, *World Medical Association Statement on Human Organ Donation*; WHO, *Statement from the Xenotransplantation Advisory Consultation, Xenotransplantation: Hopes and Concerns*, Geneva, 18–20 April 2005; OECD, *Advances in Transplantation Biotechnology and Animal to Human Organ Transplants (Xenotransplantation) Safety, Economic and Ethical Aspects* (Paris: OECD, 1996), OECD Working Papers vol. IV, No. 97; WHO, *Xenotransplantation: Guidance on Infectious Disease Prevention and Management* (1998) WHO/EMC/ZOO/98.1 (at: http://whqlibdoc.who.int/hq/1998/ WHO_EMC_ZOO_98.1.pdf, accessed 23/03/11); WHO, *Report of WHO Consultation on Xenotransplantation, Geneva, Switzerland, 28–30 October 1997* (1998) WHO/EMC/ZOO/98.2 (at: www.who.int/emc-documents/zoonoses/whoemczoo982c. html, accessed 23/03/11).

126   Regulatory responses to developing biotechnologies

Sciences joint workshop in 1998, for example, agreed that an international approach was 'valuable' and should be 'immediately [set] in motion', including international xeno-recipient databases and how to monitor xeno-recipients trans-nationally.[171] There was 'general agreement' that an 'international co-operative resource' would be helpful to report events, keep xenotransplant records and information on guidelines and regulatory issues, and the cooperation of the OECD and WHO could encourage both this and public discussion.[172] Recommendations on the required information for effective international surveillance and the international sharing of information on xenotransplantation regulations could also be developed.[173] During 1999 the WHO set up an electronic discussion group and the OECD and WHO announced a global system of international experts to monitor adverse events in xenotransplant clinical trials.[174] Furthermore, at a WHO conference it was agreed that international action prior to evidence of successful clinical xenotransplants was required and '"guidelines [put] in place as soon as possible" in all states in which xenotransplantation occurs'.[175] The potential for the WHO to have a key role was noted to encourage states to support a consensus on the basic principles for xenotransplant safety and oversight, develop recommendations for obtaining informed consent, and develop and encourage nations to agree to control and monitor xeno-recipients' travel.[176] The WHA subsequently adopted a resolution urging member states to only allow clinical xenotransplants when national regulatory control and surveillance systems existed.[177]

A number of European bodies have also considered xenotransplantation,[178] and in 1997 the Council of Europe recommended that member states' governments 'establish a mechanism for the registration and regulation' of, *inter alia*, pre-clinical and clinical trials, and

---

[171] OECD, *Xenotransplantation*, p. 10.   [172] *Ibid.*   [173] *Ibid.*, pp. 10–11.
[174] K. Birmingham, 'WHO Hosts Web Discussion on Xenotransplantation Policy' (1999) 5 *Nature Medicine* 595.
[175] WHO, *Ethics, Access and Safety in Tissue and Organ Transplantation: Issues of Global Concern – Madrid, Spain, 6–9 October 2003 – Report* (Madrid: WHO, 2003), p. 22.
[176] *Ibid.*, p. 23.
[177] WHA, *Human Organ and Tissue Transplantation* 22 May 2004, WHA57.18, Section II. Xenogeneic Transplantation, para. 1.
[178] E.g. Committee for Human Medicinal Products (CHMP), *Concept Paper on the Revision of the Points to Consider on Xenogeneic Cell Therapy Medicinal Products* (2007) EMEA/CHMP/165085/2007; CPMP, *Points to Consider on Xenogeneic Cell Therapy Medicinal Products* (2003) CPMP/1199/02; CPMP, *Note for Guidance on the Quality, Preclinical and Clinical Aspects of Gene Transfer Medicinal Products* (2001) CPMP/BWP/3088/99; EMEA, *Concept Paper on the Development of a Committee for Proprietary Medicinal Products (CMP) Points to Consider on Xenogeneic Cell Therapy* (2000) CPMP/BWP/3326/99.

Implementing the recommendations 127

the long-term monitoring of xeno-recipients.[179] Public debate was encouraged,[180] and in 1993 the Parliamentary Assembly recommended a worldwide legally binding moratorium on clinical xenotransplants.[181] This was not adopted but a multidisciplinary xenotransplantation working party was set up,[182] and a draft report and guidelines published in 2000.[183] An opinion on the state of the art in xenotransplantation was adopted in 2001 which proposed a centralised *regulatory* body to oversee therapeutic xenotransplantation because of the international health risks.[184] A recommendation on xenotransplantation was adopted by Ministers of the Council of Europe in June 2003, stating that clinical xenotransplants should not be performed in countries without a centralised *regulatory* body and xenotransplants must be authorised by a 'body officially recognised as competent for this purpose'.[185] International cooperation on xenotransplantation research and public health was again also called for.[186]

Implementing the recommendations

Unsurprisingly, not all of the above recommendations were acted on and although the regulation of xenotransplantation is not always as clear as would be hoped, given the risks, two forms of regulation are primarily identifiable; regulating via new and/or existing committees, and using general and/or xeno-specific legislation. These are not exclusive categories and combinations of these approaches are in evidence. Notably, in some of the countries in which specific xenotransplant *regulatory*

---

[179] Council of Europe, Recommendation No. R(97)15 of the Committee of Ministers to Member States on Xenotransplantation, Adopted by the Committee of Ministers on 30 September 1997 at the 602nd meeting of the Ministers' Deputies.
[180] 'Opinion on the Working Group on Organ Transplantation of the Council of Europe on Xenotransplantation (presented on March 3, 1998)', as cited in C. de Sola, 'Current Developments on Xenotransplantation in the Council of Europe', in J. Fishman *et al.*, *Xenotransplantation*, pp. 211, 212–213.
[181] Parliamentary Assembly, Council of Europe, Recommendation 1399(99) on Xenotransplantation, 29 January 1999, Article 6i–ii.
[182] Reply of the Ministers Deputies of the Council of Europe to the Recommendation 1399(1999) on Xenotransplantation of the Parliamentary Assembly, 662nd meeting, 2–8 March 1999.
[183] Council of Europe Working Party on Xenotransplantation, *State of the Art Report on Xenotransplantation* (2000) CDBI/CDSP-XENO 2000. This was amended in 2001 and the final version published in 2003: Council of Europe, *Report on the State*.
[184] European Commission, Health & Consumer Protection Directorate-General, *Opinion on the State of the Art Concerning Xenotransplantation – Adopted by the Scientific Committee on Medicinal Products and Medical Devices on 1st October 2001*, (2001) Doc. SANCO/SCMPMD/2001/0002 Final, p. 14.
[185] Council of Europe, Recommendation Rec(2003)10, Articles 4–5.
[186] *Ibid.*, Articles 31–32.

128 Regulatory responses to developing biotechnologies

regimes were initially established, these have subsequently been disbanded and regulation of this biotechnology subsumed under existing regulatory structures. This suggests that any specific issues raised by xenotransplantation have now been addressed, but this is contestable and I suggest that this approach puts public health at risk.

National committees

New

In Spain, the Subcommission on Xenotransplantation, set up by the Spanish minister of health in May 1997, was asked to review and monitor research projects involving non-human primates and/or humans, develop recommendations for conducting research, and assess, evaluate and approve clinical research applications.[187] Guidelines were published on pre-clinical and clinical research in 1998, with the latter only permitted under certain conditions.[188] In the UK, following the recommendations of the DH and Nuffield Council reports,[189] the United Kingdom Xenotransplantation Interim Regulatory Authority (UKXIRA) was established in 1997 to *advise* the secretaries of state for health on the action necessary to regulate xenotransplantation, including advising on the acceptability of clinical trial applications.[190] The role of the UKXIRA within the regulatory scheme is confusing as despite its title (*Regulatory* Authority), it was an '*advisory* body, it does not take executive decisions but offers advice on the proposals it receives to the Secretaries of State for the UK Health Departments'.[191] The DH report's recommendation that primary legislation was introduced to regulate xenotransplantation was not adopted and, despite the then secretary of state for health's recognition that a 'clear finding from the consultation exercise was that regulation of xenotransplantation should have statutory backing',[192] UKXIRA remained a non-statutory

[187] 'Recommendations for the Regulation', p. 35.
[188] OECD, 'Regulatory Developments in Xenotransplantation in Spain' (at: www.oecd.org/document/36/0,3343,en_2649_34537_2352420_1_1_1_1,00.html, accessed 25/03/11). Note that xenotransplantation is also regulated by guidelines in Japan (Ministry of Health, Labour and Welfare (MHLW), *Guidelines on Issues of Infectious Diseases in Public Health Associated with Clinical Trials of Xenotransplantation* (Tokyo: MHLW, 2001)).
[189] DH, *Animal Tissue*; Nuffield Council, *Animal-to-Human*.
[190] DH, 'Xenotransplantation and UKXIRA Terms of Reference' (2008) (at: www.dh.gov.uk/ab/Archive/UKXIRA/DH_087869, accessed 25/03/11). The terms of reference altered between 1997 and 2006 and can be tracked in UKXIRA's annual reports (at: www.dh.gov.uk/ab/Archive/UKXIRA/DH_087899, accessed 25/03/11).
[191] UKXIRA, *Guidance*, para. 4.5, emphasis supplied; also, paras. 2.2–2.3.
[192] DH, 'Press release – Frank Dobson announces steps to regulate animal to human transplants' 30 July 1998.

non-departmental advisory body.[193] Between 1997 and 2006 UKXIRA met approximately three times a year, published a number of reports including guidance on making clinical trial proposals and draft reports on surveillance and biosecurity issues.[194]

In 2004, in the light of devolution in the UK, the DH instigated a review of certain types of national organisations within the Department which undertook executive functions, but this did not include expert non-departmental advisory bodies like UKXIRA.[195] A review of such bodies was not a high priority as they did not have staff or budgets, but these bodies would be looked at 'in due course'.[196] In December 2006 with no prior notice the UKXIRA ceased to exist, with a message on the website stating that the change was due to 'amendments to the statutory framework. Other Government Committees, Research Ethics Committees, and clinical governance arrangements are absorbing the functions'.[197] UKXIRA's 'low volume of work (no application for a xenotransplantation procedure was ever made to UKXIRA)' and other regulatory developments,[198] led to the conclusion that 'the advisory role of UKXIRA was more than adequately catered for by a range of other statutory bodies, and that UKXIRA had therefore completed its interim function'.[199] When questioned on its quiet disposal and the lack of consultation on the abolition, the DH responded that there was no routine requirement for public consultation on reviews of *advisory* bodies and that 'UKXIRA was set up as an interim body and a number of standing (statutory and advisory) bodies adequately cover the issues'.[200] A DH spokesperson was also reported as saying that genetically engineered solid organ xenotransplants were unlikely in the 'short to medium term'[201] and that there were 'unlikely to be trials to prove the procedures to be safe as no one

---

[193] DH, *Animal Tissue*, paras. 6.9, 8.74, ch. 9.
[194] See www.dh.gov.uk/ab/Archive/UKXIRA/index.htm, accessed 25/03/11.
[195] DH, *Reconfiguring the Department of Health's Arm's Length Bodies* (London: DH, 2004), p. 5.
[196] 'Q and A for Arms Length Bodies Review Policy, *Reconfiguring the Department of Health's Arms Length Bodies*, published 22 July 2004' (2004) (at: www.dh.gov.uk/prod_consum_dh/groups/dh_digitalassets/@dh/@en/documents/digitalasset/dh_4086163.pdf, accessed 25/03/11).
[197] DH, 'UK Xenotransplantation Regulatory Authority (UKXIRA) (at: www.dh.gov.uk/ab/Archive/UKXIRA/index.htm?ssSourceSiteId=en, accessed 25/03/11).
[198] Lord Warner the Minister for State for the DH declared that Commission Directive 2003/63/EU and the 2004 Clinical Trials Regulations 'make specific provision for xenotransplantation proposals' (Lord Warner, Hansard, vol. 687, col. WS181).
[199] Personal communication with DH dated 9 August 2007, on file with author.
[200] *Ibid.*
[201] Similarly, Lord Warner said that 'there have been no xenotransplant procedures in the UK and very few, if any, are anticipated over the next few years' (Lord Warner, Hansard, vol. 687, col. WS180).

would consent to the operation in numbers large enough to assess, but people desperate for a cure when they have a failing organ could consent as a last resort, something witnessed in other countries'.[202]

These comments raise a number of issues. First, according to UKXIRA annual reports at least four clinical trial applications were considered by the Authority, although none were approved.[203] Secondly, as the UKXIRA considered proposals in order to advise the relevant secretary of state in reality their role was not simply advisory. Thirdly, while its title included the word 'interim' this implies that a permanent body *would* be established, but there was no indication between 1997 and 2006 that UKXIRA was merely viewed as a stopgap. Fourthly, the status of existing UKXIRA guidance and documents is not explained in the 2006 guidance, although the DH has since privately clarified that they have no legal status but remain 'helpful *guidance*'.[204] It is questionable whether prior to 2006 the UK had an effective *regulatory* framework for xenotransplantation. Finally, as highlighted in Chapter 3, it is unclear whether existing arrangements *do* appropriately cover genetically engineered solid organ xenotransplants. With regard to the ethical review, the GTAC's remit *does not* extend to genetically engineered solid organs.[205] Using the general REC system suggests that 'the fundamental ethical issues specifically associated with xenotransplantation ... will receive little, if any, further attention at governmental level in the United Kingdom ... [and] serves to normalize xeno-technologies by suggesting that they do not raise issues over and above other types of clinical research'.[206] This is not the case. RECs have been widely criticised for their inconsistent and variable determinations on and of 'ethical' research;[207] thus, it is appropriate to ask whether 'we [can] really afford to have these committees taking decisions that could result in widespread public health problems'.[208] These committees are used to focusing on ethical issues largely centring around consent but, as discussed in Chapters 5 and 6, xenotransplantation involves differing kinds of consent from the norm because of the risks to public health, and the ability

---

[202] P. Curtis, 'Ethicists fear free-for-all in animal-to-human transplants', *The Guardian*, 13 January 2007.
[203] UKXIRA, *Fifth Annual Report January 2002–September 2003* (London: DH, 2004), p. 6; UKXIRA, *Third Annual Report*, p. 12; UKXIRA, *Second Annual Report September 1998–August 1999* (London: DH, 2000), pp. 12–14.
[204] Personal communication with DH dated 9 August 2007, on file with author, emphasis supplied.
[205] DH, *Xenotransplantation*, p. 3.
[206] L. Williamson *et al.*, 'The Regulation of Xenotransplantation in the United Kingdom after UKXIRA: Legal and Ethical Issues' (2007) 34 *Journal of Law and Society* 441, 458.
[207] See Chapter 3.   [208] McLean and Williamson, 'Demise', 375.

of existing general RECs to take these into account is questionable. Additionally, NHS RECs focus on protecting the interests of *individual* research participants and are not designed to consider 'population' matters.

The DH published new guidance on xenotransplantation in December 2006 and those considering performing a xenotransplant should now follow international guidance; with the Council of Europe, European Medicines Agency, US FDA and WHO cited as providing 'key recommendations'.[209] The common themes from these recommendations are set out; xenotransplantation should only occur if there is 'an adequate regulatory framework in place', infection transmission from non-human to human animals should be minimised, patients should be traced and subject to ongoing surveillance, and public debate encouraged.[210] It is *recommended* that all xenotransplants are carried out in a research context, with a research protocol, and appropriate approval from an REC. However, as set out in Chapter 3, there are three ways in which a clinical xenotransplant can be performed in the UK: as a clinical trial under the 2004 Clinical Trials Regulations, as research involving NHS patients outside the Regulations, or as 'experimental medicine'.[211] Genetically engineered solid organ xenotransplants are thus now regulated via existing UK regulatory schemes; schemes which were not designed for nor tailored to the particular needs and demands of this biotechnology.

In the US, the regulations in place since the early 1990s were supplemented in August 1999 by the establishment of the SACX to *advise* the secretary of HHS on 'all aspects of the scientific development and clinical applications' of the biotechnology.[212] It first met in 2001 to consider 'the full range of scientific, medical, social, and ethical issues and the public health concerns raised by xenotransplantation',[213] and published two draft documents for public comment on informed consent and the state of the science in xenotransplantation.[214] The SACX was discontinued in June 2005 but the FDA remains responsible for regulating xenotransplant clinical trials applying the 2001 guidelines.[215]

---

[209] DH, *Xenotransplantation*, p. 1. This replaces HSC 1998/126 *Clinical Procedures Involving Xenotransplantation*.
[210] DH, *Xenotransplantation*, pp. 1–2.   [211] *Ibid.*, pp. 2–3.
[212] US DHHS, NIH, 'Notice of Establishment', 26 August 1999, 64 *Federal Register* 46697.
[213] 'Charter, Secretary's Advisory Committee on Xenotransplantation', as cited in McLean and Williamson, *Xenotransplantation*, pp. 149–150.
[214] US DHHS, SACX, *Informed Consent*; US DHHS, SACX, *Report on the State of the Science in Xenotransplantation* (2004) (at: www.nelsonerlick.com/PDF/NIH%20Report%20on%20State%20of%20Xenotransplantation%202005.pdf, accessed 25/03/11).
[215] Above, n. 166.

Its jurisdiction is derived from the Food Drug and Cosmetics Act and Public Health Service Act, and the regulations issued in the Code of Federal Regulations by executive agencies such as the FDA or US DHHS have the force of law.[216] The CBER of the FDA now regulates xenotransplantation via the Cellular, Tissue and Gene Therapies Advisory Committee, established in 2008, which evaluates and reviews data on the effectiveness and safety of the biotechnology.[217] The Office of Science Policy and Data of the US DHHS also coordinates and guides the development of science policy on xenotransplantation.[218] Thus, as with the UK, xenotransplantation no longer has its own specific regulatory scheme in the US.

Existing

From 1999 to 2007 in Australia the GTRAP was responsible for providing scientific advice on xenotransplantation to the relevant human REC, and it reviewed and rejected one clinical trial proposal.[219] GTRAP was replaced by the Cellular Therapies Advisory Committee (CTAC), an expert advisory committee which provided scientific, medical and technical advice to human RECs and the NHMRC on the clinical application of xenotransplantation, in 2007.[220] The CTAC no longer exists and xenotransplant clinical trials in Australia are now overseen by the TGA and the relevant human REC, but the Therapeutic Goods Act 1989 and its Regulations 'do not currently specify xenotransplantation'.[221] Amendments to the Therapeutic Goods Regulations 1990 commenced on 31 May 2011, however, 'the status of biologicals to be used in xenotransplantation, is not discussed', but will be addressed at a later date.[222] In 2004 the NHMRC recommended that clinical

---

[216] E. Cozzi et al., 'The International Xenotransplantation Association (IXA) Consensus Statement on Conditions for Undertaking Clinical Trials of Porcine Islet Products in Type 1 Diabetes – Chapter 1: Key Ethical Requirements and Progress Toward the Definition of an International Regulatory Framework' (2009) 16 *Xenotransplantation* 203, 205–206.

[217] US FDA, 'Cellular, Tissue, and Gene Therapies Advisory Committee' (2010) (at: www.fda.gov/AdvisoryCommittees/CommitteesMeetingMaterials/BloodVaccinesandOther Biologics/CellularTissueandGeneTherapiesAdvisoryCommittee/default.htm, accessed 25/03/11).

[218] US DHHS, Assistant Secretary for Planning and Evaluation, 'Office of Science and Data Policy' (at: http://aspe.hhs.gov/_/office_specific/sdp.cfm, accessed 25/03/11).

[219] NHMRC, 'Frequently Asked Questions about Xenotransplantation' (2002) (at: www.nhmrc.gov.au/media/media/rel02/xenofaq.htm, accessed 25/03/11).

[220] NHMRC, *CEO Newsletter*, June 2007 (at: www.nhmrc.gov.au/_files_nhmrc/file/about/senior_staff/newsletters/0607.pdf, accessed 25/03/11).

[221] NHMRC, Discussion Paper, p. 10.

[222] NHMRC 'Submission on Amendments to the Therapeutic Goods Regulation 1990 for the Implementation of Biologicals Framework, October 2010' (2010) (at: www.tga.

xenotransplantation was not performed for five years, and this ended in December 2009. NHMRC Council members then considered the moratorium, aided by a discussion paper,[223] and recommended that if clinical trials were to proceed, the NHMRC should consider developing 'a suite of guidance documents to provide a scaffold for researchers', and that a number of activities could contribute to developing 'a robust standard of regulation, oversight and monitoring'.[224] It was said that xenotransplantation could be included in the TGA's regulatory framework for human cellular and tissue therapies and a specific xenotransplant *advisory* committee appointed *because*, in stark contrast to the UK position, human RECs 'may lack the specific expertise required to assess new techniques or evaluate risks and benefits associated with research proposals involving animal-to-human xenotransplantation', and it could develop xenotransplant guidelines.[225] The Council recommended that clinical xenotransplants could proceed in Australia when: (i) the TGA had implemented 'a robust framework' to regulate the trials; (ii) 'a robust standard of oversight and monitoring [was] established, including for example, a surveillance strategy and a patient register'; and (iii) the NHMRC, using the Australian Health Ethics Committee and Animal Welfare Committee's advice, had issued guidance to investigators and ethics committees involved in non-human-to-human animal studies.[226] The NHMRC is to develop this guidance and consult the community on it.[227] At present in Australia, as in the UK and US, clinical xenotransplantation is not regulated via a specific system designed to address the particular issues raised by the biotechnology. However, if the recommendations in the 2009 discussion paper are adopted, the regulatory scheme in Australia would mirror the initial system introduced in the UK. In so doing, the particular issues raised by xenotransplantation are acknowledged but at the end of the discussion paper it is stated that 'the consensus is that the risk posed by animal viruses is low and *can* be managed via herd selection and screening strategies providing there is a regulatory mechanism to obligate compliance. In reality, the risks of novel infection is more likely to be greater with allotransplantation compared with

gov.au/pdf/consult/regs-biologicals-1110-submission-nhmrc.pdf, accessed 27/3/11). On the amendments, see TGA, 'Biologicals Framework' (2011) (at: www.tga.gov.au/bt/hct.htm#adverse, accessed 27/3/11).

[223] NHMRC, 'Review on Xenotransplantation' (2009) (at: www.nhmrc.gov.au/health_ethics/health/xeno_review.htm, accessed 25/03/11); NHMRC, Discussion Paper.
[224] NHMRC, Discussion Paper, p. 21.   [225] *Ibid.*, pp. 21–22.
[226] NHMRC, 'NHMRC Statement on Xenotransplantation'.
[227] NHMRC, 'Animal to Human Transplantation Research (Xenotransplantation)' (2010).

134   Regulatory responses to developing biotechnologies

xenotransplantation as human donors are not screened or held in specialised containment facilities.'[228] The validity of this statement, as Chapters 2 and 6 in particular show, is debatable.

The 1999 *Proposed Canadian Standard*'s recommendation for a national review board to consider xenotransplant clinical trials was not implemented,[229] and a Health Canada report in 2001 declared that clinical xenotransplantation was only legal if the Therapeutic Products Programme authorised the application.[230] Additional guidance on the regulation of medical devices manufactured from or incorporating viable and non-viable non-human animal tissue was issued in 2004,[231] and it was reported in 2006 that an update of the 1999 *Standard* had been initiated.[232] This has not yet occurred but would 'in the future should it become a priority'.[233] Live cells, tissues and organs from non-human animals are considered to be therapeutic products, drugs or medical devices, and xenotransplants are subject to general drugs and medical devices regulations.[234] Similarly, in New Zealand the Gene Technology Advisory Committee (GTAC), an existing standing committee of the Health Research Council (HRC), assesses the scientific merit of xenotransplant clinical trial proposals in order to obtain an exemption under the Medicines Act 1981, or as required by an accredited ethics committee, or the HRC of New Zealand.[235] The GTAC has produced guidelines on xenotransplantation,[236] and its approval is required before the relevant ethics committee reviews the proposal, with final approval coming from the minister of health.[237] A bill on therapeutic products and medicines was introduced in 2006

---

[228] NHMRC, Discussion Paper, pp. 22–23, emphasis supplied.   [229] Above, n. 137.
[230] Health Canada, *Report of the Xenotransplantation*, p. 3.
[231] Health Canada, *Guidance for Industry – Guidance Document on the Regulation of Medical Devices Manufactured from or Incorporating Viable or Non-Viable Animal Tissue or their Derivative(s)* (2004) (at: www.hc-sc.gc.ca/dhp-mps/md-im/applic-demande/guide-ld/anim_tiss-eng.php, accessed 23/03/11).
[232] Health Canada, Science & Research, 'Xenotransplantation'.
[233] Personal communication with Health Canada dated 3 December 2009, on file with author.
[234] Food and Drugs Act, the Food and Drug Regulations, the Medical Devices Regulations (Health Canada, 'Xenotransplantation').
[235] HRC of New Zealand, Te Kaunihera Rangahau Hauora o Aotearoa, 'Terms of Reference' (2004) (at: www.hrc.govt.nz/root/pages_regulatory/GTAC_Terms_of_Reference.html, accessed 25/03/11).
[236] HRC Gene Technology Advisory Committee, *Process and Guidelines for Application for Approval of Proposals Involving Administration of Gene Products to Human Subjects in New Zealand* (2008) (at: www.hrc.govt.nz/assets/pdfs/publications/GTACProcess%20and%20Guidelines%202008%20_2_.pdf, accessed 25/03/11); HRC, *Guidelines for Preparation*.
[237] HRC, *Guidelines for Preparation*, p. 1.

which would repeal the Medicines Act 1981 and, adopting the provisions from Part 7A of that Act, the minister for health could only authorise clinical xenotransplants if it 'does not pose an unacceptable risk to the health and safety of the public'[238] and 'any risks will be appropriately managed'.[239] To obtain advice on whether a clinical trial application meets these criteria, the minister may establish an *advisory committee*, ask a recognised body for advice, or request that the person making the application obtains advice on the criteria from a body comprising the minister's nominees.[240] The bill would introduce a joint New Zealand and Australian regulatory scheme for therapeutic products.[241] The bill was introduced on 5 December 2006, had its first reading on 12 December, and a select committee reported on 15 June 2007.[242] The bill was listed on the Order Paper of 24 March 2011, indicating that it is still processing through New Zealand's Parliamentary system.[243]

Legislation[244]

Under the 1998 French health and safety regulations clinical xenotransplantation must comply with biomedical research legislation and be approved by the minister for health, following the opinion of the French Agency for the Health and Safety of Health Products and the French Transplant Establishment.[245] The authorisation can be subject to specific conditions, such as long-term surveillance. In the Netherlands

---

[238] *Therapeutic Products and Medicines Bill, Government Bill, Explanatory Note* (2006), p. 16 (at: www.legislation.govt.nz/bill/government/2006/0103/latest/viewpdf.aspx, accessed 25/03/11).
[239] Clause 491(1) Therapeutic Products and Medicines Bill 2006; also, clauses 486–498.
[240] *Ibid.*, clause 492(1).
[241] *Ibid.*, Parts 1 to 5; *Therapeutic Products*, pp. 1, 16–17.
[242] New Zealand Parliament, 'Therapeutic Products and Medicines Bill' (at: www.parliament.nz/en-NZ/PB/Legislation/Bills/1/5/8/00DBHOH_BILL7738_1-Therapeutic-Products-and-Medicines-Bill.htm, accessed 25/03/11).
[243] House of Representatives, 'Order Paper', Final No. 183, 24 March 2011, p. 4 (at: www.parliament.nz/NR/rdonlyres/7B3B73E3-47FC-456C-83D3-8BA19D6A5BAC/188888/00HOH20110324_orderpaper3.pdf, accessed 25/03/11). The Order Paper lists all business before the House of Representatives and is similar to an agenda (New Zealand Parliament, 'Order Paper and Questions', at: www.parliament.nz/en-NZ/PB/Business/OrderPaper/f/f/0/00HOHOrderPaper1-Final-Order-Paper-for-Thursday-24-March-2011.htm, accessed 25/03/11).
[244] For information on legislation covering xenotransplantation as of 1 April 2000, see Council of Europe, *Report on the State*, Table 24, pp. 76–78.
[245] Article L. 209-18-3, Law No. 98-535 of 1 July 1998 on the Strengthening of Health Surveillance and the Control of the Safety to Health of Products Intended for Human Beings.

general medical research laws initially regulated xenotransplantation and the Central Committee on Research Involving Human Subjects had to approve research in which non-human animal parts were applied into or onto a human's body.[246] However, public debates on xenotransplantation were held during 2000 and 2001,[247] and in 2002 the law was amended to prohibit xenotransplantation.[248] In contrast, in Germany xenotransplants are regulated by general European directives and regulations on clinical trials and advanced therapies.[249] The applicability and suitability of such general regulations to the specific situation and problems raised by clinical genetically engineered solid organ xenotransplants is debatable.

In Switzerland existing laws were initially amended to cover xenotransplants before specific xenotransplant legislation was introduced. The Swiss Science Council noted, in 1998, that 'comprehensive legislation' on xenotransplantation was required and, in the light of the infectious disease risks, the Federal Council suggested that the regulations should be made 'more stringent'.[250] From 1999, following amendments to existing laws, xenotransplants could be performed within a clinical trial if the Federal Office of Public Health approved, and the risk of infection for the public could be 'excluded with a large degree of probability and if a therapeutic benefit can be expected'.[251] Xenotransplants could then be performed as standard treatment if infection risks to the public could be excluded and therapeutic benefit proved in clinical trials.[252] The Federal Public Health Department proposed a moratorium on clinical xenotransplants from 1 September 1998 until

---

[246] Section 1, Regulations on the Central Review of Medical Research Involving Human Subjects Decree (Central Review of Medical Research Involving Human Subjects Decree), in The Medical Research Involving Human Subjects Act 1998 (WMO) (The Hague: International Publication Series Health, Welfare and Sport, 2000), nr. 2, Appendix II.

[247] The Dutch Consumer and Biotechnology Foundation, *Xenotransplantation: Is and Should It Be Possible? Final Report in Respect of the Public Debate on Xenotransplantation* (The Hague: Dutch Consumer and Biotechnology Foundation, 2001).

[248] Law of 16 May 2002 amending the Law on Special Medical Procedures with Respect to the Introduction of a Prohibition on Xenotransplantation.

[249] Medicinal Products Act, last amended by the Act of 23 November 2007; Ordinance of the Federal Republic of Germany on the Implementation of Good Clinical Practice in the Conduct of Clinical Trials of Medicinal Products on Human Beings of 9 August 2004, last amended by the Ordinance of 3 November 2006.

[250] Swiss Science Council, *Xenotransplantation*, p. 12.

[251] Federal Law of 8 October 1999 amending the Federal Order on the Control of Blood, Blood Products and Transplants, Order of 22 March 1996; Federal Order of 18 December 1998 on the Revision of the Federal Constitution; Statement of Position, 'Medical–Ethical Principles', p. 393.

[252] Statement of Position, 'Medical–Ethical', p. 393.

2002,[253] with some xenotransplants permitted if they had 'proved safe' and that Department authorised them after an 'in-depth investigation'.[254] In 2000 there was a PubliForum on transplantation, including xenotransplantation, and a majority of the Citizens' Panel recommended that a moratorium should not be introduced as the proposed law on transplantation was sufficient.[255] During the early 2000s a number of revisions were made to laws and ordinances,[256] and clinical therapeutic xenotransplants continued to be permissible under the conditions in place since 1999.[257] In 2004 a new federal law on transplantation was introduced and this came into force on 1 July 2007.[258] Xenotransplant clinical trials must now be the subject of a notification to Swissmedic, the Swiss Agency for Therapeutic Products, and carried out in accordance with the ICH guideline on Good Clinical Practice.[259]

International regulation

The WHO has continued to play a central role in emphasising the importance of, and facilitating, international cooperation and collaboration. However, the 1999 electronic discussion group on xenotransplantation is no longer operating and it is unclear when and why this ended. Xenotransplantation is part of the WHO's Global Knowledge Base on Transplantation,[260] and in 2006 a *voluntary* inventory of clinical xenotransplants was introduced by the University Hospital Geneva, IXA[261]

---

[253] Swiss Science Council, *Xenotransplantation*, p. 12.   [254] *Ibid.*
[255] Center for Technology Assessment, Federal Office of Public Health, Swiss National Science Foundation, *Transplantation Medicine, 24–27 November 2000 at Bern: Citizen Panel Report* (2001) TA-P2/2000e, p. 37.
[256] Federal Law of 15 December 2000 on Medicinal Products and Medical Devices (Law on Therapeutic Products – LTP), updated on 1 May 2007; Federal Law of 21 June 2002 amending the Federal Order on the Control of Transplants; Ordinance on the Control of Blood, Blood Products, and Transplants (Ordinance on Blood Control, Ordinance of 26 June 1996), amendment of 23 May 2001.
[257] Federal Law of 8 October 1999.
[258] Federal Law of 8 October 2004 concerning the Transplantation of Organs, Tissues and Cells (Transplantation Law).
[259] Swissmedic, *New Regulations for Transplant Products as of 1 July 2007* (2007) (at: www.swissmedic.ch/produktbereiche/00451/00915/index.html?lang=en, accessed 25/03/11).
[260] WHO, 'Global Knowledge Base on Transplantation (at: www.who.int/transplantation/knowledgebase/en, accessed 23/03/11); WHO, 'GTK4 Xenotransplantation' (at: www.who.int/transplantation/gkt/xenotransplantation/en/index.html, accessed 23/03/11).
[261] The Ethics Committee of the IXA also produced a position paper acknowledging the ethical and regulatory issues at stake (M. Sykes *et al.*, 'Position Paper of the Ethics Committee of the International Xenotransplantation Association' (2003) 10 *Xenotransplantation* 194).

and WHO.[262] The aim is to 'allow the identification of countries where [human xenotransplantation] exist and provide information for international agencies, national health authorities, health-care workers and the public with the objective of encouraging good practices, international guidelines and regulations'.[263] As of March 2011 thirty-one trials were registered.[264] The WHO also organised and acted as the secretariat for a meeting on clinical xenotransplant trials in 2008;[265] a meeting in collaboration with the Chinese ministry of health, Central South University of China and the IXA, and attended by over fifty delegates.[266] Principles for clinical xenotransplants were subsequently compiled, along with recommendations for the WHO, member states and investigators and proposers of such trials. While a valuable indication of how those working within the field currently view xenotransplantation, its clinical implementation and the implications of this, these WHO guidelines have no legal status.

Some problems with regulating developing biotechnologies

Global health and health tourism

There are similarities in the way the regulatory systems were devised for IVF, gene therapy and xenotransplantation and in the difficulties or problems the adopted approaches highlight. Along with problems caused by regulating 'too soon' and introducing inappropriate requirements which may curtail promising advances, delaying introducing regulation and waiting for committees to report may lead to 'regulatory gap[s]'[267] and a biotechnology may be in clinical use but essentially unregulated. There may also be a replication of work with committees *within* individual countries and/or internationally sitting at the same time and considering the same biotechnology, and this may result in circular discussions and regulatory inertia.[268] International regulatory discussions may minimise these problems,[269] and although each country may have a different

---

[262] Global Inventory of Xenotransplantation (at: www.humanxenotransplant.org, accessed 23/03/11).
[263] WHO, 'GTK4 Xenotransplantation'.
[264] Also, A. Sgroi et al., 'International Human Xenotransplantation Inventory' (2010) 90 *Transplantation* 597.
[265] 'First WHO'.
[266] D.K.C. Cooper, 'Global Consultation on Regulatory Requirements for Xenotransplantation in Clinical Trials, Conference held in Changsha, China, 19–21 November 2008' (2009) 16 *Xenotransplantation* 58.
[267] Ahmed, 'Last Twist', 1544.
[268] Cooper et al., 'Report of the Xenotransplantation', 1142.   [269] *Ibid.*

cultural perspective on the implications of a developing biotechnology, the science behind it will undoubtedly be global and the peer-reviewed literature international. Where global health is at stake *because of* the nature and extent of the risks, a separate, individual country-focused consideration is not the most effective way to proceed. Developing biotechnologies thus highlight the global context within which we exist. Nevertheless, the need for and possibility of globalized regulation has been questioned.[270] In the xenotransplantation context individual countries no longer exist, borders *are* blurred, and regulatory and clinical decisions made in one country *will* affect behaviour and business in another.

The risks of xenotransplantation are borderless, personally and country-wise; thus, international and national cooperation and regulatory mechanisms *are* essential to protect those involved and to minimise or prevent 'xeno-havens'. These may develop where one country's regulatory regime is deemed to be too restrictive by investigators and so trials are conducted in countries where the controls are perceived as being more relaxed. When countries stand at different places on the regulatory prohibitive–permissive spectrum, it can be harder to enforce the stance of those at the former end of the scale *because* it is known that there are countries situated towards the other end of the spectrum. Evidence of 'bio-tourism' for IVF and stem cell research/treatments, for example, is increasing,[271] and it has been suggested that stem cell tourists travelling to China for 'treatment' led to regulations being introduced, and Indian surrogacy laws are currently under debate because of the increasing 'trade' in this area.[272] A well-known example of health tourism is the Diane Blood case in which the English Court of Appeal agreed that she could take her dead husband's sperm abroad to be used in her infertility treatment; treatment which could not be

---

[270] E.g. V. Garrafa *et al.*, 'Between the Needy and the Greedy: The Quest for a Just and Fair Ethics of Clinical Research' (2010) 36 *Journal of Medical Ethics* 500; V. Heyvaert, 'Globalizing Regulation: Reaching beyond the Borders of Chemical Safety' (2009) 36 *Journal of Law and Society* 110.

[271] E.g. D. Campbell, 'Destination Spain: The Rise and Rise of Fertility Tourism', *guardian.co.uk*, 22 August 2010; BBC News, '"Stem Cell Tourism" in Germany', 23 June 2009 (at: http://news.bbc.co.uk/1/hi/health/8115881.stm, accessed 25/03/11); House of Commons Science and Technology Committee, *Human Reproductive Technologies and the Law*, Fifth Report of Session 2004–5, HC 7–1, vol. I, paras. 380–382, 385–386.

[272] D. Cyranoski, 'Stem-Cell Therapy Faces More Scrutiny in China' (2009) 459 *Nature* 146; N. Hyder, 'India Debates New Surrogacy Laws', *BioNews* 594, 7 February 2011 (at: www.bionews.org.uk, accessed 25/03/11).

provided in the UK because the sperm had been removed without her husband's consent.[273] The (possible) xenotransplant in India in 1996 of a pig's heart, lungs and kidneys into a human,[274] and pig islet cells into twelve teenagers in Mexico in 2002[275] have been suggested as examples of xeno-tourism,[276] and the risk of such tourism has been explicitly acknowledged in Australian and US reports.[277] Indeed, the US SACX suggested that the public needs educating about the dangers of xeno-tourism and international discussions on xeno-regulation encouraged to minimise its occurrence.[278]

Bio-tourism may not be limited to those seeking to access a biotechnological 'treatment' and may include companies and investigators. Indeed, it has been suggested that one reason Novartis closed its Imutran operation in the UK and moved it to mainland Europe, and then the US, was the regulatory schemes for non-human animal experiments.[279] More recently, Lord Winston has stated that he *had* to move his research on producing transgenic pig sperm, to be used to breed genetically engineered pigs for use in xenotransplants, from the UK to the US *because of* the relevant regulatory schemes in the UK and Europe, including the time it took (two years) to receive a Home Office licence to conduct the research on 'just six pigs'.[280] Such moves may be understandable for those keen for their pre-clinical work to move to the clinic, but they are ethically questionable particularly where the developing biotechnology inherently includes risks which go beyond the intended beneficiary. The challenge is thus to regulate 'to allow for the development of a potentially beneficial new technology, while safeguarding public health',[281] and to do this within a global context.

[273] *R v. Human Fertilisation and Embryology Authority, ex parte Blood* [1997] 2 All ER 687, CA.
[274] Jayaraman, 'Pig Heart'.
[275] K. Birmingham, 'Skepticism Surrounds Diabetes Xenograft Experiment' (2002) 8 *Nature Medicine* 1047. The scientific results were not published until 2005 (R.A. Valdés-González *et al.*, 'Xenotransplantation of Porcine Neonatal Islets of Langerhans and Sertoli Cells: A 4-Year Study' (2005) 153 *European Journal of Endocrinology* 419).
[276] A. Persson, 'Research Ethics and the Development of Medical Biotechnology' (2006) 13 *Xenotransplantation* 511; Daar, 'Xenotransplantation – Science', p. 135.
[277] NHMRC, Discussion Paper, p. 18; US DHHS, SACX, *Report on the State*, pp. iv–v, 25–27, respectively.
[278] US DHHS, SACX, *Report on the State*, pp. v, 26.
[279] E.g. 'Animal lab shuts down after we reveal horrors', *Daily Express* 28 September 2000.
[280] R. Winston, 'Britain squanders pioneer work on organ transplants', *Sunday Times*, 7 September 2008.
[281] Bloom, 'Xenotransplantation', 314.

Business, finance and 'the market'

The commercial companies which finance biotechnological research may have an important influence or impact on regulatory decisions, and xenotransplantation is an example of the 'conjunction of science, commercialization of university research, venture capital, risk, need, and glamour (we must not under-estimate the need in scientists to be the first; there might even be a Nobel prize here)'.[282] This conjunction is particularly evident in the US where the DHHS has published a number of guidance documents specifically directed towards industry, indicating their prominent role in the field.[283] Such a conjunction is clearly necessary and often advantageous, but a problem is that '[t]he management and cultural practices of commerce differ from those of the traditional European professional medico-scientific approach'.[284] There may, for example, be pressure on companies to announce scientific results and advances to shareholders and 'the market' sooner than is appropriate and without the necessary peer review of the work.[285] Finance has an ever more important role in biotechnological developments and genetically engineered solid organ xenotransplants are likely to be a multimillion dollar market *if* clinical trials prolong life. Given this, calls for international collaboration may not be well received by those financing the research and accountable to shareholders and investors. Thus, while lip-service may be paid to the need for international and national cooperation, business confidentiality and financial implications may make this more difficult to achieve in practice. Indeed, there is an argument that the 'morality of the market place' should regulate science because the public are moral and will only use technologies which they consider to be ethically acceptable.[286] Under this approach, 'the market place can function to ensure ethics: Immoral or unethical uses of new technologies will not be commercially viable'.[287] This approach may, however, lead the public to perceive that they are being presented with a *fait accompli*; if the science is proved, it *must* be fine to proceed. It is then for each individual to determine whether to access the relevant development. This may be appropriate in situations of certainty where knowledge and information can be communicated and transferred and any risks remain with the intended beneficiary. Where this is not so the market cannot sufficiently protect all those who may be affected and placed at risk by such a decision. In reality market forces may *require*

---

[282] Daar, 'Xenotransplantation – Science', p. 150.   [283] E.g. nn. 165, 167, above.
[284] Johnson, 'Art of Regulation', 401.   [285] Persson, 'Research Ethics'.
[286] Sommerville, 'Searching for Ethics', p. 33.   [287] *Ibid.*

national and international effective regulatory regimes because '[w]ithout regulation by governments, there is no product that is credible product ... in the eyes of patients and consumers'.[288] Indeed, 'global markets are a crucial reality for biotechnology firms. It is the global regulatory system that concerns them and within which they must function and seek approvals ... The health product market is not a fully free competitive market. It is a managed market with complex sets of national and international regulators.'[289]

The role of the market, commerce and investment cannot be ignored, nor can the impact of the internet in providing information on and 'marketing' new 'treatments'.[290] Politicians may also be wary of regulation which can be viewed as discouraging investment, so '[l]ocal regulation ... can operate only in the shadow of whatever local political will prevails; and the prospect of regulatory arbitrage between jurisdictions competing to host technology-based business militates against the adoption and enforcement of regional or international minimum standards'.[291] This pull of competing interests was noted in the UK government's 1999 review on the regulation of biotechnologies.[292] Furthermore, it has been suggested that the 1996 version of the Declaration of Helsinki was relied on in the UK's Clinical Trials Regulations, rather than the 2000 version which existed at the time the Regulations were passed, for political reasons.[293] Thus (biotechnological) regulation necessarily involves political, commercial and global elements, and any proposed regulatory scheme must have the investigators on their side, otherwise it will be meaningless. This should not mean that their concerns or interests are allowed to dominate; rather, while it may be difficult to draft legislation on biotechnologies, it should be achievable to set ethical, professional, quality and safety assurances and standards that are 'reasonable or coherent for all members of a pluralistic

---

[288] G.B. Doern, 'Regulatory regimes for the safety and efficacy of biotechnological health products: changing pressures, products and processes – a paper prepared for the Canadian Biotechnology Advisory Committee (2003), p. 12, unpublished.
[289] Ibid., p. 14.
[290] E.g. S. Boseley, 'Government warned on DIY cancer treatments', The Guardian 28 April 2008.
[291] R. Brownsword, 'What the World Needs Now: Techno-Regulation, Human Rights and Human Dignity', in R. Brownsword (ed.), Global Governance and the Quest for Justice (Oxford: Hart, 2004), pp. 203, 222.
[292] Cabinet Office, Office of Science and Technology, The Advisory and Regulatory Framework for Biotechnology: Report from the Government's Review (London: Cabinet Office, 1999), p. 2.
[293] Biggs, Healthcare Research, pp. 57–58. The 2008 version of the Declaration has also not been incorporated into the subsequently amended Regulations (see Chapter 3).

society'.[294] If not, 'we risk being entrapped in a *dialogue of the deaf*, a policy stalemate, in which market forces undermine democratic processes'.[295]

Global regulation

Regulating a developing biotechnology at a local or national level may be difficult and introducing an international, global scheme highlights and exacerbates these problems. Despite this, global discussion and cooperation on xenotransplantation is imperative and the WHO and OECD have an important role to play here, although without effective regulatory teeth their statements are well meaning but ignorable. Furthermore, '[a]ttempts to harmonize regulation through the traditional processes of international law are cumbersome and beset by political considerations, and at best achieve agreement only in very general terms'.[296] Where a controversial and uncertain biotechnology is being regulated, it is unclear *what* form international regulation can take as there are likely to be 'different regulatory thresholds in different societies'.[297] To be effective, compliance with such regulation must be monitored and meaningful sanctions for non-compliance introduced. However, despite an apparent consensus for an international regulatory regime, there has been a marked reluctance to act on this and it is hard to see how such a regime could effectively work in practice because:

there is not a natural culture of compliance in this field [of new technologies] (indeed, one might believe that there is considerable regulatory resistance both on the part of those with commercial interests in the development of the technology as well as on the part of those wishing to access the technology); and fast-moving technology represents one of the most complex challenges at the level of regulatory design.[298]

Nevertheless, '[i]nternational standards and guidelines are indispensable for providing the direction to be followed in developing clinical research in each place around the world',[299] and if clinical genetically engineered solid organ xenotransplants are to be performed, international regulatory action must be pursued.

---

[294] R.M. Isasi and B.M. Knoppers, 'Mind the Gap: Policy Approaches to Embryonic Stem Cell and Cloning Research in 50 Countries' (2006) 13 *European Journal of Health Law* 9, 10.
[295] *Ibid.*, emphasis in original, reference removed.
[296] S. Picciotto, 'Introduction: Reconceptualizing Regulation in the Era of Globalization' (2002) 29 *Journal of Law and Society* 1, 7.
[297] Brownsword, 'What the World Needs', p. 221.
[298] *Ibid.*, p. 220, references removed. [299] Garrafa *et al.*, 'Between the Needy', 503.

Conclusion

Elements of the four problems of existing legal frameworks with regard to genetic science noted at the outset of this chapter are in evidence in the development of regulation for IVF, gene therapy and xenotransplantation. Problems raised by proactive or reactive–adaptive regulation are now widely recognised and in relation to xenotransplantation the Australian NHMRC has noted that '[i]t is not feasible to wait for efficacy data to be adequate for specific technologies before developing an appropriate framework; rather it is necessary to anticipate the regulatory processes which would be required'.[300] Whereas it might once have been viewed as reasonable or responsible to wait for clinical use before introducing regulation, this is now rarely deemed appropriate. Regulation is now appropriately viewed as a fundamental and key aspect of a biotechnology's development, particularly one which exposes more than the intended beneficiary to risks. In the regulatory histories of gene therapy and xenotransplantation this move towards proactive or pre-emptive regulation is clear, and it has been said 'that more ethical and public policy analysis ... occurred before the fact with human gene therapy than any other biomedical technology in history'.[301] Similarly, many countries have proposed or implemented regulatory schemes when no clinical genetically engineered solid organ xenotransplants have yet occurred.

However, it is of concern that the UK, one of the few countries to introduce a specific xenotransplant regulatory regime at an early stage in the biotechnology's development, has since incorporated xenotransplantation within existing regulatory schemes; schemes not designed to address the specific issues raised by it. By initially introducing a specific xeno-regime it appeared that the UK had recognised that such issues existed and that it was willing to take the lead in regulating it. However, establishing the UKXIRA as an interim, advisory/regulatory non-statutory body has been criticised as 'a knee-jerk solution to the problems which xenotransplantation presented, with little thought given to its place in a broader regulatory framework'.[302] This criticism is compounded by the UKXIRA's 'ill-considered' abolition in 2006 which 'reinforce[s] the impression that government policy on this issue has lacked a clear rationale'.[303] There is a sense that lessons have not been

---

[300] NHMRC, Discussion Paper, p. 10.
[301] E.K. Nichols, *Human Gene Therapy* (Cambridge, MA: Harvard University Press, 1988), p. 187, n. 9.
[302] Williamson *et al.*, 'Regulation', 463.   [303] Ibid.

Conclusion

learnt from the regulatory histories of other developing biotechnologies and the general regulatory framework within the UK has itself been under review since 2010.[304]

The suggestion that there is no 'clear rationale' for regulating xenotransplantation in the UK is difficult to dispute, especially as xenotransplants have now been brought within existing biotechnology regulatory schemes, perhaps indicating that it is now viewed as posing no specific issues or problems. This is the impression that xenorecipients and others could understandably draw but this is contestable and research on the infectious risks of xenotransplants continues.[305] There is no scientific consensus on this, but moving xenotransplantation within general regulatory schemes dangerously suggests otherwise and is worrying given that it also remains unclear which regulatory scheme(s) genetically engineered solid organ xenotransplants fall. The UK is not alone in adopting this strategy as in Australia, Canada, New Zealand and the US clinical xenotransplants must currently comply with existing non-xenotransplant specific regulatory regimes. It may be that this is an appropriate response because genetically engineered solid organ xenotransplants are unlikely,[306] but research on this type of xenotransplantation continues with suggestions of clinical trials in 2013.[307] Regardless of when such trials will occur, the risks 'posed by continued efforts to make it a reality surely mandate a regime much more stringent than that which is now in place in the UK'.[308] Given the disjunction between the intended beneficiary and those placed at harm, the balance between these groups should not only be determined by local RECs.[309] Additionally, consensus on some of the issues inherent in xenotransplantation has not led to uniformity in national regulatory responses nor a more concerted international response, and this requires action because '[b]iotechnology can be no nation's monopoly'.[310] This must occur *before* a clinical genetically engineered solid organ xenotransplant is performed. At the very least proactive, dynamic legally enforceable European regulation is needed. There must thus be a willingness to take the lead and produce the gold standard for others to follow. Although health tourism is inevitable, to protect individual and public health strong leadership is required, and a European regulatory

---

[304] DH, *Liberating the NHS*. [305] See Chapter 2. [306] Above nn. 201–202.
[307] E.g. D.K.C. Cooper *et al.*, 'Recent Advances'.
[308] McLean and Williamson, 'Demise', 375. [309] *Ibid.*, 374.
[310] L. Kass, *Toward a More Natural Science: Biology and Human Affairs* (New York, NY: Free Press, 1985), p. 42.

regime should be implemented which provides clear legal and ethical parameters for pre-clinical and clinical xenotransplant research.

Xenotransplant regulation has followed some of the trends evident in the regulatory histories of IVF and gene therapy, but this developing biotechnology is distinctive from other interventions and making it fit within existing regulatory structures and systems is inappropriate and fails to recognise its unique elements. Indeed, in situations of risk and uncertainty the public should participate in the decision-making process,[311] because where the 'associated social stakes are so extensive ... it is difficult to see how technical experts acting as proxy on society's behalf can address them adequately ... earlier, wider and deeper public involvement in the shaping of strategic science and technology objectives is a vital precondition in any attempt to strike such a balance'.[312] Meaningful dialogue is required so that 'the public trust those responsible for developing and regulating [xenotransplantation]'.[313] However, many Western countries have 'insufficiently developed mechanisms for engaging in a broad, in-depth public debate, which is usually pushed to the end of the agenda'.[314] Involving the public in regulatory decision-making might not be easy but as they will bear the risks of xenotransplantation their involvement has been recognised as crucial.[315] Furthermore, the UK's Better Regulation Task Force has suggested that when devising subject-specific regulation 'the Government should ensure that the public has input into the decision making process through open meetings or lay representation on committees'.[316] In situations of uncertainty this is particularly important and 'political decision-making should not take place in a vacuum ... it should seek out and take account of diverse forms of social knowledge and intelligence, and use deliberative processes to better inform its decisions'.[317]

It has been suggested that five lessons must be learned from the history of technology regulation: the central importance of public confidence and trust; not imposing discriminatory regulatory burdens on new technologies, even if the public seem to favour such; that adaptive regulatory frameworks are essential; social and moral concerns must be

---

[311] Better Regulation Task Force (BRTF), *Scientific Research: Innovation with Controls* (London: BRTF, 2003), p. 15.
[312] Welsh and Evans, 'Xenotransplantation', 212, reference removed.
[313] Persson, 'Research Ethics', 513.
[314] G. Incorvati, 'Xenotransplantation and Public Responsibility' (2003) 10 *European Journal of Health Law* 295, 302.
[315] Cozzi *et al.*, 'IXA – Chapter 1', 205.   [316] BRTF, *Scientific Research*, p. 15.
[317] Wilsdon and Willis, *See-Through Science*, p. 47.

addressed; and international harmonisation is vital.[318] These lessons resonate for xenotransplantation and some other developing biotechnologies, and in relation to social and moral concerns, it is widely accepted that xenotransplantation raises particular issues in relation to consent and that those involved should be subject to extensive, possibly lifelong, surveillance and monitoring. These are explored in Chapters 5 and 6, and further set xenotransplantation apart from other biotechnologies and necessitate a *specific* international regulatory response because 'the implementation of xenotransplantation technology cannot proceed in an *ad hoc* manner, but ... requires a collective decision to implement an institutional risk management structure capable of reconciling private benefits with public risks and potential ethical objections. It is within the design and operation of such an institutional structure that consent plays an important role.'[319] Consent is the focus of my discussion in Chapter 5.

---

[318] G.E. Marchant *et al.*, 'What Does the History of Technology Teach Us about Nano Oversight?' (2009) 37 *Journal of Law, Medicine and Ethics* 724.
[319] Gold and Adams, 'Reconciling Private Benefit', 35.

5 Challenges to legal and ethical norms: first-party consent and third parties at risk

The importance of individual, first-party consent and informed decision-making is almost universally accepted in the health context, and is viewed as a vital component of responsible health practice and research. Health care in most Western societies is based on this form of consent[1] and, for research, international and national declarations and guidelines emphasise the importance of obtaining consent,[2] as do the UK's Clinical Trials Regulations 2004.[3] Clinical trials in Europe should accord with the ethical principles set out in the Declaration of Helsinki and the consent of the *individual* participant is at the centre of this.[4] Xenotransplantation requires a reconsideration of this focus on the individual's consent because of the nature and magnitude of the risks, and '[r]esponsibility for one's choices demands consideration of how these choices will affect others'.[5] There are no reported cases on consenting to clinical research in the UK, but the UK's DH has stated that the requirements on consenting to medical treatment apply.[6] Consenting to experimental procedures is not specifically addressed in UK

---

[1] Consent from or involvement of others as well as the individual is noted for some communities or circumstances, e.g., CIOMS and WHO, *International Ethical*, Commentary on Guideline 4; Australia – NHMRC *et al.*, *National Statement*, para. 2.2.13, ch. 4.7; Canada – Canadian Institutes *et al.*, *TCPS2*, ch. 9; New Zealand – MH, *Operational Standard*, para. 4.5.

[2] E.g. WMA, *Declaration*, B24–26, 31; CIOMS and WHO, *International Ethical*, Guidelines 4–6; International Conference, *ICH Harmonised*, para. 4.8; Australia – NHMRC *et al.*, *National Statement*, ch. 2.2; Canada – Canadian Institutes *et al.*, *TCPS2*, ch. 3; New Zealand – MH, *Operational Standard*, Section 2.2; HRC, *Guidelines on Ethics*, para. 3.1; UK – GMC, *Consent to Research*; US – 45 CFR 46, (US DHHS), Code of Federal Regulations Title 45 Public Welfare, Part 46 Protection of Human Subjects, 2009, § 46.116.

[3] Sched. 1, Part 3, Medicines for Human Use (Clinical Trials) Regulations 2004, SI 2004 No. 1031, as amended.

[4] Directive 2001/20/EC; UK – Sched. 1, Part 2, para. 6, 2004 Regulations, as amended. See Chapter 3.

[5] Brazier, 'Do No Harm', 401.

[6] DH, *Reference Guide to Consent for Examination or Treatment* (2nd edn, London: DH, 2009), para. 39.

legal or ethical guidance but it is similarly assumed that the requirements for consent to treatment and research also apply. This is problematic. Medical treatment, clinical research and experimental procedures are very different in nature and different standards of information disclosure for research, especially non-therapeutic, than for treatment may be appropriate.[7]

Individual consent is undoubtedly important, can help to enhance patient autonomy, and 'frees the researcher from the suspicion that the patient's vulnerability has been exploited for the researcher's profit'.[8] However, in some societies where an individual's 'rights' and ideas of 'choice' are emphasised, there is a sense that provided a competent informed adult agrees anything is possible. Three key issues raised by the legal and ethical norm of relying on first-party consent in the xenotransplantation context are explored. First, whether competent informed individuals *should* be able to consent to a genetically engineered solid organ xenotransplant *because* the risks go beyond the intended beneficiary. It should not be assumed that it is legally possible to consent to this, and consideration must be given to an assessment of private benefit and public risk, the 'obligation to protect society from the spread of infection',[9] and the situation of those who need a transplant but cannot obtain one. Secondly, if it is possible to legally consent, is traditional 'first-party' consent appropriate for xenotransplants? To provide 'real' consent to a treatment, a clinical trial and, presumably, an experimental procedure in the UK, the participant/recipient must be: (i) competent; (ii) acting voluntarily; and (iii) informed 'in broad terms of the nature of the [experimental procedure or clinical trial]'.[10] Will the first xeno-recipients be able to meet these requirements? There is a developing consensus that the first xeno-recipients should be competent adults,[11] with those with no

---

[7] E.g. E. Chwang, 'A Puzzle about Consent in Research and in Practice' (2010) 27 *Journal of Applied Philosophy* 258; Mason and Laurie, *Mason & McCall Smith's*, pp. 629–631; M. Brazier and E. Cave, *Medicine, Patients and the Law* (London: LexisNexis Butterworths, 2007), pp. 419–420.
[8] C.L. Bosk, 'Obtaining Voluntary Consent for Research in Desperately Ill Patients' (2002) 40 *Medical Care* V-64, V-65.
[9] K.A. Bramstedt, 'Arguments for the Ethical Permissibility of Transgenic Xenografting' (2000) 7 *Gene Therapy* 633, 634.
[10] *Chatterton* v. *Gerson* [1981] 1 All ER 257, 265 *per* Bristow J.
[11] E.g. Australia – NHMRC, XWP, *Guidelines for Clinical*, Guideline 6, accompanying NHMRC, XWP, *Animal-to-Human Transplantation: Final Report*; Canada – Health Canada, *Proposed Canadian Standard*, p. 7; Netherlands – Health Council, *Xenotransplantation*, pp. 12, 43; Sweden – Swedish Committee, *From One Species*, p. 17; UK – UKXIRA, *Guidance*, para. 7.12; Council of Europe, Recommendation Rec(2003)10, Article 19.

other hope likely candidates,[12] and I consider whether they can be competent because of their health status. Concerns have long been raised about the voluntariness of *patients'* consent to involvement in research, especially when their doctor requests their participation,[13] and the health status of proposed xeno-recipients may further affect their ability to consent voluntarily. Furthermore, does the limited information available make it (im)possible for a patient to make an informed choice to be involved?

Finally, xenotransplantation challenges the centrality of individual autonomy and the relevance of first-party consent as currently conceived because of the risks to others, and I highlight some of the issues developed further in Chapter 6. Is first-party consent possible and adequate when the risks are not limited to the possible beneficiary? It is proposed that third parties are involved in post-xenotransplant surveillance, and this suggests that the 'individual-centered, rights-based approach to [informed consent is] abandoned, and replaced by more communitarian or interpersonal models of medical decision-making'.[14] If so and third-party consent is necessary, xenotransplantation is taken further out of the realms of accepted legal and ethical norms and the doctor–patient relationship transformed into, at the very least, a three-way relationship also involving the xeno-recipient's contacts and, possibly, many (unidentified) others. It should not be assumed that such changes are legally and/or ethically unproblematic or can be automatically accommodated within existing systems. Fundamental changes of this order require public discussion and debate and should not be taken lightly.[15]

Consenting to being a xeno-recipient

The first few genetically engineered solid organs xenotransplanted into humans will be experimental procedures and subsequent xeno-transplants should only be permitted as part of clinical trials. Can an individual consent to receive such a procedure and, following this, others consent to participating in xeno-clinical trials? The former has not been widely addressed,[16] but in *R* v. *Brown* the UK's House of Lords held it

---

[12] See Chapter 3.
[13] E.g. O. Corrigan, 'Empty Ethics: The Problem with Informed Consent' (2003) 25 *Sociology of Health and Illness* 768.
[14] M. Häyry and T. Takala, 'Genetic Information, Rights and Autonomy' (2001) 22 *Theoretical Medicine* 403, 406–407, references removed.
[15] S. Fovargue, 'Consenting to Bio-Risk: Xenotransplantation and the Law' (2005) 25 *Legal Studies* 404.
[16] Important exceptions include *Simms* v. *Simms; PA* v. *JA and another* [2002] EWHC 2734; Price, 'Remodelling'.

was possible to consent to certain forms of bodily harm such as that which may occur in clinical trials,[17] if the trial was 'performed in accordance with good medical practice and with the consent of the patient'.[18] If these provisos apply to experimental procedures and the elements of consent are complied with, such consent can provide the necessary legal authorisation for receiving one of the first clinical genetically engineered solid organ xenotransplants. For subsequent clinical trials, the UK's initial xenotransplant regulatory body, the UKXIRA, assumed that it was legally possible to consent to such a trial.[19] However, can a patient who is prepared to accept the risk legally be involved in *any* high-risk procedure or trial? This has again received little attention, as the focus has been on ensuring that voluntary and informed consent has been obtained from the intended recipient/participant.[20] This means that the recipient/participant is, to some extent, responsible for ensuring that she is not abused by being involved in an overly risky experimental procedure or trial. If this is so, then, at the very least, 'extra care' should be taken when obtaining consent to treatment that has not been 'fully' tested, or tested at all, on humans,[21] because 'in the medical context, there are some things which are too risky for doctors to ask their patients to face, even if, *particularly if*, the patient might agree if she *was* asked'.[22] Nevertheless, given that it is legal to consent to high-risk sports such as boxing the courts are unlikely to prevent people receiving a procedure or participating in a trial which may benefit them and/or others, and which has been approved by the relevant bodies.[23] Thus, provided the xenotransplant experimental procedure or trial protocol has been appropriately approved, there appears to be no limit to the harm to which a competent and consenting adult can be exposed. However, since the benefits of solid organ xenotransplants are as speculative as the risks, the necessary threshold of benefit which must accompany any experimental or research procedure may not be met, *or be able to be met*.[24] It thus remains contested whether it is possible to obtain valid consent to such a solid organ xenotransplant.

A broad reading of the ability to consent to experimental procedures or trials respects the highly regarded right to self-determination and

---

[17] [1993] 2 All ER 75, 79 *per* Lord Templeman, HL.
[18] *Ibid.*, p. 103 *per* Lord Mustill; Law Commission, *Consent in the Criminal Law* Consultation Paper No. 139 (London: HMSO, 1995), para. 8.51.
[19] UKXIRA, *Guidance*, paras. 7.13–7.14.
[20] Exceptions include Fox, 'Clinical Research'. [21] Jackson, *Medical Law*, p. 441.
[22] C. Foster, *The Ethics of Medical Research on Humans* (Cambridge University Press, 2001), p. 61, emphasis in original.
[23] Montgomery, *Health Care Law*, pp. 362–3. [24] See Chapters 2 and 3.

autonomy of *individuals*, but should an individual be able to consent to being a xeno-recipient when this exposes *society* to risk? Those who interpret the consent process as giving voice to and protecting the autonomy of the individual will no doubt suggest that a negative response is paternalistic.[25] At first glance it is problematic to state that a competent individual who consents should not be allowed to expose herself to extreme risk, but xenotransplantation may also involve harming others. During the 1990s it was questioned whether the level of risk had diminished to such an extent that consenting to being a xeno-recipient would, at that point, be legal.[26] While awareness of the risks has increased since then, their nature and magnitude remain undetermined and may stay so until a human receives a genetically engineered solid organ xenotransplant. Evidence on the benefits is similarly partial and it may thus not be possible to provide legally valid consent because of the significant information gaps. Rather than focusing on ideas of autonomy of the individual, a more nuanced approach to autonomy is required[27] which recognises that we are not isolated individuals but are interconnected and responsible for ourselves *and* to others.[28] As such, is it and should it be legally and morally acceptable for an individual to consent to risks which may fall on her *and* on unasked, non-consenting others? Whether people are able to consent to involvement in certain types of experiments/trials may be a matter of public policy and public acceptability,[29] but in consenting to being a xeno-recipient the individual is merely volunteering to run risks *to herself*; her consent says nothing about exposing others to risks. What is at issue is how to balance the personal freedom to volunteer for a xenotransplant with ethical requirements such as justice, non-maleficence, beneficence and respect for persons.[30] Into this equation must be added the fact that the risks to the xeno-recipient personally may be great but the available information inadequate and speculative.[31]

---

[25] E.g. C. Gavaghan, *Defending the Genetic Supermarket: The Law and Ethics of Selecting the Next Generation* (Oxford: Routledge-Cavendish, 2007), esp. ch. 2.

[26] J.K. Mason, 'Organ Donation and Transplantation', in C. Dyer (ed.), *Doctors, Patients and the Law* (Oxford: Blackwell, 1992), pp. 120, 121–2.

[27] O'Neill, *Autonomy and Trust*; Manson and O'Neill, *Rethinking Informed Consent*.

[28] See, e.g., Mason and Laurie, *Mason & McCall Smith's*, ch. 1; C. Mackenzie and N. Stoljar (eds.), *Relational Autonomy: Feminist Perspectives on Autonomy, Agency and the Social Self* (New York, NY: Oxford University Press, 2000); A.V. Campbell, 'Dependency: The Foundational Value in Medical Ethics', in K.W.M. Fulford *et al.*, *Medicine and Moral Reasoning* (New York, NY: Cambridge University Press, 1994), p. 184.

[29] Montgomery, *Health Care Law*, pp. 362–3.

[30] E.g. CIOMS and WHO, *International Ethical*, General Ethical Principles; Australia – NHMRC *et al.*, *National Statement*, Section 1; Canada – Canadian Institutes *et al.*, *TCPS2*, ch. 1; US – National Commission, *Ethical Principles*, Part B.

[31] See Chapter 2.

The Declaration of Helsinki states that the 'predictable risks and burdens' of a trial procedure 'to the individuals and communities involved in the research' should be assessed and compared with the 'foreseeable benefits *to them and to other individuals or communities affected by the condition under investigation*'.[32] There is thus a sense that the effect that an experimental procedure or clinical trial can have on others should be considered when deciding whether to perform that procedure or trial, but only the effect to others with the same condition and not all others. However, the Declaration also states that 'medical research involving human subjects may only be conducted if the importance of the objective outweighs the inherent risks and burdens *to the research subjects*'.[33] Both the UK's 2004 Regulations and the GMC's guidelines emphasise the risks and benefits *to patients* alone.[34] The former specifically declare that '*[t]he rights, safety, and well-being of the trial subjects* are the most important considerations and *shall prevail over interests of science and society*'.[35] The Declaration states that where proven therapeutic methods are ineffective or do not exist, an unproven procedure can be used if informed consent is provided and if, in the physician's judgement, 'it offers hope of saving life, re-establishing health or alleviating suffering'.[36] As there have been no clinical genetically engineered solid organ xenotransplants, there is no evidence that such a xenotransplant will improve or enhance the recipient's quality of life or extend their prospects of survival. It is thus debatable whether 'therapeutic value', required under the Declaration when medical research is combined with medical care, can be provided.[37] Nevertheless, performing medical research combined with medical care is possible without a consideration of the impact of the decision to proceed on those other than the individual recipient/participant.

The lack of consensus in guidelines on the weight to be given to the needs and interests of the recipient/participant *and* others may be because few medical advances have highlighted the need for such a balance. However, developing biotechnologies such as xenotransplantation necessitate that this is addressed and attention has to be given to the

---

[32] WMA, *Declaration*, B18, emphasis supplied.
[33] *Ibid.*, B21, emphasis supplied.
[34] Sched. 1, Part 2, para. 2, 2004 Regulations, as amended; GMC, *Good Practice in Research*, para. 9.
[35] Sched. 1, Part 2, para. 3, 2004 Regulations, as amended, emphasis supplied. Similarly, WMA, *Declaration*, A6; International Conference, *ICH Harmonised*, para. 2.3.
[36] WMA, *Declaration*, C35, but there are different requirements in the 1996 Declaration and thus the UK's 2004 Regulations. See Chapter 3.
[37] WMA, *Declaration*, C31.

needs of those who will not personally receive the xenotransplant. Although value is rightly placed on individual autonomy there are situations in which other principles have and should take precedence; '[i]f our choices endanger the public health, potentially harm innocent others, or require a scarce resource for which no funds are available, others can justifiably restrict our exercises of autonomy'.[38] For xenotransplantation, the Council of Europe has stated that 'autonomy, privacy and confidentiality ... are never *absolute* obstacles and *communities* are entitled to limit them where there is *serious harm* to the individual concerned or *to other people. A high level of risk to public health would be considered an adequate ground for limiting these principles.*'[39] The world's experiences of swine flu during 2009 showed the devastating effect a pandemic might have,[40] albeit a viral pandemic of a different nature to that which may follow a genetically engineered solid organ xenotransplant to a human. Nevertheless, in the light of the significant (un)known risks, a precautionary approach is required and it must be considered whether individuals are and should be able to consent to xenotransplantation as an experimental procedure or a clinical trial because it should not be assumed that xenotransplantation *is* like any other developing biotechnology and can fit within existing legal and ethical norms and regulatory structures. The nature and magnitude of the risks mean that even if there are patients who are willing to consent to it, a wider conversation is needed as to whether this is morally and legally acceptable. As part of this, it is necessary to explore whether those considering receiving a genetically engineered solid organ xenotransplant will be able to fulfil the three legal requirements of valid consent and, if they can, whether this is appropriate to protect themselves and others. This is an important issue because pre-clinical work continues apace with suggestions of clinical trials in 2013,[41] and the appropriate legal and ethical safeguards must exist before this occurs in order to protect public health.

Requirements of valid consent

Questions of competency

There is little international and national legal and ethical guidance specifically on competence and experimental procedures and so it is assumed that guidance on competence and clinical trials and medical

---

[38] Beauchamp and Childress, *Principles*, p. 105.
[39] Council of Europe, *Report on the State*, para. 7.5.3, emphasis supplied.
[40] See Chapter 6.
[41] D.K.C. Cooper *et al.*, 'Recent Advances'; R.N. Pierson *et al.*, 'Current Status'.

treatment also applies to these procedures. For an individual's consent to a xenotransplant to be valid she must be competent to voluntarily give her informed consent to receive it. There is a statutory test for capacity in England and Wales, and to be deemed competent to consent a patient must be able to understand, retain, use or weigh the information relevant to the decision, and communicate her decision via means appropriate for her.[42] Failure to fulfil one or more of these requirements will mean she is not competent to consent. Elements two, three and four of the statutory test are perhaps more straightforward than the first, as it may be possible to assess if information has been retained, how the information is used or weighed by the patient, and communication can also be examined. The understanding element may be harder to determine and is complicated when experimental procedures or clinical trials are under consideration, particularly ones involving a developing biotechnology and where the proposed recipient/participant may be terminally ill with no other hope.

Can a xeno-recipient with no other hope be competent to consent to a clinical trial?

It is always difficult, if not impossible, to determine what another person has understood but for the first xeno-recipients who are likely to have no other hope, their understanding may be 'particularly fragile or open to question' because of the situation they are in.[43] Special care thus needs to be taken in ensuring their understanding of information relevant to their decision, and the Declaration of Helsinki suggests that this is an appropriate role for the doctor.[44] Regardless of whether doctors are qualified to undertake this task, under the UK's 2004 Regulations the participant should have an interview with the investigator or member of the investigating team and be given the '*opportunity* to understand the objectives, risks and inconveniences of the trial and the conditions under which it is to be conducted'.[45] Alongside these requirements and the

---

[42] Section 3(1) Mental Capacity Act (MCA) 2005, as amended by the Mental Health Act 2007. For Scotland, see Adults with Incapacity Act (Scotland) 2000. There is no equivalent statute for Northern Ireland.

[43] Pattinson, *Medical Law*, p. 379.

[44] 'After *ensuring* that the subject has understood the information, the physician or another appropriately qualified individual must then seek the potential subject's freely-given informed consent, preferably in writing' (WMA, *Declaration*, B24, emphasis supplied).

[45] Sched. 1, Part 3, para.1, 2004 Regulations, as amended; also, Australia – NHMRC *et al.*, *National Statement*, para. 2.2.4; Canada – Canadian Institutes *et al.*, *TCPS2*, Article 3.2; CIOMS and WHO, *International Ethical*, Guideline 5; International Conference, *ICH Harmonised*, para. 4.8; New Zealand – HRC, *Guidelines on Ethics*, para. 3.1; US – 45 CFR 46, § 46.116; National Commission, *Ethical Principles*, Part C1.

information specific to xenotransplants, the recipient will need to understand the subtle legal distinction between experimental procedures, clinical trials and medical treatment, and what this means in terms of the regulatory framework within which the xenotransplant will be performed.[46] This is important because of the risk of 'therapeutic misconceptions' where patients/participants assume that they have the same relationship with the investigator as they do with their doctor, and that the research is in fact *treatment*.[47] If they are asked by their doctor, who is also acting as or on behalf of the investigator, to take part in an experimental procedure or a clinical trial they may assume that their doctor is asking them to get involved because it will be of benefit *to them*, rather than obtaining information which may benefit others in future. Indeed, empirical research suggests that 'the mere suggestion of enrolment in research by a patient's personal physician was interpreted by many patients to be an endorsement'.[48] Injurious misconceptions may also develop where the patient/participant not only misunderstands the distinction between care and research, but also has an overstated sense of risk and threat.[49] These issues are relevant to the voluntariness of the decision to be involved in an experimental procedure or clinical trial and are discussed further below.

The first recipients of genetically engineered solid organs will need to understand that the treatment is experimental in that it has not previously been tested in humans and so its efficacy and implications for the xeno-recipient *and* others are unknown in the short, medium and long term. They must understand that because of the limited evidence on the risks they will be subject to lifelong surveillance of an extensive and intrusive nature.[50] This is important because traditionally involvement in an experimental procedure or a trial has a limited shelf life; at some point, the participant is 'free' of it and the regime proscribed under it. Xeno-recipients will never be in this position. While easy to agree to conditions when they have no other hope, the realities of doing so will be difficult to communicate and explain to recipients because those proposing the surveillance regime will also have limited knowledge

---

[46] See Chapter 3.
[47] P.S. Appelbaum, L.H. Roth and C.W. Lidz, 'The Therapeutic Misconception: Informed Consent in Psychiatric Research' (1982) 5 *International Journal of Law and Psychiatry* 319.
[48] N.E. Kass *et al.*, 'Trust – The Fragile Foundation of Contemporary Biomedical Research' (1996) 26 *Hastings Center Report* 25, 28.
[49] C. Snowdon *et al.*, 'Declining Enrolment in a Clinical Trial and Injurious Misconceptions: Is there a Flipside to the Therapeutic Misconception?' (2007) 2 *Clinical Ethics* 193, 199.
[50] See Chapter 6.

as to what exactly may be required, when and how often. At best, educated guesses can be made based on existing evidence and experience with other biotechnologies and infectious disease pandemics and epidemics. As the xeno-recipient who is asked to agree now to a xenotransplant and be monitored for the rest of her life, I agree to both because I have no other choice and monitoring will surely not be that onerous. This may be so until it is decided that, for example, weekly blood tests are required, *all* illnesses must be reported to my GP, and I am prohibited from having any more children 'just in case'; practically meaning either sterilisation, a contraceptive implant or an intra-uterine device until menopause. What if I am informed that I am to be quarantined until it is 'clear' that I pose no infectious risk or that this may occur if I become unwell? While xeno-recipients can be given a sense of what tests and/or restrictions may be required, will xeno-recipients with no other hope truly *understand* what is being asked of them, now and for ever?

Competency status of those with no other hope

It is questionable whether previous xeno-recipients were competent to give their informed consent because of their health status,[51] and the first xeno-recipients of genetically engineered solid organ xenotransplants are likely to be in a similar position, having no other hope. Issues of competency and understanding are exacerbated by their health status and while it is appreciated why those with no other hope might be willing to consent to an experimental procedure or clinical trial,[52] it is important to consider whether they are in fact competent to consent. One problem is that '[a] dying patient is frequently desperate, and a desperate individual does not always make decisions in the best interests of society at large or even of patients as a group. Desperate people do not even always make decisions that are in their own best interests.'[53] Those with incurable illnesses may, for example, accept untried 'treatments',[54] and concerns about how claims about such treatments are presented and reported have resulted in Sense About Science publishing a report addressing this.[55] The motivations of the first xeno-recipients are likely to be complex, but little attention has been paid to this. Where the chances of success are low and the risks unknown, consenting to involvement in

---

[51] Annas, 'Baby Fae'; Bailey *et al.*, 'Baboon-to-Human'.
[52] See Chapter 3.   [53] Cooper and Lanza, *Xeno*, p. 178.
[54] E.g. stem-cell 'therapy' for cerebellar atrophy (A. Hill, 'I know the risk. It's my only hope', *The Observer*, 16 December 2007).
[55] Sense About Science, *'I've Got Nothing to Lose By Trying It.' Weighing Up Claims about Cures and Treatments for Long-Term Conditions* (2010) (at: www.senseaboutscience.org.uk/index.php/site/project/267, accessed 21/03/11).

such a trial *could* be used as evidence that the xeno-recipient is 'desperately clutching at straws and incapable of making a rational choice'.[56] But *is it* irrational for desperate people to accept poor or low odds? Accepting high risks *may* be evidence of an 'impaired capacity to make rational choices', but a patient's competence should be judged on more than this.[57] Very ill patients with no other hope may legitimately refuse life-saving treatments, so why should they not be able to consent to receiving an experimental procedure or being involved in a clinical trial? At the same time, it is important to guard against the idea that '[t]he most expendable subjects of all are those already destined to die imminently',[58] and people who are facing death require particular protection from 'over-optimistic or reckless experiments'.[59] However, it could be viewed as discriminatory and unjust not to allow them the *chance* of helping themselves and/or others because '[t]here are a lot of things that people are willing to accept as risks in the setting of being desperate enough to be basically at the door of death'.[60]

A balance is thus required between the understandable eagerness of a patient with no other hope being involved in an experimental procedure or trial, and the fact that a seemingly competent xeno-recipient may be very ill with no other hope and so 'in such a nonautonomous situation that anything at this point appears to be more attractive than death'.[61] One way to avoid these issues is to seek consent *before* that patient is:

> not so ill (but on the waiting list for transplantation). They should be asked if they are interested in receiving a pig heart *if a human heart is not available and the situation is critical* ... the patients recruited to the study should feel certain that they will only be included in any clinical trial of xenotransplantation if a human heart is definitely not available.[62]

This would circumvent some of the concerns noted here, but raise other questions including, for example, whether if the science had progressed by the time the xenotransplant was required, the early consent provided when the patient was not so ill and based on a different level of information would still be operative? This is a criticism of all advance decisions

---

[56] Hughes, 'Xenografting', p. 20.   [57] *Ibid.*   [58] BMA, *Medical Profession*, p. 213.
[59] Nuffield Council, *Animal-to-Human*, para. 7.14.
[60] Organ Farm, 'Interview with Daniel R. Salomon' (2001) (at: www.pbs.org/wgbh/pages/frontline/shows/organfarm/interviews/salomon.html, accessed 21/03/11). See Chapter 3.
[61] A. Hastillo and M.L. Hess, 'Heart Xenografting: A Route Not Yet to Trod' (1993) 12 *Journal of Heart and Lung Transplantation* 3, 4. Arguing that those who are stressed *can* consent, see E. Jackson, 'The Donation of Eggs for Research and the Rise of Neopaternalism', in M. Freeman (ed.), *Law and Bioethics: Current Legal Issues 2008*, vol. 11 (Oxford University Press, 2008), p. 286.
[62] Welin and Sandrin, 'Some Ethical Problems', 501, emphasis in original.

and such decisions, in the UK at least, are only legally valid for advance refusals of treatment and not requests for or consent to future treatment.[63] While obtaining consent should be an iterative process and the original consent confirmed at the point of xenotransplant, this will do nothing to eradicate the concerns raised by asking those who are desperately ill to consent to such a procedure at the time when they have no other hope.

In the light of these issues it cannot and should not be automatically assumed that a patient with no other hope *is* competent to consent to an experimental treatment or involvement in a clinical trial. There needs to be a sensitive and careful exploration of her competency during the process of seeking her consent because although:

[t]he argument that a patient can make a choice and should be permitted to do so is powerful ... society in deciding how best to respond to it does need to incorporate the recognition that there are things worse than death – being made to die faster, being made to die more miserably or having ones dying prolonged but with no appreciable increase in quality of life or functionality.[64]

These tensions mean that it is also questionable whether consent given in this situation *will* be voluntarily and freely given as such patients may be 'particularly vulnerable to unrealistic enticements and manipulations of hope'.[65]

Voluntariness

There may always be doubt over the voluntary nature of consenting to an experimental procedure or clinical trial because '[n]o one acts in a vacuum and some decision-making contexts are inherently pressured';[66] this increases when patients are desperately ill and have no other options available to them. As such, it may be that 'adequately voluntary' consent is only ever possible, as long as it is provided without 'controlling influences' and the opportunity to be involved is, ideally, 'one of at least two options'.[67] The voluntariness of a decision to receive an experimental procedure or participate in a clinical trial may be affected not only by the health status of the patient, but also by the dual role of the doctor and the actual process of obtaining consent.

---

[63] Sections 24–26 MCA 2005.
[64] A. Caplan, 'Is It Sound Public Policy to Let the Terminally Ill Access Experimental Medical Innovations?' (2007) 7 *American Journal of Bioethics* 1, 3.
[65] R.M. Nelson and J.F. Merz, 'Voluntariness of Consent for Research: An Empirical and Conceptual Review' (2002) 40 *Medical Care* V-69, V-72.
[66] Pattinson, *Medical Law*, p. 137.
[67] S. Hewlett, 'Consent to Clinical Research – Adequately Voluntary or Substantially Influenced?' (1996) 22 *Journal of Medical Ethics* 232, 233.

Dual role

The importance and need for experimental procedures and clinical trials is not disputed, but there are some difficulties when the doctor has a dual role and these must be acknowledged and, where possible, addressed. Where the doctor is also the investigator three issues need attention: the focus of the doctor; conflicts of interests; and the patient's perceptions. These are, to some extent, intertwined but for the former most patients are aware that doctors are supposed to act with the therapeutic intention of benefiting and minimising any harm *to them*. With an experimental procedure or trial the 'physician-investigator'[68] might *hope* that the patient before them benefits, but she is also (more?) concerned with obtaining results which can be extrapolated and used to benefit *future* patients, *and* her own career interests. The physician-investigator may be focused on persuading the patient to consent to the experimental procedure or trial, but is it 'too selfish for a patient to expect her consultant to be solely concerned with *her* welfare . . . ? Total concern for *her* will seem to have been replaced by a concern for future generations.'[69] To counter this, recipients/participants should, at the very least, be reminded that they are receiving an experimental procedure or are part of a clinical trial, and the physician-investigator should disclose the fact that there might be a conflict between what is best for the protocol and the patient-recipient's best interests.[70]

Additionally, '[p]atients, particularly those with chronic or terminal illness place immense trust in the judgement of their doctors . . . The tendency to conflate treatment and research means that patients and doctors find it difficult to perceive their roles and relationships as materially difficult in these two situations.'[71] *All* patients are dependent on their doctor to some extent and this can affect the voluntariness of their consent; indeed, the Declaration of Helsinki states that where the 'potential subject is in a dependent relationship with the physician', 'the physician should be particularly cautious' and informed consent sought by an individual independent from the relationship.[72] The position of those who are highly dependent on medical care and may be unable to consent to involvement in research has also been considered in Australia and New Zealand and, in the former, the need to balance the risk of their being exploited by being involved in research with their

---

[68] Katz, 'Human Experimentation', 7.
[69] H. Thornton, 'Clinical Trials – A Brave New Partnership?' (1994) 20 *Journal of Medical Ethics* 19, 21, emphasis in original.
[70] Snyder and Leffler, 'Ethics Manual', 576.   [71] Kong, 'Regulation', 170–171.
[72] WMA, *Declaration*, B26; also, Australia – NHMRC *et al.*, *National Statement*, paras. 3.3.17, 4.3.9, 4.4.12; US – AMA, *Opinion 8.0315*, para. (3).

entitlement to be involved in research is noted, and three conditions must be met for their involvement to be approved, with four further conditions for terminal care research.[73] These include that the research is aimed at increasing understanding of or leading to improvements in the condition from which the patient is suffering, these possible benefits are such as to justify any risks, and not exaggerating the chance of benefiting from participation.[74] On seeking consent, 'steps should be taken to minimise the risk' that 'stress or emotional factors' may impair the patient's understanding and that dependency on those providing care 'may compromise the freedom of a decision to participate'.[75] Where a doctor has a dual role as physician-investigator, an independent person should seek consent, as I argue below.[76]

Those with this dual role will also have to deal with conflicts of interests between, not least, the interests of the patient before them, future patients, their employers and those funding the research.[77] While there will be a shared desire between the physician-investigator, patient and funders of the research for the procedure/trial to succeed, 'if risk estimation can influence perceptions of risk acceptability, then there is at least an apparent [conflict of interest] in allowing those who endorse the research to be the sole arbiters of its estimated risks'.[78] These possible tensions are identifiable in the initial allotransplants in the 1960s,[79] and although conflicts of interests may not be restricted to experimental procedures or clinical trials the research setting is unique so 'a strict borderline *has* to be maintained between the two professional roles of being a doctor and being a researcher'.[80] This is necessary because in asking patients to consent to such they may assume that it *will* benefit them, 'a professional recommendation',[81] otherwise why else would *their* doctor ask *them* to participate? Thus, '[g]ranting consent to go ahead with something as complex as a xenotransplant may boil down to a matter of trust between patient and surgeon',[82] and a patient may not

---

[73] NHMRC et al., *National Statement*, ch. 4.4, paras. 4.4.2, 4.4.1, 4.4.4; New Zealand – MH, *Operational Standard*, Appendix 5.
[74] NHMRC et al., *National Statement*, para. 3.3.9.   [75] *Ibid.*, paras. 3.3.16, 4.4.11.
[76] *Ibid.*, paras. 3.3.17, 4.4.12.
[77] K.C. Glass and T. Lemmens, 'Conflict of Interest and Commercialization of Biomedical Research', in T.A. Caulfield and B. Williams-Jones (eds.), *The Commercialization of Genetic Research: Ethical, Legal and Policy Issues* (New York, NY: Kluwer Academic Press, 1999), p. 79.
[78] Waring and Lemmens, 'Integrating Values', p. 182.
[79] Fox and Swazey, *Courage*, ch. 3.
[80] M.O. Hansson, 'Balancing the Quality of Consent' (1998) 24 *Journal of Medical Ethics* 182, 185, emphasis supplied.
[81] Katz, 'Human Experimentation', 29.   [82] Cooper and Lanza, *Xeno*, p. 208.

feel able to say no to her doctor as she wants to help and please her, and doctors need to be aware of this.[83] There may be limited opportunities to question their doctor about the procedure or trial, and trust may play such a central role in this relationship that it 'short-circuit[s] a consent policy founded upon individuals making as rational a choice as possible on the basis of complete information as possible under the circumstances'.[84] Patients may also develop therapeutic misconceptions that it is treatment not research or that the procedure or drug *will* benefit them, *because of* the trust they have in the medical professional generally and their own doctors in particular.[85] These may develop because of the difficulties doctors face in explaining, and patients in understanding, the important but subtle differences between medical treatment, experimental procedures and clinical trials. Empirical studies have suggested that for those involved in research there is a 'theme of hope ... often wedded to despair' because their involvement was preceded by failed standard interventions so that 'they viewed the investigational "treatment" as a last hope for improvement or amelioration of their conditions'.[86]

In the UK the BMA's Working Party on Consent recognised some of these issues and noted that '[p]atients may be too intimidated to raise questions with doctors. Lack of knowledge about the proposed treatment can also mean that patients are not in a position to formulate pertinent questions.'[87] If so, surely '[c]onsent by patients in clinical research must often be only partially voluntary, because it lies within the context of illness or the doctor–patient relationship. The duty of health care professionals is to ensure that partially voluntary consent is *adequately* voluntary'.[88] However, as doctors control the decision-making process with regard to research, if the ideology of medical professionalism is imported into this context this 'permits *not* fully informing patient-subjects about uncertainties and risks inherent in clinical research on grounds of beneficence which physicians traditionally invoke for clinical practice'.[89] Information issues are considered below and, at the very least, patients should be told that their physician-investigator has a dual role with divided loyalties and that their

---

[83] On why patients participate in trials, see, e.g., P.R. Ferguson, 'Human "Guinea Pigs": Why Patients Participate in Clinical Trials', in S.A.M. McLean (ed.), *First Do No Harm – Law, Ethics and Healthcare* (Aldershot: Ashgate, 2006), p. 165.
[84] C.L. Bosk, 'Obtaining Voluntary Consent', V-64.
[85] Above, n. 47; Kass *et al*., 'Trust'. [86] Kass *et al*., 'Trust', 25, references removed.
[87] BMA, *Report of the Consent Working Party: Incorporating Consent Toolkit* (London: BMA, 2001), p. 7.
[88] Hewlett, 'Consent to Clinical Research', 236, emphasis supplied.
[89] Katz, 'Human Experimentation', 20, emphasis supplied.

focus may be more on future patients than the individual in front of them.[90] Such disclosure is necessary because when their doctor asks them to consent to a novel, untried and untested procedure this may unduly influence the patient to accede to the request. As 'investigators often look more like clinicians, than scientists. They wear white coats, work in hospitals, perform medical tests, and provide medications',[91] it is vital that their dual role and different professional perspectives and tensions are explained. The inherent conflicts and power imbalance in this situation are obvious and must be addressed. The process of obtaining consent, who asks a patient if they want to be involved, and how information is framed and presented are thus crucial.

Obtaining consent

There may be problems in obtaining consent to new medical treatments from patients who may be vulnerable due to their condition, dependency or desperation for *any* treatment or hope. These are exacerbated in an experimental procedure or clinical trial situation, particularly where the potential recipients are required to understand complex issues including the lack of information about risks and benefits, and that the risks go beyond the individual. These complexities are highlighted when the doctor has a dual role and so the process of obtaining consent assumes greater importance. The possibility of undue influence and exploitation from physician-investigators, family members or other health professionals must be acknowledged, and two inextricably linked issues addressed. First, *who* poses the question about involvement is important because of the existing doctor–patient relationship, and the *doctor's* role of benefiting *that* patient and an *investigator's* focus on benefiting *others*. The power (im)balance in the traditional doctor–patient relationship is exacerbated where a doctor is proposing to perform an experimental procedure or involve a patient in a clinical trial, '[b]ecause many patients are often fearful and unequal to their physicians in status, knowledge and power, they may be particularly susceptible to manipulations of this type'.[92] Careful thought must thus be given to who raises questions about involvement, presents the required information, and seeks consent from

---

[90] WMA, *Declaration*, B24; CIOMS and WHO, *International Ethical*, Guideline 5.
[91] D. Wendler and C. Grady, 'What Should Research Participants Understand to Understand that They Are Participants in Research?' (2008) 22 *Bioethics* 203, 206.
[92] President's Commission for the Study of Ethical Problems in Medicine and Biomedical and Behavioral Research, *Making Health Care Decisions: The Ethical and Legal Implications of Informed Consent in the Patient–Practitioner Relationship, Volume One: Report* (Washington, DC: President's Commission for the Study of Ethical Problems in Medicine and Biomedical and Behavioral Research, 1982), p. 67.

patients. Many UK RECs may request that, where practicable, consent is obtained by someone independent from the research team to address these issues. However, this is not currently mandatory, but should be. In some respects, then, the 'who' can be more easily addressed than the 'how' information is presented. Those seeking consent should 'share information in a way that the patient can understand',[93] but this may not be as straightforward as it sounds because '[i]f desperate patients come in search of help, and an investigational intervention is available that is targeted for their condition, it is very difficult to present information about the risk and value of the intervention without in some way stimulating patients' hope'.[94] Is it possible to 'objectively' provide the necessary information on the matters raised by xenotransplantation as 'it is difficult to present a highly complex subject, particularly in the early stages of development, to patients and expect them to fully comprehend what they are agreeing to'?[95] If the information is being provided by those invested (professionally, financially, personally, emotionally) in the procedure, it will be even harder to present information 'in an objective way to persons who are made vulnerable to hearing only good news by their very plight'.[96]

Thus, and the second issue, the *way* in which information is presented can influence and affect the decision of those interpreting it because it:

can powerfully affect the recipient's response to it. The tone of voice and other aspects of the practitioner's manner of presentation can indicate whether a risk of a particular kind with a particular incidence should be considered serious. Information can be emphasized or played down without altering the content. And it can be framed in a way that affects the listener – for example, 'this procedure succeeds most of the time' versus 'this procedure has a 40 per cent failure rate'.[97]

As a minimum, when obtaining consent to an experimental procedure or clinical research there is 'an obligation to translate scientific information into language which is relevant to patient-subjects' life and interests'.[98] Language and the presentation of information are central aspects of informed decision-making and although it may be difficult to present medical information to those without medical training, this is not an

---

[93] GMC, *Consent*, para. 18.   [94] Kass *et al.*, 'Trust', 27.
[95] Cooper and Lanza, *Xeno*, p. 207. On involving psychologists in devising ways to present and provide information, see G. Kent, 'Shared Understandings for Informed Consent: The Relevance of Psychological Research on the Provision of Information' (1996) 43 *Social Science and Medicine* 1517.
[96] Caplan, 'Is It Sound?', p. 2.
[97] President's Commission, *Making Health Care Decisions*, p. 67.
[98] Katz, 'Human Experimentation', 36.

excuse for not providing it as 'no condition is so complex that it cannot be explained in simple, intelligible language. To clothe illness in unintelligible terminology only increases the patient's anxiety.'[99] Those seeking to obtain consent must provide information in the most accessible format possible and be imaginative because the order in which information is given, for example, can influence its interpretation and the decisions which are conditional on it.[100] Not only do 'people process medical information given to them in ways that often do not follow the expectation of the person supplying the information', but 'information is mediated through a range of socio-economic factors such as educational level, class, race, and gender'.[101] Patients may thus not respond to information provided in 'rational' or expected ways. Perhaps because of this it has been claimed that patients misunderstand information and are unable to recall what has been provided to them, thus there is little point in disclosing information to them.[102] This has been contested,[103] and current thinking is that potential participants should be provided with an 'adequate opportunity to ask questions about the study, before agreeing to participate'.[104] Such space is particularly crucial with a biotechnology as complex and complicated as xenotransplantation, as the UKXIRA recognised.[105]

Some of these issues have been recognised by professional and regulatory bodies,[106] and the UK's GMC guidance on consent notes the importance of the doctor–patient relationship being 'a partnership based on openness, trust and good communication' with 'each person [having] a role to play in making decisions about treatment or care'.[107]

---

[99] H.L. Blumgart, 'The Medical Framework for Viewing the Problem of Human Experimentation' (1969) 98 *Daedalus* 248, 255.

[100] For examples of different ways to provide information about risk and the problems of so doing for treatment, see C. Breitsameter, 'Medical Decision-Making and Communication of Risks: An Ethical Perspective' (2010) 36 *Journal of Medical Ethics* 349; Edwards and Elwyn, 'Understanding Risk'.

[101] S. Guttmacher, 'HIV Infection: Individual Rights v. Disease Control' (1990) 17 *Journal of Law and Society* 66, 74.

[102] Beauchamp and Childress, *Principles*, pp. 127–131; A.J. Lloyd, 'The Extent of Patients' Understanding of the Risk of Treatments' (2001) 10 (suppl. I) *Quality in Health Care* i14.

[103] Discussed in P.R. Ferguson, 'Patients' Perceptions of Information Provided in Clinical Trials' (2002) 28 *Journal of Medical Ethics* 45.

[104] *Ibid.*, p. 48. [105] UKXIRA, *Draft Report*, A5.8.

[106] Australia – NHMRC *et al.*, *National Statement*, ch. 2.2, paras. 3.3.13, 5.2.16, 5.2.17; Canada – Canadian Institutes *et al.*, *TCPS2*, Article 3.2; New Zealand – Code of Health and Disability Services Consumers' Rights, Right 5 (at: www.hdc.org.nz/media/24833/brochure-code-white.pdf, accessed 21/03/11); UK – RCP, *Guidelines*, para. 2.39; US – 45 CFR 46, §46.116.

[107] GMC, *Consent*, para. 3.

Information should be 'share[d] in a way that the patient can understand', giving them time to reflect before and after making a decision, involving other members of the healthcare team where appropriate, and encouraging patients to ask questions.[108] Information should be given 'in a balanced way', patients' understanding of it checked, as should whether they would like more before making a decision, or whether they need additional support to understand it.[109] With regard to risk, information should be 'clear [and] accurate', provided according to the individual patient, using 'clear, simple and consistent language'.[110] Again, patients' understanding should be checked, and 'simple and accurate written information or visual or other aids' used to explain risk if this will help their understanding.[111] In devising written information for patients, material provided by the Plain English Campaign, for example, may be of use.[112] The effect of the health status of potential xeno-recipients on their competence has been noted, but if it is determined that a patient with no other hope is competent to consent their thinking may still be 'frequently impaired and partially compromised, thus necessitating sensitive and responsive information giving processes'.[113] These issues are not confined to xenotransplants, but focusing on this developing biotechnology highlights the need to re-evaluate the *process* of obtaining consent, particularly with regard to an experimental procedure or a clinical trial, to minimise some of the concerns highlighted here. Even if this occurs, the limited information currently available on some aspects of xenotransplantation (see Chapter 2) means that the possibility of providing *informed* consent needs exploring.

Informed decision-making

The amount of information a xeno-recipient receives is important because she can only give her valid consent if she has been informed of the risks and benefits, and who decides how much information is disclosed and what should be disclosed, generally and for xenotransplants, are significant. As with consent and competency, there are no UK cases on information disclosure and experimental procedures or clinical trials but the common law on information and medical treatment presumably also applies to these, very different, situations.

---

[108] *Ibid.*, paras. 10, 18, also, 28.   [109] *Ibid.*, paras. 11, 18, 21, 33.
[110] *Ibid.*, paras. 28, 30, 34.   [111] *Ibid.*, para. 34.
[112] www.plainenglish.co.uk, accessed 21/03/11.   [113] Price, 'Remodelling', p. 137.

Who decides what should be disclosed?

In the UK a professional standard of information disclosure applies in the context of medical advice, diagnosis and treatment; doctors essentially decide what and how much a patient should be told, and failing to meet this standard could lead to a claim in negligence.[114] The courts retain the ultimate responsibility for determining the standard of care in negligence, and although the courts could challenge whether a body of medical opinion was responsible, in the majority of cases expert opinion would be likely to support the 'reasonableness of that opinion'.[115] It was unclear whether the latter applied to information disclosure as this was specifically excluded from Lord Browne-Wilkinson's consideration in *Bolitho*,[116] but the Court of Appeal has held that 'if there is a significant risk which would affect the judgement of a *reasonable patient*, then in the normal course it is the responsibility of a doctor to inform the patient of that significant risk, if the information is needed so that the patient can determine for him or herself as to what course he or she should adopt'.[117] 'Significant risk' was not defined and 'it is not possible to talk in precise percentages',[118] but in *Fitzpatrick* v. *White*, an Irish case, it was said that 'significant' and 'material' are interchangeable.[119] This has not been judicially approved in England and Wales and is academically debated.[120] It is especially disappointing that in the experimental procedure and clinical trial context this key issue remains undefined because there are issues which a specific individual may place weight on because of their particular circumstances. Indeed, as the GMC recognises, physician-investigators need to be aware that information which may seem irrelevant to them may be highly pertinent to the patient,[121] as 'the only judge of what is "grave" or "adverse" can be the patient'.[122] Nevertheless, English

---

[114] *Sidaway* v. *Bethlem Royal Hospital Governors and others* [1985] 1 All ER 643, HL adopting the decision in *Bolam* v. *Friern Hospital Management Committee* [1957] 2 All ER 118.
[115] *Bolitho* v. *City and Hackney Health Authority* [1997] 4 All ER 771, 779, HL *per* Lord Browne-Wilkinson.
[116] *Ibid.*
[117] *Pearce* v. *United Bristol Healthcare NHS Trust* [1999] PIQR 53, 59, *per* Lord Woolf MR. Emphasis supplied.
[118] *Ibid.* [119] [2008] 3 IR 551, para. 35 *per* Kearns J.
[120] Supporting this interpretation see, e.g., J. Miola, 'On the Materiality of Risk: Paper Tigers and Panaceas' (2009) 17 *Medical Law Review* 76, 98. Maclean has, however, argued that a significant risk is one that might change the patient's mind – it is significant to that patient (A. Maclean, 'Giving the Reasonable Patient a Voice: Information Disclosure and the Relevance of Empirical Evidence' (2005) 7 *Medical Law International* 1, 7–10).
[121] GMC, *Consent*, para. 8; also, paras. 5, 7, 9, 31.
[122] Kennedy and Grubb, *Medical Law*, p. 693.

law only requires that materiality is viewed from the perspective of the reasonable, and not the particular, patient. The UK's 2004 Regulations do, however, make it clear that ethics committees have a key role in determining 'the adequacy and completeness of the written information to be given, and the procedure to be followed for the purpose of obtaining informed consent'.[123]

What should be disclosed?

Legal guidance in the UK on the amount of information to disclose (significant risks) is limited, with the 2004 Regulations stating that the potential participant should be informed 'of the nature, significance, implications and risks of the trial'.[124] Article 5 of the European Convention on Human Rights and Biomedicine requires disclosure of 'appropriate information' on the purpose, nature, consequences and risks,[125] and the 2005 Additional Protocol to the Convention emphasised the importance of giving 'adequate information in a comprehensible form'.[126] This should cover 'the purpose, the overall plan and the possible risks and benefits ... and ... the opinion of the ethics committee'.[127] Participants should be 'specifically informed' about seven issues, including the nature, extent, duration and burdens of the procedures and project, and 'arrangements to ensure respect for private life',[128] and information to be provided to the ethics committee is also described.[129] The UK has not signed or ratified the Convention or the Additional Protocol, so these are of limited value within this jurisdiction. The physician-investigator wanting to perform an experimental procedure or clinical trial is thus, essentially, in control of what and how much information is disclosed. In deciding this they may rely on their professional judgement, and international and national non-statutory professional and ethical codes may guide them. However, the Declaration of Helsinki is as vague as the law in the UK, requiring participants to be 'adequately informed' of the aims, methods, anticipated benefits and risks, sources of funding, possible conflicts of interest, the investigator's

---

[123] Reg. 15(5)(g), 2004 Regulations, as amended. Similarly, Australia – NHMRC *et al.*, *National Statement*, paras. 5.2.16–5.2.17; Canada – Canadian Institutes *et al.*, *TCPS2*, Article 3.2; New Zealand – MH, *Operational Standard*, para. 134; HRC, *Guidelines on Ethics*, para. 3.1; US – 45 CFR 46, § 46.109.

[124] Sched. 1, Part 1, para. 3(1)(a), 2004 Regulations, as amended.

[125] Convention for the Protection of Human Rights and Dignity of the Human Being with regard to the Application of Biology and Medicine (Convention on Human Rights and Biomedicine (1997) ETS no. 164).

[126] Additional Protocol to the Convention on Human Rights and Biomedicine, concerning Biomedical Research, Article 13(1).

[127] *Ibid.*, Article 13(2). [128] *Ibid.* [129] *Ibid.*, Appendix.

institutional affiliations and 'any other relevant aspects of the study'.[130] In contrast, the CIOMS and WHO guidelines list twenty-six pieces of information which should be disclosed, and the ICH Harmonised Tripartite Guideline twenty.[131]

Nationally, the UK's DH notes that the common law applies to treatment and research, and states that if an experimental procedure is being offered not as part of a research trial this must be explained before consent is sought and information on standard alternatives provided.[132] It would also be good practice to give information about the national and international evidence on the effectiveness of the experimental procedure and in the practitioner's experience, including known possible side effects.[133] The National Research Ethics Service (NRES) and RCP have published guidance on information sheets which can be used as part of the consent process, including how to design these sheets and examples of the types of information which should be disclosed.[134] The GMC's 2008 consent guidance sets out more extensive provisions with regard to providing information on treatment than the common law,[135] and the principles outlined therein 'apply more widely, including decisions on taking part in research'.[136] Twelve pieces of information are listed which a patient may 'want or need' to know,[137] but beyond making clear that the 'proposed investigation or treatment is part of a research programme or is an innovative treatment designed specifically for their benefit' and how it differs from usual methods, why it is being offered, and additional risks or uncertainties,[138] information disclosure for experimental procedures is not directly addressed.[139] This is surprising as 'innovative treatments designed to benefit individual patients' are not covered by the GMC's 2010 guidance on research as these 'treatments' are said to be covered by the 2008 consent guidance.[140] Sharing information is emphasised in the 2008 guidance, and '[h]ow much information you share with patients will vary, depending on their individual circumstances'.[141] Assumptions should not be made about how much and what

---

[130] WMA, *Declaration*, B24.
[131] CIOMS and WHO, *International Ethical*, Guideline 5; International Conference, *ICH Harmonised*, para. 4.8.10.
[132] DH, *Reference Guide*, paras. 39–40.   [133] *Ibid.*, para. 40.
[134] National Research Ethics Service (NRES), *Information Sheets & Consent Forms: Guidance for Researchers and Reviewers* (London: NRES, 2009), Section. 6; RCP, *Guidelines*, paras. 5.46–5.58.
[135] S. Fovargue and J. Miola, 'One Step Forward, Two Steps Back?: The GMC, the Common Law and "Informed" Consent' (2010) 36 *Journal of Medical Ethics* 494.
[136] GMC, *Consent*, p. 4.   [137] *Ibid.*, para. 9.   [138] *Ibid.*, para. 9(f) n. 4.
[139] GMC, *Consent*, para. 9(f).   [140] GMC, *Good Practice in Research*, para. 4.
[141] GMC, *Consent*, para. 7.

information a person may want or need, 'the clinical or other factors the patient might consider significant', or their knowledge or understanding of what is proposed.[142] The BMA refers health professionals to the GMC consent guidance,[143] states that providing 'sufficient accurate information' is essential to seeking consent,[144] and that in the research context it is preferable for information to be written.[145] Six pieces of information to be provided are set out, and an REC should approve this written information in advance.[146] The RCP also stresses that 'adequate or sufficient information' is required as it is impractical to give 'full information';[147] but neither the BMA nor the RCP specifically consider consenting to experimental procedures. NICE has produced a leaflet for patients who may be offered procedures which NICE has declared to have uncertain risks and benefits, and this may apply to some experimental procedures. Eight questions are listed that a patient might want to ask health professionals before agreeing to such a procedure, including what it involves, the benefits and chances of them benefiting, the risks and their extent, nature and likelihood of occurring, and the alternatives.[148]

In contrast, in other jurisdictions attention has been paid to providing information on experimental procedures and for clinical trials. Thus, physician-investigators following the American Medical Association guidelines should disclose their intention to use an experimental procedure, give a 'reasonable explanation' of the nature of it, expected risks and possible benefits, and offer to answer any questions.[149] They should disclose any alternatives, be 'completely objective' when discussing the details of the procedure, the anticipated pain and discomfort, 'known risks and possible hazards', expected quality of life, persuasion should not be used, and unjustifiable expectations not unreasonably or unrealistically encouraged.[150] Where the experimental procedure is the 'only potential treatment' and 'full disclosure' of information on the nature or risks of it 'would pose such a psychological threat of detriment to the patient as to be medically contraindicated' that information may be withheld from the patient.[151] For clinical trials, it must be disclosed that an investigational procedure is to be used, 'a reasonable explanation' of the nature of it and expected risks provided, and the physician-investigator should offer to

---

[142] Ibid., para. 8.
[143] BMA, Consent Tool Kit (5th edn, London: BMA, 2009), Card 2, para. 2.
[144] Ibid., para. 1.   [145] Ibid., Card 10, para. 2.   [146] Ibid.
[147] RCP, Guidelines, para. 5.23.
[148] NICE, Consent – Procedures for which the Benefits and Risks are Uncertain (London: NICE, 2003), p. 7.
[149] AMA, Opinion 2.07, para. (4)(b).   [150] Ibid.   [151] Ibid., para. (4)(b)(i).

Requirements of valid consent

answer any questions about it.[152] The federal regulations make no distinction between experimental procedures and clinical trials, and eight pieces of information are set out as the basic elements of informed consent, with six additional elements to be provided when appropriate.[153] It is, however, unclear whether these regulations apply to experimental procedures as it has been suggested that if a surgeon does not label her innovative surgery as research she is under no legal obligation to disclose the nature of the procedure to the patient, regardless of whether it is untested, but that if the procedure is designated 'research' informed consent is required.[154]

The Australian NHMRC sets out thirteen pieces of information which should be communicated so that the decision to participate is based on 'sufficient information and adequate understanding' of the research and implications of participation.[155] For clinical trials it should be made clear whether there is any intended benefit to the participant, and whether the procedure is 'innovative and/or experimental'.[156] In Canada 'full disclosure of all information necessary for making an informed decision to participate' must occur, and this includes twelve pieces of information, but there is no specific reference to experimental procedures.[157] Similarly, fifteen pieces of information are listed by the New Zealand Ministry of Health to be provided to all research participants so that 'adequate information is provided to enable an informed judgement to be made'.[158] Although the standard contains a specific section on 'innovative practice' no additional information is required for those considering receiving such practices; rather, seventeen pieces of information should be provided to an ethics committee in this situation.[159] Additionally, under Right 6 of the Code of Health and Disability Services Consumers' Rights 'every consumer has the right to the information that a reasonable consumer, in that consumer's circumstances would expect to receive', including seven pieces of information. Patients can only receive health care procedures if they have made 'an informed choice' and informed consent to research or experimental procedures must be written.[160]

It does not, of course, matter *how many* pieces of information guidelines suggest should be disclosed, as *what* is provided and the *quality* of it

---

[152] *Ibid.*, para. (5)(b).   [153] 45 CFR 46, § 46.116(a)–(b).
[154] Ahmed, 'Last Twist', 1540.
[155] NHMRC *et al.*, *National Statement*, paras. 2.2.1, 2.2.6.
[156] *Ibid.*, paras. 3.3.14–3.3.15.
[157] Canada – Canadian Institutes *et al.*, *TCPS2*, Article 3.2.
[158] MH, *Operational Standard*, paras. 29–30.   [159] *Ibid.*, para. 135.
[160] *Ibid.*, Right 7.

is crucial. However, despite existing guidance in the UK and some other jurisdictions, it remains unclear *what* should be disclosed to potential recipients/participants of experimental procedures and clinical trials. At the very least, they should be told that the procedure is experimental or that they are involved in a clinical trial, as to do otherwise would be negligent for failing to disclose a material fact.[161] Beyond this, investigators have wide discretion on disclosure, which is worrying with a developing biotechnology such as xenotransplantation because of the nature and magnitude of the risks.

What should be disclosed to xeno-recipients?
In the UK's DH report on xenotransplantation it was recommended that seven issues needed to be disclosed so that xeno-recipients were 'properly informed', including the current status of clinical and pre-clinical xenotransplantation, infection risks, alternatives and 'such information [on the nature of the procedure] as enables the patient to make a personal decision about the acceptability of xeno-transplantation'.[162] The Nuffield Council was also concerned that patients gave 'properly informed consent' based on 'proper information', but noted that there were two particular problems for consent and xenotransplantation, discussed below.[163] Patients should be made aware of the experimental nature of the biotechnology, 'an estimation of likely success, attendant risks and subsequent quality of life', the need for post-xenotransplant monitoring and that consent to the xeno-transplant includes consent to this.[164] UKXIRA's 1998 guidance on information provision for investigators stated that '[it] will wish to be satisfied that: ... the patient will be informed of the procedures involved at all stages (that is, *sufficient information* will be given to the patient to enable consent to be based on an appreciation and understanding of the relevant facts)'.[165] 'Sufficient information' appears to mean details being given in the application of the information to be provided to the recipient and her contacts, how it will be provided, and details of any post-xenotransplant regimes for the recipient and her contacts.[166] In an Annex to the 1999 draft surveillance report, it was again stated that 'patients must receive *sufficient information* to enable them to reach a balanced judgement before valid consent can be given

---

[161] Jackson, *Medical Law*, p. 441.
[162] DH, *Animal Tissue*, para. 7.11; also, paras. 7.12–7.13.
[163] Nuffield Council, *Animal-to-Human*, paras. 7.15–7.16.
[164] *Ibid.*, paras. 7.18–7.19; also, para. 7.20.
[165] UKXIRA, *Guidance*, para. 7.13, emphasis supplied.   [166] *Ibid.*, paras. 7.16–7.17.

to a procedure. UKXIRA would expect to see a *very high standard of information* supplied to the patients to ensure they are advised about *all the material foreseeable risks* in a way that they can use in their decision-making.'[167] The xeno-recipient must consent explicitly and in advance to the xenotransplant *and* a post-xenotransplant surveillance regime, with contacts consenting to some monitoring, and '[t]he UKXIRA will expect to see evidence of a *well prepared* programme to inform and prepare patients and their close contacts for the realities of the procedure and the follow-up programme'.[168] These key phrases are not defined so xeno-investigators can, essentially, determine what and how much to disclose. This minimal guidance contrasts unfavourably with that provided by the UK's GTAC which has long set out the information to be provided to those considering involvement in gene therapy trials, including the content of participant information sheets.[169] In not adopting a similar approach, the UKXIRA permitted the (im)balance of power to move further away from the xeno-recipient and this delegation of responsibility did not appropriately protect the interests and well-being of those involved.

Despite UKXIRA's dissolution in December 2006, its guidance remains valid,[170] but there are now three routes through which a xenotransplant may be performed in the UK.[171] First, as a clinical trial under the UK's 2004 Regulations. The xeno-recipient must thus be informed of the 'nature, significance, implications and risks of the trial',[172] *and* the investigator must comply with either the NRES guidance on consent and information sheets or that of the GTAC, whichever is relevant.[173] NRES has produced a comprehensive (196-page) document on information sheets noting that 'one size will not fit all' and discussing length, language and writing style, and the presentation of the sheets.[174] Part 1 should set out the study title, an invitation paragraph, and address fifteen questions or issues, including the purpose of the study, why they have been invited, whether they have to take part, and what will happen if they do, alternatives, risks and benefits.[175] In Part 2 a further eleven questions or issues should be discussed, including withdrawing from the study, what happens if there is a problem, confidentiality, and what

---

[167] UKXIRA, *Draft Report*, A5.4, emphasis supplied.   [168] *Ibid.*, emphasis supplied.
[169] GTAC, *Guidance on the Content of a Proposal and Participant Information Sheets* (London: DH, 2009).
[170] See Chapter 4.   [171] DH, *Xenotransplantation*, pp. 2–3. Discussion in Chapter 3.
[172] Sched. 1, Part 1, para. 3(1)(a), 2004 Regulations, as amended.
[173] NRES, *Information Sheets*; GTAC, *Guidance on the Content*.
[174] NRES, *Information Sheets*, paras. 5.1.2–5.1.5, and Section 5 generally.
[175] *Ibid.*, paras. 6.1.2–6.1.7, 6.1.10–6.1.12, 6.1.15, and Section 6 generally.

174 Challenges to legal and ethical norms

happens to any samples provided.[176] An example of a consent form is also provided.[177] The GTAC guidance was written specifically for gene therapy trials and requires that '[t]he detailed arrangements for the clinical and technical procedures involved in the research should be specified in the study protocol ... [including] an outline of the clinical procedures and the tests used to monitor the patient'.[178] Eleven headings are set out to structure the proposal, including objectives and rationale, risk/benefit, prior studies, criteria for inclusion/exclusion and monitoring.[179] The proposal must also 'detail the arrangements for informing prospective subjects ... about the research before seeking consent to take part in the study'.[180] The GTAC must see copies of the patient information leaflets; a 'simple introductory document' explaining the aims, objectives and what is proposed in 'non-technical language'.[181] There must also be arrangements for providing further written and/or oral information, with investigators referred to the NRES website for advice on preparing 'clear patient information material'.[182] Further guidance on writing information leaflets for gene therapy research participants is provided, some of which may be relevant to solid organ xeno-recipients, but it is unclear whether these paragraphs must be complied with in the xenotransplant context.[183]

The second route for performing a xenotransplant in the UK is as research not under the 2004 Regulations, and again NRES or GTAC guidance, as appropriate, must be adhered to. Finally, if the xenotransplant is classified as experimental medicine the relevant Trust's CGC must approve it and notify the Interventional Procedures Programme at NICE if the procedure is not already listed by NICE.[184] If a xenotransplant is performed under the first two routes, investigators now have more general guidance on what to disclose to xeno-recipients and non-compliance with such will lead to rejection of the proposal by the NRES or GTAC. However, it is unclear whether this is the case for xenotransplantation as experimental medicine, as NICE's Interventional Procedures Programme merely states that 'all patients offered the procedure [should be] made aware of the special status of the procedure and the lack of experience of its use. This should be done as part of the consent process and should be clearly recorded.'[185] Each Trust's CGC may also have its own guidance on information provision, and inconsistency and

---

[176] Ibid., paras. 6.2.2–6.2.4, 6.2.6.   [177] Ibid., p. 28.
[178] GTAC, Guidance on the Content, para. 01.   [179] Ibid., paras. 03–29.
[180] Ibid., para. 30.   [181] Ibid., para. 31.   [182] Ibid.   [183] Ibid., paras. 59–91.
[184] DH, Xenotransplantation, p. 3.
[185] HSC 2003/011, para. 8.

uncertainty may thereby be introduced. Crucially, *none* of the three routes require consent to, and compliance with, a post-xenotransplant surveillance regime.

Elsewhere, one of the proposed guidelines of the Australian NHMRC's Xenotransplantation Working Party required a xenotransplant research protocol to include 'clear patient information sheets' to enable patients to make an informed decision, procedures which would ensure that '*appropriate information*' was provided, and the need for ongoing long-term surveillance for recipients and others made clear.[186] The Council of Europe has stated that recipients should be '*adequately informed* in a comprehensible manner of the nature, objectives, possible benefits, potential risks and consequences of the procedure, as well as of any constraints that may be linked to it'.[187] Eight items were listed for the recipient to be informed of for post-xenotransplant monitoring, along with provisions relating to the information to be provided to their contacts and health professionals.[188] The Health Council of the Netherlands recognised the 'right to information' with xeno-recipients informed of the nature, consequences, risks and 'other relevant matters in a way which is clear and comprehensible to the individuals in question'.[189] Guideline 8 of the New Zealand HRC's guidance sets out nine 'points for consideration' on informed consent, derived from US FDA documents, including potential and 'specific desired' benefits, risks, subsequent treatment options and the need for lifelong monitoring.[190] Whereas the Swedish Committee's report states that informed consent 'requires special work as regards the content of the information and as regards the procedure surrounding how the information is presented and consent obtained',[191] the French CCNE did not view xenotransplantation as raising different consent issues from allotransplantation apart from the need for 'detailed and prolonged epidemiological monitoring'.[192] This must be specifically consented to and patients '*completely informed*' of the experimental nature of xenotransplantation, the phases, risks and alternatives.[193] In contrast, in Canada the need for specific xenotransplant informed consent requirements, information on minimising disease transmission, insurance and

---

[186] NHMRC, XWP, *Guidelines for Clinical*, Guideline 6, accompanying NHMRC, XWP, *Animal-to-Human Transplantation: Final Report*, emphasis supplied. Guideline 7 speaks of '*necessary information*'.
[187] Council of Europe, Recommendation Rec(2003)10, Article 13(1), emphasis supplied.
[188] *Ibid.*, Articles 13(2), 14–15.   [189] Health Council, *Xenotransplantation*, p. 43.
[190] HRC, *Guidelines for Preparation*, Guideline 8.
[191] Swedish Committee, *From One Species*, p. 16.
[192] CCNE, *Opinion on Ethics*, pp. 7–8.   [193] *Ibid.*, emphasis supplied.

employment implications, and long-term monitoring were noted, and it was proposed that an 'information package' was available for xeno-recipients.[194] Information on the nature, risks, alternatives, psychological and social effects, and current status of xenotransplantation should be provided.[195]

Most attention has been paid to informed consent issues in the US, and in the 2001 guideline thirteen points were set out which should be addressed 'at a minimum' in the informed consent discussion and document, including xeno-centres 'develop[ing] appropriate xeno-transplantation procedure-specific educational materials' for educating and counselling the recipient and her contacts.[196] In 2004 the SACX published a draft report on informed consent, including a draft consent form.[197] In obtaining consent, discussions should include eight pieces of information, including the need for lifelong monitoring, with the information disclosed *'sufficiently complete'*.[198] Notably, in the ten principles for the regulation of xenotransplant clinical trials developed by the WHO 2008 it was merely stated that '[p]atients and close contacts should be *effectively educated* about their treatment to encourage compliance, and to minimize risks for themselves and for society'.[199] The IXA has also suggested that, with regard to porcine islet clinical trials, consent forms should follow a particular format, contain information on twelve topics, with the aim being to provide *'fully informed consent'*.[200] There is no reason to assume that such topics will not also apply to solid organ xenotransplants and included are purposes of the research, alternatives, risks, an estimation of rejection or failure rates, and post-xenotransplant monitoring. Within the latter, patients should be informed of ten 'responsibilities expected and required', such as 'timely reporting of all unexplained illnesses', behavioural guidelines with regard to 'exchanges of bodily fluids with intimate contacts', and limits on future donations of sperm, fluids, tissues and organs.[201]

Guidance on providing information for potential xeno-recipients and others is as varied, and in some cases vague, as it is for experimental procedures and clinical trials generally. This is not appropriate because

[194] Health Canada, *Proposed Canadian Standard*, p. 6. [195] *Ibid.*, p. 7.
[196] US DHHS, FDA, *PHS Guideline*, para. 2.5.
[197] US DHHS, SACX, *Informed Consent*.
[198] *Ibid.*, pp. ii–iii, vi, 5–6, 28, emphasis supplied.
[199] 'First WHO Global', Principle 6, emphasis supplied.
[200] H.Y. Vanderpool, 'The International Xenotransplantation (IXA) Association Consensus Statement on Conditions for Undertaking Clinical Trials of Porcine Islet products in Type 1 Diabetes – Chapter 7: Informed Consent and Xenotransplantation Clinical Trials' (2009) 16 *Xenotransplantation* 255, 259–260, emphasis supplied.
[201] *Ibid.*, p. 259.

of the nature and magnitude of the risks, and in order to protect and safeguard public health more directed xeno-guidance is vital. Even if this were developed, providing information to others is always difficult and this is exacerbated when what is involved is an experimental procedure, with risks going beyond the potential beneficiary, and it is thus necessary to also consider whether it is possible to provide 'informed consent' in the way traditionally conceived in the health care and research contexts.

Problems disclosing information

The problems of providing adequate information were discussed in the Nuffield Council's report with two issues highlighted: the difficulty of assessing the risk–benefit ratio because of the novelty of xenotransplantation; and the risk of overestimating the chance of success because of investigators' desires to perform a genetically engineered solid organ xenotransplant.[202] With the former, the Council recognised that although the results of pre-clinical trials might suggest a clinical xenotransplant would be successful, the risks might only be known after a number had been performed.[203] Knowledge in this area has not sufficiently increased and as investigators themselves will lack adequate information about the risks, it is unclear how xeno-recipients can be informed of them. Some or all of the risks might not be identified or evidenced for a number of years following a xenotransplant, because of latent infections. The US Institute of Medicine (IOM) has thus queried whether it will ever be possible to know the level of risk involved in order to balance it against possible benefits,[204] and as uncertainty still surrounds the risks the value that can be attributed to the information provided to initial recipients is necessarily questionable. In all research contexts it is important to inform the patient of the known risks and that there may be unknown and unknowable risks. However, it is unclear whether and how these sorts of risk can be explained, particularly to someone who is desperately ill with no other hope.[205] Their competency may be impaired because of their health status, which places further strain on their ability to comprehend these complexities and to provide their sufficiently informed consent. As the extent of the information which can be provided is limited, an informed discussion about

---

[202] Nuffield Council, *Animal-to-Human*, paras. 7.16–7.17. Similarly, France – CCNE, *Opinion on Ethics*, p. 8.
[203] Nuffield Council, *Animal-to-Human*, para. 7.16.
[204] Institute of Medicine (IOM), *Xenotransplantation: Science, Ethics and Public Policy* (Washington, DC: National Academy Press, 1996), p. 15.
[205] See Chapter 2.

involvement is unlikely as so much is not known about xenotransplantation, including the fact that *'nothing* is known as to the long-term viability of xenografts in human beings'.[206] This may mean that '[f]uture legal questions could arise as to the adequacy of the information given, seeing that the medical profession is itself unable to state with precision the extent of these dangers. Questions could arise ... as to whether they fully understood the information they were given or the extent of the restrictions they were placing on themselves.'[207]

As to overestimating the chance of success, this may be a problem with all research and, with xenotransplantation, the US IOM has highlighted the fact that '[o]verly optimistic judgments have appeared repeatedly in public statements by treating physicians and in consent forms'.[208] Although 'it remains morally reprehensible not to give the individual patient as honest and realistic a picture as possible of the potential benefits and risk',[209] the Nuffield Council acknowledged that 'innovators may be more dismissive of the risks, and pains and stresses, of a particular procedure than may be their patients'.[210] Those involved in developing or performing xenotransplants may find it difficult to present the risks and benefits in an unbiased and 'objective' manner (is this ever possible?),[211] particularly as '[s]ubtle changes in the manner of presentation may influence the perception of risk and a patient's decision'.[212] This is not to suggest that health professionals will deliberately misrepresent information but highlights the significance of the skills of those obtaining consent, and the need to ensure that those involved in experimental procedures or clinical trials are adequately protected. The dual role of, and the problems with, health professionals acting as physician-investigators are particularly emphasised here.

There may also be a third problem with disclosing information: patients may be faced with 'information overload'. Although much is still unknown and uncertain about xenotransplantation, investigators may seek to protect themselves by providing details about all known and possible, however remote, risks, thus making it difficult for patients

---

[206] Caplan, 'Ethical Issues', 3343, emphasis in original.
[207] Bach *et al.*, 'Ethical and Legal Issues', 290.
[208] IOM, *Xenotransplantation*, p. 62, citing the Baby Fae xenotransplant in 1985 as an example (Bailey *et al.*, 'Baboon-to-Human'). Recent claims in the media about when clinical xenotransplants will begin include S.-K. Templeton, 'Lord Winston to farm pigs for transplants', *Sunday Times*, 7 September 2008.
[209] Cooper and Lanza, *Xeno*, p. 208.
[210] Nuffield Council, *Animal-to-Human*, para. 7.17.
[211] T. Tomlinson, 'The Physician's Influence on Patients' Choices' (1986) 7 *Theoretical Medicine and Bioethics* 105, 116.
[212] Nuffield Council, *Animal-to-Human*, para. 7.17.

to evaluate the risks and benefits. It is unclear whether patients will be able to 'fully assimilate and evaluate such quantities of information'[213] which may 'unnecessarily frighten or confuse' them.[214] Indeed, '[i]nformation overload may prevent adequate understanding, and physicians exacerbate these problems if they use unfamiliar terms or if patients cannot meaningfully organize information. Patients and potential subjects may also rely on modes of selective perception, and it is often difficult to determine when words have special meaning for them, when preconceptions distort their processing of the information, and when other biases intrude.'[215] This problem was recognised in the UK's DH report in which it was suggested that regularly updated information packs and individual counselling might be needed to aid the potential recipients through the consent process.[216] These ideas have been adopted by some regulators, discussed below, and the problems indicate that the practical and legal challenges which xenotransplantation poses to traditional individual consent based systems requires recognition and action.

Changes to first-party consent for xenotransplantation

The nature of consent

To afford greater protection to recipients and affected others, fundamental changes to first-party consent for xenotransplantation are required, and it has been proposed that the nature of consent should be revised to *require* written consent, especially to surveillance.[217] Others have considered whether a more contractual form of consent might be necessary to ensure compliance with surveillance.[218] The UK's 2004 Regulations require 'informed consent' to involvement in a clinical trial to be 'evidenced in writing, dated and signed',[219] but this is not required for experimental procedures. The GMC states that written consent should be obtained if 'the treatment is part of a research programme or is an innovative treatment designed specifically for their benefit',[220] but written consent has no greater legal value or effect than other types of consent. It merely constitutes evidence that consent has been obtained

---

[213] Fox, 'Clinical Research', p. 270. [214] BMA, *Report of the Consent*, p. 7.
[215] Beauchamp and Childress, *Principles*, pp. 129–130.
[216] DH, *Animal Tissue*, paras. 7.12–7.13.
[217] E.g. Canada – Health Canada, *Proposed Canadian Standard*, p. 7; Sweden – Swedish Committee, *From One Species*, p. 17.
[218] See Chapter 6.
[219] Sched. 1, Part 1, para. 3(1)(b)(i), 2004 Regulations, as amended.
[220] GMC, *Consent*, para. 49(d).

and may be relevant if there is an adverse incident or event. A written consent document emphasising the extent of the consent could, however, be useful by setting out the surveillance conditions that xeno-recipients must comply with; but without sanctions for non-compliance simply changing the nature of consent in this way will not enhance protection for recipients or others. I explore this further in Chapter 6.

The process

If changing the nature of first-party consent will not enhance the protection of xeno-recipients and others, altering the process of obtaining consent may help. In the UK problems with the process of obtaining consent to post-mortems and retaining organs were recognised at the end of the 1990s and start of the 2000s, with some of the difficulties relating to the complicated and confusing questions which were asked at a time of recent bereavement and distress. There were misunderstandings regarding what had been agreed, and it was recommended that bereavement advisers were introduced in all hospitals to supply bereaved parents with 'clear, factual, unbiased information', explain the need for consent, and develop and use information packs on deaths in hospitals for relatives.[221] Although in a different context, xeno-recipients will be asked to consent to a procedure at a time of significant ill-health and distress, when their health status may affect their ability to understand and retain information, and to a procedure for which the benefits and the risks at the time and in the future are unknown. The process through which consent is obtained is thus vitally important and the skills of those seeking to obtain consent crucial. It has been suggested that the decision-making process 'must take place *before* preterminal deterioration and thus avoid a situation where desperation overwhelms concerns of dignity, science, and common sense',[222] but the first xeno-recipients are likely to be desperately ill and with no other hope. Given this, '[c]areful attention must be paid to both the content of the consent disclosure *and* the manner in which consent is obtained',[223] and whoever obtains consent must take particular care in leading discussions and framing and asking questions to ensure that the xeno-recipient understands the complexity and implications of her decision. Leading questions and misleading impressions need to be minimised; for example, the xeno-recipient

---

[221] *Royal Liverpool Children's Inquiry*, para. 12.1.5, chs. 11, 12.
[222] R.N. Pierson *et al.*, 'Ethical Considerations in Clinical Cardiac Xenografting – Letter' (1993) 12 *Journal of Heart and Lung Transplantation* 876, 877, emphasis supplied.
[223] AMA, *Report of the Council on Ethical*, Recommendation 3, emphasis supplied.

must not be left with the idea or impression that they have no choice but to consent to the procedure even though, medically at least, it may be their only realistic chance of staying alive. They also need to understand that they are likely to die even if they have the xenotransplant, but the nature of their death and duration of the dying process might be more uncertain.

Given the complexities surrounding xenotransplantation, three changes to the process of obtaining consent are essential. First, a person independent from the xenotransplant team, with a similar but more extensive remit to that of the bereavement adviser noted above, must be introduced to seek consent. An independent person involved in the consent process was mooted in Sweden ('a person with psychological training') and the UK ('a suitably qualified person'),[224] but in no country is this currently required. Similarly, the New Zealand HRC has stated that it is 'essential' that xeno-participants have the opportunity to receive information and advice from an independent relevant specialist before consent is sought.[225] Introducing an independent person changes the traditional first-party consent process as consent is usually sought by those performing the procedure as they are more likely to understand the risks and benefits involved. However, the extraordinary risks justify a departure from accepted norms, and this should be mandatory for *all* xenotransplants regardless of their regulatory classification. Such a change will give legal effect to the ethical duty set out in the Declaration of Helsinki for an 'appropriately qualified individual who is completely independent of this relationship' to seek informed consent if the participants are in a 'dependent relationship' with the investigator.[226] A person independent of the xenotransplant team must seek consent to minimise the problems raised by the likely dual role of the xenotransplant physician-investigator, the power and control inherent in this position, and the potential for selective information provision.

The second necessary change also involves introducing another party into the process of seeking consent. The Australian NHMRC states that a participant advocate should be appointed for research '[w]here potential participants are especially vulnerable or powerless', and the UKXIRA and US DHHS have similarly suggested that an independent third party or patient advocate should or might observe the xenotransplant consent process.[227] Such advocates could 'ask questions on

---

[224] Sweden – Swedish Committee, *From One Species*, pp. 16–17; UK – UKXIRA, *Draft Report*, A5.5.
[225] HRC, *Guidelines for Preparation*, p. 18.   [226] Above, n. 71.
[227] Australia – NHMRC *et al.*, *National Statement*, para. 4.3.2; UK – UKXIRA, *Guidance on Making Proposals*, para. 7.13; US – US DHSS, FDA, *PHS Guideline*, para. 2.5.

the patients' behalf, act as an impartial sounding board, and deter the doctor from pressurising or hurrying the patient'.[228] A lay advocate might be unable to interpret technical details and may, as a patient might, feel too intimidated to ask questions so a non-doctor health professional may be a more appropriate advocate.[229] Such professionals may still be seen as part of the experimental procedure or research team and as having a vested interest in persuading patients to be involved, and so 'a trained advocate, perhaps funded by the health authority or trust, could be specifically trained and supervised by the research ethics committee. Such posts, separate from any research or care team, have the potential to develop into an independent advocacy system.'[230] The nature of xenotransplantation is such that an independent patient advocate is vital to support those considering a xenotransplant, and to help minimise the effect of the conflicts of interest inherent in the dual role of the physician-investigator on the xeno-recipient. At the very least, as suggested by the Australian NHMRC, xeno-participants should be encouraged to discuss their involvement with 'someone who is able to support them in making their decision'.[231]

Finally, all xeno-recipients *must* be counselled pre- and post-xenotransplant. For gene therapy trials the UK's GTAC 'advocates appropriate counselling, independent of the research team and the institution involved in the study, wherever possible'.[232] Xenotransplant counselling has been suggested in Australia, Canada and the US, and by the Council of Europe and WHO;[233] but in no country is it currently mandatory. Counselling will not be a panacea to the problems discussed here, but it may help the xeno-recipient to gain some sense and understanding of what may happen to them and the effect this may have on others. There may be problems with counselling, as with the physician-investigator or an independent person seeking consent, with

---

[228] Hewlett, 'Consent', 235.
[229] M. Brazier, 'Patient Autonomy and Consent to Treatment: The Role of the Law?' (1987) 7 *Legal Studies* 169; C. Faulder, *Whose Body Is It? The Troubling Issue of Informed Consent* (London: Virago Press, 1985), p. 115.
[230] Hewlett, 'Consent', 235. [231] NHMRC *et al.*, *National Statement*, para. 4.3.2.
[232] GTAC, *Guidance on the Content*, para. 32; also, paras. 25, 63–64, 79.
[233] Australia – NHMRC, XWP, *Guidelines for Clinical*, Guideline 6, accompanying NHMRC, XWP, *Animal-to-Human Transplantation: Final Report*; Canada – Health Canada, *Proposed Canadian Standard*, pp. 6, 27; UK – UKXIRA, *Draft Report*, A5.2; DH, *Animal Tissue*, para. 7.13; Nuffield Council, *Animal-to-Human*, para. 7.18; US – US DHHS, FDA, *PHS Guideline*, paras. 2.5, 2.5.13; Council of Europe, Recommendation Rec(2003)10, Article 17; WHO, *Report of the WHO Consultation*, paras. 3.4, 8.1.6, 8.1.7.

regard to non-directiveness and framing.[234] It is questionable whether a xenotransplant counsellor would be able to present information in an unbiased manner, and patients may perceive the offering of a xenotransplant as an implicit endorsement. Tensions in genetic counselling have been highlighted and the effectiveness of xenotransplantation counselling might similarly be questioned, particularly if it is correct that:

> aware of the limitations to what can be offered, the clinician at some level may attempt to compensate by presenting an optimistic picture, this being for the benefit of both professional and patient. Similarly aware of the huge uncontrollable implications of the new genetics, the clinician may try to restore some sense of personal control by following a carefully pre-set agenda which, therefore, is not oriented to the emotional concerns of the patient.[235]

The outcome of genetic counselling may also differ depending on who is the counsellor: an obstetrician, clinical geneticist or genetic nurse.[236] Careful thought must thus be given as to who the xenotransplant counsellor is and they should, at the very least, have successfully completed the postgraduate training which is currently available for medically and non-medically qualified genetic counsellors.[237] For such training to be effective, courses or options directed to the specific issues raised by xenotransplantation, such as the uncertainty, risks to others and post-operative lifelong surveillance regime, may need to be developed.

Third-party consent to xenotransplantation

Xenotransplantation also necessitates some form of third-party consent because it invokes the interests of the public and identifiable others. Whereas with conventional medical treatment or research if the individual patient has consented to it nothing else is required as the only interests at stake are those of the individual, 'the unique risk xenotransplantation poses to the public health *requires* approval not just on scientific and individual grounds but also by the community at large'.[238] In Chapter 2, I argued that the public must participate in decisions

---

[234] E.g. J.A. Smith *et al.*, 'Certainty and Uncertainty in Genetic Counselling: A Qualitative Case Study' (2000) 15 *Psychology and Health* 1; L. Sherr, 'Counselling and HIV Testing: Ethical Dilemmas', in R. Bennett and C.A. Erin (eds.), *HIV and AIDS; Testing, Screening and Confidentiality* (Oxford University Press, 1999), p. 39.

[235] Smith, 'Certainty and Uncertainty', 11.

[236] T. Marteau *et al.*, 'Counselling Following Diagnosis of a Fetal Abnormality: The Differing Approaches of Obstetricians, Clinical Geneticists and Genetic Nurses' (1994) 31 *Journal of Medical Genetics* 864.

[237] Association of Genetic Nurses and Counsellors, 'Training to Become a Genetic Counsellor' (2010) (at: www.agnc.org.uk/howtobecomeaGC.htm, accessed 21/03/11).

[238] AMA, *Report of the Council*, p. 3, emphasis supplied.

184 Challenges to legal and ethical norms

about xenotransplantation *because* their interests are engaged by it and that if this does not occur 'the many' have no say or choice about being exposed to risks in order to benefit 'the few'. Without such, 'imposing risks of infection on healthy members of the general public ... raises serious legal questions because it could constitute a form of involuntary human experimentation'.[239] Genetically engineered solid organ xenotransplants also place at risk the health of identifiable third parties: the xeno-recipient's contacts. It has been widely recognised that these people are in a unique position because although not the subject of the procedure, it has been proposed that *they* also receive counselling *and/or* consent to post-xenotransplant surveillance regimes *for themselves*.[240] The technical issues raised by obtaining consent from contacts are similar to those concerning xeno-recipients, but *requiring* Y's consent to a surveillance regime following a xenotransplant to X necessitates careful consideration. Can Y's refusal to agree to surveillance *prevent* the xenotransplant to X? This has not been widely explored by regulators to date but must be because requiring such consent further sets xenotransplantation apart from other developing biotechnologies. The Council of Europe has considered this and said that:

> [i]f, after ... xenotransplantation ... the recipient or his or her close personal contacts refuse to comply with the constraints associated with xenotransplantation, public health authorities should intervene and take appropriate measures, where public health protection so requires, in conformity with principles of necessity and proportionality. Depending on the circumstances and in accordance with the procedures provided for by national law, such measures might include registration, compulsory medical follow-up and sampling.[241]

Going further, the Health Council of the Netherlands has suggested that direct contact would not be possible if a third party refused to comply with post-operative checks and it might be necessary to limit the number of people the xeno-recipient has contact with 'so as to keep

---

[239] A. Fano, 'If Pigs Could Fly, They Would: The Problems with Xenotransplantation', in B. Tokar (ed.), *Redesigning Life? The Worldwide Challenge to Genetic Engineering* (London: Zed Books, 2001), pp. 182, 189.

[240] Australia – NHMRC, XWP, *Guidelines for Clinical*, Guidelines 6–8, accompanying NHMRC, XWP, *Animal-to-Human Transplantation: Final Report*; Canada – Health Canada, *Proposed Canadian Standard*, pp. 6–7, 27, 31–3; Netherlands – Health Council, *Xenotransplantation*, pp. 12, 43; New Zealand – HRC, *Guidelines for Preparation*, Section 7; UK – UKXIRA, *Draft Report*, A5.2; US – US DHHS *et al.*, *Guidance for Industry – Source Animal*, VIII.F.4; US DHHS, FDA, *PHS Guideline*, paras. 2.5, 2.5.4, 2.5.11; Council of Europe, Recommendation Rec(2003)10, Article 9; Council of Europe, *Report on the State*, para. 7.5.3.

[241] Council of Europe, Recommendation Rec(2003)10, Article 21.

the postoperative monitoring programme to tolerable proportions'.[242] The particular provisions of the surveillance regime with which xeno-recipients and their contacts may have to comply are considered in Chapter 6, but it cannot simply be assumed that requiring the consent of these third parties is straightforward and takes xenotransplantation further out of existing legal and ethical norms. As such, this cannot and should not be imposed 'quietly' and, at the very least, these identifiable third parties should receive mandatory counselling.

Conclusion

Where the benefits and risks of a developing biotechnology are unclear, the risks go beyond the intended beneficiary, and that beneficiary is desperately ill with no other hope, challenges are posed to the familiar conception of first-party consent in many Western countries. Such consent is 'not an appropriate way to respond to xenotransplantation'[243] and it is problematic that 'policy decisions concerning xenotransplantation have been made on the basis of principles and processes that are traditionally associated with biomedical ethics and medical law, rather than being derived from a responsive assessment of xenotransplantation itself or from public health ethics'.[244] This is not to dismiss the importance of first-party informed consent but it must be recognised that for clinical genetically engineered solid organ xenotransplants to be performed more than this is required to protect individual *and* public health. Public participation in the decision-making process is necessary because of the risks, and protecting public health in this context means adopting a precautionary approach informed by the harm principle.[245] However, because of the nature and magnitude of the risks more than this is required. First, it must be clarified whether consent to a xenotransplant has legal authority, given the uncertain benefits and risks to the recipient and others. Secondly, if it is possible to give valid consent, then the three elements of consent must be considered in the specific context of xenotransplantation. Thirdly, the suggested changes to first-party consent to xenotransplantation set out above must be implemented, and the nature and role of third-party consent explicitly addressed.

Seeking consent to a genetically engineered solid organ xenotransplant *must* involve a team so that xeno-recipients and their contacts

---

[242] Health Council, *Xenotransplantation*, pp. 12, 44.
[243] L. Williamson *et al.*, 'Regulation', 459, references removed.   [244] *Ibid.*, 460–461.
[245] Fovargue and Ost, 'When Should Precaution Prevail?'.

186   Challenges to legal and ethical norms

have the opportunity to discuss with a number of health professionals what a xenotransplant entails, particularly post-operative requirements.[246] The team should include an independent person who will seek to obtain the necessary consent, a patient advocate, and a counsellor. Using a team is important because '[i]nformed consent gives desperately ill patients information precisely at the moment at which they are least able to process it. Then, it asks for an independent decision precisely at the moment when the individual is most dependent on others – caretakers, families, and friends.'[247] Providing the time and space for team and individual discussions with the xeno-recipient and their contacts will, it is to be hoped, minimise the chance of 'the lower status of grievously sick persons [being used] as a means toward the ends of our personal and scientific pursuits'.[248] A key component in achieving this is the information which these first and third parties receive because 'if patients are denied the information that they require to consent validly to treatment [and research], they are effectively turned into slaves for medical purposes'.[249] However, the varying guidance which exists on how much and what information should be disclosed with regard to experimental procedures and clinical trials is insufficient and inadequate for xenotransplantation because of the health status of the recipients, the risks and complexity of understanding required for the available information, and its consequences. It is regrettable that the provisions of the UK's 2004 Regulations on information disclosure were not amended in the light of the concerns raised about information and consent in the aborted TGN1412 drug trial in the UK in March 2006.[250] These issues were highlighted to the Expert Scientific Group which considered this trial but it was beyond their remit to explore them.[251]

There is an emerging consensus on the categories of information which should be disclosed for xenotransplantation and in the light of the particular issues involved specific xenotransplantation legislation should be introduced to, among other things, address this. The minimum information to be disclosed should be legislatively set out in, at the very least, an EU regulation. Consistency across member states would

---

[246] Also, Vanderpool, 'IXA – Chapter 7', 258, 260; US DHHS, SACX, *Informed Consent*, pp. vi, 6–7, 28.
[247] Bosk, 'Obtaining Voluntary Consent', V-66.
[248] Vanderpool, 'Informed Consent', 354.
[249] L. Doyal, 'Informed Consent: Moral Necessity or Illusion?' (2001) 10 (suppl. I) *Quality in Health Care* i29, i31.
[250] Discussed in Expert Scientific Group on Phase One Clinical Trials, *Final Report* (London: Stationery Office, 2006), Introduction, ch. 3.
[251] *Ibid.*, p. 1.

thus be ensured and this might influence regulatory activities in other jurisdictions. The GTAC's guidance on what information to provide to potential gene therapy trial participants and on writing participant information sheets could be a useful basis for such a regulation,[252] along with those contained within NRES's guidance.[253] The New Zealand Code of Health and Disability Services Consumer's Rights might also be of assistance and serve as a practical model.[254] In this way it might be possible to obtain *adequately informed* consent to xenotransplantation within Europe which would help to 'redress the balance by providing patients with the "right" to be given that information, or ... impos[e] a duty on doctors to provide it'.[255] The Council of Europe has already provided a useful basis for this regulation in its Recommendation Rec (2003)10 which, along with a general statement on disclosure, lists eight pieces of information on monitoring to be provided to a xeno-recipient, and provisions regarding what should be provided to contacts (current and future), and to health professionals.[256]

The legislation should also statutorily refine the process of seeking consent to a xenotransplant to include an independent person seeking the consent, a patient advocate to support the xeno-recipient, and mandatory counselling of recipients and *their* current contacts. Introducing this team approach, along with sanctions for non-compliance, should help to minimise some of the problems with obtaining first-party consent to xenotransplantation under existing schemes. Although it is unusual for consent schemes to experimental procedures, clinical research and (possibly eventually) medical treatment to be statutorily defined, there is a precedent in the UK at least: IVF.[257] The unique nature of xenotransplantation demands a similar approach. Furthermore, the role of third parties and their consent to post-xenotransplant surveillance in particular *must* be statutorily addressed,[258] and it is difficult to see how practically anything other than a legislative response will suffice to protect the health of the xeno-recipient, those close to her and the public. Key issues to address are the position of contacts at the time of the xenotransplant but who cease to be so, the situation of those who

---

[252] GTAC, *Guidance on the Content*, Sections 2, 4; above, p. 174.
[253] NRES, *Information Sheets*, chs. 5–6, Annexes 2–5, 8–10, 29; above, p. 173.
[254] Code of Health, Rights 6, 7; above, p. 175.
[255] M.A. Jones, 'Informed Consent and Other Fairy Stories' (1999) 7 *Medical Law Review* 103, 129.
[256] Articles 13–15.
[257] Human Fertilisation and Embryology Act 1990, as amended by the Human Fertilisation and Embryology Act 2008.
[258] See Chapter 6.

become close to the recipient *post*-xenotransplant, the effect of a contact's refusal to consent, withdrawal from the regime, and sanctions for non-compliance. All of this sets xenotransplantation *outside* existing legal and ethical norms, and the challenges posed by this must be explicitly addressed and not assumed to be addressable at a later stage. It should not, must not and cannot be the case that 'issues surrounding informed consent do not achieve prominence until other critically important moral prerequisites of research ethics are dealt with – in particular, harm–benefit considerations ... When clinicians-researchers move xenotransplantation into clinical trials, informed consent emerges from behind the curtains to play a pivotal role on center stage.'[259] Detailed consideration of how consent can and will work is necessary *prior* to clinical xenotransplantation, and this is supported by the comprehensive and extensive requirements of the proposed surveillance schemes which xeno-recipients and others must consent to and comply with. I explore these requirements in Chapter 6.

---

[259] Vanderpool, 'IXA – Chapter 7', 261.

6 Surveillance and monitoring: balancing public health and individual freedom

An inherent risk of xenotransplantation is that known and unknown infectious diseases might be transmitted to the recipient and others, and the implications are such that it is widely recognised that the human and non-human animals involved must be monitored pre- and post-xenotransplant.[1] While an effective and efficient regime is necessary, 'the importance of the safeguards lies *not* in their ability to prevent the emergence of infectious diseases – because they are incapable of doing so – but in their ability to provide the foundation for a *rapid response* to emerging infectious diseases'.[2] Interventions to control infectious diseases include vaccination, medical examination, surveillance, isolation, quarantine, contact tracing and travel restrictions or warnings about travel. Their applicability will depend on the nature of the disease, its ease and method of transmission, the incubation and infectious period and severity of its clinical manifestation.[3] A surveillance regime should identify infectious diseases and prevent their spread; however, xeno-schemes are necessarily limited because it is not currently possible to detect or even know all the diseases which may be transmitted post-xenotransplant. Xenotransplantation is thus similar to SARS which 'took society back to a pretherapeutic era with no definitive diagnostic test, a nonspecific definition, and no effective vaccine or treatment'.[4] Nevertheless, if a surveillance scheme is to successfully protect individual

---

[1] On monitoring the non-human animals see, e.g., Health Canada, *Proposed Canadian Standard*, pp. 10–17; Home Office, *Code of Practice for the Housing and Care of Pigs Intended for Use as Xenotransplant Source Animals* (London: Home Office, 1999); UKXIRA, *Draft Guidance Notes on Biosecurity Considerations in Relation to Xenotransplantation* (London: DH, 1999); US DHSS *et al.*, *Guidance for Industry: Source Animal*.

[2] P.S. Florencio and E.D. Ramanathan, 'Are Xenotransplantation Safeguards Legally Viable?' (2001) 16 *Berkeley Technology Law Journal* 937, 941, emphasis supplied.

[3] Nuffield Council, *Public Health*, paras. 4.56–4.57.

[4] L.O. Gostin *et al.*, 'Ethical and Legal Challenges Posed by Severe Acute Respiratory Syndrome: Implications for the Control of Severe Infectious Disease Threats' (2003) 290 *Journal of the American Medical Association* 3229, 3329, reference removed.

and public health it 'must be consistent with public values as expressed in culture and law'[5] and 'in times of crisis, the most potent variable distinguishing the community that survives a plague from that which does not is not a community's degree of scientific knowledge but rather its legal system's responsiveness and stability'.[6]

A proposed public health measure should meet five 'justificatory conditions': be likely to meet its goal; the probable public health benefits should outweigh any private infringements; be necessary to achieve the goal; be the minimal possible infringement; and be explained and justified to the public.[7] I examine the proposed regimes in the UK, US and Canada to determine whether they can/will protect individual and public health by sufficiently controlling and monitoring xeno-risks, locally, nationally and internationally. These were among the first schemes to be published and are some of the most comprehensive proposed to date. Do they 'allow for the development of a potentially beneficial new technology, while safeguarding public health'?[8] Experiences with SARS are helpful here to consider the impact and effect of xeno-surveillance regimes, determine their practicability, and the appropriate legal and ethical responses to them. The structure and key elements of xeno-schemes are noted and the particular surveillance xeno-recipients, their contacts, and relevant health workers may be subject to discussion.[9]

The need for international collaboration and cooperation is acknowledged in many schemes, but is it possible to devise, implement and enforce an effective and appropriate regime in the light of problems of monitoring global risks and enforcing regimes at these different levels? If not, should a developing biotechnology requiring such a regime be permitted, or do the limitations of global surveillance and the opportunities for xeno-tourism mean that society is, essentially, presented with a *fait accompli*? Xenotransplantation risks necessitate further re-evaluations of legal and ethical norms, beyond those relating to autonomy and consent, and I consider the implications of surveillance regimes for the xeno-recipient, her contacts, and others. These are not inconsiderable and may mean that by consenting to a xenotransplant the recipient also

---

[5] Rothstein, 'Traditional Public Health Strategies', 182.
[6] W.E. Parmet, 'Introduction: The Interdependency of Law and Public Health', in R.A. Goodman *et al.*, (eds.), *Law in Public Health Practice* (2nd edn, New York, NY: Oxford University Press, 2007), p. xxxi.
[7] J.F. Childress *et al.*, 'Public Health Ethics: Mapping the Terrain' (2002) 30 *Journal of Law, Medicine and Ethics* 170, 173.
[8] Bloom, 'Xenotransplantation', 314.
[9] On surveillance of non-human animal workers, see, e.g., UKXIRA, *Draft Report*, paras. 2.5, 2.8, Annexes 3 and 4; US DHHS *et al.*, *Guidance for Industry: Source Animal*, Sections V and VII; US DHHS, FDA, *PHS Guideline*, Section 3.

consents to a surveillance regime *and* not withdrawing from it, otherwise such regimes will be ineffective and meaningless. This raises enforcement and compliance issues and sits uneasily with the well-established legal and ethical right to withdraw from a trial.[10] I explore how an individual's compliance with the regimes has been addressed and discuss whether alternative forms of enforcement, within the English and Welsh legal system, are possible or required to protect health. I highlight the problems which are likely to be encountered in adopting such proposals, problems which are unlikely to be jurisdiction specific. Finally, the involvement of third parties in these surveillance schemes places them in an unusual role, but what effect will their refusal to comply with such a regime have for the recipient? Will or should this mean the xeno-transplant cannot proceed?

Surprisingly the human rights implications of xeno-surveillance regimes have been minimally addressed to date, but it is unclear how the necessary requirements can be legally and ethically accommodated if currently accepted notions of protecting an individual's human rights are to continue. Or is it acceptable to *require* that these rights are sacrificed where the risks an individual takes may also harm others? The nature of the suggested obligations of/on xeno-recipients and others are such that their human rights *will* be limited, but this could be viewed by those with no other hope as a necessary compromise which gives them the chance to benefit from the biotechnology and, to some extent, remain 'free' within society, but also seeks to protect public health.[11] Such changes require public discussion and justification because they entail a reconsideration of traditional consent-based schemes for experimental procedures and clinical trials and surveillance regimes; '[a]s soon as any part of a person's conduct affects prejudicially the interests of others, society has a jurisdiction over it, and the question whether the general welfare will or will not be promoted by interfering with it becomes open to discussion'.[12]

Pre-2000 proposed surveillance regimes

In 1996 the US DHHS published a draft xenotransplantation guideline which included surveillance.[13] This was revised in 2001 following

---

[10] E.g. UK – Sched. 1, Part 3, para. 2, 2004 Regulations, as amended; US – 45 CFR 46, § 46.116(8); WMA, *Declaration*, B24; CIOMS and WHO, *International Ethical*, Guideline 5; International Conference, *ICH Harmonised*, para. 4.8.10(m).
[11] Florencio and Ramanathan, 'Xenotransplantation Safeguards', p. 971.
[12] J.S. Mill, 'On Liberty', in *On Liberty*, pp. 83–84.
[13] US DHHS, 'Draft PHS Guideline'. These were wholeheartedly adopted in Spain: 'Recommendations for the Regulation'.

192   Surveillance and monitoring

written comments and public workshops.[14] As the 2001 guidelines built on the 1996 document they are considered here along with subsequent US guidance and the 1999 reports published by the UKXIRA, the UK's then xenotransplant regulator, and Health Canada.[15] The UKXIRA's report was published as *draft* guidance but was never finalised even though UKXIRA's work was declared complete when it was disbanded in 2006.[16] The draft report remains valid guidance[17] even though 'no policy position had been reached at this time regarding the issues [it] examined'.[18] There is consensus in the three regimes that information should be collected on/from the non-human animals, their workers, xeno-recipients, their contacts and relevant health workers, and that the schemes required local and national levels.[19] International dimensions were, however, minimally recognised.

Local

Under the three schemes an individual or team at the site where the xenotransplant is performed is responsible for surveillance,[20] and each team determines what information, samples and tissues are taken and when.[21] The UKXIRA and US DHHS set out pre- and post-xenotransplant minimum testing schedules,[22] the latter noting that the intervals of post-xenotransplant screening might decrease if 'evidence of infection remains absent'.[23] All three schemes require provisions for an untoward event, significant exposure, or when it is suspected or known that there are xenogeneic infectious agents in the xenotransplanted organ.[24] In the US biological specimens obtained for public health investigations will be archived for fifty years after the date of the xenotransplant,[25]

---

[14] US DHHS, FDA, *PHS Guideline*, pp. 2–3.
[15] Health Canada, *Proposed Canadian Standard*; UKXIRA, *Draft Report*.
[16] Lord Warner, Hansard, vol. 687, col. WS181 12 December 2006.
[17] See Chapter 4.   [18] L. Williamson *et al.*, 'Regulation', 461.
[19] Health Canada, *Proposed Canadian Standard*, p. 32; UKXIRA, *Draft Report*, para. 2.5; US DHHS, FDA, *PHS Guideline*, para. 2.4.
[20] Health Canada, *Proposed Canadian Standard*, p. 29; UKXIRA, *Draft Report*, para. 2.3, Annex One; US DHHS, FDA, *PHS Guideline*; paras. 2.1, 2.4.
[21] Health Canada, *Proposed Canadian Standard*, pp. 30, 32–33; UKXIRA, *Draft Report*, paras. 2.6–2.7; US DHHS, FDA, *PHS Guideline*, para. 4.1.2; also, New Zealand – HRC, *Guidelines for Preparation*, para. 7.
[22] UKXIRA, *Draft Report*, para. 2.6, Annexes Three, Four; US DHHS, FDA, *PHS Guideline*, paras. 4.1.1.2, 4.1.2.
[23] US DHHS, FDA, *PHS Guideline*, para. 4.1.1.2.
[24] Health Canada, *Proposed Canadian Standard*, p. 33, Section F; UKXIRA, *Draft Report*, paras. 2.5–2.6, 2.8, Section 3, Annex Seven; US DHHS, FDA, *PHS Guideline*, paras. 4.1.1.2, 4.1.2.3.
[25] US DHHS, FDA, *PHS Guideline*, para. 4.1.2; also, 2.5.10, 4.1.2.2, 4.3, 5.2.

but there are no time limits in the UK or Canadian provisions.[26] The effectiveness of these schemes in protecting public health is questionable, given the delegation of responsibility for determining what samples are obtained and archived to individuals or xeno-teams. Allowing different material to be collected and stored for different periods must make it harder to identify infection trends and protect individual and public health. Health Canada has recognised that clarification on this is required,[27] but nothing has been published to date. Additionally, the UKXIRA's scheme permits a number of bodies to collate information on infections, thereby increasing the risk of error and mismanagement of information.[28] This is not the most effective way of protecting health.

Sampling and archiving
Xeno-recipients

Under all three schemes a xeno-recipient has to consent to the xeno-transplant *and* to the 'post-operative procedures and constraints' with which they have 'a *commitment* to comply'.[29] In Canada xeno-recipient monitoring is to be 'long term',[30] unspecified, and individual xeno-teams must describe the protocol for collecting and archiving baseline sera, peripheral blood lymphocytes, 'or other materials' pre-xenotransplant.[31] An appropriate post-xenotransplant schedule of clinical and laboratory monitoring should be provided by the team 'to the extent possible',[32] and the recipient's long-term surveillance will include physical examinations and archiving tissues and/or serum samples.[33] Testing schedules were considered in 2001 and it was recommended that these were established before clinical trials began,[34] but as of March 2011 nothing has been published. Individual teams can also determine the xeno-recipient's clinical and laboratory surveillance in the UK and US, and the UKXIRA noted that the 'biological "samples and specimens" required and what needs to be tested for [need] to be defined'.[35] Nevertheless, these schemes

---

[26] Health Canada, *Proposed Canadian Standard*, pp. 30, 32; UKXIRA, *Draft Report*, paras. 2.7–2.8.
[27] Health Canada, *Report of the Xenotransplantation*, p. 4.
[28] UKXIRA, *Draft Report*, Section Two.
[29] *Ibid.*, A5.4, emphasis supplied; Health Canada, *Proposed Canadian Standard*, p. 6; US DHHS, FDA, *PHS Guideline*, para. 2.5.7.
[30] Health Canada, *Proposed Canadian Standard*, pp. 6 and 33.
[31] *Ibid.*, p. 32. In Norway recipients must have 'regular health checks', be included in the xenotransplant register, and 'biological samples' collected and stored in the xenobiobank (Gjørv, 'Political Considerations', 57).
[32] Health Canada, *Proposed Canadian Standard*, p. 33.   [33] *Ibid.*, pp. 6, 33.
[34] Health Canada, *Report of the Xenotransplantation*, pp. 14–20.
[35] UKXIRA, *Draft Report*, Annex Three.

set out minimum pre- and post-xenotransplant screening schedules; screening which will be lifelong.[36] Sets of samples should be taken in the US at the time of the xenotransplant, 'in the immediate post-xenotransplantation period', one and six months after it, annually for the first two years, and then every five years for the rest of the recipient's life.[37] Serum, peripheral blood mononuclear cells, tissue or 'other body fluids' will be analysed at 'frequent' intervals (two, four and six weeks suggested) immediately post-xenotransplant for known or suspected xenogeneic agents.[38] In the UK tissue and blood samples will be taken and archived at the time of the xenotransplant, specimens tested at zero, one-to-two days, two, four and six weeks, one and two years, and then continuous clinical assessment will begin.[39] The scheduling timeline is zero to six months, six months to two years, two years to life, and specimens taken at one and six months and at one and two years will be archived. After two years the frequency of future sampling will be reviewed.[40]

Subsequent US guidance recommends introducing a 'passive screening' programme, with 'appropriate clinical samples such as blood, plasma and urine' obtained 'periodically' and archived for future retrospective testing of asymptomatic xeno-recipients.[41] The frequency of the tests could follow the 2001 guideline but the *sponsor* would be responsible for proposing the schedule and the tests used.[42] An 'active screening' programme should be considered where samples are tested immediately after collection, 'periodic' tests conducted on the samples collected under the passive programme, or there could be centralised review of routinely collected clinical data to look for trends.[43] This would involve screening for evidence of asymptomatic infections and provide a 'prospective understanding of the patterns of infection and diseases that may be occurring in recipients'.[44] Active surveillance could occur at two, four and six weeks post-xenotransplant, and if it is known that a xenotransplant contains an infectious agent, active screening for that agent should be instigated and samples archived.[45] *Sponsors* should

---

[36] UKXIRA, *Draft Report*, para. 2.5, A5.2; US DHHS *et al.*, *Guidance for Industry: Source Animal*, Section VIII J2a iv; US DHHS, FDA, *PHS Guideline*, paras. 2.5.7, 4.1.1.1, 4.1.1.2. Similarly, e.g., New Zealand – HRC, *Guidelines for Preparation*, Guideline 8; Norway – Gjørv, 'Political Considerations', p. 56; Spain – 'Recommendations for the Regulation', p. 40; Council of Europe, Recommendation Rec(2003)10, Article 13; 'First WHO', Principle 7.
[37] US DHHS, FDA, *PHS Guideline*, para. 4.1.2.   [38] *Ibid.*, para. 4.1.1.2.
[39] UKXIRA, *Draft Report*, Annex Three.   [40] *Ibid.*
[41] US DHHS *et al.*, *Guidance for Industry: Source Animal*, Section VIII F3c i; also, Section VIII H1.
[42] *Ibid.*, Section VIII F3 ci.   [43] *Ibid.*, Section VIII F3 cii.   [44] *Ibid.*   [45] *Ibid.*

'develop a plan to address the possibility that a recipient tests positive for the presence of PERV or other similar xenogeneic infectious agents', including strategies to identify the source of a positive result, determine the infectivity of an agent, notify the FDA, relevant sponsors and investigators, provisions for acute and follow-up care and counselling of recipients, and additional actions to protect the recipient, contacts and public health.[46] A plan for the clinical follow-up of the recipient should be provided to the FDA when applying to conduct a clinical trial.[47]

Close contacts

Under Health Canada's scheme, contacts (who are not defined in the *Standard*) will be tracked for developing infections via a central registry.[48] Individual xeno-teams must describe the protocol for collecting and archiving pre-xenotransplant baseline sera, peripheral blood lymphocytes, 'or other materials' from contacts, which will be archived for public health purposes.[49] In contrast, the US 2001 guideline did not discuss contact surveillance as xeno-recipients were to 'educate' them about the risks and how to reduce them.[50] In 2003, however, the US DHHS recommended that a programme was developed to monitor 'other intimate contacts of recipients'; 'persons with whom recipients repeatedly engage in activities that could result in intimate exchange of body fluids'.[51] Such contacts should be advised and counselled about potential risks and 'passive[ly] screening'.[52] As with recipients, pre-xenotransplant baseline plasma samples should be taken and archived.[53] A similar scheme was envisaged by the UKXIRA whereby 'household/close contacts'[54] would be seen by the xeno-team prior to the xenotransplant and informed about the possible risks and how to minimise them.[55] Baseline blood samples would be

---

[46] *Ibid.*, Section VIII F3 d.   [47] *Ibid.*, Section VIII G.
[48] Health Canada, *Proposed Canadian Standard*, p. 31.   [49] *Ibid.*, p. 32.
[50] US DHHS, FDA, *PHS Guideline*, para. 2.5.4; US DHHS, SACX, *Informed Consent*, p. 22; also, New Zealand – HRC, *Guidelines for Preparation*, Guideline 7.11; Spain – 'Recommendations for the Regulation', p. 41; Switzerland – Statement of Position, 'Medical–Ethical Principles', p. 391.
[51] US DHHS *et al.*, *Guidance for Industry: Source Animal*, Sections VIII F4 and VIII J2a i. Adopted in New Zealand: HRC, *Guidelines for Preparation*, Guideline 8.
[52] US DHHS *et al.*, *Guidance for Industry: Source Animal*, Section VIII F4.
[53] *Ibid.*, pp. 48–49.
[54] '[H]ousehold members and sexual partners and others with whom the xenotransplant recipient may engage in activities in which bodily fluid may be exchanged' (UKXIRA, *Draft Report*, para. 2.5, Annex Seven).
[55] *Ibid.*, para. 2.5. Contacts might also be monitored in, e.g., Australia and the Netherlands: NHMRC, XWP, *Guidelines for Clinical*, Guideline 8, accompanying

taken, samples and records maintained and 'archived indefinitely', and a clinical history taken.[56] Post-xenotransplant, contacts will have samples tested and archived if an untoward event occurs.[57] Samples may be taken and archived at one year, with future sampling needs reviewed and clinical surveillance continued at the xeno-recipient's scheduled visits.[58] Contacts will thus be subject to active surveillance via scheduled follow-up visits,[59] and the laboratory tests on contacts linked to national reporting schemes.[60]

Health workers

Health Canada's 1999 document did not consider health workers, but in 2001 they suggested that their baseline and investigative samples should be provided if an adverse event occurs, but a sampling schedule was not set out.[61] The UKXIRA requires the 'xenotransplant team and others at risk of significant exposure to a recipient's body fluids' to have access to an occupational health service (OHS), up-to-date occupational health record, and pre-xenotransplant baseline blood samples taken for archiving 'indefinitely'.[62] Post-xenotransplant significant exposures and untoward events should be reported 'immediately' to 'relevant local teams and national bodies', with the follow-up to such incidents including 'appropriate laboratory testing' and sample archiving.[63] Active surveillance here is the responsibility of the OHS, and laboratory and clinical surveillance will be linked to national surveillance schemes for occupational exposures to blood-borne viruses, and could involve requesting monthly information from the xeno-centre and associated OHS.[64] Health workers will thus not be subject to active surveillance via laboratory tests and clinical assessment at minimum scheduled follow-up visits and will only undergo such tests if there is a significant exposure or an untoward event.[65]

An OHS is also central to the US scheme and xeno-trial *sponsors* are required to ensure that an OHS programme is available to educate workers about the risks of xenotransplantation and to monitor possible

---

NHMRC, XWP, *Animal-to-Human Transplantation: Final Report*; Health Council, *Xenotransplantation*, para. 5.3.2.

[56] UKXIRA, *Draft Report*, para. 2.5.
[57] *Ibid.*; similarly, Sweden – Swedish Committee, *From One Species*, p. 17.
[58] UKXIRA, *Draft Report*, para. 2.5, Annex Three. [59] *Ibid.*, para. 2.8, Annex Three.
[60] *Ibid.*, Annex Three. [61] Health Canada, *Report of the Xenotransplantation*, p. 16.
[62] UKXIRA, *Draft Report*, para. 2.5, Annex Three. [63] *Ibid.*
[64] *Ibid.*, para. 2.8, Annex Three.
[65] Similarly, Sweden – Swedish Committee, *From One Species*, p. 17.

infections.[66] The trial sponsor and OHS should develop protocols for monitoring workers, describing methods for storing and retrieving personnel records and collecting serologic specimens.[67] Pre-xenotransplant, baseline sera should be provided by those who 'provide direct care to xenotransplantation product recipients, and laboratory personnel who handle, or are likely to handle, animal cells, tissues and organs or biologic specimens from xenotransplantation product recipients'.[68] The sera can then be compared to that collected following an occupational exposure and, as with xeno-recipients, the samples should be stored for fifty years.[69] Written protocols should be devised for evaluating health care workers who experience, for example, a needlestick injury, with such exposures immediately reported to the OHS and the information which the protocol should require to be reported set out.[70] The health exposure log should be maintained for at least fifty years post-xenotransplant and continue even if the worker is no longer employed at the centre or the centre stops performing xenotransplants.[71] It was also recommended that a programme is developed to monitor, educate, counsel and advise health care providers of the risks and 'passive screening' adopted, including baseline samples.[72] The differences in the monitoring schemes of health workers is important because in the event that an infectious disease is transmitted these workers may not only have the greatest knowledge and understanding but also be more likely to succumb to any infection.

Additional requirements
Xeno-recipients

The UK and US schemes must be complied with even if the xenotransplant is unsuccessful, and all xeno-recipients should agree to anonymised information being released for research or analysis.[73] Under all three regimes xeno-recipients must remain contactable,[74] with UK recipients allowing relevant health authorities to be informed if they move abroad.[75] They will also have to inform any doctor they register

---

[66] US DHHS, FDA, *PHS Guideline*, paras. 4.2.3, 4.2.3.1, 4.2.3.2. Similarly, New Zealand: HRC, *Guidelines for Preparation*, Guideline 7.11; Spain – 'Recommendations for the Regulation', pp. 41–42.
[67] US DHHS, FDA, *PHS Guideline*, para. 4.2.3.2.   [68] Ibid.   [69] Ibid.
[70] Ibid., para. 4.2.3.3.   [71] Ibid.
[72] US DHHS *et al.*, *Guidance for Industry: Source Animal*, Section VIII F4.
[73] UKXIRA, *Draft Report*, A5.2; US DHHS, FDA, *PHS Guideline*, para. 2.5.10.
[74] Health Canada, *Proposed Canadian Standard*, p. 6; UKXIRA, *Draft Report*, A5.2; US DHHS *et al.*, *Guidance for Industry: Source Animal*, Section VIII J2a vi; US DHHS, FDA, *PHS Guideline*, para. 2.5.8.
[75] UKXIRA, *Draft Report*, A5.2.

with of their status as a xeno-recipient, declare their status to any doctor who provides them with emergency treatment and advice, and identify possible contacts beyond close contacts if an 'adverse event' occurs, although no means of policing these requirements is stated.[76] Under the UKXIRA and Health Canada's schemes xeno-recipients 'must' consent to their contacts being told about their condition, the procedure, subsequent treatment and possible side effects for both the xeno-recipient and symptoms in themselves[77] and, in the UK, xeno-recipients' consent to passing personal information on to others 'must' be obtained.[78] Health Canada also noted that xeno-transplantation might raise insurance and employment issues,[79] and under the US scheme xeno-recipients should be informed that they might be subject to 'confinement, reverse isolation or other specialized medical housing', isolated if they are hospitalised and, following discharge, might have to undertake specific precautions to minimise the infection risk.[80] Health Canada noted the possibility of quarantine in the event of infection,[81] and the Health Council of the Netherlands has stated that 'during the clinical experimentation phase at least, it would be necessary to restrict the number of people with whom a patient had contact ... so as to keep the postoperative monitoring programme to tolerable proportions. As a result, the organ recipient's freedom of movement would need to be restricted.'[82]

Procreation

In 1999 the UKXIRA stated that xeno-recipients are 'likely to [be] *require[d]*' to use barrier contraception 'consistently and for life' and 'refrain from pregnancy/fathering a child';[83] but in 2001 this was changed, without explanation, to barrier contraception being '*recommended*' and recipients *should* 'seek advice' before having children.[84] It was noted that xeno-recipients' personal circumstances and relationships

---

[76] *Ibid.*
[77] Health Canada, *Proposed Canadian Standard*, p. 6; UK – *ibid.* Similarly, Switzerland – Statement of Position, 'Medical–Ethical Principles', p. 391.
[78] UKXIRA, *Guidance*, para. 7.14.
[79] Health Canada, *Proposed Canadian Standard*, p. 6.
[80] US DHHS *et al.*, *Guidance for Industry: Source Animal*, Section VIII J2b ii; US DHHS, FDA, *PHS Guideline*, para. 2.5.5.
[81] Health Canada, *Proposed Canadian Standard*, p. 6. Similarly, France – CCNE, *Opinion on Ethics*, p. 8; New Zealand – HRC, *Guidelines for Preparation*, Guideline 8; Spain – 'Recommendations for the Regulation', p. 41; WHO, *Xenotransplantation*, para. 6.6.3.
[82] Health Council, *Xenotransplantation*, para. 5.3.2.
[83] UKXIRA, *Draft Report*, A5.2, emphasis supplied. This was discounted in Nuffield Council, *Animal-to-Human*, para. 6.36.
[84] UKXIRA, *Third Annual Report*, p. 15, emphasis supplied.

might not remain constant, so when seeking consent to the surveillance regime the xeno-recipient 'may' need to be counselled about informing future sexual partners of their status as a xeno-recipient.[85] Both the Canadian and US schemes noted the risks associated with procreation, with the former stating that recipients and their contacts would have to be informed and counselled that barrier contraception should minimise these risks.[86] However, Health Canada offers conflicting advice with two sections stating that the consent form should make it clear that xeno-recipients and their contacts should '*never*, subsequent to receiving the transplant ... engage in unprotected sex',[87] but later stating this is merely 'recommended'.[88] The US DHHS also recommended that the potential risk to sexual partners was made clear and that infection transmission to 'their offspring during conception, embryonic/fetal development and/or breast-feeding cannot be excluded',[89] and xeno-recipients provided with advice on using contraceptive barriers.[90]

These limitations raise important issues about enforceability and the human rights of xeno-recipients and connected others, but were only minimally explored in UKXIRA's report and not at all by Health Canada or the US DHHS.[91] The effectiveness of any requirement limiting procreation will depend on the disclosure and compliance of sexual contacts, and a legally enforceable requirement to use barrier contraception would not be possible. 'Safe sex is premised on an awareness and acceptance of risk and, in turn, on the production of trust',[92] and as the risks of xenotransplants are uncertain, it is questionable whether recipients will understand and accept them, and whether they and their sexual partners (current and future) will then act appropriately. Xeno-recipients are likely to 'assess their own risk in light of their own circumstances and belief';[93] thus, if the xenotransplant survives for any length of time and no sign of ill health is detected, their perception of the need for behaviour modification may

---

[85] UKXIRA, *Draft Report*, A5.2.   [86] Health Canada, *Proposed Canadian Standard*, p. 6.
[87] *Ibid.*, p. 7, emphasis supplied; 'the patient is *obligated* to follow up all of the requirements of the program which include: ... safe sex practice' (p. 6, emphasis supplied).
[88] *Ibid.*, p. 33.   [89] US DHHS, FDA, *PHS Guideline*, para. 2.5.12.
[90] US DHHS *et al.*, *Guidance for Industry: Source Animal*, Section VIII J2 iii.
[91] UKXIRA, *Draft Report*, A5.3.
[92] S. Scott and R. Freeman, 'Prevention as a Problem of Modernity: The Example of HIV and AIDS', in J. Gabe (ed.), *Medicine, Health and Risk: Sociological Approaches* (Oxford: Blackwell, 1995), pp. 151, 162.
[93] L. Johnson, 'Particular Issues of Public Health: Infectious Disease', in R. Martin and L. Johnson (eds.), *Law and the Public Dimension of Health* (London: Cavendish, 2001), pp. 243, 256.

decrease. The most that may be hoped of sexually active, fertile xeno-recipients is that they understand the importance of and need for using precautions, although this is not fail-safe as precautions are sometimes unsuccessful. If clinical xenotransplants are to proceed and if we are serious about limiting the risk of infection transmission via these routes, then who is offered a xenotransplant becomes important if compliance with the limits on procreation is to be assured. The 'safest' recipients in this context are post-menopausal women, the infertile, and those who have been sterilised. Clinical xenotransplants could thus be limited to these groups. Alternatively, those who want a xenotransplant could be compulsorily sterilised. These options have not been publicly considered, nor has there been discussion regarding what would happen if the agreement not to reproduce were ignored and a pregnancy established; would a termination be imposed? The practicalities of limiting the procreative capacity of xeno-recipients and the reality of expecting future sexual partners to be bound by arrangements made by their current partners before their relationship existed must be addressed.

Donation, post-mortems and tissue storage

All three schemes acknowledged the dangers of donation following a xenotransplant; in the UK xeno-recipients 'must' refrain from donating blood or organs,[94] and in the US and Canada 'Whole Blood, blood components, including Source Plasma and Source Leukocytes, tissues, breast milk, ova, sperm, or any other body parts for use in humans'.[95] In the US potential organ, tissue and blood donors should be asked if they have received an organ, skin graft or other tissue transplant from another human in the past twelve months, and if they have any donation should be deferred.[96] Potential donors should also be asked if they, their sexual partner or a member of their household have received a transplant or other medical procedure involving organs, tissues or cells from a non-human animal, with a positive response leading to further questioning. Even though a system which involves questioning potential donors relies on honest responses, the more detailed provisions of the US and Canadian schemes on donation and questioning should be internationally adopted to protect individual and public health. Such a system exists

---

[94] UKXIRA, *Draft Report*, A5.2.
[95] US DHHS *et al.*, *Guidance for Industry: Source Animal*, Section VIII J2a ii; US DHHS, FDA, *PHS Guideline*, para. 2.5.11; Health Canada, *Proposed Canadian Standard*, p. 7 and p. 33. Also US DHHS *et al.*, *Guidance for Industry: Precautionary Measures*, p. 5.
[96] US DHHS *et al.*, *Guidance for Industry: Precautionary Measures*, p. 6.

in the UK for blood donation,[97] and all donors should be made aware that they will be asked about their, and others', medical history. A central national xeno-register will aid here, as it can be checked to see whether a potential donor was listed as a xeno-recipient, contact or involved health workers. The xeno-recipient and others must accept that as a condition of receiving a xenotransplant their names will be held on the register and their status disclosed to others in specified circumstances. This appears to breach confidentiality but is essential to protect public health and would fall within accepted exceptions to the principle.[98] Furthermore, all three schemes recognised the importance of xeno-recipients undergoing post-mortems ('should' Canada, 'must' UK, 'request' US) and the need to tell family members of this agreement,[99] with xeno-recipients having to agree to samples being stored following the post-mortem in the UK.[100] Consideration must be given as to whether these must be mandatory because of the risks.

Contacts

The UKXIRA required those proposing xeno-trials to provide 'details of any information to be provided to [close contacts/relatives of the patient] – or requirements to be imposed on them'.[101] Contacts 'may need to be asked to comply with' keeping their current name and address on a register so they are contactable and divulging anonymised information to others for research or analysis.[102] They 'should' refrain from donating blood and organs,[103] and their GP will be made aware that they are a xeno-recipient's contact as they will receive information about the tests the contacts have undergone.[104] Similarly, in Canada contacts need to remain contactable and *recipients* should report 'any serious or unexplained illness' in their contacts to the *recipient's* doctor.[105] The xeno-recipient should also discuss insurance and employment issues with 'family members who may be affected',[106] and contacts should be subject to the same limits on donation as recipients.[107] Only xeno-recipients

---

[97] NHS Blood and Transplant, 'Donor Health Check' (at: www.blood.co.uk/can-i-give-blood/donor-health-check, accessed 18/03/11).
[98] For the UK see GMC, *Confidentiality*.
[99] Health Canada, *Proposed Canadian Standard*, pp. 6, 33; UKXIRA, *Draft Report*, A5.2; US DHHS *et al.*, *Guidance for Industry: Source Animal*, Section VIII J2a viii; US DHHS, FDA, *PHS Guideline*, para. 2.5.9; also, New Zealand – HRC, *Guidelines for Preparation*, Guideline 8; Norway – Gjørv, 'Political Considerations', 57; Spain – 'Recommendations for the Regulation', p. 40.
[100] UKXIRA, *Draft Report*, A5.2.   [101] UKXIRA, *Guidance*, para. 7.16.
[102] UKXIRA, *Draft Report*, A5.2.   [103] *Ibid.*   [104] *Ibid.*
[105] Health Canada, *Proposed Canadian Standard*, p. 6, emphasis supplied.
[106] *Ibid.*   [107] *Ibid.*, pp. 7 and 33.

must remain contactable in the US, with the approach to contacts based on education, including educating them of the need to report 'any significant unexplained illness' to their health care provider.[108] '[P]ersons who have engaged *repeatedly* in activities that could result in intimate exchange of body fluids with a xenotransplantation product recipient' should indefinitely defer from donating blood, tissues, breast milk, semen and ova or other body parts for use in humans,[109] and 'individuals who have had *repeated* exposure to blood and any body fluids through percutaneous inoculation (such as accidental needlestick) or through contact with an open wound, non-contact skin, or mucous membranes' should defer donation.[110] This emphasis on repeated exposure implies that a single exposure is 'safe', but this is not explained or justified. Both Health Canada and the US DHHS noted that xeno-recipients (and in Canada their contacts) should be alerted to the fact that 'infants, pregnant women, the elderly, chronically ill or immuno-suppressed individuals' might be at increased risk of infection transmission,[111] but it is unclear whether this means that recipients with contacts in these categories should not receive a xenotransplant.

Health workers

Health workers in the UK and Canada are not subject to further surveillance provisions, whereas in the US 'individuals who have had repeated exposure to blood and any body fluids through percutaneous inoculation (such as accidental needlestick) or through contact with an open wound, non-contact skin, or mucous membranes' should defer donation.[112] Health workers may fall within this category, and the US DHHS included in the definition of a xeno-recipient's intimate contacts 'health care workers or laboratory personnel with repeated percutaneous, mucosal or other direct exposures'.[113] No explanation is

---

[108] US DHHS, FDA, *PHS Guideline*, paras. 2.5.4 and 2.5.8, respectively; also, Spain – 'Recommendations for the Regulation', p. 41.

[109] US DHHS, FDA, *PHS Guideline*, para. 2.5.11, emphasis supplied; US DHHS *et al.*, *Guidance for Industry: Precautionary Measures*, pp. 2 and 5; US DHHS *et al.*, *Guidance for Industry: Source Animal*, Section VIII J2a i.

[110] US DHHS *et al.*, *Guidance for Industry: Precautionary Measures*, p. 5, emphasis supplied.

[111] Health Canada, *Proposed Canadian Standard*, p. 6; US DHHS *et al.*, *Guidance for Industry: Source Animal*, Section VIII J2a i; also, New Zealand – HRC, *Guidelines for Preparation*, Guideline 8.

[112] Above, n. 108.

[113] US DHHS *et al.*, *Guidance for Industry: Precautionary Measures*, p. 2; US DHHS *et al.*, *Guidance for Industry: Source Animal*, Section VIII J2a i; US DHHS, FDA, *PHS Guideline*, para. 2.5.11. Adopted in New Zealand: HRC, *Guidelines for Preparation*, Guideline 7.11.

provided for this, nor for the lack of additional provisions relating to health workers in the UK and Canada.

National

The importance of national surveillance is acknowledged in the schemes, with Canada and the US recommending setting up a national database to aid public health surveillance.[114] In Canada, within seventy-two hours of a xenotransplant being performed the national registry should be informed of specified information to, *inter alia*, provide baseline information and enable recipients to be tracked.[115] It should be 'immediately' notified of adverse events, and information from the registry should be 'reasonably available to the public' with any identifying information about the xeno-recipient or confidential commercial information protected.[116] In the US a national xenotransplantation database (NXD) was proposed to collect data from the centres conducting xenotransplantation and providing the non-human animals, and a pilot project was performed in 2001.[117] The NXD was to monitor public health by identifying rates of occurrence and clustering of adverse health events, nationally providing accurate links of these events to exposures, notifying individuals and clinical centres of significant adverse events connected to xenotransplantation, and facilitating biological and clinical research assessments.[118] The xenotransplant sponsor would be responsible for providing requested information to the NXD in 'an accurate and timely manner', and information obtained would be publicly available while maintaining commercial or individual confidentiality.[119] A tripartite system of public health protection was envisaged in the US as alongside the NXD, a biologic specimen archive (to be maintained by the sponsor and linked to the NXD with samples deposited in a centrally held archive if introduced), and the (now defunct) SACX were listed under the heading 'Public Health Needs'.[120]

In contrast, under the UKXIRA guidance current public health infection surveillance models and existing UK health and public health structures will be used for infection surveillance purposes, and the information gathered locally will identify 'the necessary data for the

---

[114] Health Canada, *Proposed Canadian Standard*, p. 31; US DHHS, FDA, *PHS Guideline*, para. 5.1. Similarly, Switzerland – Statement of Position, 'Medical–Ethical Principles', p. 391; WHO, *Report of WHO Consultation*, para. 3.3.
[115] Health Canada, *Proposed Canadian Standard*, p. 32.   [116] *Ibid.*, pp. 31–32.
[117] US DHHS, FDA, *PHS Guideline*, para. 5.1. Similarly, Sweden – Swedish Committee, *From One Species*, p. 16; also, pp. 17–18, 23–31.
[118] US DHHS, FDA, *PHS Guideline*, para. 5.1.   [119] *Ibid.*   [120] *Ibid.*, para. 5.

national surveillance system'.[121] 'A specified minimum data set for public health surveillance is required' which should be 'simple, easily collected data to meet defined output'.[122] A 'summary of basic information requirements' was set out,[123] with pre-xenotransplant information required on any 'untoward events' relating to the non-human animal from which the organ is taken, and for recipients 'information [is] required for linkage with all sources of information, patient identifiers, demographic details, and basic baseline clinical details'.[124] Post-xenotransplant information with regard to the non-human animal from which the organ is taken, their workers, the xeno-recipient, their health workers and the recipient's contacts were also listed.[125] Data will be collated and analysed on a 'regular', undefined, basis at one central location with a designated xenotransplantation public health surveillance coordinator, but other centres may also conduct national surveillance.[126] Communication between the local and national teams, to the national surveillance scheme, and to the UKXIRA 'will need to be clearly defined before any xenotransplantation trials take place',[127] and the xeno-recipients and contacts' laboratory tests are to be linked to national laboratory reporting schemes.[128]

The UKXIRA scheme is particularly weak with regard to surveillance at a national level given that only 'basic information requirements' are set out and the failure to set up a national database significantly diminishes the effectiveness of the scheme. If clinical genetically engineered solid organ xenotransplants are to proceed and infection surveillance taken seriously, a *national* central xenotransplant register and database must be established in each country to hold the information on those involved. Specified samples must be provided for testing, archived for agreed periods, and held locally *and* at the national central registry. This registry should be linked to an international database, and international agreement on the information, samples, testing schedule and archiving periods encouraged and sought.

International

International dimensions were not initially discussed by Health Canada or in the US, although they have since been recognised by the former.[129] The international context was consistently recognised by the

---

[121] UKXIRA, *Draft Report*, paras. 1.2, 2.3.   [122] *Ibid.*, para. 2.8.   [123] *Ibid.*
[124] *Ibid.*, Annex Four.   [125] *Ibid.*   [126] *Ibid.*, para. 2.8.   [127] *Ibid.*, para. 2.3.
[128] *Ibid.*, Annex Three.   [129] Health Canada, *Report of the Xenotransplantation*, p. 21.

UKXIRA,[130] but the draft report merely states that 'every effort' should be made to ensure that UK surveillance 'complement[s] international requirements', that international groups performing xenotransplants communicate,[131] and the basic minimum data to 'meet the needs of international surveillance' outlined.[132] In contrast, during the 1990s others acknowledged the need for international cooperation,[133] including the OECD and WHO.[134] One aim was to ensure that internationally 'adequate guidelines are promptly in place ... to prevent possible public health hazards, at the same time allowing medical progress and equitable technology transfer'.[135] The OECD suggested it could facilitate information sharing 'through various means',[136] and both it and the WHO recommended an international register of xeno-recipients and compatibility between national archives and registry procedures to facilitate international cooperation and communication.[137] International collaboration and cooperation is essential because of the risks, national xeno-databases must be established and linked so that if xeno-recipients travel or emigrate surveillance can continue elsewhere.[138] Xenotransplants, their outcomes and adverse events should also be internationally reported.

Effective surveillance?

These surveillance requirements raise many issues; for example, key terms in the UKXIRA's scheme are undefined which is worrying given that by its demise in December 2006 it had considered four clinical trial applications.[139] These lacunae and the ability of individual xeno-teams to decide what is tested and when undermines the attempt to establish national and international surveillance schemes. International guidelines on sampling, testing and archiving schedules are required so that all xeno-teams adhere to a predetermined and clearly defined schedule in

---

[130] See the annual reports: www.dh.gov.uk/ab/Archive/UKXIRA/DH_087899, accessed 18/03/11.
[131] UKXIRA, *Draft Report*, para. 2.4.   [132] *Ibid.*, para. 2.8.
[133] E.g. papers published in J. Fishman *et al.*, *Xenotransplantation*, pp. 202–250.
[134] OECD, *Xenotransplantation*, pp. 43–58, 74–81; WHO, *Report of WHO Consultation*, paras. 7, 8.1.14; OECD, *Advances in Transplantation*, p. 18. See Chapter 4.
[135] OECD, *Advances in Transplantation*, p. 22.   [136] OECD, *Xenotransplantation*, p. 77.
[137] *Ibid.*, p. 76; WHO, *Report of WHO Consultation*, para. 3.3. On the OECD and WHO, see Chapter 4.
[138] J.A. Holland, 'The "Catch-22" of Xenotransplantation: Compelling Compliance with Long-Term Surveillance' (2007) 7 *Houston Journal of Health Law and Policy* 151, 157.
[139] UKXIRA, *Fifth Annual Report*, para. 2.3; UKXIRA, *Third Annual*, para. 4.3; UKXIRA, *Second Annual Report*, paras. 3.15, 3.17.

order to protect the xeno-recipient's and public health. Furthermore, under the UK's Human Tissue Act 2004 appropriate consent to the storage and use of body parts, tissues, cells and organs must be obtained and any UK surveillance scheme must now reflect this.[140] Details of the samples to be taken, where, why and for how long they will be stored should be provided, and best practice would be to discuss this with the xeno-recipient's next of kin and relatives. Employment issues also need to be considered because although the initial recipients are likely to be very ill and their opportunity to work restricted, if a xenotransplant does improve the recipient's health to such an extent that they can return to work, they need to know if their health status will, or should, be disclosed and whether legislation such as the UK's Disability Discrimination Act 1995 will apply. There may be insurance implications as a xeno-recipient who discloses their status may be refused life or health cover, and being a recipient may also affect their employment opportunities. This may have to be accepted as a necessary consequence of their decision, but this should not be assumed. Debate and consultation is important and the possibility of isolation and quarantine must also be publicly aired because of the impact on xeno-recipients' and others' lives and resource implications. Over a decade ago the WHO noted that 'containment steps' might be appropriate to limit infection transmission,[141] and this possibility must be attended to so that xeno-recipients and others know what they are agreeing to when they consent to a xenotransplant. At the very least, the circumstances under which isolation or quarantine can be imposed must be made clear.

The practicalities of obtaining consent to surveillance were not specifically addressed in the schemes;[142] nevertheless, those affected must be informed of, agree to *and* comply with the requirements in order to ensure effective international, national and local surveillance. Compliance, enforcement and sanctions for non-compliance have also received minimal attention in official reports to date, even though lifelong schemes are necessary because of the uncertainty about and possible latency of infections. Recipients may agree to the conditions at the time of xenotransplant and then renege on their agreement. This possibility has not been publicly explored, but there is a sense that xeno-recipients *will* be 'willing to participate in ... an enduring experiment'.[143]

---

[140] See Human Tissue Authority, 'Model Consent Forms' (2010) (at: www.hta.gov.uk/legislationpoliciesandcodesofpractice/modelconsentforms.cfm, accessed 18/03/11).
[141] WHO, *Xenotransplantation*, paras. 6.6.3, 7.   [142] See Chapter 5.
[143] J.A. Fishman, 'Infection and Xenotransplantation', in Fishman *et al.*, *Xenotransplantation*, p. 61.

Allo-recipients do not always comply with their post-operative regimes, particularly once the initial months have passed 'successfully', and xeno-recipients may act likewise.[144] But xenotransplant risks *demand* more than this and consent, compliance and enforcement deserve careful consideration. Furthermore, effective surveillance of contacts will depend on the recipient providing details of their friends and family, but they may not and cannot currently be forced to do so in the UK,[145] so some may be excluded from the regime. Legislation could be introduced to require such disclosures, but without effective enforcement and sanctions it would be meaningless and it is difficult to envisage how gaps can be eliminated without this. The implications of such legislation necessitate public discussion and debate, and more than merely educating contacts of the risks and ways to minimise them, as under the US scheme,[146] is necessary to protect individual and public health. The UKXIRA recognised the important position of contacts and that their changing nature was also a concern,[147] but none of the schemes make clear whether a contact at the time of the xenotransplant but who ceases to be so is obliged to continue to comply with the surveillance regime. These issues must be addressed and clarified in advance to ensure that all parties are aware of their rights and responsibilities.

Most of the xeno-surveillance schemes were devised at an early stage of the biotechnology's development and so regulators can be forgiven for not addressing some issues whose importance has since become clear. However, these schemes have not been revised, perhaps because genetically engineered solid organ xenotransplants are not expected to reach the clinical stage. This is a dangerous assumption to make and national, international and global health security must be taken seriously. The schemes must be revised *before* such solid organs are xenotransplanted into a human, and it is concerning that cellular xenotransplants are occurring without effective post-operative surveillance. The revised schemes must consider the impact on recipients and others, something which is missing from the existing schemes even though, as they stand, their lives will be fundamentally altered. Indeed, '[h]ow will patients react to ongoing tests and treatment? ... Will patients find themselves more identified with the transplant experience because of intense attention and monitoring? Will the emotional burden of possible delayed

---

[144] E.g., L.B. Hilbrands *et al.*, 'Medication Compliance after Renal Transplantation' (1995) 60 *Transplantation* 914. On compliance in other contexts, see J. Dunbar-Jacob and M.K. Mortimer-Stephens, 'Treatment Adherence in Chronic Disease' (2001) 54 *Journal of Clinical Epidemiology* S57.
[145] UKXIRA, *Draft Report*, A5.3.   [146] US DHHS, FDA, *PHS Guideline*, para. 2.5.4.
[147] UKXIRA, *Draft Report*, A5.2; also, US DHHS, SACX, *Informed Consent*, p. 22.

infection and disease or public health risks be stressful? What will monitoring and reporting of sexual contacts do to relationships?'[148] The human rights implications of the proposals are barely explored but are such that alternative forms of consent, discussed below, have been proposed to take account of the particular circumstances of the xeno-recipient and their contacts.

Post-2000 regimes

It might be presumed that the lack of detail in the schemes was due to their development when the science was still advancing; but similarly vague provisions were proposed to, but not endorsed by, the Australian NHMRC in 2004.[149] Similarly, a 2009 NHMRC Discussion Paper stated that 'if deemed appropriate'[150] local, national and international cooperation was needed for '[e]ffective monitoring and surveillance',[151] including a national patient register, health authorities being responsible for implementing a surveillance scheme, and debates required on whether existing frameworks were sufficient to monitor xeno-diseases or specific xeno-legislation was needed.[152] A central xenotransplant register was also recommended in Norway along with a 'special xeno-biobank' to hold 'blood and tissue samples, micro-organisms, biological material' from xeno-recipients, their contacts and the source non-human animal.[153] No timescale for holding such materials was set out but it was noted that '[i]nternationally' fifty years had been suggested.[154] The New Zealand HRC's 2007 guidelines noted the need for post-xenotransplant recipient monitoring, but no local, national or international structures are discussed and individual researchers are to set out the detail in their clinical trial applications.[155] More detail was provided in the National Health Committee's consideration in 2008 of an application to conduct pig cell xenotransplants, with a xenotransplant register and biological specimen archive supported as 'interim solutions' to appropriately managing the risks of a cellular xenotransplant.[156] The director of public

---

[148] M.A. Clark, 'This Little Piggy Went to Market: The Xenotransplantation and Xenozoonose Debate' (1999) 27 *Journal of Law, Medicine and Ethics* 137, 141.
[149] NHMRC, *Guidelines for Clinical*, Guideline 8, accompanying NHMRC, WXP, *Animal-to-Human Transplantation: Final Report*. Also Guidelines 7, 9–11. Similarly, Switzerland – Statement of Position, 'Medical–Ethical Principles'.
[150] NHMRC, Discussion Paper, p. 21.   [151] *Ibid.*, p. 19.   [152] *Ibid.*; also, pp. 21–22.
[153] Gjørv, 'Political Considerations', 56.   [154] *Ibid.*
[155] HRC, *Guidelines for Preparation*, Guideline 7.
[156] *National Health Committee's Advice on Living Cell Technologies Application for Xenotransplantation Clinical Trials in New Zealand* (2008), criterion 2 (at: www.nhc. health.govt.nz/moh.nsf/pagescm/7547/$File/nhc-living-cell-technologies-report-oct082. pdf, accessed 18/03/11).

health was to be responsible for developing and approving a policy framework and an implementation plan for it, 'an official long term register and archive' should be overseen by the director and established within eighteen months of approving a clinical trial.[157] The need for 'lifelong monitoring' was noted, as was engaging in international discussions on public health risk management.[158] This document relates to a specific application to conduct pig cell xenotransplants and these recommendations have not translated into a specific xenotransplant surveillance scheme.[159] Furthermore, the 2006 UK xenotransplant guidance merely states that '[t]raceability and ongoing surveillance of patients is essential'.[160] This is despite the fact that the National Expert Panel on New and Emerging Infections (NEPNEI) had referred the issue of xeno-tourism to the UKXIRA which stated it was 'not looking at the issue ... and agreed the surveillance mechanisms were inadequate in the UK to monitor and identify xenotourists'.[161] The NEPNEI's chair then consulted the WHO, raised the issue of xeno-tourism and 'the need for UKXIRA to do a risk assessment on this and to look into the feasibility of a national register of patients'.[162] As yet nothing has been published on this.

Additionally, although it is widely accepted that an international response to xenotransplantation is needed,[163] minimal practical steps have been taken to achieve this and, for example, the WHO's xenotransplantation inventory website remains optional and has no surveillance remit.[164] In 2003 the Council of Europe recommended that to protect public health biological samples should be collected and stored, xeno-recipients and others traced and monitored, and a 'public health protection plan' needed in member states to 'address any events, in particular of infection, possibly related to a xenotransplantation which could comprise public health'.[165] Member states 'should communicate without delay to national public health authorities of other member states and other concerned states any events, in particular of infection, possibly related to a xenotransplantation which could compromise

---

[157] *Ibid*; also, section 2.3.   [158] *Ibid.*, criterion 2, sections 2.3, 6.10.
[159] See Chapter 4.   [160] DH, *Xenotransplantation*, p. 2.
[161] National Expert Panel on New and Emerging Infections (NEPNEI), *Combined Report 2006–2007* (London: DH, 2008), p. 7.
[162] *Ibid.*
[163] E.g., 'First WHO', Principle 9, Key Recommendations to WHO 1–8; WMA, *World Medical Association Statement on Human Organ Donation*, Section I; WHO, *Statement from the Xenotransplantation*; WHA, *Human Organ and Tissue*. See Chapter 4.
[164] Global Inventory of Xenotransplantation (at: www.humanxenotransplant.org, accessed 18/03/11).
[165] Council of Europe, Recommendation Rec(2003)10, Articles 8, 9, 7, respectively.

public health'.[166] Little has been done to set up or facilitate systems of notification and communication, and no specific xenotransplant infectious diseases, such as PERVs, are listed as a notifiable disease on the European Centre for Disease Prevention and Control website.[167] This is notable because the Centre is an EU agency which aims to '[strengthen] Europe's defences against infectious diseases'[168] and 'identify, assess and communicate current and emerging threats to human health posed by infectious diseases'.[169] As cellular xenotransplants *have* been performed, it is questionable whether infection transmission is being effectively monitored within the EU.

If genetically engineered solid organ xenotransplants are to clinically proceed, international surveillance mechanisms must be instituted otherwise national claims of protecting public health are nugatory, because 'the best efforts at minimizing ... risks in countries with appropriate regulatory oversight may be thwarted by the free travel of individuals undergoing unmonitored xenotransplantation in countries lacking such regulation'.[170] The OECD and WHO have already performed much of the groundwork in this regard but it is disappointing that reports have not been acted upon, given continued pre-clinical research. International surveillance may be difficult,[171] but without it health is endangered because 'global surveillance is the primary tool of prevention'[172] and 'the key to successful management of epidemics is the determination of who is infected'.[173] The importance of securing and protecting global public health has been highlighted by recent experiences of SARS, H5N1 influenza and H1N1 influenza, particularly as

---

[166] *Ibid.*, Article 32.
[167] European Centre for Disease Prevention and Control (ECDC), 'Reportable Communicable Diseases in the EU' (at: http://ecdc.europa.eu/en/healthtopics/spotlight/spotlight_surveillance/Pages/Communicable_diseases.aspx, accessed 18/03/11).
[168] ECDC, 'Mission' (at: www.ecdc.europa.eu/en/aboutus/Pages/AboutUs_Mission.aspx, accessed 18/03/11).
[169] Article 3, Regulation (EC) No. 851/2004 of the European Parliament and of the Council of 21 April 2004 establishing a European centre for disease prevention and control.
[170] M. Sykes *et al.*, 'International Cooperation on Xenotransplantation' (2004) 10 *Nature Medicine* 119, 119.
[171] E.g., criticism of the WHO's handling of the H1N1 influenza pandemic of 2009 (Parliamentary Assembly, Council of Europe, 'The Handling of the H1N1 Pandemic: More Transparency Needed' (2010) AS/Soc. (2010), 12).
[172] House of Lords Select Committee on Intergovernmental Organisations, *Diseases Know No Frontiers: How Effective Are Intergovernmental Organisations in Controlling Their Spread?* (2008) vol. I: Report HL Paper 143-I, para. 50.
[173] D.P. Fidler, 'Constitutional Outlines of Public Health's "New World Order"' (2004) 77 *Temple Law Review* 247, 287.

information on the former was not provided in a timely manner by local health authorities so epidemiologic investigations were delayed.[174] These experiences may have improved the prospects for global health governance,[175] and the WHO's legally binding International Health Regulations which require 194 countries to report outbreaks of certain diseases and public events to the WHO may also help.[176] These Regulations are required because '[i]n the globalized world, diseases can spread far and wide via international travel and trade. A health crisis in one country can impact livelihoods and economies in many parts of the world',[177] and 'effective surveillance programmes are not simply a national matter'.[178] The specific risks of xenotransplantation demand meaningful international collaboration prior to clinical application, and sharing data on infections via such collaboration 'would provide a window of opportunity to limit the impact of future epidemics'.[179] The WHO is well placed to, and must more actively, implement an international xeno-surveillance scheme,[180] but its inability to enforce the standards it sets means that sanctions are required nationally.

Consent, compliance and enforcement

Discussions on the effect of consent, compliance and enforcement to and with xeno-surveillance on established Western legal and ethical norms and their practical effect is largely absent. Rather, there is a sense that these will be dealt with once the science is mastered and that at the clinical stage 'informed consent emerges from behind the curtains to play a pivotal role'.[181] If individual and public health is to be protected, this is too late and these challenges to established norms require earlier consideration otherwise there is a danger that the ball will have gained such momentum that any legal and/or ethical concerns are steamrolled by the understandable desire to save lives. In the majority of medical and

---

[174] J.A. Fishman, 'SARS, Xenotransplantation and Bioterrorism: Preventing the Next Epidemic' (2003) 3 *American Journal of Transplantation* 909.
[175] Fidler, 'Constitutional Outlines', 287.
[176] WHO, *International Health Regulations (2005)* (2nd edn, Geneva: WHO, 2008), as amended in 2008.
[177] WHO, 'What are the International Health Regulations?' (2008) (at: www.who.int/features/qa/39/en/index.html, accessed 18/03/11).
[178] Nuffield Council, *Public Health*, para. 4.48.   [179] Fishman, 'SARS', 911.
[180] On the key role of the WHO, see, e.g., House of Lords, *Diseases Know No Frontiers*, Foreword, paras. 94–119; Nuffield Council, *Public Health*, para. 4.75. Note the WHO's, Global Outbreak Alert & Response Network (at: www.who.int/csr/outbreaknetwork/en, accessed 18/03/11).
[181] Vanderpool, 'IXA – Chapter 7', 261.

scientific literature there is a presumption that effective surveillance *can* be established,[182] but this may not be so as 'there are limits to the enforcement measures that the law will be prepared to accommodate'.[183] Three situations are of especial concern: the xeno-recipient who consents to surveillance but does not comply with it; the role of third parties and the effect of their refusal to consent to or non-compliance with surveillance; and whether xeno-recipients and others can withdraw their consent to a surveillance regime.

Consent and non-compliance

There is unanimity that for xeno-recipients compliance with surveillance can only come through consent.[184] In the US post-xenotransplant surveillance should be raised when seeking consent,[185] and it is 'essential' that xeno-recipients are 'fully informed' that compliance with lifelong surveillance is 'critical'.[186] The UKXIRA also made it clear that consent to surveillance *and* the xenotransplant should be sought '*explicitly* and *in advance*'.[187] Those proposing xenotransplantation are to 'present plans to maximise the compliance of patients and their close contacts'[188] and in both the UK and US the importance of assessing the likely compliance of potential recipients in the selection process was noted.[189] Xeno-recipients 'will need to comply' (Canada), should have 'the commitment to comply' (UK), and understand their 'responsibilities' and give their 'understanding and agreement to comply' (US) with the schemes.[190] Health Canada also said '[c]onsent should indicate

---

[182] E.g., E. Cozzi *et al.*, 'IXA – Chapter 1'.
[183] P.S. Florencio and E.D. Ramanathan, 'Legal Enforcement of Xenotransplantation Public Health Safeguards' (2004) 32 *Journal of Law, Medicine and Ethics* 117, 118.
[184] E.g., Australia – NHMRC, *Guidelines for Clinical*, Guidelines 7–8, accompanying NHMRC, WXP, *Animal-to-Human Transplantation: Final Report*; Canada – Health Canada, *Proposed Canadian Standard*, pp. 6–7, 30; Netherlands – Health Council, *Xenotransplantation*, para. 5.3.2; Sweden – Swedish Committee, *From One Species*, p. 18; Council of Europe, Recommendation Rec(2003)10, Article 16(1)(i); WHO, *Report of WHO Consultation*, para. 4.3.
[185] US DHHS *et al.*, *Guidance for Industry: Source Animal*, Section VIII D; US DHHS, FDA, *PHS Guideline*, para. 2.5.
[186] US DHHS and SACX, *Informed Consent*, pp. vi and 20.
[187] UKXIRA, *Draft Report*, A5.4, emphasis in original; also, A5.3–A5.6
[188] *Ibid.*, para. A5.6.
[189] *Ibid.*, para. A5.7; US DHHS *et al.*, *Guidance for Industry: Source Animal*, Section VIII D.
[190] Health Canada, *Proposed Canadian Standard*, p. 33; UKXIRA, *Draft Report*, A5.4; US DHHS and SACX, *Informed Consent*, pp. ii, vi, 20, 28. In Switzerland '[t]he recipient *must be convinced of his moral obligation*, after the transplantation has been carried out, to adhere to the instructions contained in the protocol, in his own interest and in that of those around him' (Statement of Position, 'Medical–Ethical Principles', p. 391,

that the patient is *obligated* to follow all of the requirements of the program',[191] suggesting they could be compelled to adhere to the regime; but this is not explained or supported. In contrast, the UKXIRA was clear that *only* voluntary compliance was possible because no UK legislation required or forced patients to do so, and legislation to that effect was 'probably not needed'.[192] This was because xeno-recipients will 'perceive the need to attend regular check-ups and to comply with an immunosuppressive drug regime to maintain their health'.[193] However, there is nothing to prevent a xeno-recipient from agreeing to surveillance and then not complying with it; although the US DHHS and SACX and UKXIRA agree that if there were an infection, public health laws might apply.[194] In contrast, the OECD states that 'it is unlikely that public health officials will be able to enforce strict compliance or restrain young patients in particular who have returned to good health and who are looking forward to leading a normal life'.[195] However, under Article 21 of the Council of Europe's Recommendation Rec(2003)10 if the xeno-recipient does not comply with 'the constraints associated with xenotransplantation, public authorities should intervene and take appropriate measures, where public health protection so requires, in conformity with principles of necessity and proportionality'. This might include, if provided for by national laws, 'registration, compulsory medical follow-up and sampling'.[196] The IXA has also suggested that 'governments may consider whether research subjects should be informed that certain government services will be withheld from subjects who do not honor their original promises to abide by practices that will minimize infectious disease risks'.[197]

Given the complex and restrictive nature of the proposals, ensuring compliance will be difficult and it is hard to see how, without more, public health will be safeguarded. It is not unreasonable to predict that xeno-recipients, as with allo-recipients, might initially understand the need for compliance but that this may change in the medium or long term, particularly if no infection is identified and/or they remain asymptomatic. Geography and convenience may influence how compliant the key groups

---

emphasis supplied). In Australia recipients must be 'aware of the need for' surveillance: NHMRC, *Guidelines for Clinical*, Guideline 6, accompanying NHMRC, WXP, *Animal-to-Human Transplantation: Final Report*.

[191] Health Canada, *Proposed Canadian Standard*, p. 6, emphasis supplied.
[192] UKXIRA, *Draft Report*, A5.3.   [193] *Ibid*.
[194] US DHHS and SACX, *Informed Consent*, p. 20; UKXIRA, *Draft Report*, A5.3.
[195] OECD, *Xenotransplantation*, p. 72.
[196] Council of Europe, Recommendation Rec(2003)10, Article 21.
[197] Sykes *et al.*, 'Position Paper', p. 198.

are,[198] but long-term commitment is crucial given the risks and possibility of latent infections. Compliance is 'presumably of the highest order of significance otherwise it would not be required in the first place',[199] but if public health is to be protected it cannot be left to goodwill and the vagaries of human nature. The law must intervene to protect individual and public health but this raises a number of issues because, as with other communicable infectious diseases, the xeno-recipient can be seen as both an individual victim with needs, interests and rights and a potential disease vector, a threat to the wider community.[200]

Third parties

As with recipients, in some countries it has been suggested that contacts should consent to the surveillance scheme[201] with, in Canada, the xeno-recipient's partner 'at a minimum' also consenting.[202] In the US, the consent of third parties has 'no legal foundation' unless they are specifically involved in the research; thus, reliance is placed on the xeno-recipient 'educating' her contacts.[203] Nevertheless, it is more legally and ethically appropriate for contacts to consent to surveillance because of the limitations which may be placed on how they live their lives. The Council of Europe has recognised that requiring consent from others 'might set aside other moral principles like autonomy, privacy and confidentiality' but that '[t]hese principles are never absolute obstacles and communities are entitled to limit them where there is serious harm to the individual concerned or to other people'.[204] 'A high level of risk to public health' would fall within this.[205] Affected third parties are not limited to contacts, but the consent of health professionals has not been specifically

---

[198] Holland, '"Catch-22"', p. 157.
[199] S.A.M. McLean and L. Williamson, 'Xenotransplantation: A Pig in a Poke?' (2004) 57 *Current Legal Problems* 443, 459.
[200] C.B. Smith *et al.*, 'Are There Characteristics of Infectious Diseases that Raise Special Ethical Issues?' (2004) 4 *Developing World Bioethics* 1, 2.
[201] E.g. Netherlands – Health Council, *Xenotransplantation*, para. 5.3.2; Sweden – Swedish Committee, *From One Species* p. 18; UK – UKXIRA, *Draft Report*, A5.4; also, Council of Europe, *State of the Art*, para. 7.5.3; WHO, *Report of WHO Consultation*, para. 8.1.7. In Australia contacts must be 'aware of the need for' surveillance: NHMRC, *Guidelines for Clinical*, Guideline 6, accompanying NHMRC, WXP, *Animal-to-Human Transplantation: Final Report*, and in Norway 'close relatives' should be informed in writing of the xeno-recipients surveillance regime as this may also 'directly influence their lives' (Gjørv, 'Political Considerations', 57).
[202] Health Canada, *Proposed Canadian Standard*, p. 7.
[203] US DHHS and SACX, *Informed Consent*, pp. 21–22. Educating 'those in close personal relationships with the recipient' is also suggested in Council of Europe, *State of the Art*, para. 7.5.3.
[204] Council of Europe, *State of the Art*, para. 7.5.3.   [205] *Ibid.*

addressed so far. The US DHHS and SACX emphasised the need for their education,[206] and it may be that their consent can be implied as part of their contract of employment, but involved health professionals should explicitly consent to any surveillance regime *because* their 'personal privacy' is also involved.[207] They must know who will have access to any results and what will happen if, for example, a 'difficult or embarrassing infection' is revealed.[208] Such specific consent will ensure that health professionals considering being involved in xenotransplantation are clear about their current and future roles and responsibilities, thereby, it is hoped, increasing the effectiveness of the surveillance scheme. However, as with xeno-recipients, there is nothing to prevent a contact or health professional from agreeing to surveillance and then not complying, although the Council of Europe's Article 21 also applies to contacts.

The involvement of third parties, particularly contacts, in surveillance sets xenotransplantation apart from other developing biotechnologies, but many reports have not explained whether having a contact without capacity or one who refuses to consent to surveillance *prevents* a patient being a xeno-recipient. The UKXIRA said it would 'probably not' allow a recipient with contacts who could not consent to receive a xeno-transplant, which seems to exclude those with non-competent children.[209] The Council of Europe has noted that there are ethical issues in selecting xeno-recipients on this basis and 'the danger is a move away from treating the individual ... as an end in him or her self'.[210] However, 'it is important to recognise that close contacts do have obligations' and health professionals should judge whether contacts are likely to comply and provide xeno-recipients with the required support.[211] The Health Council of the Netherlands has gone further stating that while 'the voluntary and informed cooperation of [immediate] contacts [to constant monitoring] is required ... further direct contact between the patient and anyone who declines to cooperate in this regard would not be possible'.[212] The behaviour of contacts would thus not prevent the selection of a xeno-recipient, 'merely' their ability to interact with them. How such restrictions would be introduced and enforced is not addressed, but allowing the decisions of third parties to influence the selection or freedom of xeno-recipients further sets xenotransplantation

---

[206] US DHHS and SACX, *Informed Consent*, pp. 22–23; also, US DHHS, FDA, *PHS Guideline*, para. 4.2.3.1.
[207] H.Y. Vanderpool, 'Critical Ethical Issues in Clinical Trials with Xenotransplants' (1998) 351 *The Lancet* 1347, 1348.
[208] *Ibid.*   [209] UKXIRA, *Draft Report*, A5.5.
[210] Council of Europe, *State of the Art*, para. 7.5.3.   [211] *Ibid.*
[212] Health Council, *Xenotransplantation*, para. 5.3.2.

apart from other developing biotechnologies and this distinction requires support, justification and public discussion. Nevertheless, if clinical genetically engineered solid organ xenotransplants are to be performed and individual and public health are to be protected, it *must* be accepted that the refusal of a contact to consent to surveillance negates the xeno-recipient's consent *unless* restrictions on who recipients can have contact with are considered a viable alternative.

Furthermore, while contacts at the time of a xenotransplant might understand the need for and thus agree to being monitored, what if they cease to be so close to the recipient; do they remain obligated to the scheme? Similarly, what of 'new', post-xenotransplant contacts: can and should they be bound to surveillance, or is consent required from them? What if they refuse? It may be that if the xeno-recipient survives long enough and is able to make new, intimate contacts that suggests that the health risk is minimal and thus they need not be involved in any surveillance. But this would be mere speculation and it would be safer and preferable for new contacts to agree to surveillance. They may, however, not understand the importance of following the regime or may feel aggrieved at being restricted by an agreement made prior to their involvement with the recipient. None of these questions have been addressed to date, although the UKXIRA recognised that relationships were not static and that recipients might need counselling about informing future sexual partners of their status.[213] Given the unanimity on the need for post-xenotransplant monitoring and the fact that 'if these [recipients and their contacts] fail to cooperate, the entire surveillance and public health system would be undermined', the status quo cannot remain.[214] Issues of compliance and enforcement of such must thus be considered.

Withdrawing consent

Protecting public health via the voluntary, informed consent of xeno-recipients and their contacts may also be undermined by the well-established right of those involved in a clinical trial to withdraw from it.[215] The UKXIRA declared that the right to withdraw 'at any time' would be retained but 'it [was] necessary and possible to insist' that, as a minimum, xeno-recipients '[would] be deemed to have agreed to allow their NHS number to be used to trace them *in an emergency*'.[216] The implications of such withdrawals were not addressed, nor were the

---

[213] Above, n. 145. [214] Fano, 'If Pigs Could Fly', p. 189. [215] Above, n. 10.
[216] UKXIRA, *Draft Report*, A5.4, emphasis in original; also, UKXIRA, *Guidance*, para. 7.14.

positions of contacts or health workers. However, in permitting xeno-recipients and others to withdraw from the surveillance regime, individual and public health is placed at risk. In the light of this, provided the xeno-recipient and her contacts have been counselled and consented to the xenotransplant, post-xenotransplant there must be no right to withdraw from the surveillance regime. While a recipient can change her mind and withdraw from the trial itself, she *must* be legally required to remain within the surveillance scheme because the potential for transmitting (latent) infectious diseases means that those who consent to be involved in a xenotransplant have responsibilities to others.[217] Consenting to a xenotransplant *is* different to consenting to other experimental procedures or trials and permitting withdrawal from surveillance has implications for individual and public health. The IXA recently recommended this for porcine islet xenotransplants, but the legal and ethical implications were not explored other than that informing recipients of non-withdrawal would 'resolve' the conflict with the provisions of the Declaration of Helsinki, CIOMS and WHO guidelines, and US federal regulations.[218] The law must be involved to implement this proposal and, if this occurs, 'consent now will need to be enforceable in a direction different from that in the past – this time against the best interests of the subject, and in favour of the public'.[219]

Alternative methods of ensuring compliance

It is clear that reliance *cannot* be placed on traditionally conceived first-party consent to a xeno-surveillance regime to protect individual and public health from the risks. The extraordinary risks mean that xenotransplantation *cannot* simply be slotted into existing legal and ethical structures and so 'something more binding and contractual' may be required; something 'which then would dramatically alter the traditional doctor–patient relationship'.[220] No report has adopted anything other than a consent-based system, although alternative methods to 'encourage' compliance could include withholding government services from non-compliant parties, financial incentives for compliance, and fines for non-compliance.[221] But can existing civil or criminal law be used to secure compliance with a xeno-surveillance scheme, or is new legislation required?

---

[217] Recommended in Norway (Gjørv, 'Political Considerations', 57).
[218] Vanderpool, 'IXA – Chapter 7', p. 260.
[219] Daar, 'Xenotransplantation – Science', p. 134.
[220] A.S. Daar, 'Ethics of Xenotransplantation: Animal Issues, Consent, and Likely Transformation of Transplant Ethics' (1997) 21 *World Journal of Surgery* 975, 977.
[221] Above, n. 195; Florencio and Ramanathan, 'Legal Enforcement', 119.

Contract law

Should those involved in a xenotransplant have to sign a binding contract agreeing to comply with, among other things, the surveillance regime?[222] For a legally binding contract to exist, there must be an agreement expressed in a sufficiently certain form for the courts to be able to enforce it, and it should be supported by consideration.[223] There are some requirements regarding the form which the agreement should take and the parties must have an intention to create legal relations, presumed in commercial but not domestic and social arrangements.[224] Both parties must have the capacity to enter into a legal contract, consent to do so freely and voluntarily, and the purpose of the contract must not be illegal or contrary to public policy.[225] On the face of it, a contract to abide by the necessary surveillance regime for the xeno-recipient, her contacts and involved health professionals could be drawn up. However, a number of issues require clarification, including who the contract would be between; the hospital in which the operation was performed, the regulator, the state or the company which supplied the non-human source animals? Health care provision in the UK, via the NHS, is not based on a contract between the patient and another, but if a contractual approach to ensuring compliance is adopted, a new approach to health provision would be introduced, which would require careful consideration and public debate and discussion.

A binding contract forcing participation with lifelong monitoring would, however, be 'inconsistent with current legal principles' given that 'consent to medical treatment is characterized not as a *contract*, but as a *permission*'.[226] Given the pressure on and desire of potential recipients to agree to a xenotransplant, they could argue that they did not have the capacity to consent to a surveillance contract or that they had been coerced into signing it because of the situation they were in: no other hope.[227] To counter this, 'outline' consent to surveillance could be sought while the xeno-recipient is on the allotransplant waiting list so that any issues about coercion or capacity could be addressed over

---

[222] E.g., Holland, '"Catch-22"', 174–179; Florencio and Ramanathan, 'Xenotransplantation Safeguards', 949–953; Caulfield and Robertson, 'Xenotransplantation'; Cooper and Lanza, *Xeno*, p. 218.
[223] E. McKendrick, *Contract Law – Text, Cases and Materials* (4th edn, Oxford University Press, 2010), pp. 19–20.
[224] *Ibid.*
[225] E. McKendrick, *Contract Law* (8th edn, Basingstoke: Palgrave MacMillan, 2009), chs. 15–16.
[226] Caulfield and Robertson, 'Xenotransplantation', 86, emphasis in original.
[227] See Chapters 3 and 5.

Alternative methods of ensuring compliance 219

time.[228] But this would not alter the fact that consent would still have to be obtained *at the time of the xenotransplant*. Thus, concerns about asking those who are desperately ill to consent to surveillance *at the time when they have no other hope* will not be eradicated. However, under the MCA 2005 competent adults in England and Wales *can* refuse treatment *in advance* for when they are no longer competent.[229] An analogy could be drawn and an argument constructed that xeno-recipients and others can be legally bound to a lifelong surveillance contract to which they have consented in advance. The OECD and WHO have considered this option; 'the Ulysses contract' where someone 'binds him-/herself in advance to a future therapeutic course of action'.[230] Such contracts have been mooted for those with fluctuating capacity so that treatment can be provided against their will when needed and when they are not competent to consent to it. For xenotransplantation, the binding consent/contract would be enforced to protect *others* and not just the recipient herself.[231] Despite this, such a contract could be ethically justifiable as there *are* alternatives to xenotransplantation,[232] and if public health is to be protected this possibility merits public discussion. At the very least, using a Ulysses contract to remove the right to withdraw from the surveillance scheme should be considered.

There may also be policy reasons for not viewing consent as a binding contract including the patient's vulnerability, the balance of knowledge and power between doctor and patient, and if the xeno-recipient, contact, etc., can show that they were unduly influenced to enter into the contract, that contract can be set aside.[233] Undue influence cases tend to involve some form of advantage-taking and it is not inconceivable that an argument could be constructed that the other party to the contract had taken advantage of the relationship of trust and confidence in her to the substantial detriment of the recipient. Furthermore, a surveillance contract may be unenforceable as being against public policy because of

---

[228] Note that the UK RCP's states that when considering proposals to involve those with no other hope, RECs should review them 'sympathetically' and that 'innovative methods of consent, such as the use of advance directives' might be used (RCP, *Guidelines*, para. 8.68).
[229] Sections 24–26.
[230] OECD, WHO, *OECD/WHO Consultation on Xenotransplantation Surveillance: Summary* (2001) WHO/CDS/CSR/EPH/2001.1, p. 21.
[231] *Ibid.*
[232] M.A. Spillman and R.M. Sade, 'Clinical Trials of Xenotransplantation: Waiver of the Right to Withdraw from a Clinical Trial Should Be Required' (2007) 35 *Journal of Law, Medicine and Ethics* 265.
[233] McKendrick, *Contract Law – Text*, ch. 19.

the necessary restrictions of liberty.[234] Even if these issues are addressed, the effectiveness of contract law to protect individual and public health will rest on its ability to enforce the contract. If the xeno-recipient breaches that contract by refusing to comply with the surveillance regime, monetary damages can be claimed for loss caused by the breach, with the aim being to put the claimant in the position she would have been in had the contract been performed.[235] But the claimant can only be the other party to the contract and it may not be this party who suffers loss by being infected because of the breach. Even if this party is infected and so affected by the breach, the damage has been done and no amount of money will put her in the position she would have been in if the breach had not occurred. Also, the damage from the transmitted infection may not be evident for some time after the breach, so would the xeno-recipient remain liable fifteen years post-xenotransplant, and would it be possible to show that the breach caused the loss suffered by the other party after such a lapse of time? It is similarly unclear whether a court would order specific performance of a surveillance contract and make the person breaching the contract comply with it.[236] Thus, contract law does not seem the most appropriate way of enforcing compliance with a xeno-surveillance regime as such a contract would be of little value if the signatory could not be *made* to follow the regime.

Existing public health law

When the UKXIRA published its 1999 draft report on surveillance the relevant statute was the Public Health (Control of Disease) Act 1984, and this has been substantially amended by the Health and Social Care Act 2008.[237] Under section 45A of the amended 1984 Act if an infection 'presents or could present significant harm to human health', the appropriate minister can make regulations giving effect to international agreements or arrangements,[238] and when giving effect to such health protection regulations can amend any enactment and may 'provide for the execution of restrictions and requirements imposed by or under the regulations'.[239] The minister can make regulations for 'preventing danger to public health' because of international travel and from persons

---

[234] *Horwood v. Millar's Timber* [1917] 1 KB 305.
[235] McKendrick, *Contract Law*, chs. 19–20.
[236] McKendrick, *Contract Law – Text*, ch. 24.
[237] In the event of an 'emergency', 'an event or situation which threatens serious damage to human welfare in a place in the United Kingdom' (section 1(1)(a)), the provisions of the Civil Contingencies Act 2004 will also apply.
[238] Section 45B 1984 Act, as amended. [239] Section 45F(2)(d).

arriving at any place,[240] and might include provisions for 'medical examination, detention, isolation or quarantine of persons',[241] 'prohibiting or regulating ... the entry or exit of persons', and 'requiring persons to provide information or answer questions (including information or questions relating to their health)'.[242] Regulations can be made to prevent, protect against, control or respond to the incidence or spread of infection in England and Wales, whether or not the risk originated there.[243] These can be in relation to infection generally, particular forms of infection, and can make general, contingent or specific provisions.[244] Examples of particular provisions include: (i) imposing notification and recording duties on registered medical practitioners for infection and suspected infection cases;[245] (ii) giving local authorities monitoring of public health risks functions;[246] and (iii) imposing restrictions or requirements on persons 'in the event of, or in response to, a threat to public health'.[247] The latter includes 'a special restriction or requirement' which can only be imposed by a magistrate.[248] A restriction or requirement with regard to threats to public health cannot be made unless the appropriate minister, when making the regulations, considers that the measures are 'proportionate to what is sought to be achieved by imposing it'.[249] Regulations under section 45C cannot include provisions imposing a special restriction or requirement to require submission to medical examination, removal to or detention in hospital or another suitable establishment, or isolation or quarantine.[250] Provisions enabling the imposition of a special restriction or requirement can only be included if there is: (i) a 'serious and imminent threat to public health' when the regulations are made; or (ii) the decision to impose the restrictions or requirements in the regulations is 'contingent on there being such a threat at the time when it is imposed'.[251] Notably, health protection regulations cannot create an offence triable on indictment, punishable by imprisonment, or by a fine over £20,000.[252]

---

[240] Section 45B.
[241] Medical examination includes 'microbiological, radiological and toxicological tests' (section 45T(3)).
[242] Section 45B(2)(b), (e) and (g), respectively. [243] Section 45C(1).
[244] Section 45C(2).
[245] E.g., Health Protection (Notification) Regulations 2010, SI 2010/659.
[246] E.g., Health Protection (Local Authority Powers) Regulations 2010, SI 2010/657.
[247] Section 45C(3) 1984 Act, as amended. [248] Section 45C(4) and (6).
[249] Section 45D(1)–(2). [250] Sections 45D(3), 45E.
[251] Section 45D(4). Note that under s 1(1) and Schedule 1 Part 2 Human Tissue Act 2004 in England, Wales and Northern Ireland tissue from a living person *can* be stored for use *without* consent for the purposes of public health monitoring.
[252] Section 45F(5).

Magistrates can now order a person to, *inter alia*, submit to medical examination, be removed to or detained in a hospital or other suitable establishment, be kept in quarantine or isolation, provide information, have their health monitored, attend training or advice sessions, and be restricted as to where they go or with whom they have contact, a Part 2A Order.[253] Such an Order can be made if the magistrate is 'satisfied' that: (i) the person 'is or may be infected'; (ii) with an infection 'which presents or could present significant harm to human health'; (iii) there is 'a risk' that the person might infect others; and (iv) the order is 'necessary ... in order to remove or reduce that risk'.[254] Magistrates can order a person who is or may be infected to provide information about the identity of others who may also be infected and there is a risk that that they might infect others; contact tracing.[255] The Health Protection Regulations 2010 set out what evidence must be available to the magistrate before they can be satisfied that there are grounds for making a Part 2A Order.[256] Such an Order[257] may, in addition to the restrictions or requirements in the provision under which it is made, include 'such other restrictions or requirements as the justice considers necessary for the purpose of reducing or removing the risk in question'.[258] A measure in a Part 2A Order may be conditional, a magistrate can include in it directions as to any action that might be appropriate to give effect to the order, and, in some circumstances, the authority to enter premises.[259] Any restriction or requirement in an Order must have a specified time limit, but this can be extended.[260] If the Order imposes detention in a hospital or other suitable establishment, quarantine, or isolation of a person, then the initial period specified in the order or any extension of it cannot exceed twenty-eight days, and the appropriate minister can specify in regulations the maximum period for which any restriction or requirement other than one for detention in those circumstances may be imposed and the maximum period of any extension.[261] Only local authorities may apply for a Part 2A Order, but an affected person[262] can apply for it to be varied or revoked.[263] It is an offence, punishable with a fine of up to £20,000, to fail to comply, without reasonable

---

[253] Section 45G(2). [254] Section 45G(1). [255] Section 45G(3)–(4).
[256] Health Protection (Part 2A Orders) Regulations 2010, SI 2010/658.
[257] Those made under sections 45G-I 1984 Act, as amended.
[258] Section 45K(2). [259] Sections 45K(3), (5)–(6), respectively.
[260] Sections 45K(6), 45L(1)–(2), respectively. [261] Section 45L(3)–(4).
[262] Defined in section 45M(6) as that person, a person with parental responsibility for that person, a person living with that person as husband, wife or civil partner, and such others as prescribed by regulations.
[263] Sections 45M(1) and (5).

excuse, with a restriction or requirement imposed by or under an Order of a magistrate or to wilfully obstruct anyone executing it.[264] If a person leaves a place at which a Part 2A Order requires them to be detained, isolated or quarantined, then a constable may take them into custody and return them to that place.[265]

While the amended 1984 Act could be of some use for clinical xenotransplants, any regulation made under the Act would still not *ensure* compliance with a surveillance regime. Some of the most relevant provisions are time limited and the value of imposing a fine for non-compliance or returning a person to their place of detention, isolation or quarantine (for no more than twenty-eight days) is questionable in this context. Although the amendments to the Act are welcome in the general scheme of infectious disease control and management, they do not significantly aid in protecting health from xenotransplant risks. North American public health statutes are similarly unlikely to be of use in regulating xenotransplantation because of difficulties with invoking and applying them to asymptomatic individuals and the need, in some cases, for a state of public health emergency to be declared.[266]

Existing criminal law

Criminal law might encourage compliance with a xeno-surveillance regime via its deterrent effect and ability to influence behaviour generally and, after the fact, by punishing those not complying with the regime. Indeed, widespread publication of such prosecutions and/or punishment may persuade others to comply with the regimes.[267] It is difficult to prove murder or attempted murder under the English criminal law against someone who infected another with human immunodeficiency virus (HIV),[268] and this will also hold true for those infected by a xeno-recipient. However, the Offences Against the Person Act 1861 might be relevant. There is no specific offence of transmitting a communicable infectious disease, but sections 23 and 24 of the 1861 Act relate to

---

[264] Section 45O(1)–(2). [265] Section 45O(4)–(5).
[266] See, e.g., Holland, '"Catch-22"', 167–172; Caulfield and Robertson, 'Xenotransplantation', 92–93; Florencio and Ramanathan, 'Xenotransplantation Safeguards', 953–960.
[267] E.g., K. Connolly, 'German singer Nadja Benaissa sentenced for infecting lover with HIV', guardian.co.uk, 26 August 2010; K. Connolly, '"In those days I was careless" says pop star accused of infecting man with HIV', guardian.co.uk, 16 August 2010.
[268] S. Bronitt, 'Spreading Disease and the Criminal Law' [1994] *Criminal Law Review* 21; D.C. Ormerod and M.J. Gunn, 'Criminal Liability for the Transmission of HIV' [1996] 1 *Web Journal of Current Legal Issues*; K.J.M. Smith, 'Sexual Etiquette, Public Interest and the Criminal Law' (1991) 42 *Northern Ireland Legal Quarterly* 309.

maliciously administering 'any poison or other destructive or noxious thing' to endanger the life of another or inflict grievous bodily harm on them (s. 23), or intending to injure, aggrieve or annoy them (s. 24). Section 23 involves subjective recklessness,[269] and section 24 requires recklessness and the requisite intention. Section 47 is concerned with an assault occasioning actual bodily harm, 'any hurt or injury calculated to interfere with the health or comfort' of the victim,[270] and it has to be shown that there was an assault or battery, the victim suffered actual bodily harm, the harm was caused by the defendant's assault or battery, and the defendant intended or was reckless as to whether the victim would suffer an assault or battery.[271] Alternatively, under section 18 it is an offence to cause grievous bodily harm, a really serious injury,[272] with intent,[273] and the Court of Appeal has confirmed that if A is HIV positive and has consensual sexual intercourse with B, causing B to become HIV positive, A is guilty of a section 18 offence if A intends to cause B to suffer grievous bodily harm as a result of the sex and it is irrelevant whether B consents to the risk of HIV infection.[274] Thus, intentional transmission is likely to constitute a criminal offence under section 18.

A xeno-recipient who fails to comply with the procreation requirements of a xeno-surveillance regime and thereby infects another appears to fall within one of these sections; however, there are problems with applying these sections in this context. Proving intention may not be straightforward and for sections 23 or 24 an infectious disease must be construed as a poison or destructive or noxious thing and it must be established that the poison or destructive or noxious thing had been 'administered' by the xeno-recipient to a named other.[275] The 1861 Act will also only apply if an infection is identified in the xeno-recipient and the victim, and this may not happen for some time because of difficulties in diagnosis, limits of existing tests and problems of latency. It is unclear whether the Act applies where the xeno-recipient has infected another but did not know they were infected themselves at the relevant time;[276] is that xeno-recipient then liable on the basis that she was informed at the time of the xenotransplant of the risk of infection, hence the need to comply with the surveillance scheme? The causal link

---

[269] R v. Cunningham [1957] 2 QB 396.
[270] R v. Donovan [1934] 2 KB 498, 509, CCA, per Swift J.
[271] R v. Savage; R v. Parmenter [1992] 1 AC 699, HL.
[272] DPP v. Smith [1961] AC 290, HL.
[273] For discussion of mens rea in English law, see J. Herring, Criminal Law: Text, Cases and Materials (4th edn, Oxford University Press, 2010), ch. 3.
[274] R v. Dica [2004] EWCA Crim. 1103; R v. Konzani [2005] EWCA Crim. 706.
[275] See further, Ormerod and Gunn, 'Criminal Liability'. [276] Ibid.

between the xeno-recipient and the person infected must be established, and until a case is brought before the court it is unclear whether these sections apply to communicable infectious diseases.

Section 20, under which it is an offence to unlawfully and maliciously wound or inflict any grievous bodily harm upon any other person, may be of more use. With no legal justification the defendant must have wounded the victim or caused grievous bodily harm to them and have intended or foreseen that the victim might suffer some harm, not necessarily grievous bodily harm. Successful prosecutions have been obtained under this section for HIV transmission.[277] Where C knows he is HIV positive, or has some other serious sexual disease, and he has consensual sexual intercourse with D, causing D to become HIV positive, C will be guilty of a section 20 offence if he is aware of the risk that by having unprotected sex he may cause D to suffer some harm and D does not consent to that risk. Thus, if a xeno-recipient is told she may be suffering from a communicable infectious disease and not to have unprotected sex but does so, without telling her partner she may be infected, she has committed a section 20 offence. Her defences would be that she believed there was no risk that she would infect her partner, or she told her partner of the risk and they agreed to take it. As the xeno-recipient should be told from the outset of the risks of unprotected sex, only the latter may be relevant here.

While the criminal law may be used after the fact to punish the xeno-recipient who infects another, will this help to protect public health?[278] Using the criminal law in this way might have symbolic value but could prove counter-productive for public health initiatives aimed at controlling the spread of infectious disease by stopping people going for testing.[279] The extent to which the criminal law affects and influences people's behaviour is questionable and trying a xeno-recipient for transmitting PERVs to their partner, for example, does little for public health; if the infection has already been transmitted, then it is too late. To protect public health, action must be taken *before* this point. Furthermore, it is unclear whether the OAPA offences only apply where infections are transmitted between sexual partners or in other situations. Criminal law's ability to protect public health is thus unclear and it is debatable whether its use in this area is appropriate.

---

[277] E.g., *R* v. *Dica*; *R* v. *Konzani*.
[278] UNAIDS, *Criminal Law, Public Health and HIV Transmission: A Policy Options Paper* (Geneva: UNAIDS, 2002).
[279] R. Martin, 'The Role of Law in Public Health', in A. Dawson (ed.), *The Philosophy of Public Health* (Surrey: Ashgate, 2009), pp. 11, 19–20.

Introducing specific xenotransplantation legislation

To establish an effective surveillance regime and secure compliance with it, specific xenotransplant legislation may be required; legislation which, in the UK, must comply with the Human Rights Act 1998.[280] Introducing a specific Act would further set xenotransplantation apart from other biotechnologies as it is not common in the UK for statutes to deal with specific medical procedures or treatments;[281] however, such a statute has been proposed in other countries.[282] If introduced, a legal framework for enforcing compliance without a public health emergency could be set out, further taking this biotechnology outside of legal and ethical norms. Nevertheless, if public health cannot be effectively otherwise protected a statute is required because 'in a society where individuals have little control over their living environments, the public expects the state to intervene to prevent known threats to health. The failure of the state to intervene suggests that the threat is minimal, imaginary, or unimportant.'[283] Furthermore, *'restrictions on civil liberties should not be permitted unless they have unambiguous legislative authorization'*,[284] and the risks of xenotransplantation necessitate such a response. Legislation must address compliance and sanctions for non-compliance, the removal of the right to withdraw from the surveillance scheme, and the role of contacts and health workers. It must clearly set out the requirements of the regime with regard to regular sampling and storage (who, what, when, for how long), post-mortems and storage, procreation, donation, isolation and/quarantine, insurance and employment. A contingency plan in the event of infection should also be included. Attention must be given to the possibility of and need for anticipatory action *prior to* established infection transmission and whether and in what circumstances this might be appropriate and/or required, because if action can only be taken on proof of infection this could be too late. Indeed, 'because the threat to public health from xenotransplant recipients is unknown and unpredictable, the crucial language in any law seeking to protect the community from the spread or outbreak of an analogous disease situation will lie in how the statute addresses *potential* risks or threats'.[285]

---

[280] Section 3 Human Rights Act 1998.
[281] Notable exceptions are the Human Fertilisation and Embryology Acts 1990 and 2008.
[282] See Chapter 4.
[283] R. Coker and R. Martin, 'Introduction: The Importance of Law for Public Health Policy and Practice' (2006) 120 suppl. 1 *Public Health* 2, 5.
[284] Sunstein, *Laws of Fear*, p. 211, emphasis in original.
[285] Holland, '"Catch-22"', 181, emphasis in original.

In drafting the legislation, note should be taken of the schemes proposed so far, the critiques of them, and how the adopted scheme might fit into international structures. The issues highlighted here must be addressed, and an effective way of doing this would be to introduce a central xenotransplantation registry to hold the names of all involved parties, their samples and results of tests. Access to this registry must be clearly delineated in order to maintain confidentiality as far as possible. While drafted for an emergency, the proposed US Model State Emergency Health Plan Act could be used as a base for a Xeno Act.[286] The Model Act was developed in response to bioterrorist and epidemic threats, and provides that each state should develop a 'comprehensive plan' so that in a public health emergency there is a 'coordinated, appropriate response'.[287] Emergencies would be detected at an early stage by collecting and reporting data and records and the need to, as far as possible, balance the rights of individuals with 'the common good' was recognised.[288] The Act contains extensive provisions in relation to situations of a declared public health emergency, including medical examination and testing, treatment, isolation and quarantine, but also relates to health threats.[289]

With regard to enforcement powers, it must be considered how best to balance the freedom of those who have sought to benefit from a xenotransplant with their obligations to protect others from the risks they have taken. There must be statutory support for compulsory isolation and quarantine in clearly specified circumstances, as this may be needed to protect the health of the recipient and others. If it proves difficult to clearly limit the scope of these powers, then it must be questioned whether such a biotechnology should be clinically introduced. If this hurdle is crossed, it must also be discussed whether there are situations in which it is legitimate to *impose* obligations on those who take risks with the health of others, albeit indirectly. As it is currently impossible to determine the extent and nature of the risks, must xeno-recipients accept that as well as the potential benefits they must also bear the burdens and obligations which are necessary to protect themselves and others? These changes to accepted legal and ethical norms

---

[286] Suggested in *ibid.*, 178–179, referring to the Center for Law and the Public's Health at Georgetown and Johns Hopkins Universities, *The Model State Emergency Health Powers Act: A Draft for Discussion* (December 21, 2001) (at: www2a.cdc.gov/phlp/docs/msehpa2.pdf, accessed 18/03/11).
[287] Center for Law, *The Model State Emergency*, p. 1, Article I, section 103 (a), Article II, section 202.
[288] *Ibid.*, Article III, sections 301–303, Article I, section 102 (f), (i).
[289] *Ibid.*, Articles IV–VII, section 302.

228 Surveillance and monitoring

demand public consultation and discussion, particularly as they will impact on currently established and protected human rights.

Surveillance and human rights

Between November 2002 and July 2003 8,096 people worldwide were suspected of contracting SARS, of whom 774 died.[290] A range of measures and approaches were adopted to protect health including name reporting, contact tracing for the ten days prior to when it was thought the symptoms had developed, mandatory or voluntary taking of body temperatures, answering health questionnaires, wearing 'fever-free' stickers, travel restrictions, isolation and quarantine.[291] In some countries the police, military and private detectives were involved in implementing the relevant measures, and in others hospitals were responsible. There were also differences in publicly naming those infected, and how quarantine was viewed, as either voluntary or enforceable. Nevertheless, participants in the global consultation on SARS epidemiology agreed that 'early identification and isolation of patients, vigorous contact tracing, management of close contacts by home confinement or quarantine, and public information and education to encourage prompt reporting of symptoms' supported the WHO's view that SARS 'can be contained and driven back out of its new human host'.[292] Many of the approaches noted above impinge on the human rights of those subject to them, and 'infectious disease control implicates the right to life, liberty and security of person, privacy, health, an adequate standard of living, food, housing, education, development, and other rights. Infectious diseases cut across both civil and political rights and economic, social, and cultural rights.'[293] The tension between individual human rights and public health infectious disease control have not, however, been addressed in detail in xenotransplant reports to date,[294] and this is surprising for the UK at least, as the UKXIRA report was published

---

[290] WHO, 'Summary of Probable SARS Cases with Onset of Illness from 1 November 2002 to 31 July 2003' (2004) (at: www.who.int/csr/sars/country/table2004_04_21/en/index.html, accessed 18/03/11).
[291] Gostin et al., 'Ethical and Legal Challenges'.
[292] WHO, 'Update 58 – First Global Consultation on SARS Epidemiology, Travel Recommendations for Hebei Province (China), Situation on Singapore' (2003) (at: www.who.int/csr/sars/archive/2003_05_17/en, accessed 18/03/11).
[293] D.P. Fidler, *International Law and Infectious Diseases* (Oxford: Clarendon Press, 1999), p. 169.
[294] E.g., The Health Council of the Netherlands stated that xeno-recipients' freedom of movement *could* be limited but did not explore how this was compatible with the ECHR (see above, n. 80).

after the ECHR was incorporated into UK law via the Human Rights Act 1998. But if effective xeno-surveillance is to occur, can and should xeno-recipients and others be legally *required* to forego certain rights to protect public health? The Council of Europe has suggested that, in some circumstances, rights or freedoms can be limited and that '[i]t is ethically permissible for patients to choose to set aside such human rights such as the right to begin a family or the freedom to donate blood, if there is some overwhelming public good to be attained or public harm avoided'.[295] Similarly, the WHO has noted that '[e]xceptions to the rights of patients are usually anticipated in law when it is deemed necessary for public good. This often means limitations which apply for reasons of public order, public health and other persons human rights.'[296] However, '[t]he guiding rule in such exceptions is always that patients can be subjected only to such limitations as are compatible with human rights instruments and in accordance with a procedure prescribed by law'.[297] For North America, although elements of a xeno-surveillance scheme might be unconstitutional, existing constitutional doctrines might justify these violations in the 'fundamental interest of protecting the public health'.[298] It is thus not clear whether a xeno-surveillance scheme would or could comply with, for the UK, the ECHR and 1998 Act because of the limits that *need* to be placed on currently statutorily protected rights and/or freedoms.

Xeno-surveillance regimes clearly engage a number of ECHR rights, including the right to life (Article 2), the right not to be subjected to inhuman and degrading treatment (Article 3), the right to liberty and security of the person (Article 5), the right to respect for private and family life (Article 8), the right to freedom of association with others (Article 11), and the right to marry and to found a family (Article 12).[299] Isolation, quarantine and other surveillance provisions, such as remaining contactable and holding personal information on databases, must comply with Article 8(1) which includes the right to individual self-determination.[300] This can only be interfered with by a public authority where this is in accordance with the law and necessary in the interests of, *inter alia*, public safety for the protection of health or the rights and

---

[295] Council of Europe, *State of the Art*, para. 7.5.2.
[296] WHO, *Report of WHO Consultation*, para. 4.3.   [297] *Ibid.*
[298] Florencio and Ramanathan, 'Legal Enforcement', 120, reference removed.
[299] Similarly, Universal Declaration of Human Rights 1948, International Covenant on Civil and Political Rights 1966, American Convention on Human Rights 1969, Canadian Charter of Rights and Freedoms 1982.
[300] S. Wheatley, 'Human Rights and Human Dignity in the Resolution of Certain Ethical Questions in Biomedicine' (2001) *European Human Rights Law Review* 312, 315.

freedoms of others, Article 8(2). A xeno-surveillance scheme would seem to fall within Article 8(2), but the UKXIRA declared that without an emergency, specific legislation providing for the routine surveillance of xeno-recipients to protect public health might fall outside its scope.[301] This is debatable and difficult to understand as no explanation was provided. *Routine* surveillance might have been considered problematic, rather than that which occurs once an infection has been established, as the UKXIRA stated that if a 'demonstrable emergency such as the emergence of a highly infectious disease' existed it would be 'feasible to introduce rapid emergency legislation' which could include detaining people for testing purposes to protect public health.[302] While it is not unreasonable to assume that the government can protect society via enforceable measures in this situation, the suggestion that the public may not ordinarily be protected from the risks of clinical xenotransplantation is worrying. Human rights schemes are generally premised on the idea that in the absence of harm to others the state should not interfere in an individual's choices, and the European Court of Human Rights has recognised the importance of protecting the public and the vulnerable, albeit in different contexts.[303] But it is difficult to see how a law which explicitly allowed for routine surveillance in order to ensure public protection would not be encompassed by Article 8(2). If this is not so and *routine* surveillance is the problem, a xeno-surveillance regime could not fall within Article 8(2) as the point is to act *in advance* of established infection. It would be alarming if such regimes were held to be incompatible with this Article because of their purpose; to protect public health *before* infection is widespread. Without a case reaching court or a statute explicitly addressing this, the status of these regimes is debatable.

If the Article 8(2) exception does apply to a xeno-surveillance regime, is enforcing compliance with it compatible with the ECHR? Xeno-recipients and others will be aware and informed of their obligations and responsibilities in advance, and the former are hoping to benefit from the xenotransplant. Can, or should, a trade-off be implied or expected? Compulsory measures to protect against threats to public health may be compatible with the ECHR provided the sanctions are 'proportionate, non-discriminatory, and not ... applied arbitrarily',[304] the interventions are authorised by law, and there is a right to a fair

---

[301] UKXIRA, *Draft Report*, A5.3.   [302] *Ibid.*
[303] E.g., *Pretty* v. *United Kingdom* (2002) 35 EHHR 1; *Laskey, Jaggard and Brown* v. *United Kingdom* (1997) 24 EHHR 39.
[304] R.J. Coker *et al.*, 'Public Health Law and Tuberculosis Control in Europe' (2007) 121 *Public Health* 266, 271.

public hearing including an appeal (Article 6). Interventions must be in response to a 'pressing public health need', be proportional to the aim of protecting public health, and no more restrictive than necessary to achieve that aim.[305] Compulsory detention has been held to be compatible with the Convention on this basis.[306] However, establishing that detaining a non-compliant xeno-contact, for example, is proportionate may be difficult as it is unclear what threat to health is being faced and what alternatives, if any, might also protect public health. It may also be difficult to establish a 'pressing public health need', but compliance is required *before* infection is established in order to identify and monitor such infections. This is another reason why xenotransplantation necessitates a precautionary approach.[307]

If a UK surveillance scheme includes provision for the xeno-recipient to be isolated or their contacts quarantined, these restrictions must comply with Article 5. The European Court has confirmed that the conditions for depriving someone of their liberty must be clearly set out in domestic law, it must be foreseeable that the law will be applied to a person, and detention must be proportionate to preventing disease transmission, not arbitrary, the least restrictive alternative, and necessary.[308] The person must have an infectious disease whose spread would be dangerous to others, and detention must be appropriate because of the disease's nature.[309] Where risk cannot be proved, laws which enable detention for public health purposes may not comply with Article 5;[310] clearly a problem for xenotransplantation. Nevertheless, xenotransplantation necessitates adopting a precautionary approach informed by the harm principle and the risks justify restricting liberty provided the conditions of Article 5 are met. Although a precautionary approach has not been expressly adopted it has 'implicitly guided public health interventions designed to limit or forestall epidemic outbreaks',[311] and 'the harm principle justifies restrictions on liberty to avert tangible harms to third parties'.[312] Despite this, where infection is unconfirmed or an individual has merely been exposed or might have been exposed to it, it is harder to justify restricting liberty;[313] but this is what xenotransplantation demands. When determining the legal and ethical

---

[305] *Ibid.*, references removed.
[306] *Acmanne* v. *Belgium* (1984) 40 Decision & Reports 251, European Commission on Human Rights.
[307] See Chapter 2.
[308] *Enhorn* v. *Sweden* (2005) 41 EHRR 30, European Court of Human Rights, paras. 36, 46.
[309] *Ibid.*, para. 44.   [310] R. Martin, 'Exercise of Public Health', 141.
[311] Gostin *et al.*, 'Ethical and Legal Challenges', 3232.
[312] *Ibid.*, 3233–3234, reference removed.   [313] *Ibid.*, 3234.

justifications for isolation and quarantine, it is important to consider the scientific assessment of risk, target (where possible) restrictive measures to those infected, provide a safe and humane environment for those restricted, provide fair treatment and social justice, observe procedural due process, and employ the least restrictive options.[314] But if faced with 'the prospect of a significant risk – measured in terms of the probability of transmission and the severity of harm – populations should be protected, even in the context of medical uncertainty'.[315] Xenotransplantation falls within this so 'from a public health perspective, individual movement can be restricted to avert transmission until potential infectiousness has been ruled out'.[316] The 'precautionary principle – even when limited by the least restrictive/intrusive alternative, justice, and transparency – dictated that restrictive measures be imposed to halt the spread of SARS',[317] and xenotransplantation mirrors this.

If clinical genetically engineered solid organ xenotransplants are to be performed compliance with a surveillance regime *must* be ensured, and the xeno-recipient's human rights limited if required. Provided recipients and others are informed of this in advance and consent to it, this change to established legal and ethical norms is acceptable and necessary because of the risks. The Council of Europe has recommended that public authorities can take necessary and proportionate 'appropriate measures' when xeno-recipients and their contacts do not comply with 'the constraints associated with xenotransplantation',[318] and the Siracusa Principles, which set out when the International Covenant on Civil and Political Rights 1966 can be departed from, permit restrictions on human rights in similar circumstances.[319] For clinical xenotransplants to proceed the human rights of those involved *must* be restricted to protect public health, but this does not mean that any and all restrictions are possible or desirable. Rather, '[t]he law needs to maintain a degree of proportionality between the extent to which those infected with diseases are required to bear additional burdens and the public good achieved by such constraints'.[320] At issue with xenotransplantation is whether a *risk* of harm is sufficient. This can only be statutorily determined or in a court case.

---

[314] Gostin *et al.*, 'Ethical and Legal Challenges', 3233–3235.   [315] *Ibid.*, 3234.
[316] *Ibid.*   [317] *Ibid.*, 3236.
[318] Council of Europe, Recommendation Rec(2003)10, Article 21; above n. 194.
[319] United Nations, Economic and Social Council, UN Sub-Commission on Prevention of Discrimination and Protection of Minorities, Siracusa Principles on Limitation and Derogation of Provisions in the International Covenant on Civil and Political Rights, Annex, UN Doc E/CN.4/1984/4 (1984), Part I B15–16, 25–26, and 35.
[320] J. Montgomery, 'Medicalising Crime? Criminalising Health?', in C. Erin and S. Ost (eds.), *The Criminal Justice System and Health Care* (Oxford University Press, 2007), pp. 257, 270.

Conclusion

There is a consensus that clinical genetically engineered solid organ xenotransplants must not be performed without the safeguard of an appropriate surveillance regime, but the proposed regimes will not necessarily protect individual or public health. Regulators have not been sufficiently active on surveillance to date and, perhaps because of their desire for clinical xenotransplants to proceed, scientists have taken the initiative.[321] Before such xenotransplants are performed, the omissions highlighted here must be addressed and, with regard to the UK, as the general emerging infections surveillance structures have changed since the publication of the UKXIRA's 1999 draft report,[322] new guidance on xeno-surveillance is required which reflects this and the lacunae noted here. A central database should be established in each country to hold the details of xeno-recipients, their current contacts, relevant health workers and, subsequently, their samples and any test results. These national databases must then be globally linked to facilitate international surveillance. International communication, cooperation and action is vital because of the possibility of xeno-tourism and decisions in country X will affect country Y as 'diseases know no frontiers'.[323] Without an international body able to impose global quarantine, for example, it will be hard for national governments to protect their populations from such trans-boundary threats.[324] A chain is only as strong as its weakest link and developing countries will require financial assistance to ensure that appropriate surveillance infrastructures exist.[325] International surveillance is not easy because of different legal and cultural norms, histories, agendas, and issues of accountability, but '[t]he question is not how can we afford to invest in better systems of community surveillance,

---

[321] E.g., Cozzi *et al.*, 'IXA – Chapter 1'; 'First WHO'.
[322] E.g., the establishment of the NEPNEI in November 2003 to '[identify] emerging and potential infectious threats to the public health both nationally and internationally, [place] emerging infections in the wider clinical and public health contexts, [advise] on prevention and control measures, [prioritise] areas for surveillance and for information needs, [advise] on research, including technological development needs' (NEPNEI, *First Annual Report (November 2003–December 2004)* (London: NEPNEI, 2006), p. 3). The Human Animal Infections and Risk Surveillance Group was also established in 2004 as a 'horizon scanning group' which meets monthly (Health Protection Agency (HPA), *The Human Animal Infections and Risk Surveillance (HAIRS) Group, First Report 2004–2007* (London: HPA, 2008), p. 3).
[323] House of Lords, *Diseases Know No Frontiers*.
[324] E.S. Michelson, 'Individual Freedom or Collective Welfare? An Analysis of Quarantine as a Response to Global Infectious Disease', in M.J. Selgelid *et al.*, *Ethics and Infectious Diseases* (Oxford: Wiley-Blackwell, 2006), pp. 53, 54.
[325] House of Lords, *Diseases Know No Frontiers*, Foreword, paras. 37, 44, 52, 56, 65, 87.

diagnosis and treatment, but how can we afford not to? Failure to establish safe systems of infection control and appropriate community services in high-risk areas increases risks to individual health, public health and corporate liability.'[326] Without global action, our ability to protect public health is weakened and the possibility of xeno-tourism heightened. If a clinical genetically engineered solid organ xenotransplant is performed somewhere in the world without an effective surveillance regime, *everyone's* health is at risk. This unpalatable possibility should not prevent responsible countries from introducing structures and systems to act as, at the very least, damage limitation measures.

Introducing national legislation might help to achieve global regulatory action because '[t]he history of infectious disease has ... demonstrated the need for domestic regulation to ensure effective health strategies within States in order for there to be effective transnational and international health regulation'.[327] Clinical xenotransplants should not proceed without such legislation, but it is unclear whether a surveillance regime can be devised and implemented which will sufficiently protect the interested parties, given the uncertainties discussed in Chapter 2. As the UKXIRA noted, even if introducing legislation requiring xeno-recipients to participate in a surveillance programme was justified, it would not be possible to force them, for example, to disclose details on their contacts.[328] It must thus be considered whether, as suggested in the Netherlands, recipients should have limits placed on whom they can have contact with.[329] Without such restrictions the regimes may not be effective in limiting disease transmission and protecting public health. Jacobs's compelling discussion of the surveillance required in the SARS crisis and its impact, also indicates that monitoring is not straightforward in practice and has legal, social, psychological and other effects on those subjected to it.[330] These must not be taken lightly as complying with the necessary lifelong xeno-surveillance is 'a critically unique component of xenotransplantation research trials'.[331]

While it is clearly preferable for surveillance to be voluntarily complied with, coercive action may, at times, be necessary. Compliance cannot remain solely consent based because '[p]ublic health is

---

[326] A. Harris, R. Martin, 'The Exercise of Public Health Powers In An Era Of Human Rights: The Particular Problems of Tuberculosis' (2004) 118 *Public Health* 313, 318.
[327] Johnson, 'Particular Issues of Public Health', 259, reference removed.
[328] UKXIRA, *Draft Report*, A5.3.   [329] Above, nn. 80, 210.
[330] L.A. Jacobs, 'Rights and Quarantine During the SARS Global Health Crisis: Differentiated Legal Consciousness in Hong Kong, Shanghai, and Toronto' (2007) 41 *Law and Society Review* 511.
[331] Caulfield and Robertson, 'Xenotransplantation', p. 85.

about keeping society healthy by *preventing* individuals from doing things that endanger others'.[332] Without more, surveillance schemes are no more than symbolic but empty reassurances that public health is being protected. Specific legislation is therefore needed to regulate and enforce compliance with the necessary xeno-surveillance regime. The right to withdraw from that regime must be removed, and sanctions for non-compliance introduced. A statutory scheme is the only way of ensuring that xeno-recipients, their contacts and relevant health professionals are effectively monitored, and public health protected. Such legislation would 'impose onerous obligations on recipients, [but] it ... represents a fair compromise between outright prohibition of clinical xenotransplantation and unduly jeopardizing the public's health through non-existent, inadequate or ineffective regulation'.[333] It would further set xenotransplantation apart from other developing biotechnologies and so public consultation and debate is required, something which may occur if a bill is introduced. Xenotransplantation necessitates such developments, but if these are deemed legally and/or ethically unacceptable, then a move from laboratory to clinic threatens us all.

If clinical xenotransplants are performed, what are currently viewed as fundamental human rights *must* be breached to protect public health, because '[t]here is no way to avoid the dilemmas posed by acting without full scientific knowledge. Failure to move aggressively can have catastrophic consequences.'[334] The UK's Nuffield Council agreed that 'where harm to the population could be prevented through implementing measures that restrict civil liberties (isolation and quarantining) and challenge the notion of individual consent, this may be justified, particularly when the risks to the individual are minimal and/or the potential harms to others are substantial'.[335] With xenotransplantation there is scientific uncertainty but some situations *demand* action in conditions of uncertainty *because of* the consequences of inaction. These intrusions run counter to the trend of protecting individual human rights but are necessary because of the potentially wide ranging effects of xenotransplantation. Indeed, '[p]ublic health ... puts the community's interests before those of the individual patient. Although the health and the autonomy of the individual are protected to the extent possible, they

---

[332] E.P. Richards and K.C. Rathbun, 'The Role of the Police Power in 21st Century Public Health' (1999) 26 *Sexually Transmitted Disease* 350, 356, emphasis supplied.
[333] Florencio and Ramanathan, 'Are Xenotransplantation Safeguards', 962.
[334] Gostin *et al.*, 'Ethical and Legal Challenges', 3236.
[335] Nuffield Council, *Public Health*, para. 4.73.

are secondary. Public health rejects the patient's right to have sole control of his/her treatment.'[336] If a recipient, her contacts and health workers consent to being involved in a xenotransplant they *must* accept that their future rights have to be restricted to safeguard public health. Detailed and clear information must be provided to all parties who may be involved in or affected by a decision to receive a xenotransplant during the consent process, and refusal to consent to this *must* mean the xenotransplant is not performed. For those who accept a xenotransplant and subsequently fail to comply with surveillance, provisions must be in place for compulsory quarantine and isolation. Without such it is hard to see how the state is fulfilling its obligations to protect public health. The different nature of the consent which xenotransplantation requires, the necessary enforcement of the xeno-surveillance regime, and the challenges this poses to protected human rights means that this biotechnology *cannot* automatically fit into existing legal and ethical regulatory structures, despite contrary assumptions. The public must thus be consulted on these matters, particularly whether some currently protected rights have to be relinquished in order to protect the health and interests of others. Is it agreed that she who seeks to benefit should carry the burden under the social contract?

---

[336] Richards and Rathbun, 'Role of the Police Power', 355, reference removed.

7 Summary and concluding thoughts: looking to the future

> Advancements in biotechnology have the potential to alter not just our environment but our physical embodiment as well. In altering not merely our social, cultural, economic or political environments, but the physical foundations of life itself, the decision to adopt a particular biotechnology may be irrevocable and the results irreversible. There can be no turning back from a decision to alter our biological destiny.[1]

It is indisputable that there is a significant and costly disparity between the number of patients who require an organ transplant and the number of organs currently available for transplantation. The desire to support or promote xenotransplantation as part of the solution to this shortage is understandable but the implications of doing so must be acknowledged and addressed because '[a]dvances which may seem to be the answer to a pressing problem may well entail consequences of such a drastic nature as to cause researchers to halt and take stock of their situations before proceeding further'.[2] The science behind xenotransplantation continues to develop and although some of the initial barriers to placing a non-human animal organ into a human appear to have been addressed, it remains unclear whether a solid organ xenotransplant will be able to support a human life. In addition, performing such a transplant may transfer infectious diseases across the species boundary to the xeno-recipient *and* others, and it is this risk which requires global legal and regulatory attention. While porcine endogenous retroviruses have been the main focus to date, it is anticipated that other organisms will need investigating and that latent diseases may be transmitted to the xeno-recipient and others. These risks and their unknown nature and magnitude make xenotransplantation a useful case study through which to explore the role of science in society, public involvement in science and decision-making, risk, responsibility (individual, societal, governmental), regulation, public health and the

---

[1] Gold and Adams, 'Reconciling Private Benefit', 31–32.
[2] C.G. Weeramantry, *Xenotransplantation: The Ethical and Legal Concerns* (Sri Lanka: Weeramantry International Centre for Peace Education and Research, 2007), p. xv.

global 'market'. These themes have underpinned the discussions within this book, along with the idea that developing biotechnologies may pose challenges to established legal and ethical norms.

In Chapter 2, I explored the risks posed by genetically engineered solid organ xenotransplants and argued that in situations of uncertainty a precautionary approach informed by the harm principle is an appropriate response because where the risk is significant with regard to the probability of transmission and the severity of harm, action should be taken to *prevent* harm to public health.[3] This approach is required because '[t]oo often ... public health and environmental policies are based on a principle of *reaction* rather than precaution' with regulatory agencies 'having to wait until evidence of harm is established beyond all reasonable doubt before they can act to prevent harm'.[4] Adopting a precautionary approach does not necessarily mean that such xenotransplants cannot be performed, but it does require society to consider whether it is appropriate to proceed to clinical use when possible individual benefit may place public health at risk. Xenotransplantation is thus a useful reminder that health care involves protecting and enhancing the health of individuals *and* that of the public, and that 'a shift from reaction to precaution is entirely consistent with the core values of public health practice'.[5] The UK government has acknowledged the importance of public health and commented that:

> [m]odern biotechnology is an important area of scientific advance which offers enormous opportunity for improving our quality of life. But there is also understandable public concern about a technology which allows scientific advances which we would have hardly imagined possible only a few years ago. The Government's overriding responsibilities are to protect the health of the public and to protect the environment.[6]

Xenotransplantation raises important issues about whose health needs should be prioritised; those of the individual requiring the xenotransplant or those of other members of a society who may be affected if it is performed. The interests of more than the intended beneficiary are engaged by xenotransplantation in a way outside of the norm *because* everyone is placed at risk if genetically engineered solid organ clinical xenotransplants occur. At the same time, if this biotechnology can help to reduce or eliminate the number of people on organ waiting lists

---

[3] Gostin *et al.*, 'Ethical and Legal Challenges'.
[4] Kriebel and Tickner, 'Reenergizing Public Health', 1354, emphasis in original.
[5] *Ibid.*
[6] Cabinet Office, *Advisory and Regulatory Framework*, Foreword.

society would also benefit. Nevertheless, 'society should be wary of those innovations that cannot or have not been tested, particularly where human life is at stake',[7] and it is unacceptable to expose and/or expect the public to bear the risks when they have had no opportunity to explore or debate them. Indeed, 'the decision whether to undertake the procedure involves more than ensuring the ability of the surgeon and the transplant team, the capacity of the institution, and the willingness of the patient'.[8] In the light of this, the public has a crucial role to play in discussing the clinical application of xenotransplantation. This may not be easy to negotiate but any difficulties should not be used as an excuse to not involve the public. Rather, 'meaningful opportunities for public voices to influence decision-making' must be provided,[9] and methods of consulting the public matched to the purpose in order to 'improve opportunities to inform and empower the public, accommodate change, build mutual confidence, and make better decisions'.[10] Such discussions between scientists, policy-makers and the public are particularly important in the xenotransplant context to determine whether the potential benefits to the individual recipient outweigh the burden which society may carry. Engaging in public discussion will help to 'ensure that science and its applications can advance with public consent, contribution and active support, shaped through varied and open discussion of what society wants and needs'.[11] Experiences in the UK with BSE and GM foods, for example, have highlighted how 'trust in the processes by which science and its applications are developed and regulated' may be affected and that this may lead to 'fear of change and the blocking of the potentially huge benefits of science and technology'.[12] Public confidence in and an understanding of science, and trust and confidence in scientists and regulators is thus vital. For xenotransplantation it is also important that the risks of infectious disease transmission are effectively communicated 'to avoid or minimize excessive fear; to engage patients and the public in decisions and actions aimed at reducing risks; and to provide a basis for dialogue among health providers, the public, scientists, and government'.[13]

The UK's House of Lords has warned that it would be 'retrograde and repressive' to prohibit scientific progress without advance, express public

---

[7] Ahmed, 'Last Twist', 1546.
[8] Bach et al., 'Uncertainty in Xenotransplantation', 142.
[9] Wilsdon et al., Public Value, p. 26.
[10] Coote and Franklin, 'Negotiating Risks', p. 192.
[11] Jackson et al., 'Strengths of Public Dialogue', 357. [12] Ibid.
[13] Glanz and Yang, 'Communicating about Risk', p. 253.

240 Summary and concluding thoughts

support,[14] and commented that 'in modern democratic conditions, science like any other player in the public arena ignores public attitudes and values at its peril. Our recommendation for increased and integrated dialogue with the public is intended to *secure* science's "licence to practise", not to *restrict* it.'[15] The importance of public involvement in decision-making is thus becoming more widely recognised because '[s]cientists themselves, while responsible for the production of the knowledge, *cannot* be solely accountable for the (ab)uses of ensuing technologies'.[16] Equally, '[e]thics is no longer solely the concern of scientists, engineers or health care professionals. It has ... transcended the exclusive domain of experts, showing that science is first of all a public enterprise, a social activity, a cultural good.'[17] Public debate may help to ensure that scientific and technological advances are occurring within an appropriate ethical framework,[18] and is necessary because a 'health and human rights approach mandates ... that the adoption of any public health strategy be informed by evidence and debated openly and that public health decisions, whether or not rights are to be restricted, are made through transparent and accountable processes'.[19] As discussed in Chapter 6, the vital post-xenotransplant surveillance schemes *must* limit well-established and protected human rights and civil liberties in order to effectively safeguard individual and public health. If a patient is willing to benefit from a solid organ xenotransplant, then they must also carry the burdens of so consenting, in the form of relinquishing some of their rights in order to protect the health and interests of others who may be affected by their personal choice. Thus, '[s]ituations of manufactured risk shift the relation between collective and individual responsibility in many risk situations'.[20] Limiting legally protected rights in this way is controversial but necessary if clinical xenotransplants are performed and the risks taken seriously. Provided the xeno-recipient, her contacts and health professionals are informed of the restrictions prior to consenting to involvement, then this is appropriate and laws may need amending to reflect this. Similarly, our often individual-focused ethical antennae will require retuning to a more collective wavelength because:

---

[14] House of Lords, *Science and Society*, para. 5.49.
[15] *Ibid.*, para. 5.50, emphasis in original.
[16] Knoppers, 'Reflections', 565, emphasis supplied.
[17] ten Have, 'UNESCO and Ethics of Science and Technology', p. 11.   [18] *Ibid.*
[19] S. Gruskin, 'Is There a Government in the Cockpit: A Passenger's Perspective or Global Public Health: The Role of Human Rights' (2004) 22 *Temple Law Review* 313, 324.
[20] Giddens, 'Risk and Responsibility', 9.

although the community of (human) rights is designed to promote individual autonomy, there are limits to the choices that individuals may be permitted to make. Most obviously, each individual is required to exercise his or her autonomy in a way that is compatible with respect for the entitlements of fellow humans ... the way in which choice is exercised must not damage the context in which a community of rights-respecting humans is itself possible.[21]

Concerns over the effectiveness of first-party consent in this context, the role of third-party consent, and the need to enforce compliance with the required surveillance regime, further support my argument for public involvement in the decision-making process on xenotransplantation. With regard to consent, in Chapter 5 I argued that where the benefits and risks are unclear, the risks go beyond the intended beneficiary, and that beneficiary is desperately ill with no other hope, first-party consent, as conceived in many Western countries, to the xenotransplant procedure itself and the necessary post-xeno surveillance is challenged in significant ways. For example, it is unclear whether it is possible to give legally valid consent to a solid organ xenotransplant given the uncertain benefits and the nature and magnitude of the risks. If it is possible to consent, the competency, voluntary and informed elements of consent must be considered in the context of xenotransplantation and the health status of proposed initial recipients; those with no other hope. These elements raise important legal, ethical and policy questions which merit public discussion. One way to minimise some of the concerns is to introduce xeno-specific legislation, possibly an EU regulation to ensure consistency across member states, which sets out that a team should be involved in the process of obtaining consent and outlines the information which must be disclosed to xeno-recipients, contacts and relevant health professionals. The uncertainties which surround this biotechnology and the emerging consensus on the categories of information which should be disclosed support this unusual move. The role of third parties and their consent to post-xenotransplant surveillance in particular must also be addressed, and it is difficult to see how practically anything other than a legislative response will suffice to protect the health of the recipient, those close to her and the public. All of this sets xenotransplantation outside existing legal and ethical norms; but the challenges posed by this biotechnology must be explicitly addressed prior to clinical introduction.

The omissions in the xeno-surveillance schemes, highlighted in Chapter 6, must be addressed. In particular, all countries should establish national central databases, regardless of whether clinical xenotransplants are performed there, to hold details of xeno-recipients, their current

---

[21] Brownsword, 'What the World Needs', p. 212.

contacts and relevant health workers and, subsequently, their samples and test results. These databases must then be globally linked to facilitate international surveillance. Although such surveillance will not be easy, without global cooperation and action the ability to protect public health is weakened and the possibility of xeno-tourism heightened. One way to facilitate international action is via the introduction of national xenotransplant-specific legislation which sets out a regulatory scheme for its clinical use, details the requirements of the surveillance regime, its enforcement and sanctions for non-compliance, and prohibits withdrawal from that regime. Introducing such provisions must not be taken lightly because the suggested requirements are invasive and limit the freedom of the xeno-recipient, her contacts, and involved health professionals. Nevertheless, a statutory scheme is the most effective way of ensuring that these parties are monitored and their health and those of others protected, but would set xenotransplantation apart from other developing biotechnologies. The WHO has acknowledged that xenotransplantation may demand amendments to existing, or the introduction of new, legislation 'to establish a regulatory infrastructure for this technology',[22] and public involvement in doing such is crucial.

Xenotransplantation not only highlights the need for public consultation and involvement in decision-making but also emphasises the fallacy in assuming that developing biotechnologies can automatically fit into existing regulatory schemes and structures. I thus argued in Chapter 3 that xenotransplantation calls attention to the deficiencies within the different existing regulatory schemes for experimental procedures and medical research, particularly in the UK. It is imperative that these are aligned because experimentation, research and treatment are part of a spectrum, and the paucity of legal regulation and ethical guidance on experimental procedures in the UK makes it questionable whether involved parties are appropriately protected when participating in activities which carry risks. At the very least, experimental procedures should be reviewed by an ethics committee which will, amongst other things, consider patient selection decisions to help minimise the possibility that advantage is taken of those with no other hope. While in the UK a general NHS research ethics committee as currently constituted may be able to undertake this task for many experimental procedures and medical research, their ability to consider solid organ xenotransplant protocols is questionable because of the risks involved, the need to assess uncertain and unknown dangers, and balance potential predominantly

---

[22] WHO, *Report of WHO Consultation*, p. 6.

private benefit with public risk. Such committees are more experienced at evaluating individual and not public risk–benefit ratios, but where risks go beyond the individual it is not appropriate for the clinical judgement of physician-investigators to be the main or only basis on which the decision to proceed to clinical use and/or participant selection decisions are made. A sufficiently robust regulatory regime is required to cope with the specific issues this developing biotechnology raises. However, as described in Chapter 4, historically law's engagement with science has been problematic, especially where the science is evolving. Regulation has tended to be ad hoc, technology led and not based on a unifying ethical theory. It was once common to wait for clinical application before introducing regulation but the trend is now for proactive rather than reactive activity, with regulatory discussions perceived as an aspect of a biotechnology's development. Indeed, whereas when IVF and gene therapy were clinically introduced there was minimal regulation of these biotechnologies throughout the world, including in the countries where they were first performed, many countries have already proposed or implemented regulatory schemes even though no clinical genetically engineered solid organ xenotransplants have yet occurred. Despite this, xenotransplantation highlights what may happen if law fails to keep up with and address the implications of biotechnological advances; there is uncertainty as to whether existing systems apply, existing rules may under- or over-regulate the advance, the advance may make existing rules obsolete, and specialist laws may be required to regulate it.[23]

Although this proactive xenotransplant regulatory activity is commendable given the risks involved, it is notable that there is now a trend for incorporating this biotechnology within existing regulatory structures; structures which were not designed with xeno-specific issues in mind. In Australia, Canada, New Zealand, the UK and US, for example, clinical xenotransplants must comply with existing non-xenotransplant specific regulatory regimes. This trend is alarming because of the risks and legal and ethical issues discussed in this book, but the use of existing regulatory schemes could be read as an acceptance or indication that xenotransplants do not raise any specific issues or problems. This is not so and a specialist xenotransplantation regulatory authority should be established in every country *before* clinical use, in order to protect individual and public health. Indeed, 'an adequate regulatory framework needs to have the profile of the technology-to-be-regulated clearly in its

---

[23] L.B. Moses, 'Recurring Dilemmas: The Law's Race to Keep Up with Technological Change' (2007) 2 *Journal of Law, Technology and Policy* 239, 248.

sights; in particular, insofar as the regulatory framework is intended to play a protective function, the risk side of the profile needs to be in focus'.[24] Without this, it is debatable whether lessons from the regulatory histories of other developing biotechnologies have been learnt.

It is also noticeable that despite longstanding calls for international activity and cooperation on xenotransplantation and evidence of emerging consensus on some of the key issues, concrete action in this regard has been minimal. This must change given the global nature of health care and advances in it, the increase in health tourism, and the fact that 'the risks associated with xenotransplantation ... cannot be confined to geopolitical borders. States cannot necessarily protect their own domestic welfare calculus from the unilateral actions of other states that may not have reached an identical assessment of the optimal balance between costs and benefits ... in the international arena, the possibility of an involuntary assumption of risk remains.'[25] Implementing and enforcing such global regulation will not be easy and may prove impossible; does this, along with the availability of cheaper global travel, mean that for practical reasons all medical advances have to be permitted because if country A prohibits it and country B does not, the prohibition will effectively be pointless? This problem and the possibility of xeno-tourism has long been recognised,[26] but it does not intuitively seem correct that the existence of such 'xeno-havens' are able to influence or determine another country's regulatory stance. Nevertheless, without a global and universal legally enforceable system for xenotransplantation it is hard to see how xeno-recipients and others can be protected, and other regulatory options will be second best, if not meaningless. Does this mean that it is not possible to effectively regulate clinical solid organ xenotransplants? In the light of the risks this cannot be an acceptable result, and countries must regulate this biotechnology even if on an individual basis and even if this means accepting that this is only 'good enough' regulation because of the xeno-havens which may exist. Such regulation may be a necessary compromise, but if the introductions of these regulatory systems are preceded by public discussion on

---

[24] R. Brownsword, 'Biotechnology and Rights: Where Are We Coming from and Where Are We Going?', in M. King, A. Murray (eds.), *Human Rights in the Digital Age* (London: Glass House Press, 2005), pp. 219, 219, reference removed.
[25] Gold and Adams, 'Reconciling Private Benefit', 43.
[26] E.g., Australia – NHMRC, Discussion Paper; UK – NEPNEI, *Combined Report 2006–2007*, pp. 4, 7; US – US DHHS and SACX, *Report on the State of the Science*, pp. iv–v; Cozzi *et al.*, 'IXA – Chapter 1', p. 205; Sykes, '2007 IXA Presidential Address', p. 10; Sykes *et al.*, 'International Cooperation'; Sykes *et al.*, 'Position Paper', p. 198.

xenotransplantation then potential recipients may be thereby educated on the risks and some, at least, may decide not to access this option.

Conclusion

the new science has moved us from chance to choice in many matters ... With choice comes the responsibility to use that choice ethically. Doing so requires two kinds of courage: the courage to go forward with the new science and technology when it is morally and ethically acceptable to do so, and the courage to exercise restraint when it is morally and ethically required.[27]

As no clinical genetically engineered solid organ xenotransplants have yet been performed, we are able to make a choice as to whether we proceed in the light of the risks to the xeno-recipient and others, given that it may not be possible to practically, legally and ethically protect those at risk. If, following public consultation and debate, the decision is made to clinically proceed then the issues highlighted in this book must be addressed. Xenotransplantation draws attention to the fact that at times difficult choices have to be made and, as lawyers have long acknowledged, hard cases can make bad law. Rather than resolve the difficulties raised by recourse to the law after the event, proactive regulation is required with public regulatory discussions occurring prior to the clinical application of xenotransplantation. Xenotransplantation emphasises the need for effective communication, competent regulatory structures, and international legal and ethical cooperation in a global market. Where the risks go beyond the intended beneficiary introducing a development without such regulation may harm us all and as '[t]hese decisions concern the future of mankind. They should not be left simply to individuals and the market'.[28] Rather, '[t]he parameters of medicine must be something other than professional self-limitation'.[29]

The legal and ethical implications of implementing effective and enforceable regulation must be explicitly considered, and I have shown that the paradigms and accepted norms of health care law and ethics are not appropriate for xenotransplantation as the issues stretch beyond the physician-investigator and patient-subject or doctor–patient relationship. Although attention has been drawn to the fact that the surveillance requirements of xenotransplantation, for example, cannot currently be legally supported,[30] policy-makers and regulators have not acted on

---

[27] Sommerville, 'Searching for Ethics', p. 29.
[28] Furger and Fukuyama, 'A Proposal', 20.
[29] Price, 'Remodelling', p. 123, reference removed.
[30] E.g., Caulfield and Robertson, 'Xenotransplantation'.

these warnings. Instead xenotransplantation has, in a number of countries, been subsumed within existing regulatory schemes, and it appears to have been assumed that legal and ethical norms regarding first-party consent, for example, can be stretched to fit the specific issues raised by this biotechnology. However, in making this assumption without careful analysis individual and public health is placed at risk because xenotransplantation inherently challenges existing legal and ethical norms. Indeed, for xenotransplantation 'we lack a framework for dealing with the nuanced and complex set of scientific and technological choices that confront us'.[31] This must be rectified and the challenges of doing so should be an immediate project for policy-makers before it is too late and law and society are once again caught out by a biotechnological advance.

---

[31] Wilsdon *et al.*, *The Public Value*, p. 26. Similarly, Bach *et al.*, 'Ethical and Legal Issues', 283.

Bibliography

Academy of Medical Sciences, *A New Pathway for the Regulation and Governance of Health Research* (London: Academy of Sciences, 2011).
Addicott, D.C. 'Regulating Research on the Terminally Ill: A Proposal for Heightened Safeguards' (1999) 15 *Journal of Contemporary Health Law and Policy* 479.
Agriculture and Environment Biotechnology Commission (AEBC), *Crops on Trial – A Report by the AEBC* (London: AEBC, 2001).
Ahmed, A.S. 'The Last Twist of the Knife: Encouraging the Regulation of Innovative Surgical Procedures' (2005) 105 *Columbia Law Review* 1529.
Allspaw, K.M. 'Engaging the Public in the Regulation of Xenotransplantation: Would the Canadian Model of Public Consultation Be Effective in the US?' (2004) 13 *Public Understanding of Science* 417.
American Fertility Society, 'Ethical Considerations of the New Reproductive Technologies' (1986) 46 suppl. 1 *Fertility and Sterility* 1S.
American Medical Association (AMA), Council on Ethical and Judicial Affairs, *Opinions of the Council on Ethical and Judicial Affairs: Gene Therapy and Surrogate Mothers*, Report E (1–88) (Chicago, IL: AMA, 1988).
  Opinion 2.07 – Clinical Investigation (1998) (at: www.ama-assn.org/ama/pub/physician-resources/medical-ethics/code-medical-ethics/opinion207.shtml, accessed 22/03/11).
  Report of the Council on Ethical and Judicial Affairs: The Ethical Implications of Xenotransplantation (2000) CEJA Report 4-I-00 (at: www.ama-assn.org/ama1/pub/upload/mm/code-medical-ethics/2169a.pdf, accessed 25/03/11).
  Opinion 8.0315 – Managing Conflicts of Interest in the Conduct of Clinical Trials (2001) (at: www.ama-assn.org/ama/pub/physician-resources/medical-ethics/code-medical-ethics/opinion80315.shtml, accessed 22/03/11).
  Opinion 2.169 The Ethical Implications of Xenotransplantation (2001) (at: www.ama-assn.org/ama/pub/physician-resources/medical-ethics/code-medical-ethics/opinion2169.shtml, accessed 25/03/11).
Anderson, W.F. and Fletcher, J.C. 'Gene Therapy in Humans: When Is It Ethical to Begin?' (1980) 303 *New England Journal of Medicine* 1293.
Andorno, R. 'The Precautionary Principle: A New Legal Standard for a Technological Age' (2004) 1 *Journal of International Biotechnology Law* 11.
Angell, E., Sutton, A.J., Windridge, K. and Dixon-Woods, M. 'Consistency in Decision Making by Research Ethics Committees: A Controlled Comparison' (2006) 32 *Journal of Medical Ethics* 662.

Annas, G.J. 'Baby Fae: The "Anything Goes" School of Human Experimentation' (1985) *Hastings Center* 15.
'The Changing Landscape of Human Experimentation: Nuremberg, Helsinki and Beyond' (1992) 2 *Health Matrix* 119.
'First WHO Global Consultation on Regulatory Requirements for Xenotransplantation Clinical Trials, Changsha, China, 19–21 November 2008' (2009) 16 *Xenotransplantation* 61.
'Recommendations for the Regulation of Xeno Activities in Spain – Extracted from the Report of the Xenotransplantation Commission of the National Transplant Commission' (1998) 18 suppl. 7 *Nefrologia* 35.
Appelbaum, P.S., Roth, L.H. and Lidz, C.W. 'The Therapeutic Misconception: Informed Consent in Psychiatric Research' (1982) 5 *International Journal of Law and Psychiatry* 319.
Arthur, C. 'Transplant patients to get organs from pigs', *The Independent*, 13 September 1995.
Bach, F.H., Fishman, J.A., Daniels, N., Proimos, J., Anderson, B., Carpenter, C.B., Forrow, L., Robson, S.C. and Fineberg, H.V. 'Uncertainty in Xenotransplantation: Individual Benefit versus Collective Risk' (1998) 4 *Nature Medicine* 141.
Bach, F.H., Ivinson, A.J. and Weeramantry, C. 'Ethical and Legal Issues in Technology: Xenotransplantation' (2001) 27 *American Journal of Law and Medicine* 283.
Bailey, L.L., Nehlsen-Cannarella, S.L., Concepcion, W. and Jolley, J.B. 'Baboon-to-Human Cardiac Xenotransplantation in a Neonate' (1985) 254 *Journal of the American Medical Association* 3321.
Baldan, N., Rigotti, P., Calabrese, F., Cadrobbi, R., Dedja, A., Iacopetti, I., Boldrin, M., Seveso, M., Dall'Olmo, L., Frison, L., De Benedictis, G., Bernardini, D., Thiene, G., Cozzi, E. and Ancona, E. 'Ureteral Stenosis in HDAF Pig-to-Primate Renal Xenotransplantation: A Phenomenon Related to Immunological Events?' (2004) 4 *American Journal of Transplantation* 475.
Barnard, C.N. 'A Human Cardiac Transplant: An Interim Report of a Successful Operation Performed at the Groote Schuur Hospital, Cape Town' (1967) 41 *South African Medical Journal* 1271.
Bateman, D., Hilton, D., Love, S., Zeidler, M., Beck, J. and Collinge, J. 'Sporadic Creutzfeldt–Jakob Disease in a 18-year-old in the UK' (1995) 346 *The Lancet* 1155.
Beauchamp, T.L. and Childress, J.F. *Principles of Biomedical Ethics* (6th edn, New York, NY: Oxford University Press, 2009).
Beck, U. *Risk Society: Towards A New Modernity* (London: Sage, 1992).
Beddard, S., Lyons, D. *The Science and Ethics of Xenotransplantation* (Sheffield: Uncaged Campaigns, 1997).
Bennett, P. 'Understanding Responses to Risk: Some Basic Findings', in P. Bennett and K. Calman (eds.), *Risk Communication and Public Health* (Oxford University Press, 2001), p. 3.
Bennett, P., Coles, D. and McDonald, A. 'Risk Communication as a Decision Process', in P. Bennett and K. Calman (eds.), *Risk Communication and Public Health* (Oxford University Press, 2001), p. 207.

Berg, P., Baltimore, D., Brenner, S., Roblin, R.O. and Singer, M.F. 'Summary Statement of the Asilomar Conference on Recombinant DNA Molecules' (1975) 72 *Proceedings of the National Academy of Science* 1981.
Better Regulation Commission (BRC), *Risk, Responsibility and Regulation – Whose Risk Is It Anyway?* (London: BRC, 2006).
Better Regulation Task Force (BRTF), *Scientific Research: Innovation with Controls* (London: BRTF, 2003).
Beyleveld, D. and Brownsword, R. *Human Dignity in Bioethics and Biolaw* (Oxford University Press, 2001).
Beyleveld, D., Finnegan, T. and Pattinson, S.D. 'The Regulation of Hybrids and Chimeras in the UK', in J. Taupitz and M. Weschka (eds.), *Chimbrids: Chimeras and Hybrids in Comparative European and International Research: Scientific, Ethical, Philosophical and Legal Aspects* (Berlin: Springer, 2009), p. 645.
Biggs, H. *Healthcare Research Ethics and Law: Regulation, Review and Responsibility* (London: Routledge-Cavendish, 2010).
Bier, V.M. 'On the State of the Art: Risk Communication to the Public' (2001) 71 *Reliability Engineering and System Safety* 139.
Birmingham, K. 'WHO Hosts Web Discussion on Xenotransplantation Policy' (1999) 5 *Nature Medicine* 595.
  'Skepticism Surrounds Diabetes Xenograft Experiment' (2002) 8 *Nature Medicine* 1047.
Blaese, R.M., Culver, K.W., Miller, A.D., Carter, C.S., Fleisher, T., Clerici, M., Shearer, G., Chang, L., Chiang, Y., Tolstoshev, P., Greenblatt, J.J., Rosenberg, S.A., Klein, H., Berger, M., Mullen, C.A., Ramsey, W.J., Muul, L., Morgan, R.A. and Anderson, W.F. 'T Lymphocyte-Directed Gene Therapy for ADA Deficiency SCID: Initial Trial Results after 4 Years' (1995) 270 *Science* 475.
Bloom, E.T. 'Xenotransplantation: Regulatory Challenges' (2001) 12 *Current Opinion in Biotechnology* 312.
Blumgart, H.L. 'The Medical Framework for Viewing the Problem of Human Experimentation' (1969) 98 *Daedalus* 248.
Boisson de Chazournes, L. 'New Technologies, the Precautionary Principle, and Public Participation', in T. Murphy (ed.), *New Technology and Human Rights* (Oxford University Press, 2009), p. 161.
Boseley, S. 'Government warned on DIY cancer treatments', *The Guardian*, 28 April 2008.
Bosk, C.L. 'Obtaining Voluntary Consent for Research in Desperately Ill Patients' (2002) 40 *Medical Care* V-64.
Bramstedt, K.A. 'Arguments for the Ethical Permissibility of Transgenic Xenografting' (2000) 7 *Gene Therapy* 633.
Brazier, M. 'Patient Autonomy and Consent to Treatment: The Role of the Law?' (1987) 7 *Legal Studies* 169.
  'Do No Harm – Do Patients Have Responsibilities Too?' (2006) 65 *Cambridge Law Journal* 397.
Brazier, M. and Cave, E. *Medicine, Patients and the Law* (London: LexisNexis Butterworths, 2007).

Brazier, M. and Harris, J. 'Public Health and Private Lives' (1996) 4 *Medical Law Review* 171.
Breitsameter, C. 'Medical Decision-Making and Communication of Risks: an Ethical Perspective' (2010) 36 *Journal of Medical Ethics* 349.
British Medical Association (BMA) Working Group on In Vitro Fertilization, 'Interim Report on Human In Vitro Fertilization and Embryo Replacement and Transfer' (1983) 286 *British Medical Journal* 1594.
 The Medical Profession and Human Rights: Handbook for a Changing Agenda (London: Zed Books, 2001).
 Report of the Consent Working Party: Incorporating Consent Toolkit (London: BMA, 2001).
 Consent Tool Kit (5th edn, London: BMA, 2009).
Britton, T.C., Al-Sarraj, S., Shaw, C., Campbell, T. and Collinge, J. 'Sporadic Creutzfeldt–Jakob Disease in a 16-year-old in the UK' (1995) 346 *The Lancet* 1155.
Bronitt, S. 'Spreading Disease and the Criminal Law' [1994] *Criminal Law Review* 21.
Brownsword, R. 'What the World Needs Now: Techno-Regulation, Human Rights and Human Dignity', in R. Brownsword (ed.), *Global Governance and the Quest for Justice* (Oxford: Hart, 2004), p. 203.
 'Biotechnology and Rights: Where Are We Coming from and Where Are We Going?', in M. King and A. Murray (eds.), *Human Rights in the Digital Age* (London: Glass House Press, 2005), p. 219.
Bubela, T., Nisbet, M.C., Borchelt, R., Brunger, F., Critchley, C., Einsiedel, E., Geller, G., Gupta, A., Hampel, J., Hyde-Lay, R., Jandciu, E.W.,
 Jones, A.A., Kolopack, P., Lane, S., Lougheed, T., Nerlich, B., Ogbogu, U., O'Riordan, K., Ouellette, C., Spear, M., Strauss, S., Thavaratnam, T., Willemse, L. and Caulfield, T. 'Science Communication Reconsidered' (2009) 27 *Nature Biotechnology* 514.
Butler, D. 'Last Chance to Stop and Think on Risks of Xenotransplants' (1998) 391 *Nature* 320.
Cabezuelo, J.B., Ramirez, P., Chavez, R., Majado, M., Munitiz, V., Muñoz, A., Hernandez, Q., Palenciano, C.G., Pino-Chávez, G., Loba, M.,
 Yélamos, J., Vizcaino, A.S., Cayuela, M., Segura, B., Marin, F., Rubio, A., Fuente, T., Gago, M.R., Rios, A., Montoya, M., Esteban, A., Bueno, F.S., Robles, R., Cozzi, E., White, D.J.G. and Parrilla, P. 'Assessment of Renal Function During the Postoperative Period Following Liver Xenotransplantation From Transgenic Pig to Baboon' (2002) 34 *Transplantation Proceedings* 321.
Cabinet Office, Office of Science and Technology, *The Advisory and Regulatory Framework for Biotechnology: Report from the Government's Review* (London: Cabinet Office, 1999).
Calman, K.C. 'Cancer: Science and Society and the Communication of Risk' (1996) 313 *British Medical Journal* 799.
Campbell, A.V. 'Dependency: The Foundational Value in Medical Ethics', in K.W.M. Fulford, G. Gillett and J.M. Soskice (eds.), *Medicine and Moral Reasoning* (New York, NY: Cambridge University Press, 1994), p. 184.

Campbell, D. 'Destination Spain: the rise and rise of fertility tourism', guardian.co.uk, 22 August 2010.

Canadian Institutes of Health Research, Natural Sciences and Engineering Research Council of Canada, Social Sciences and Humanities Research Council of Canada, *TCPS2 – Tri-Council Policy Statement: Ethical Conduct for Research Involving Humans* (2010) (at: www.pre.ethics.gc.ca/pdf/eng/tcps2/TCPS_2_FINAL_Web.pdf, accessed 22/03/11).

Canadian Public Health Association (CPHA), *Animal-to-Human Transplantation: Should Canada Proceed? A Public Consultation on Xenotransplantation* (Ontario: CPHA, 2001).

Caplan, A. 'Is It Sound Public Policy to Let the Terminally Ill Access Experimental Medical Innovations?' (2007) 7 *American Journal of Bioethics* 1.

Caplan, A.L. 'Ethical Issues Raised by Research Involving Xenografts' (1985) 254 *Journal of the American Medical Association* 3339.

Catholic Bishops' Joint Committee on Bioethical Issues, *Genetic Intervention on Human Subjects: The Report of a Working Party of the Catholic Bishops' Joint Committee on Bioethical Issues* (London: Catholic Bishops' Joint Committee, 1996).

Catholic Health Association of the United States, Research Group on Ethical Issues in Early Human Development and Genetics, *Human Genetics: Ethical Issues in Genetic Testing, Counseling, and Therapy* (St Louis, MO: Catholic Health Association of the United States, 1990).

Caulfield, T.A. and Robertson, G.B. 'Xenotransplantation: Consent, Public Health and Charter Issues' (2001) 5 *Medical Law International* 81.

Center for Law and the Public's Health at Georgetown and Johns Hopkins Universities, *The Model State Emergency Health Powers Act: A Draft for Discussion* (21 December 2001) (at: www2a.cdc.gov/phlp/docs/msehpa2.pdf, accessed 18/03/11).

Center for Technology Assessment, Federal Office of Public Health, Swiss National Science Foundation, *Transplantation Medicine, 24–27 November 2000 at Bern: Citizen Panel Report* (2001) TA-P2/2000e.

Chahal, M. 'Off-Trial Access to Experimental Cancer Agents for the Terminally Ill: Balancing the Needs of Individuals and Society' (2010) 36 *Journal of Medical Ethics* 367.

Chapman, L. 'Speculation, Stringent Reasoning, and Science' (1999) 77 *Bulletin of the World Health Organization* 68.

Chapman, L.E. and Bloom, E.T. 'Clinical Xenotransplantation' (2001) 285 *Journal of the American Medical Association* 2304.

Chari, R.S., Collins, B.H., Magee, J.C., DiMaio, J.M., Kirk, A.D., Harland, R.C., McCann, R.L., Platt, J.L. and Meyers, W.C. 'Brief Report: Treatment of Hepatic Failure with Ex Vivo Pig-Liver Perfusion Followed by Liver Transplantation' (1994) 331 *New England Journal of Medicine* 234.

Childress, J.F. and Bernheim, R.G. 'Beyond the Liberal and Communitarian Impasse: A Framework and Vision for Public Health' (2003) 55 *Florida Law Review* 1191.

Childress, J.F., Faden, R.R., Gaare, R.D., Gostin, L.O., Kahn, J., Bonnie, R.J., Kass, N.E., Mastroianni, A.C., Moreno, J.D. and Nieburg, P. 'Public

Health Ethics: Mapping the Terrain' (2002) 30 *Journal of Law, Medicine and Ethics* 170.
Chwang, E. 'A Puzzle about Consent in Research and in Practice' (2010) 27 *Journal of Applied Philosophy* 258.
Cichutek, K. and Krämer, I. 'Gene Therapy in Germany and in Europe: Regulatory Issues' (1997) 2 *Quality Assurance Journal* 141.
Clark, M.A. 'This Little Piggy Went to Market: The Xenotransplantation and Xenozoonose Debate' (1999) 27 *Journal of Law, Medicine and Ethics* 137.
Code of Health and Disability Services Consumers' Rights (at: www.hdc.org.nz/media/24833/brochure-code-white.pdf, accessed 21/03/11).
Coggon, J. 'Public Health, Responsibility and English Law: Are There Such Things as No Smoke Without Ire or Needless Clean Needles?' (2009) 17 *Medical Law Review* 127.
  'Harmful Rights-Doing? The Perceived Problem of Liberal Paradigms and Public Health' (2008) 34 *Journal of Medical Ethics* 798.
Cohen-Haguenauer, O. 'Overview of Regulation of Gene Therapy in Europe: A Current Statement Including Reference to US Regulation' (1995) 6 *Human Gene Therapy* 773.
Cohen-Haguenauer, O., Rosenthal, F., Gänsbacher, B., Bolhuis, R., Dorsch-Häsler, K., Eshhar, Z., Gahrton, G., Hokland, P., Melani, C., Rankin, E., Thielemans, K., Vile, R., Zwierzina, H. and Cichutek, K. for the Euregenethy Network 'Opinion Paper on the Current Status of the Regulation of Gene Therapy in Europe' (2002) 13 *Human Gene Therapy* 2085.
Coker, R. and Martin, R. 'Introduction: The Importance of Law for Public Health Policy and Practice' (2006) 120 suppl. 1 *Public Health* 2.
Coker, R.J., Mounier-Jack, S. and Martin, R. 'Public Health Law and Tuberculosis Control in Europe' (2007) 121 *Public Health* 266.
Coles, D. 'The Identification and Management of Risk: Opening Up the Process', in P. Bennett and K. Calman (eds.), *Risk Communication and Public Health* (Oxford University Press, 2001), p. 195.
Collinge, J., Sidle, K.C.L., Meads, J., Ironside, J. and Hill, A.F. 'Molecular Analysis of Prion Strain Variation and the Aetiology of "New Variant" CJD' (1996) 383 *Nature* 685.
Comité Consultatif National d'Ethique pour les Sciences de la Vie et de la Santé (CCNE), *Opinion on Ethical Problems Arising Out of Assisted Reproductive Techniques. Report* (1984) No. 3 (at: www.ccne-ethique.fr/docs/en/avis003.pdf, accessed 25/03/11).
  Opinion on Research and Use of In-Vitro Human Embryos for Scientific and Medical Purposes. Report (1986) No. 8 (at: www.ccne-ethique.fr/docs/en/avis008.pdf, accessed 25/03/11).
  Opinion on Gene Therapy (1990) No. 22 (at: www.ccne-ethique.fr/docs/en/avis022.pdf, accessed 25/03/11).
  Opinion on the Use of Somatic Gene Therapy Procedures. Report (1993) No. 36 (at: www.ccne-ethique.fr/docs/en/avis036.pdf, accessed 25/03/11).
  Opinion on Ethics and Xenotransplantation (1999) No. 61 (at: www.ccne-ethique.fr/docs/en/avis061.pdf, accessed 16/03/11).

Commission of the European Communities, *Communication from the Commission on the Precautionary Principle* COM.(2000) 1 Final.

Committee to Consider Social, Ethical and Legal Issues Arising from In Vitro Fertilization, *Report on the Disposition of Embryos Produced by In Vitro Fertilization* (Melbourne: Parliament of the State of Victoria, 1984).

Committee for Human Medicinal Products, *Concept Paper on the Revision of the Points to Consider on Xenogeneic Cell Therapy Medicinal Products* (2007) EMEA/CHMP/165085/2007.

Committee to Investigate Artificial Conception and Related Matters (Hobart: Director-General of Health Services, 1985).

Committee for Proprietary Medicinal Products (CPMP), *Note for Guidance on the Quality, Preclinical and Clinical Aspects of Gene Transfer Medicinal Products* (2001) CPMP/BWP/3088/99.

  Points to Consider on Xenogeneic Cell Therapy Medicinal Products (2003) CPMP/1199/02.

Committee on Xenograft Transplantation: Ethical Issues and Public Policy, Division of Health Sciences Policy, Division of Health Care Services, Institute of Medicine, *Xenotransplantation – Science, Ethics and Public Policy* (Washington, DC: National Academy Press, 1996).

Connolly, K. '"In those days I was careless" says pop star accused of infecting man with HIV', guardian.co.uk, 16 August 2010.

  'German singer Nadja Benaissa sentenced for infecting lover with HIV', guardian.co.uk, 26 August 2010.

Cook, P.S. 'What Constitutes Adequate Public Consultation? Xenotransplantation Proceeds in Australia' (2011) 8 *Bioethical Inquiry* 67.

Cook-Deegan and R.M. 'Human Gene Therapy and Congress' (1990) 1 *Human Gene Therapy* 163.

Cooper, D.K.C. 'Global Consultation on Regulatory Requirements for Xenotransplantation in Clinical Trials, Conference held in Changsha, China, 19–21 November 2008' (2009) 16 *Xenotransplantation* 58.

Cooper, D.K.C., Ezzelarab, M., Hara, H. and Ayares, D. 'Recent Advances in Pig-to-Human Organ and Cell Transplantation' (2008) 8 *Expert Opinion in Biological Therapeutics* 1.

Cooper, D.K.C., Gollackner, B. and Sachs, D.H. 'Will the Pig Solve the Transplantation Backlog?' (2002) 53 *Annual Review of Medicine* 133.

Cooper, D.K.C., Keogh, A.M., Brink, J., Corris, P.A., Klepetko, W., Pierson, R.N., Schmoeckel, M., Shirakura, R. and Warner Stevenson, L. 'Report of the Xenotransplantation Advisory Committee of the International Society for Heart and Lung Transplantation: The Present Status of Xenotransplantation and Its Potential Role in the Treatment of End-Stage Cardiac and Pulmonary Diseases' (2000) 19 *Journal of Heart and Lung Transplantation* 1125.

Cooper, D.K.C. and Lanza, R.P. *Xeno – The Promise of Transplanting Animal Organs into Humans* (Oxford University Press, 2000).

Coote, A. and Franklin, J. 'Negotiating Risks to Public Health – Models for Participation', in P. Bennett and K. Calman (eds.), *Risk Communication and Public Health* (Oxford University Press, 2001), p. 183.

Corrigan, O. 'Empty Ethics: The Problem with Informed Consent' (2003) 25 *Sociology of Health and Illness* 768.

Council of Europe Working Party on Xenotransplantation, *State of the Art Report on Xenotransplantation* (2000) CDBI/CDSP-XENO 2000.

Council of Europe, Recommendation Rec(2003)10 of the Committee of Ministers to member states on xenotransplantation and explanatory memorandum, Adopted by the Committee of Ministers on 19 June 2003 at the 844th meeting of the Ministers' Deputies.

Council of Europe, *Report on the State of the Art in the Field of Xenotransplantation*, CDBI/CDSP-XENO (2003) 1 (at: www.coe.int/t/dg3/healthbioethic/activities/06_xenotransplantation_en/XENO(2003)1_SAR.pdf, accessed 16/03/11).

Council for International Organizations of Medical Sciences (CIOMS), The Declaration of Inuyama, adopted by the XXIVth Round Table Conference of CIOMS on Genetics, Ethics and Human Values: Human Genome Mapping, Genetic Screening and Gene Therapy (Tokyo, 22–7 July 1990).

CIOMS and World Health Organization (WHO), *International Ethical Guidelines for Biomedical Research Involving Human Subjects* (Geneva: CIOMS, 2002).

Council for Responsible Genetics, 'Position Paper on Human Germ Line Manipulation Presented by Council for Responsible Genetics, Human Genetics Committee Fall, 1992' (1993) 4 *Human Gene Therapy* 35.

Cozzi, E., Tallacchini, M., Flanagan, E.B., Pierson, R.N., Sykes, M. and Vanderpool, H.Y. 'The International Xenotransplantation Association Consensus Statement on Conditions for Undertaking Clinical Trials of Porcine Islet Products in Type 1 Diabetes – Chapter 1: Key Ethical Requirements and Progress Toward the Definition of an International Regulatory Framework' (2009) 16 *Xenotransplantation* 203.

Cranor, C.F. 'Learning from the Law to Address Uncertainty in the Precautionary Principle' (2001) 7 *Science and Engineering Ethics* 313.

Curtis, P. 'Ethicists fear free-for-all in animal-to-human transplants', *The Guardian*, 13 January 2007.

Cyranoski, D. 'Stem-Cell Therapy Faces More Scrutiny in China' (2009) 459 *Nature* 146.

Daar, A.S. 'Ethics of Xenotransplantation: Animal Issues, Consent, and Likely Transformation of Transplant Ethics' (1997) 21 *World Journal of Surgery* 975.

'Xenotransplantation – Science, Risk and International Regulatory Efforts', in T.A. Caulfield and B. William-Jones (eds.), *The Commercialization of Genetic Research – Ethical, Legal and Policy Issues* (New York, NY: Kluwer Academic, 1999), p. 129.

'Xenotransplantation: Three Questions to Advance the Discourse' (2000) *British Medical Journal* (at: www.bmj.com/content/320/7238/868/reply#bmj_el_7566, accessed 16/03/11).

Dawson, A. and Garrard, E. 'In Defence of Moral Imperialism: Four Equal and Universal Prima Facie Principles' (2006) 32 *Journal of Medical Ethics* 200.

Dawson, A. and Verweij, M. (eds.), *Ethics, Prevention and Public Health* (Oxford University Press, 2007).

Department for Environment, Food and Rural Affairs (DEFRA), Scottish Executive Environment and Rural Affairs Department, Welsh Assembly Government, Department of the Environment in Northern Ireland, *The GM Dialogue: Government Response* (London: DEFRA, 2004).
The GM Public Debate: Lessons Learned from the Process (London: DEFRA, 2004).
Department of Health (DH), *Report of the Committee on the Ethics of Gene Therapy* Cm 1788 (London: HMSO, 1992).
Animal Tissue into Humans (London: DH, 1996).
Communicating About Risks to Public Health: Pointers to Good Practice (London: DH, 1997).
'Press release – Frank Dobson announces steps to regulate animal to human transplants' 30 July 1998.
Learning from Bristol: The Report of the Public Inquiry into Children's Heart Surgery at the Bristol Royal Infirmary 1984–1995 (London: Stationery Office, 2001) Cm. 5207(I).
Reconfiguring the Department of Health's Arm's Length Bodies (London: DH, 2004).
Report of the Ad Hoc Advisory Group on the Operation of NHS Research Ethics Committees (London: DH, 2005).
Research Governance Framework for Health and Social Care (2nd edn, London: DH, 2005).
Xenotransplantation Guidance (2006) (at: www.dh.gov.uk/prod_consum_dh/groups/dh_digitalassets/@dh/@en/documents/digitalasset/dh_063074.pdf, accessed 16/03/11).
Reference Guide to Consent for Examination or Treatment (2nd edn, London: DH, 2009).
Liberating the NHS: Report of the Arm's Length Bodies Review (London: DH, 2010).
Department of Health and Social Security, *Report of the Committee of Inquiry into Human Fertilisation and Embryology* (London: HMSO, 1984), Cmnd 9314.
Department of Trade and Industry (DTI), *GM Nation? The Findings of the Public Debate* (London: DTI, 2003).
Di Nicuolo, G., D'Alessandro, A., Andria, B., Scuderi, V., Scognamiglio, M., Tammaro, A., Mancini, A., Cozzolino, S., Di Florio, E., Bracco, A., Calise, F. and Chamuleau, R.A.F.M. 'Long-Term Absence of Porcine Endogenous Infection in Chronically Immunosuppressed Patients after Treatment with the Porcine Cell-Based Academic Medical Center Bioartificial Liver' (2010) 17 *Xenotransplantation* 431.
Dickson, D. 'Pig Heart Transplant "Breakthrough" Stirs Debate over Timing of Trials' (1995) 377 *Nature* 185.
Dieckhoff, B., Petersen, B., Kues, W.A., Kurth, R., Niemann, H. and Denner, J. 'Knockdown of Porcine Endogenous Retroviruses (PERV) Expression by PERV-Specific shRNA in Transgenic Pigs' (2008) 15 *Xenotransplantation* 36.

Director-General's Notice, Pharmaceutical Affairs Bureau, Ministry for Health and Welfare, *Guidance for Quality and Safety Assurance in Drugs for Gene Therapy* (Tokyo: Ministry for Health and Welfare, 1995).

Dobson, J.M. and Dark, J.H. *The Physiology of Xenotransplantation* (London: DH, 2002).

Doern, G.B. 'Regulatory regimes for the safety and efficacy of biotechnological health products: changing pressures, products and processes – a paper prepared for the Canadian Biotechnology Advisory Committee (2003)', unpublished.

Dossetor, J.B. 'Innovative Treatment Versus Clinical Research: An Ethics Issue in Transplantation' (1990) 22 *Transplantation Proceedings* 966.

Doyal, L. 'Informed Consent: Moral Necessity or Illusion?' (2001) 10 (suppl. I) *Quality in Health Care* i29.

Dratwa, J. 'Taking Risks with the Precautionary Principle: Food (and the Environment) for Thought at the European Commission' (2002) 4 *Journal of Environmental Policy and Planning* 197.

Dunbar-Jacob, J. and Mortimer-Stephens, M.K. 'Treatment Adherence in Chronic Disease' (2001) 54 *Journal of Clinical Epidemiology* S57.

Dutch Consumer and Biotechnology Foundation, *Xenotransplantation: Is and Should It Be Possible? Final Report in Respect of the Public Debate on Xenotransplantation* (The Hague: Dutch Consumer and Biotechnology Foundation, 2001).

Dutton, D.B. *Worse than the Disease: Pitfalls of Medical Progress* (New York, NY: Cambridge University Press, 1988).

Edwards, A. and Elwyn, G. 'Understanding Risk and Lessons for Clinical Risk Communication about Treatment Preferences' (2001) 10 (suppl. I) *Quality in Health Care* i9.

Edwards, R.G., Bavister, B.D. and Steptoe, P.C. 'Early Stages of Fertilization *In Vitro* of Human Oocytes Matured *In Vitro*' (1969) 221 *Nature* 632.

Edwards, R.G. and Sharpe, D.J. 'Social Values and Research in Human Embryology' (1971) 231 *Nature* 87.

Edwards, R.G., Steptoe, P.C. and Purdy, J.M. 'Fertilization and Cleavage *In Vitro* of Preovulator Human Oocytes' (1970) 227 *Nature* 1307.

Einsiedel, E.F. 'Assessing a Controversial Medical Technology: Canadian Public Consultations on Xenotransplantation' (2002) 11 *Public Understanding of Science* 315.

Einsiedel, E.F. and Ross, H. 'Animal Spare Parts? A Canadian Public Consultation on Xenotransplantation' (2002) 8 *Science and Engineering Ethics* 579.

Elliott, R.B., Escobar, L., Garkavenko, O., Croxson, M.C., Schroeder, B.A., McGregor, M., Ferguson, G., Beckman, N. and Ferguson, S. 'No Evidence of Infection with Porcine Endogenous Retrovirus in Recipients of Encapsulated Porcine Islet Xenografts' (2000) 9 *Cell Transplantation* 895.

Elliott, R.B., Escobar, L., Tan, P.L.J., Muzina, M., Zwain, S. and Buchanan, C. 'Live Encapsulated Porcine Islets from A Type 1 Diabetic Patient 9.5 Years after Xenotransplantation' (2007) 14 *Xenotransplantation* 157.

Enquête Commission, 'An Extract from Prospects and Risks of Gene Technology: The Report of the Enquête Commission to the Bundestag of the Federal Republic of Germany' (1988) 2 *Bioethics* 254.
Ethics Advisory Board, Department of Health, Education and Welfare, *Reports and Conclusions: HEW Support Involving Human In Vitro Fertilization and Embryo Transfer* (1979) (at: http://bioethics.georgetown.edu/pcbe/reports/past_commissions/HEW_IVF_report.pdf, accessed 23/03/11).
Ethics Committee of the Transplantation Society, 'Human Xenotransplantation – Position Paper' (1993) 1 *Transplantation Society Bulletin* 8.
  'The Transplantation Society and Xenotransplantation (Draft Guidelines)' (1997) 6 *Transplantation Society Bulletin* 11.
European Agency for the Evaluation of Medicinal Products (EMEA), *Gene Therapy Product Quality Aspects in the Production of Vectors and Genetically Modified Somatic Cells* (1994) (at: www.ema.europa.eu/docs/en_GB/document_library/Scientific_guideline/2009/09/WC500003449.pdf, accessed 25/03/11).
  Committee for Proprietary Medicinal Products Safety Working Party and Biotechnology Working Party, *Safety Studies for Gene Therapy Products – Annex to Note for Guidance on Gene Therapy Quality Aspects in the Production of Vectors and Genetically Modified Somatic Cells*, CPMP/SWP/112/98 draft (London: EMEA, 1998).
  Concept Paper on the Development of a Committee for Proprietary Medicinal Products (CMP) Points to Consider on Xenogeneic Cell Therapy (2000) CPMP/BWP/3326/99.
European Commission, Health and Consumer Protection Directorate-General, *Opinion on the State of the Art Concerning Xenotransplantation – Adopted by the Scientific Committee on Medicinal Products and Medical Devices on 1st October 2001*, (2001) Doc.SANCO/SCMPMD/2001/0002 Final.
European Medical Research Councils (EMRC), 'Recommendations on Human In Vitro Fertilization and Embryo Transfer' (1983) 322 *The Lancet* 1187.
  'Gene Therapy in Man: Recommendations of European Medical Research Councils' (1988) 2 *The Lancet* 1271.
Expert Scientific Group on Phase One Clinical Trials, *Final Report* (London: Stationery Office, 2006).
Family Law Council, *Creating Children: A Uniform Approach to the Law and Practice of Reproductive Technology in Australia* (Canberra: Australian Government Publishing Service, 1985).
Fano, A. 'If Pigs Could Fly, They Would: The Problems with Xeno-transplantation', in B. Tokar (ed.), *Redesigning Life? The Worldwide Challenge to Genetic Engineering* (London: Zed Books, 2001), p. 182.
Faulder, C. *Whose Body Is It? The Troubling Issue of Informed Consent* (London: Virago Press, 1985).
Feinberg, J. *The Moral Limits of the Criminal Law: Harm to Others Volume One* (New York, NY: Oxford University Press, 1984).
Feintuck, M. 'Precautionary Maybe, But What's the Principle? The Precautionary Principle, the Regulation of Risk, and the Public Domain' (2005) 32 *Journal of Law and Society* 371.

Ferguson, P.R. 'Patients' Perceptions of Information Provided in Clinical Trials' (2002) 28 *Journal of Medical Ethics* 45.
  'Human "Guinea Pigs": Why Patients Participate in Clinical Trials', in S.A.M. McLean (ed.), *First Do No Harm – Law, Ethics and Healthcare* (Aldershot: Ashgate, 2006), p. 165.
Fidler, D.P. *International Law and Infectious Diseases* (Oxford: Clarendon Press, 1999).
  'Constitutional Outlines of Public Health's "New World Order"' (2004) 77 *Temple Law Review* 247.
Fiebig, U., Stephan, O., Kurth, R. and Denner, J. 'Neutralizing Antibodies against Conserved Domains of p15E of Porcine Endogenous Retroviruses: Basis for a Vaccine for Xenotransplantation?' (2003) 307 *Virology* 406.
Fischbacher-Smith, D. and Calman, K. 'A Precautionary Tale: The Role of the Precautionary Principle in Policy-Making for Public Health', in P. Bennett, K. Calman, S. Curtis and D. Fischbacher-Smith (eds.), *Risk Communication and Public Health* (2nd edn, Oxford University Press, 2010), pp. 202–206.
Fisher, E. *Risk Regulation and Administrative Constitutionalism* (Oxford: Hart, 2007).
Fisher, E. and Harding, R. 'The Precautionary Principle: Towards a Deliberative, Transdisciplinary Problem-Solving Process', in R. Harding and E. Fisher (eds.), *Perspectives on the Precautionary Principle* (New South Wales: Federation Press, 1999), p. 292.
Fishman, J. 'Infection and Xenotransplantation: Developing Strategies to Minimize Risk', in J. Fishman, D. Sachs and R. Shaikh (eds.), *Xenotransplantation: Scientific Frontiers and Public Policy* (New York, NY: New York Academy of Sciences, 1998), p. 52.
Fishman, J.A. 'SARS, Xenotransplantation and Bioterrorism: Preventing the Next Epidemic' (2003) 3 *American Journal of Transplantation* 909.
Fishman, J., Sachs, D. and Shaikh, R. (eds.), *Xenotransplantation: Scientific Frontiers and Public Policy* (New York, NY: New York Academy of Sciences, 1998).
Fisk, D. 'Perception of Risk – Is the Public Probably Right?', in P. Bennett and K. Calman (eds.), *Risk Communication and Public Health* (Oxford University Press, 2001), p. 133.
Fleck, L.M. 'Can We Trust "Democratic Deliberation"?' (2007) 37 *Hastings Center Report* 22.
Fletcher, J.C. 'Moral Problems and Ethical Issues in Prospective Human Gene Therapy' (1983) 69 *Virginia Law Review* 515.
Florencio, P.S. and Ramanathan, E.D. 'Are Xenotransplantation Safeguards Legally Viable?' (2001) 16 *Berkeley Technology Law Journal* 937.
  'Legal Enforcement of Xenotransplantation Public Health Safeguards' (2004) 32 *Journal of Law, Medicine and Ethics* 117.
Foster, C. *The Ethics of Medical Research on Humans* (Cambridge University Press, 2001).
Fovargue, S. 'Consenting to Bio-Risk: Xenotransplantation and the Law' (2005) 25 *Legal Studies* 404.

'"Oh Pick Me, Pick Me": Selecting Participants for Xenotransplant Clinical Trials' (2007) 15 *Medical Law Review* 176.
Fovargue, S. and Miola, J. 'One Step Forward, Two Steps Back?: The GMC, the Common Law and "Informed" Consent' (2010) 36 *Journal of Medical Ethics* 494.
Fovargue, S. and Ost, S. 'When Should Precaution Prevail? Interests in (Public) Health and the Risk of Harm: The Xenotransplantation Example' (2010) 18 *Medical Law Review* 302.
Fowler, G., Juengst, E.T. and Zimmerman, B.Z. 'Germ-Line Gene Therapy and the Clinical Ethics of Medical Genetics' (1989) 10 *Theoretical Medicine* 151.
Fox, M. 'Research Bodies: Feminist Perspectives on Clinical Research', in S. Sheldon and M. Thomson (eds.) *Feminist Perspectives on Health Care Law* (London: Cavendish, 1998), p. 115.
  'Clinical Research and Patients: The Legal Perspective', in J. Tingle and A. Cribb (eds.) *Nursing Law and Ethics* (2nd edn, Oxford: Blackwell, 2002), p. 252.
Fox, R.C. and Swazey, J.P. *The Courage to Fail – A Social View of Organ Transplants and Dialysis* (New Brunswick, NJ: Transaction, 2002).
Frewer, L.J. 'Public Risk Perceptions and Risk Communication', in P. Bennett and K. Calman (eds.), *Risk Communication and Public Health* (Oxford University Press, 2001), p. 20.
Frewer, L. and Salter, B. 'Public Attitudes, Scientific Advice and the Politics of Regulatory Policy: The Case of BSE' (2002) 29 *Science and Public Policy* 137.
Friedmann, T. 'A Brief History of Gene Therapy' (1992) 2 *Nature Genetics* 93.
Furger, F. and Fukuyama, F. 'A Proposal for Modernizing the Regulation of Human Biotechnologies' (2007) 37 *Hastings Center Report* 16.
Garrafa, V., Solbakk, J.H., Vidal, S. and Lorenzo, C. 'Between the Needy and the Greedy: The Quest for A Just and Fair Ethics of Clinical Research' (2010) 36 *Journal of Medical Ethics* 500.
Gavaghan, C. *Defending the Genetic Supermarket: The Law and Ethics of Selecting the Next Generation* (Oxford: Routledge-Cavendish, 2007).
GM Science Review Panel, *GM Science Review: First Report* (London: DTI, 2003).
  GM Science Review: Second Report (London: DTI, 2004).
Gene Therapy Advisory Committee (GTAC), *Guidance on Making Proposals to Conduct Gene Therapy Research on Human Subjects* (London: DH, 1994).
  First Annual Report November 1993–December 1994 (London: DH, 1995).
  Seventh Annual Report January 2000–December 2000 (London: DH, 2001).
  Guidance on the Content of a Proposal and Participant Information Sheets (London: DH, 2009).
General Medical Council (GMC), *Consent: Patients and Doctors Making Decisions Together* (London: GMC, 2008).
  Confidentiality (London: GMC, 2009).
  Consent to Research (London: GMC, 2010).
  Good Practice in Research (London: GMC, 2010).

Giddens, A. 'Risk and Responsibility' (1999) 62 *Modern Law Review* 1.
Gjørv, I.L. 'Political Considerations of Controversial Medical Issues: Xenotransplantation and Society. A Presentation of the Work of the Norwegian National Working Group on Xenotransplantation' (2004) 45 (suppl. 1) *Acta Veterinaria Scandinavica* S53.
Glanz, K. and Yang, H. 'Communicating About Risk of Infectious Diseases' (1996) 275 *Journal of the American Medical Association* 253.
Glass, K.C. and Lemmens, T. 'Conflict of Interest and Commercialization of Biomedical Research: What Is the Role of Research Ethics Review', in T.A. Caulfield and B. Williams-Jones (eds.), *The Commercialization of Genetic Research: Ethical, Legal and Policy Issues* (New York, NY: Kluwer Academic Press, 1999), p. 79.
Glover, J. *Ethics of New Reproductive Technologies: The Glover Report to the European Commission – Studies in Biomedical Policy* (DeKalb, IL: Northern Illinois Press, 1989).
Gold, E.R. and Adams, W.A. 'Reconciling Private Benefit and Public Risk in Biotechnology: Xenotransplantation as a Case Study in Consent' (2002) 10 *Health Law Journal* 31.
Gostin, L.O. *Public Health Law: Power, Duty, Restraint* (2nd edn, Berkeley, CA: University of California Press, 2008).
Gostin, L.O., Bayer, R. and Fairchild, A.L. 'Ethical and Legal Challenges Posed by Severe Acute Respiratory Syndrome: Implications for the Control of Severe Infectious Disease Threats' (2003) 290 *Journal of the American Medical Association* 3229.
Green, E., Short, S.D., Duarte-Davidson, R. and Levy, L.S. 'Public and Professional Perceptions of Environmental and Health Risks', in P. Bennett, K. Calman (eds.), *Risk Communication and Public Health* (Oxford University Press, 2001), p. 51.
Grießler, E., Littig, B., Hüsing, B., Zimmer, R., Santos, D., Munoz, E., Ponce, G., Gronke, H. and Dordoni, P. *Final Report – Increasing Public Involvement in Debates on Ethical Questions of Xenotransplantation* (Vienna: Institute for Advanced Studies, 2004).
Griffin, G. and Muir, D. *Infection Risks in Xenotransplantation* (London: DH, 2001).
Griffiths, S. and Lau, J. 'The Influence of SARS on Perceptions of Risk and Reality' (2009) 31 *Journal of Public Health* 466.
Groth, C.G. 'Editorial – Looking Back, Heading Forward' (2008) 15 *Xenotransplantation* 1.
Groth, C.G., Korsgren, O., Tibell, A., Tollemar, J., Möller, E., Bolinder, J., Östman, J., Reinholt, F.P., Hellerström, C. and Andersson, A. 'Transplantation of Porcine Fetal Pancreas to Diabetic Patients' (1994) 344 *The Lancet* 1402.
Gruskin, S. 'Is There a Government in the Cockpit: A Passenger's Perspective or Global Public Health: The Role of Human Rights' (2004) 22 *Temple Law Review* 313.
Guest, S. 'Compensation for Subjects of Medical Research: The Moral Rights of Patients and the Power of Research Ethics Committees' (1997) 23 *Journal of Medical Ethics* 181.

Gunning, J. and English, V. *Human In Vitro Fertilisation – A Case Study in the Regulation of Medical Innovation* (Aldershot: Dartmouth, 1993).
Guttmacher, S. 'HIV Infection: Individual Rights v. Disease Control' (1990) 17 *Journal of Law and Society* 66.
Haller, J.D. and Cerruti, M.M. 'Heart Transplantation in Man: Compilation of Cases – January 1 1964 to October 23 1968' (1968) 22 *American Journal of Cardiology* 840.
Halliday, S. 'A Comparative Approach to the Regulation of Human Embryonic Stem Cell Research in Europe' (2004) 12 *Medical Law Review* 40.
Halliday, S., Steinberg, D.L. 'The Regulated Gene: New Legal Dilemmas' (2004) 12 *Medical Law Review* 2.
Halpern, S.A. *Lesser Harms: The Morality of Risk in Medical Research* (Chicago, IL: University of Chicago Press, 2006).
Hanson, M.J. 'The Seductive Sirens of Medical Progress – The Case of Xenotransplantation' (1995) *Hastings Center Report* 5.
Hansson, M.O. 'Balancing the Quality of Consent' (1998) 24 *Journal of Medical Ethics* 182.
Hansson, S.O. 'Philosophical Perspectives on Risk' (2004) 8 *Techné* 10.
Harcourt, B.E. 'The Collapse of the Harm Principle' (1999) 90 *Journal of Criminal Law and Criminology* 109.
Hardy, J.D. and Chavez, C.M. 'The First Heart Transplant in Man – Developmental Animal Investigations with Analysis of the 1964 Case in the Light of Current Clinical Experience' (1968) 22 *American Journal of Cardiology* 772.
Hardy, J.D., Chavez, C.M., Kurrus, F.D., Neely, W.A., Eraslan, S., Turner, M.D., Fabian, L.W. and Labecki, T.D. 'Heart Transplantation in Man' (1964) 188 *Journal of the American Medical Association* 1132.
Harrington, J.A. 'Deciding Best Interests: Medical Progress, Clinical Judgment and the "Good Family"' [2003] 3 *Web Journal of Current Legal Issues*.
Harris, A. and Martin, R. 'The Exercise of Public Health Powers In An Era Of Human Rights: The Particular Problems of Tuberculosis' (2004) 118 *Public Health* 313.
Harris, J. 'Research on Human Subjects, Exploitation, and Global Principles of Ethics', in M. Freeman, A.D.E. Lewis (eds.), *Law and Medicine: Current Legal Issues*, vol. 3 (Oxford University Press, 2000), p. 379.
Hastillo, A. and Hess, M.L. 'Heart Xenografting: A Route Not Yet to Trod' (1993) 12 *Journal of Heart and Lung Transplantation* 3.
Hattenstone, S. 'Who's mad now?', *The Guardian*, 5 March 2001.
Häyry, M. and Takala, T. 'Genetic Information, Rights and Autonomy' (2001) 22 *Theoretical Medicine* 403.
Health Canada, TPP, *Report of the National Forum on Xenotransplantation: Clinical, Ethical, and Regulatory Issues November 6–8, 1997* (Ottawa: Health Canada, 1998).
  Proposed Canadian Standard for Xenotransplantation (Ottawa: Health Canada, 1999).
  Therapeutic Products Programme (TPP), *Survey on Human Organ Donation and Xenotransplantation* (1999) (at: www.hc-sc.gc.ca/dhp-mps/alt_formats/hpfb-dgpsa/pdf/brgth erap/xeno_survey-enquete-eng.pdf, accessed 25/03/11).

Report from the Planning Workshop: Public Involvement on Xenotransplantation – Government Conference Centre, April 10–11 2000, Ottawa, Ontario (2000) (at: www.hc-sc.gc.ca/dhp-mps/alt_formats/hpfb-dgpsa/pdf/brgtherap/ awsreport-rapportvif-eng.pdf, accessed 16/03/11).

Report of the Xenotransplantation Surveillance Workshop – Infection Control Database and Sample Archiving (2001) 27S1 *Canada Communicable Disease Report.*

Guidance for Industry – Guidance Document on the Regulation of Medical Devices Manufactured from or Incorporating Viable or Non-Viable Animal Tissue or their Derivative(s) (2004) (at: www.hc-sc.gc.ca/dhp-mps/md-im/ applic-demande/guide-ld/anim_tiss-eng.php, accessed 23/03/11).

'Expert Advisory Committee on Xenograft Regulation' (2009) (at: www.hc-sc.gc.ca/dhp-mps/brgtherap/activit/com/eacx-ccerx/index-eng.php, accessed 25/03/11).

Health Canada, Science and Research, 'Xenotransplantation' (2006) (at: www. hc-sc.gc.ca/sr-sr/biotech/about-apropos/xeno-eng.php, accessed 16/03/11).

Health Council of the Netherlands, *Artificial Procreation* (The Hague: Health Council of the Netherlands, 1986).

Heredity: Science and Society – On the Possibilities and Limits of Genetic Testing and Gene Therapy (The Hague: Health Council of the Netherlands, 1989).

Health Council of the Netherlands, Committee on Gene Therapy, *Gene Therapy* (Rijswijk: Health Council of the Netherlands, 1997) Publication no. 1997/12E.

Committee on Xenotransplantation, *Xenotransplantation* (Rijswijk: Health Council of the Netherlands, 1998), No. 1998/01E.

Health Protection Agency (HPA), *The Human Animal Infections and Risk Surveillance (HAIRS) Group, First Report 2004–2007* (London: HPA, 2008).

Health Research Council (HRC), *Guidelines on Ethics in Health Research* (2002) revised 2005 (at: www.hrc.govt.nz/assets/pdfs/publications/Ethics% 20Guidelines%20July%202006.pdf, accessed 22/03/11).

HRC Gene Technology Advisory Committee, *Guidelines for Preparation of Applications Involving Clinical Trials of Xenotransplantation in New Zealand* (2007) (at: www.hrc.govt.nz/assets/pdfs/publications/Guidelines%20for% 20Preparation%20of%20Applications%20Involving%20Clinical%20Trials %20of%20Xenotransplantation%20in%20NZ.pdf, accessed 16/03/11).

Process and Guidelines for Application for Approval of Proposals Involving Administration of Gene Products to Human Subjects in New Zealand (2008) (at: www.hrc.govt.nz/assets/pdfs/publications/GTACProcess%20and%20 Guidelines%202008%20_2_.pdf, accessed 25/3/11).

Herring, J. *Medical Law and Ethics* (Oxford University Press, 2010).

Criminal Law: Text, Cases and Materials (4th edn, Oxford University Press, 2010).

Hewlett, S. 'Consent to Clinical Research – Adequately Voluntary or Substantially Influenced?' (1996) 22 *Journal of Medical Ethics* 232.

Heyvaert, V. 'Globalizing Regulation: Reaching Beyond the Borders of Chemical Safety' (2009) 36 *Journal of Law and Society* 110.

Hilbrands, L.B., Hoitsma, A.J. and Koene, R.A.P. 'Medication Compliance After Renal Transplantation' (1995) 60 *Transplantation* 914.

Hill, A. 'I know the risk. It's my only hope', *The Observer*, 16 December 2007.

Holder, J. and Elworthy, S. 'The BSE Crisis: A Study of the Precautionary Principle and the Politics of Science in Law', in H. Reece (ed.), *Law and Science: Current Legal Issues*, vol. 1 (Oxford University Press, 1998), p. 129.

Holland, J.A. 'The "Catch-22" of Xenotransplantation: Compelling Compliance with Long-Term Surveillance' (2007) 7 *Houston Journal of Health Law and Policy* 151.

House of Commons Science and Technology Committee, *Human Reproductive Technologies and the Law*, 5th Report of Session 2004–5, HC 7–1, vol. I. *Scientific Advice, Risk and Evidence Based Policy Making*, 7th Report of Session 2005–6, vol. I. (London: Stationery Office, 2006) HC 900-I.

House of Lords Select Committee on Science and Technology, *Science and Society*, 3rd Report (London: House of Lords, 2000).

House of Lords Select Committee on Intergovernmental Organisations, *Diseases Know No Frontiers: How Effective Are Intergovernmental Organisations in Controlling Their Spread?* (2008) vol. I: Report HL Paper 143-I.

HSC 2003/011 *The Interventional Procedures Programme: Working with the National Institute for Clinical Excellence to Promote Safe Clinical Innovation*.

Hughes, J. 'Xenografting: Ethical Issues' (1998) 24 *Journal of Medical Ethics* 18.

Hughes, V. 'When Patients March In' (2010) 28 *Nature Biotechnology* 1145.

Human Gene Therapy Subcommittee, NIH Recombinant DNA Advisory Committee, 'Points to Consider in the Design and Submission of Protocols for the Transfer of Recombinant DNA into the Genome of Human Subjects' (1986) 11 *Recombinant DNA Research* 119.

Hyder, N. 'India Debates New Surrogacy Laws', *BioNews* 594, 7 February 2011 (at: www.bionews.org.uk, accessed 25/03/11).

Ibrahim, Z., Ezzelarab, M., Kormos, R. and Cooper, D.K.C. 'Which Patients First? Planning the First Clinical Trial of Xenotransplantation: A Case for Cardiac Bridging' (2005) 12 *Xenotransplantation* 168.

Incorvati, G. 'Xenotransplantation and Public Responsibility' (2003) 10 *European Journal of Health Law* 295.

Institute of Medicine (IOM), *Xenotransplantation: Science, Ethics and Public Policy* (Washington, DC: National Academy Press, 1996).

International Advisory Board of the III World Congress on In Vitro Fertilisation and Embryo Transfer, 'Helsinki Statement on Human In Vitro Fertilization' (1985) 442 *Annals of New York Academy of Sciences* 571.

International Conference on Harmonisation of Technical Requirements for Registration of Pharmaceuticals for Human Use, *ICH Harmonised Tripartite Guideline – Guideline for Good Clinical Practice E6(R1)* (1996) (at: www.ich.org/LOB/media/MEDIA482.pdf, accessed 22/03/11).

Isasi, R.M. and Knoppers, B.M. 'Mind the Gap: Policy Approaches to Embryonic Stem Cell and Cloning Research in 50 Countries' (2006) 13 *European Journal of Health Law* 9.

Jackson, E. 'The Donation of Eggs for Research and the Rise of Neopaternalism', in M. Freeman (ed.), *Law and Bioethics: Current Legal Issues 2008*, vol. 11 (Oxford University Press, 2008), p. 286.
  Medical Law: Text, Cases and Materials (Oxford University Press, 2010).
Jackson, R., Barbagallo, F. and Haste, H. 'Strengths of Public Dialogue on Science-Related Issues' (2005) 8 *Critical Review of International Social and Political Philosophy* 349.
Jacobs, L.A. 'Rights and Quarantine During the SARS Global Health Crisis: Differentiated Legal Consciousness in Hong Kong, Shanghai, and Toronto' (2007) 41 *Law and Society Review* 511.
Jamieson, D. 'The Precautionary Principle and Electric and Magnetic Fields' (2001) 91 *American Journal of Public Health* 1355.
Jasanoff, S. 'Civilization and Madness: The Great BSE Scare of 1996' (1997) 6 *Public Understanding of Science* 221.
Jayaraman, K.S. 'Pig Heart Transplant Surgeon Held in Jail' (1997) 385 *Nature* 378.
Johnson, L. 'Particular Issues of Public Health: Infectious Disease', in R. Martin and L. Johnson (eds.), *Law and the Public Dimension of Health* (London: Cavendish, 2001), p. 243.
Johnson, M.H. 'The Art of Regulation and the Regulation of ART: The Impact of Regulation on Research and Clinical Practice' (2002) 9 *Journal of Law and Medicine* 399.
  'Regulating the Science and Therapeutic Application of Human Embryo Research: Managing the Tension Between Biomedical Creativity and Public Concern', in J.R. Spence and A. du Bois-Pedain (eds.), *Freedom and Responsibility in Reproductive Choice* (Oxford: Hart, 2006), p. 91.
Jones, K.E., Patel, N.G., Levy, M.A., Storeygard, A., Balk, D., Gittleman, J.L. and Daszak, P. 'Global Trends in Emerging Infectious Diseases' (2008) 451 *Nature* 990.
Jones, M. *Medical Negligence* (4th edn, London: Sweet & Maxwell, 2008).
Jones, M.A. 'Informed Consent and other Fairy Stories' (1999) 7 *Medical Law Review* 103.
Kass, L. *Toward a More Natural Science – Biology and Human Affairs* (New York, NY: Free Press, 1985).
Kass, N.E., Sugarman, J., Faden, R. and Schoh-Spana, M. 'Trust – The Fragile Foundation of Contemporary Biomedical Research' (1996) 26 *Hastings Center Report* 25.
Katz, J. 'Human Experimentation and Human Rights' (1993) 38 *Saint Louis University Law Journal* 7.
Keeney, R.L. and von Winterfeldt, D. 'Appraising the Precautionary Principle – A Decision Analysis Perspective' (2001) 4 *Journal of Risk Research* 191.
Kennedy, I. *Treat Me Right – Essays in Medical Law and Ethics* (Oxford University Press, 1988).
Kennedy, I. and Grubb, A. *Medical Law* (3rd edn, London: Butterworths, 2000).
Kent, G. 'Shared Understandings for Informed Consent: The Relevance of Psychological Research on the Provision of Information' (1996) 43 *Social Science and Medicine* 1517.

King, N. 'Experimental Treatment: Oxymoron or Aspiration?' (1995) 25 *Hastings Center Report* 6.
  'Defining and Describing Benefit Appropriately in Clinical Trials' (2000) 28 *Journal of Law, Medicine and Ethics* 332.
Knoppers, B.M. 'Reflections: The Challenge of Biotechnology and Public Policy' (2000) 45 *McGill Law Journal* 559.
Kong, W.M. 'The Regulation of Gene Therapy Research in Competent Adult Patients, Today and Tomorrow: Implications of EU Directive 2001/20/EC' (2004) 12 *Medical Law Review* 164.
  'Legitimate Requests and Indecent Proposals: Matters of Justice in the Ethical Assessment of Phase I Trials Involving Competent Patients' (2005) 31 *Journal of Medical Ethics* 205.
Kriebel, D. and Tickner, J. 'Reenergizing Public Health Through Precaution' (2001) 91 *American Journal of Public Health* 1351.
Kumar, P.D. 'Xenotransplantation in the New Millennium: Moratorium or Cautious Experimentation?' (2000) 4 *Perspectives in Biology and Medicine* 562.
Laing, J. 'Incompetent Patients, Experimental Treatment and the "*Bolam* Test" – *JS* v. *An NHS Trust*; *JA* v. *An NHS Trust*' (2003) 11 *Medical Law Review* 237.
Langford, I.H., Marris, C. and O'Riordan, T. 'Public Reactions to Risk: Social Structures, Images of Science, and The Role of Trust', in P. Bennett and K. Calman (eds.), *Risk Communication and Public Health* (Oxford University Press, 2001), p. 33.
Langley, G. and D'silva, J. *Animal Organs in Humans – Uncalculated Risks & Unanswered Questions* (1998) (at: www.ciwf.org.uk/includes/documents/cm_docs/2008/a/animal_organs_in_humans_1998.pdf, accessed 25/03/11).
Law Commission, *Consent in the Criminal Law Consultation Paper* No 139 (London: HMSO, 1995).
Law Reform Commission of Canada, *Biomedical Experimentation Involving Human Subjects, Working Paper* 61 (Ottawa: Law Reform Commission of Canada, 1989).
Le Bas-Bernardet and S., Blancho, G. 'Current Cellular Immunological Hurdles in Pig-to Primate Xenotransplantation' (2009) 21 *Transplant Immunology* 60.
Le Tissier, P., Stoye, J.P., Takeuchi, Y., Patience, C., Weiss, R.A. 'Two Sets of Human-Tropic Pig Retrovirus' (1997) 389 *Nature* 681.
Lee, R.G. and Morgan, D. *Human Fertilisation and Embryology – Regulating the Reproductive Revolution* (Oxford: Blackstone, 2001).
Lenoir, N. 'Biotechnology, Bioethics and Law: Europe's 21st Century Challenge' (2006) 69 *Modern Law Review* 1.
Levine, R.J. 'The Impact of HIV Infection on Society's Perception of Clinical Trials' (1994) 4 *Kennedy Institute of Ethics Journal* 93.
Levy, G.A., Ghanekar, A., Mendicino, M., Phillips, M.J. and Grant, D.R. 'The Present Status of Xenotransplantation' (2001) 33 *Transplantation Proceedings* 3050.
Little, G. 'BSE and the Regulation of Risk' (2001) 64 *Modern Law Review* 730.

Lloyd, A.J. 'The Extent of Patients' Understanding of the Risk of Treatments' (2001) 10 (suppl. I) *Quality in Health Care* i14.

Louz, D., Bergmans, H.E., Loos, B.P. and Hoeben, R.C. 'Reappraisal of Biosafety Risks Posed by PERVs in Xenotransplantation' (2008) 18 *Reviews in Medical Virology* 53.

Lupton, D. 'Risk as Moral Danger: The Social and Political Functions of Risk Discourse in Public Health' (1993) 23 *International Journal of Health Services* 425.

Macintosh, K.L. *Illegal Beings: Human Clones and the Law* (New York, NY: Cambridge University Press, 2005).

Mackenzie, C. and Stoljar, N. (eds.) *Relational Autonomy: Feminist Perspectives on Autonomy, Agency and the Social Self* (New York, NY: Oxford University Press, 2000).

Maclean, A. 'Giving the Reasonable Patient a Voice: Information Disclosure and the Relevance of Empirical Evidence' (2005) 7 *Medical Law International* 1.

Malhotra, P., Malu, S. and Kanpur, S. 'Immunology of Transplant Rejection' (2009) (at: http://emedicine.medscape.com/article/432209-overview, accessed 16/03/11).

Manson, N., O'Neill, O. *Rethinking Informed Consent in Bioethics* (Cambridge University Press, 2007).

Marchant, G.E., Sylvester, D.J. and Abbott, K.W. 'What Does the History of Technology Teach Us About Nano Oversight?' (2009) 37 *Journal of Law, Medicine and Ethics* 724.

Marteau, T., Drake, H. and Bobrow, M. 'Counselling Following Diagnosis of a Fetal Abnormality: The Differing Approaches of Obstetricians, Clinical Geneticists, and Genetic Nurses' (1994) 31 *Journal of Medical Genetics* 864.

Martin, R. 'The Exercise of Public Health Powers in Cases of Infectious Disease: Human Rights Implications: *Enhorn* v. *Sweden* European Court of Human Rights: [2005] ECHR 56529/00' (2006) 14 *Medical Law Review* 132.

'The Role of Law in Public Health', in A. Dawson (ed.) *The Philosophy of Public Health* (Surrey: Ashgate, 2009), p. 11.

Mason, J.K. 'Organ Donation and Transplantation', in C. Dyer (ed.), *Doctors, Patients and the Law* (Oxford: Blackwell, 1992), p. 120.

Mason, J.K., Laurie, G.T. *Mason & McCall Smith's Law and Medical Ethics* (8th edn, Oxford University Press, 2011).

Mattiuzzo, G., Scobie, L. and Takeuchi, Y. 'Strategies to Enhance the Safety Profile of Xenotransplantation: Minimizing the Risk of Viral Zoonoses' (2008) 13 *Current Opinion in Organ Transplantation* 184.

Maxwell, R.J. 'The British Government's Handling of Risk: Some Reflections on the BSE/CJD Crisis', in P. Bennett and K. Calman (eds.), *Risk Communication and Public Health* (Oxford University Press, 2001), p. 95.

McGregor, C.G.A., Byrne, G.W., Vlasin, M., Walkjer, R.C., Tazelaar, H.D., Davies, W.R., Chandrasekaran, K., Oehler, E.A., Boilson, B.A., Wiseman, B.S. and Logan, J.S. 'Preclinical Orthotopic Cardiac Xenotransplantation' (2009) 28 *Xenotransplantation* S224.

McKee, M., Coker, R. 'Trust, Terrorism and Public Health' (2009) 31 *Journal of Public Health* 462.

McKendrick, E. *Contract Law* (8th edn, Basingstoke: Palgrave MacMillan, 2009).
  Contract Law – Text, Cases and Materials (4th edn, Oxford University Press, 2010).
McLean, S. 'Gene Therapy – Cure or Challenge?', in M. Freeman and A. Lewis (eds.), *Law and Medicine: Current Legal Issues*, vol. 3 (Oxford University Press, 2000), p. 205.
McLean, S. and Williamson, L. 'The Demise of UKXIRA and the Regulation of Solid-Organ Xenotransplantation in the UK' (2007) 33 *Journal of Medical Ethics* 373.
  'Xenotransplantation: A Pig in a Poke?' (2004) 57 *Current Legal Problems* 443.
  Xenotransplantation: Law and Ethics (Aldershot: Ashgate, 2005).
Medical Research Council (MRC), 'Statement on Research Related to Human Fertilization and Embryology' (1982) 285 *British Medical Journal* 1480.
  MRC Guidelines for Good Clinical Practice in Clinical Trials (London: MRC, 1998).
Medical Research Council of Canada, *Guidelines for Research on Somatic Cell Gene Therapy in Humans* (Ottawa: Minister of Supply and Services, 1990).
Medical Research Modernization Committee, *Of Pigs, Primates and Plagues: A Layperson's Guide to the Problems with Animal-to-Human Organ Transplants* (1997) (at: www.crt-online.org/mrmc.html, accessed 25/03/11).
Medicines and Healthcare products Regulatory Agency (MHRA), *A Guide to What Is a Medicinal Product* (London: MHRA, 2007) MHRA Guidance Note No. 8.
Michael, M. and Brown, N. 'The Meat of the Matter: Grasping and Judging Xenotransplantation' (2004) 13 *Public Understanding of Science* 379.
  'Scientific Citizenships: Self-Representations of Xenotransplantation's Public' (2005) 14 *Science as Culture* 39.
Michelson, E.S. 'Individual Freedom or Collective Welfare? An Analysis of Quarantine as a Response To Global Infectious Disease', in M.J. Selgelid, M.P. Battin and C.B. Smith (eds.), *Ethics and Infectious Diseases* (Oxford: Wiley-Blackwell, 2006), p. 53.
Michie, C. 'Xenotransplantation: Endogenous Pig Retroviruses and the Precautionary Principle' (2001) 7 *Trends in Molecular Medicine* 62.
Mill, J.S. *On Liberty and Other Essays* (Oxford University Press, 2008).
Millard, A.-L. and Mueller, N.J. 'Critical Issues Related to Porcine Xenograft Exposure to Human Viruses: Lessons from Allotransplantation' (2010) 15 *Current Opinion in Organ Transplantation* 230.
Miller, D. and Macintyre, S. 'Risk Communication: The Relationships between the Media, Public Beliefs, and Policy-Making', in P. Bennett and K. Calman (eds.), *Risk Communication and Public Health* (Oxford University Press, 2001), p. 229.
Miola, J. 'On the Materiality of Risk – Paper Tigers and Panaceas' (2009) 17 *Medical Law Review* 76.
Ministry for Agriculture, Food and Fisheries (MAFF), Department of Health (DH), *Report of the Working Party on Bovine Spongiform Encephalopathy* (London: MAFF/DH, 1989).
  Consultative Committee on Research into Spongiform Encephalopathies, Interim Report (London: MAFF, 1990).

Ministry of Health (MH), *Operational Standard for Ethics Committees* (Wellington: MH, 2006).
Ministry of Health, Labour and Welfare (MHLW), *Guidelines on Issues of Infectious Diseases in Public Health Associated with Clinical Trials of Xenotransplantation* (Tokyo: MHLW, 2001).
Ministry of Health and Social Affairs, *Swedish Act Concerning the Use of Gene Technology on Human Beings and Experiments with Fertilised Ova* (Stockholm: The Ministry, 1991).
Mohiuddin, M.M. 'Clinical Transplantation of Organs: Why Aren't We There Yet?' (2007) c e75 *PLoS Medicine* 0429.
Montgomery, J. *Health Care Law* (2nd edn, Oxford University Press, 2002).
  'Medicalising Crime? Criminalising Health?', in C. Erin and S. Ost (eds.), *The Criminal Justice System and Health Care* (Oxford University Press, 2007), p. 257.
Moran, C. 'Xenotransplantation: Benefits, Risks and Relevance of Reproductive Technology' (2008) *Theriogenology* 1269.
Moran, N. 'Pig-to-Human Heart Transplant Slated to Begin in 1996' (1995) 1 *Nature Medicine* 987.
Morgan, D. *Issues in Medical Law and Ethics* (London: Cavendish, 2001).
Moses, L.B. 'Recurring Dilemmas: The Law's Race to Keep up with Technological Change' (2007) 2 *Journal of Law, Technology and Policy* 239.
Muir, D.A., Griffin, G. *Infection Risks in Xenotransplantation* (London: DH, 2001).
Mullen, C., Hughes, D. and Vincent-Jones, P. 'The Democratic Potential of Public Participation: Healthcare Governance in England' (2011) 20 *Social and Legal Studies* 21.
Murphy-Lawless, J. 'The Impact of BSE and FMD on Ethics and Democratic Process' (2004) 17 *Journal of Agricultural and Environmental Ethics* 385.
National Bioethics Committee, *Gene Therapy* (1991) (at: www.palazzochigi.it/bioetica/eng/opinions.html, accessed 25/03/11).
National Commission for the Protection of Human Subjects of Biomedical and Behavioral Research, *Research on the Fetus: Report and Recommendations* (1975) (at: http://bioethics.georgetown.edu/pcbe/reports/past_commissions/research_fetus.pdf, accessed 25/03/11).
  Ethical Principles and Guidelines for the Protection of Human Subjects of Research (1979) (at: http://ohsr.od.nih.gov/guidelines/belmont.html, last accessed 22/03/11).
National Council of Churches, Panel on Bioethical Concerns, *Genetic Engineering: Social and Ethical Consequences* (New York, NY: Pilgrim Press, 1984).
National Expert Panel on New and Emerging Infections (NEPNEI), *First Annual Report (November 2003–December 2004)* (London: NEPNEI, 2006) *Combined Report 2006–2007* (London: DH, 2008).
  National Health Committee's Advice on Living Cell Technologies Application for Xenotransplantation Clinical Trials in New Zealand (2008) (at: www.nhc. health.govt.nz/moh.nsf/pagescm/7547/$File/nhc-living-cell-technologies-report-oct082.pdf, accessed 18/3/11).

National Health and Medical Research Council (NHMRC), 'Ethics in Medical Research', *Report of the NHMRC Working Party on Ethics in Medical Research* (Canberra: Australian Government Publishing Service, 1982).

Ethics in Medical Research Involving the Human Fetus and Human Fetal Tissue (Canberra: Australian Government Publishing Service, 1983).

Ethical Aspects of Research on Human Gene Therapy: Report to the NHMRC by the Medical Ethics Committee of NHMRC (Canberra: Australian Government Publishing Service, 1987).

Human Gene Therapy and Related Procedures: An Information Paper to Assist in the Consideration of Ethical Aspects of Human Gene Therapy (Canberra: Australian Government Publishing Service, 1995).

Guidelines for Ethical Review of Research Proposals for Human Somatic Cell Gene Therapy and Related Therapies (Canberra: NHMRC, 1999).

Discussion Paper – Xenotransplantation: A Review of the Parameters, Risks and Benefits (2009) (at: www.nhmrc.gov.au/_files_nhmrc/file/about/committeess/expert/gtrap/nhmrc_xeno_discussion_paper_website.pdf, accessed 16/03/11).

Xenotransplantation Working Party (XWP), *Draft Guidelines and Discussion Paper on Xenotransplantation – Public Consultation 2002* (2002) (at: www.nhmrc.gov.au/_files_nhmrc/file/about/committeess/expert/gtrap/xeno.pdf, accessed 16/03/11).

'NHMRC Statement on Xenotransplantation' (2009) (at: www.nhmrc.gov.au/media/noticeboard/notice09/091210-xenotransplantation.htm, accessed 25/03/11).

'Animal to Human Transplantation Research (Xenotransplantation) – Definition: What is Animal to Human Transplantation' (2010) (at: www.nhmrc.gov.au/health_ethics/health/xeno.htm, accessed 16/03/11).

'Animal-to-Human Transplantation Research (Xenotransplantation)' (2010) (at: www.nhmrc.gov.au/health_ethics/health/xeno.htm, accessed 16/03/11).

Australian Research Council, Australian Vice-Chancellor's Committee, *National Statement on Ethical Conduct in Human Research* (Canberra: Australian Government, 2007).

XWP, *Animal-to-Human Transplantation Research: How Should Australia Proceed? Response to the 2002 Public Consultation on Draft Guidelines and Discussion Paper on Xenotransplantation – Public Consultation 2003–04* (2003) (at: www.nhmrc.gov.au/_files_nhmrc/file/publications/synopses/e55.pdf, accessed 16/03/11).

XWP, *Animal-to-Human Transplantation Research: A Guide for the Community – Public Consultation on Xenotransplantation 2003/4* (2003) (at: www.nhmrc.gov.au/_files_nhmrc/file/publications/synopses/e54.pdf, accessed 16/03/11).

XWP, *Animal-to-Human Transplantation (Xenotransplantation): Final Report and Advice to the National Health and Medical Research Council* (Canberra: NHMRC, 2004).

XWP, *Guidelines for Clinical Animal-to-Human Transplantation (Xeno-transplantation) Research DRAFT for NHMRC Consideration* (2004), accompanying NHMRC, XWP, *Animal-to-Human Transplantation (Xenotransplantation): Final Report* (Canberra: NHMRC, 2004).

NHS Blood and Transplant, *Activity Report 2009–2010, Transplant Activity in the UK* (2010) (at: www.uktransplant.org.uk/ukt/statistics/transplant_activity_report/transplant_activity_report.jsp, accessed 16/03/11).

National Institute for Health and Clinical Excellence (NICE), 'About Interventional Procedures' (at: www.nice.org.uk/aboutnice/whatwedo/about_interventional_procedures/about_interventional_procedures.jsp, accessed 22/03/11).

NICE, *Consent – Procedures for which the Benefits and Risks are Uncertain* (London: NICE, 2003).

The Legal Implications of NICE Guidance (2004) (at: www.nice.org.uk/media/8BD/2B/Legal_context_nice_guidance.pdf, accessed 22/03/11).

National Research Ethics Service (NRES), *Information Sheets & Consent Forms: Guidance for Researchers and Reviewers* (London: NRES, 2009).

Nelson, R.M. and Merz, J.F. 'Voluntariness of Consent for Research: An Empirical and Conceptual Review' (2002) 40 *Medical Care* V–69.

Nichols, E.K. *Human Gene Therapy* (Cambridge: Harvard University Press, 1988).

Nowak, R. 'Xenotransplants Set to Resume' (1994) 266 *Science* 1148.

Nuffield Council on Bioethics, *Animal-to-Human Transplants – The Ethics of Xenotransplantation* (London: Nuffield Council on Bioethics, 1996).

Genetically Modified Crops: The Ethical and Social Issues (London: Nuffield Council on Bioethics, 1999).

Public Health: Ethical Issues (London: Nuffield Council on Bioethics, 2007).

O'Brien, M. 'Have Lessons Been Learned from the UK Bovine Spongiform Encephalopathy (BSE) Epidemic?' (2000) 29 *International Journal of Epidemiology* 730.

O'Neill, O. *Autonomy and Trust in Bioethics* (Cambridge University Press, 2002).

O'Riordan, T., Jordan, A. 'The Precautionary Principle in Contemporary Environmental Politics' (1995) 4 *Environmental Values* 191.

Obasogie, O. 'Ten Years Later: Jesse Gelsinger's Death and Human Subjects Protection' (2010) *Bioethics Forum* (at: www.thehastingscenter.org/Bioethicsforum/Post.aspx?id=4034&blogid=140, accessed 25/03/11).

Office of Science and Technology, 'Proposal for a Coordinated Framework for Regulation of Biotechnology', 31 December 1984, 49 *Federal Register* 50856.

Oliver, I. and Lewis, D. 'Public Trust is Necessary to Protect the Population from Threats to Public Health' (2009) 31 *Journal of Public Health* 468.

Ontario Law Reform Commission, *Report on Human Artificial Reproduction and Related Matters* (Ontario: Ministry of the Attorney-General, 1985) vols. 1 and 2.

Opinion of the Group of Advisers on the Ethical Implications of Biotechnology to the European Commission, *The Ethical Implications of Gene Therapy* (1994) No 4 (at: http://ec.europa.eu/european_group_ethics/docs/opinion4_en.pdf, accessed 25/03/11).

Organisation for Economic Co-operation and Development (OECD), 'Regulatory Developments in Xenotransplantation in France' (at: www.oecd.org/document/29/0,3343,en_2649_34537_1887773_1_1_1_1,00.html, accessed 25/03/11).

'Regulatory Developments in Xenotransplantation in Germany' (at: www.oecd.org/document/62/0,3343,en_2649_34537_1887806_1_1_1_1,00.html, accessed 25/03/11).

'Regulatory Developments in Xenotransplantation in Spain' (at: www.oecd.org/document/36/0,3343,en_2649_34537_2352420_1_1_1_1,00.html, accessed 25/03/11).

Working Papers, *Advances in Transplantation Biotechnology and Animal to Human Organ Transplants (Xenotransplantation) Safety, Economic and Ethical Aspects*, vol. IV, No. 97 (Paris: OECD, 1996).

Xenotransplantation: International Policy Issues (Paris: OECD, 1999).

World Health Organization (WHO), *OECD/WHO Consultation on Xenotransplantation Surveillance: Summary* (2001) WHO/CDS/CSR/EPH/2001.1.

Orme, N.M., Fletcher, J.G., Siddiki, H.A., Scott Harmsen, W., O'Byrne, M.M., Port, J.D., Tremaine, W.J., Pitot, H.C., McFarland, E.G., Robinson, M.E., Koenig, B.A., King, B.F. and Wolf, S.M. 'Incidental Findings in Imaging Research: Evaluating Incidence, Benefit, and Burden' (2010) 170 *Archives of Internal Medicine* 1525.

Ormerod, D.C. and Gunn, M.J. 'Criminal Liability for the Transmission of HIV' [1996] 1 *Web Journal of Current Legal Issues*.

Paradis, K., Langford, G., Long, Z., Heneine, W., Sandstrom, P., Switzer, W.M., Chapman, L.E., Lockey, C., Onions, D., the XEN 111 Study Group and Otto, E. 'Search for Cross Species Transmission of Porcine Endogenous Retrovirus in Patients Treated with Living Pig Tissue' (1999) 285 *Science* 1236.

Parliamentary Assembly, Council of Europe, 'The Handling of the H1N1 Pandemic: More Transparency Needed' (2010) AS/Soc (2010) 12.

Patience, C., Scobie, L. and Quinn, G. 'Porcine Endogenous Retrovirus – Advances, Issues and Solutions' (2002) 9 *Xenotransplantation* 373.

Patience, C., Takeuchi, Y. and Weiss, R.A. 'Infection of Human Cells by Endogenous Retrovirus of Pigs' (1997) 3 *Nature Medicine* 282.

Pattinson, S. *Medical Law and Ethics* (2nd edn, London: Sweet & Maxwell, 2009).

Pennisi, E. 'FDA Panel OKs Baboon Marrow Transplant' (1995) 269 *Science* 293.

Perico, N., Benigni, A., Remuzzi, G. 'Xenotransplantation in the 21st Century' (2002) 20 *Blood Purification* 45.

Persak, N. *Criminalising Harmful Conduct: The Harm Principle, Its Limits and Continental Counterparts* (New York, NY: Springer-Verlag, 2007).

Persson, A. 'Research Ethics and the Development of Medical Biotechnology' (2006) 13 *Xenotransplantation* 511.

Peters, P.G. *How Safe is Safe Enough? Obligations to the Children of Reproductive Technology* (New York, NY: Oxford University Press, 2004).

Lord Phillips, 'Lessons from the BSE inquiry' (2001) 17 *FST Journal* 3.

Lord Phillips, Bridgeman, J. and Ferguson-Smith, M. *The BSE Inquiry: Report: Evidence and Supporting Papers of the Inquiry into the Emergence and Identification of Bovine Spongiform Encephalopathy (BSE) and variant Creutzfeldt–Jakob Disease (CJD) and the Action Taken in Response to it up to 20 March 1996* (London: Stationery Office, 2000).

Picciotto, S. 'Introduction: Reconceptualizing Regulation in the Era of Globalization' (2002) 29 *Journal of Law and Society* 1.

Pidgeon, N., Henwood, K. and Maguire, B. 'Public Health Communication and The Social Amplification of Risks: Present Knowledge and Future Prospects', in P. Bennett and K. Calman (eds.), *Risk Communication and Public Health* (Oxford University Press, 2001), p. 65.

Pidgeon, N., Kasperson, R. and Slovic, P. *The Social Amplification of Risk* (Cambridge University Press, 2003).

Pierson, R.N., Dorling, A., Rees, M.A., Seebach, J.D., Fishman, J.A., Hering, B.H. and Cooper, D.K.C. 'Current Status of Xenotransplantation and Prospects for Clinical Application' (2009) 16 *Xenotransplantation* 263.

Pierson, R.N., White, D.J.G. and Wallwork, J. 'Ethical Considerations in Clinical Cardiac Xenografting – Letter' (1993) 12 *Journal of Heart and Lung Transplantation* 876.

Plomer, A. 'Beyond the HFE Act? The Regulation of Stem Cell Research in the UK' (2002) 10 *Medical Law Review* 132.

Pontifical Academy for Life, *Prospects for Xenotransplantation – Scientific Aspects and Ethical Considerations* (2001) (at: www.vatican.va/roman_curia/pontifical_academies/acdlife/documents/rc_pa_acdlife_doc_20010926_xenotrapianti_en.html, accessed 25/03/11).

Powell, D. and Leiss, W. *Mad Cows and Mother's Milk: The Perils of Poor Risk Communication* (Quebec: McGill-Queen's University Press, 1997).

President's Commission for the Study of Ethical Problems in Medicine and Biomedical and Behavioral Research, *Making Health Care Decisions: The Ethical and Legal Implications of Informed Consent in the Patient–Practitioner Relationship, Volume One: Report* (Washington, DC: President's Commission for the Study of Ethical Problems in Medicine and Biomedical and Behavioral Research, 1982).

Splicing Life: The Social and Ethical Issues of Genetic Engineering with Human Beings (Washington, DC: President's Commission for the Study of Ethical Problems in Medicine and Biomedical and Behavioral Research, 1982).

Price, D. *Legal and Ethical Aspects of Organ Transplantation* (Cambridge University Press, 2000).

'Remodelling the Regulation of Postmodern Innovation in Medicine' (2005) 1 *International Journal of Law in Context* 121.

Rainsbury, J.M. 'Biotechnology on the RAC – FDA/NIH Regulation of Human Gene Therapy' (2000) 55 *Food and Drug Law Journal* 575.

Ramsoondar, J., Vaught, T., Ball, S., Mendicio, M., Monahan, J., Jobst, P., Vance, A., Duncan, J., Wells, K. and Ayares, D. 'Production of Transgenic Pigs that Express Porcine Endogenous Retrovirus Small Interfering RNAs' (2009) 16 *Xenotransplantation* 164.

Ravelingien, A. 'Xenotransplantation and the Harm Principle: Factoring Out Foreseen Risk' (2007) 16 *Journal of Evolution and Technology* 127.

Ravelingien, A., Mortier, F., Kerremans, I. and Braeckman, J. 'Proceeding with Clinical Trials of Animal to Human Organ Transplantation: A Way out of the Dilemma' (2004) 30 *Journal of Medical Ethics* 92.

Reemtsma, K., McCracken, B.H., Schlegel, J.U., Pearl, M.A., Pearce, C.W., DeWitt, C.W., Smith, P.E., Hewitt, R.L., Flinner, R.L. and Creech, O. 'Renal Heterotransplantation in Man' (1964) 160 *Annals of Surgery* 384.

Report of the Working Party on In Vitro Fertilization and Artificial Insemination by Donor (Adelaide: South Australian Health Commission, 1984).

Resnik, D.B. 'Is the Precautionary Principle Unscientific?' (2003) 34 *Studies in History and Philosophy of Biological and Biomedical Sciences* 329.

Richards, E.P. and Rathbun, K.C. 'The Role of the Police Power in 21st Century Public Health' (1999) 26 *Sexually Transmitted Disease* 350.

Roberts, L. 'Human Gene Therapy Test' (1988) 241 *Science* 419.

'A Heartbeat from History', *Sunday Times*, 29 September 1996.

Rothstein, M.A. 'Are Traditional Public Health Strategies Consistent With Contemporary American Values?' (2004) 77 *Temple Law Review* 175.

Royal College of Obstetricians and Gynaecologists (RCOG), *Report of the RCOG Ethics Committee On In Vitro Fertilization and Embryo Replacement or Transfer* (London: RCOG, 1983).

Royal College of Physicians (RCP), *Guidelines on the Practice of Ethics Committees in Medical Research with Human Participants* (London: RCP, 2007).

Royal Commission, *Report of the Royal Commission on Genetic Modification* (2002) (at: www.mfe.govt.nz/publications/organisms/royal-commission-gm/, accessed 25/03/11).

Royal Commission on New Reproductive Technologies, *Proceed with Care: Final Report of the Royal Commission on New Reproductive Technologies* (Ottawa: Ministry of Supply and Services, 1993).

Royal Liverpool Children's Inquiry Report (London: Stationery Office, 2001).

Rule, S. 'Fatal cow illness stirs British fear', *New York Times*, 20 May 1990.

Sandin, P., Peterson, M., Hansson, S.O., Rudén, C. and Juthe, A. 'Five Charges Against the Precautionary Principle' (2002) 5 *Journal of Risk Research* 287.

Schumacher, F. *Small is Beautiful* (London: Vintage, 1973).

Science and Technology Policy Research Unit, Environment and Science Research Unit, Policy Studies Institute, 'Deliberative Mapping: Briefing 5 Using the Multi-Criteria Mapping Technique' (2004) (at: www.deliberative-mapping.org/papers/f-briefing-5.pdf, accessed 16/03/11).

Scobie, L. and Takeuchi, Y. 'Porcine Endogenous Retrovirus and Other Viruses in Xenotransplantation' (2009) 14 *Current Opinion in Organ Transplantation* 175.

Scott, S. and Freeman, R. 'Prevention as a Problem of Modernity: The Example of HIV and AIDS', in J. Gabe (ed.) *Medicine, Health and Risk: Sociological Approaches* (Oxford: Blackwell, 1995) p. 151.

Sgroi, A., Bühler, L.H., Morel, P., Sykes, M. and Noel, L. 'International Human Xenotransplantation Inventory' (2010) 90 *Transplantation* 597.

Sharkey, K., Savulescu, J., Aranda, S. and Schofield, P. 'Clinician Gate-Keeping in Clinical Research Is Not Ethically Defensible: An Analysis' (2010) 36 *Journal of Medical Ethics* 363.

Sherr, L. 'Counselling and HIV Testing: Ethical Dilemmas', in R. Bennett, C.A. Erin (eds.), *HIV and AIDS; Testing, Screening and Confidentiality* (Oxford University Press, 1999), p. 39.

Shimizu, A., Hisashi, Y., Kuwaki, K., Tseng, Y.-L., Dor, F.J.M.F., Houser, S.L., Robson, S.C., Schuurman, H.-J., Cooper, D.K.C., Sachs, D.H., Yamada, K. and Colvin, R.B. 'Thrombotic Microangiopathy Associated with Humoral Rejection of Cardiac Xenografts from Alpha 1,3-Galactosyltransferase Gene-Knockout Pigs in Baboons' (2008) 172 *American Journal of Pathology* 1471.

Shimm, D.S. and Spece, R.G. 'An Introduction to Conflicts of Interest in Clinical Research', in R.G. Spece, D.S. Shimm and A.E. Buchanan (eds.), *Conflicts of Interest in Clinical Practice and Research* (Oxford University Press, 1996), p. 361.

Siegrist, M. 'The Influence of Trust and Perceptions of Risks and Benefits on the Acceptance of Gene Technology' (2000) 20 *Risk Analysis* 195.

Slovic, P. 'Perception of Risk' (1987) 236 *Science* 280.

Smith, C.B., Battin, M.P., Jacobsen, J.A., Francis, L.P., Botkin, J.R., Aslund, E.P., Domek, G.J. and Hawkins, B. 'Are There Characteristics of Infectious Diseases that Raise Special Ethical Issues?' (2004) 4 *Developing World Bioethics* 1.

Smith, J.A., Michie, S., Allanson, A. and Elwy, R. 'Certainty and Uncertainty in Genetic Counselling: A Qualitative Case Study' (2000) 15 *Psychology and Health* 1.

Smith, K.J.M. 'Sexual Etiquette, Public Interest and the Criminal Law' (1991) 42 *Northern Ireland Legal Quarterly* 309.

Smith, R. 'All Changed, Changed Utterly' (1998) 316 *British Medical Journal* 1917.

Smith, S.L. 'Xenotransplantation Action Plan: US Food and Drug Administration Approach to the Regulation of Xenotransplantation' (2000) 1 *Medscape Transplantation*.

Snowdon, C., Elbourne, D. and Garcia, J. 'Declining Enrolment in a Clinical Trial and Injurious Misconceptions: Is there a Flipside to the Therapeutic Misconception?' (2007) 2 *Clinical Ethics* 193.

Snyder, L. and Leffler, C., for the Ethics and Human Rights Committee, American College of Physicians, 'Position Paper – Ethics Manual Fifth Edition' (2005) 142 *Annals of Internal Medicine* 560.

Sola, C.de. 'Current Developments on Xenotransplantation in the Council of Europe', in J. Fishman, D. Sachs and R. Shaikh (eds.), *Xenotransplantation: Scientific Frontiers and Public Policy* (New York, NY: New York Academy of Sciences, 1998), p. 211.

Sommerville, M.A. 'Searching for Ethics in a Secular Society', in *Ethics of Science and Technology, Explorations of the Frontiers of Science and Ethics* (Paris: UNESCO, 2006).

Somsen, H. 'Cloning Trojan Horses: Precautionary Regulation of Reproductive Technologies', in R. Brownsword and K. Yeung (eds.), *Regulating Technologies: Legal Futures, Regulatory Frames and Technological Fixes* (Oxford: Hart, 2008), p. 221.

Soule, E. 'Assessing the Precautionary Principle' (2000) 14 *Public Affairs Quarterly* 309.

Specke, V., Rubant, S. and Denner, J. 'Productive Infection of Human Primary Cells and Cell Lines with Porcine Endogenous Retroviruses' (2001) 285 *Virology* 177.

Spillman, M.A. and Sade, R.M. 'Clinical Trials of Xenotransplantation: Waiver of the Right to Withdraw from a Clinical Trial Should Be Required' (2007) 35 *Journal of Law, Medicine and Ethics* 265.

Standing Committee of European Doctors, *Recommendations on the Ethical Problems Concerning Artificial Insemination* (1985) (at: http://cpme.dyndns.org:591/adopted/cp%201985_93.pdf, accessed 25/03/11).

Starzl, T.E., Fung, J., Tzakis, A., Todo, S., Demetris, A.J., Marino, I.R., Doyle, H., Zeevi, A., Warty, V., Michaels, M., Kusne, S., Rudert, W.A. and Trucco, M. 'Baboon-to-Human Liver Transplantation' (1993) 341 *The Lancet* 65.

Statement of Position of the SAMS (Swiss Academy of Medical Sciences), 'Medical–Ethical Principles of Xenotransplantation' (2001) 131 *Swiss Medical Weekly* 388.

Steele, K. 'The Precautionary Principle: A New Approach to Public Decision-Making' (2006) 5 *Law, Probability and Risk* 19.

Steering Committee on Bioethics (CDBI), European Health Committee (CDSP), *Explanatory Report to Recommendation Rec(2003)10 of the Committee of Ministers to member states on xenotransplantation* CDBI/INF (2003) 12.

Stirling, A. *On Science and Precaution in the Management of Technological Risk, Volume I A Synthesis of Case Studies* (Seville: European Commission Institute for Prospective Technological Studies, 1999) EUR 19056 EN.

Strategy Unit, *Field Work: Weighing Up the Costs and Benefits of GM Crops* (London: Cabinet Office, 2003).

Strategy Unit, Cabinet Office, *Risk: Improving Government's Capability to Handle Risk and Uncertainty: Full Report – A Source Document* (London: Cabinet Office, 2002).

Sunstein, C.R. *Laws of Fear: Beyond the Precautionary Principle* (Cambridge University Press, 2005).

Swedish Committee on Xenotransplantation, *From One Species to Another – Transplantation from Animals to Humans: Summary and Statutory Proposals* (Stockholm: Swedish Committee on Xenotransplantation, 1999) Swedish Government Official Report No. 1999: 120.

Swiss Science Council, *Xenotransplantation – Tested on Heart and Kidneys – Short version of the TA study of Xenotransplantation* (1998) (at: www.ta-swiss.ch/incms_files/filebrowser/1998_TA30A_KF_xenotransplantation_e.pdf, accessed 25/03/11).

Sykes, M. '2007 IXA Presidential Address: Progress Toward an Ideal Source Animal: Opportunities and Challenges in a Changing World' (2008) 15 *Xenotransplantation* 7.

Sykes, M., d'Apice, A. and Sandrin, M. 'Position Paper of the Ethics Committee of the International Xenotransplantation Association' (2003) 10 *Xenotransplantation* 194.

Sykes, M., Sandrin, M. and Cozzi, E. 'International Cooperation on Xenotransplantation' (2004) 10 *Nature Medicine* 119.

Tallacchini, M. 'Community and Public Participation in the Risk Assessment of Experimental Clinical Trials' (2007) 14 *Xenotransplantation* 356.

Taylor, I.E. 'Political Risk Culture: Not Just A Communication Failure', in P. Bennett and K. Calman (eds.), *Risk Communication and Public Health* (Oxford University Press, 2001), p. 152.

ten Have, H. *'UNESCO and Ethics of Science and Technology' in Ethics of Science and Technology, Explorations of the Frontiers of Science and Ethics* (Paris: UNESCO, 2006).

Templeton, S.-K. 'Lord Winston to farm pigs for transplants', *Sunday Times*, 7 September 2008.

Thornton, H. 'Clinical Trials – A Brave New Partnership?' (1994) 20 *Journal of Medical Ethics* 19.

Toi te Taiao, Bioethics Council, *The Cultural, Spiritual and Ethical Aspects of Xenotransplantation: Animal-to-Human Transplantation – Final Report* (Wellington: New Zealand, 2005).

The Cultural, Spiritual and Ethical Aspects of Xenotransplantation: Animal-to-Human Transplantation – A Discussion Document (Wellington: New Zealand, 2005).

Tomlinson, T. 'The Physician's Influence on Patients' Choices' (1986) 7 *Theoretical Medicine and Bioethics* 105.

Townsend, M. 'Doubts on pig organ transplants ignored', *The Observer*, 29 June 2003.

Transplantation Society of Australia and New Zealand, *Xenotransplantation Ad Hoc Working Party* (1998).

Trent, R.J.A. 'Oversight and Monitoring of Clinical Research with Gene Therapy in Australia' (2005) 182 *Medical Journal of Australia* 441.

Ullman, E. 'Tissue and Organ Transplantation' (1914) 60 *Annals of Surgery* 195.

United Kingdom Xenotransplantation Interim Regulatory Authority (UKXIRA), *Guidance on Making Proposals to Conduct Xenotransplantation on Human Subjects* (London: DH, 1998).

Draft Guidance Notes on Biosecurity Considerations in Relation to Xenotransplantation (London: DH, 1999).

Draft Report of the Infection Surveillance Steering Group of the UKXIRA (London: DH, 1999).

Second Annual Report September 1998-August 1999 (London: DH, 2000).

Third Annual Report September 1999-November 2000 (London: DH, 2001).

Fifth Annual Report January 2002-September 2003 (London: DH, 2004).

UNAIDS, *Criminal Law, Public Health and HIV Transmission: A Policy Options Paper* (Geneva: UNAIDS, 2002).

United Nations Educational, Scientific and Cultural Organization (UNESCO), *Report on Human Gene Therapy* (1998) (at: www.eubios.info/UNESCO/ibc1994.pdf, accessed 25/03/11).

UNESCO, World Commission on the Ethics of Scientific Knowledge and Technology (COMEST), *The Precautionary Principle* (2005) (at: http://unesdoc.unesco.org/images/0013/001395/139578e.pdf, accessed 16/03/11).

US Congress, Office of Technology Assessment (OTA), *Human Gene Therapy – A Background Paper* (Washington, DC: OTA, 1984).

New Developments in Biotechnology, Volume 2: Background Paper: Public Perceptions of Biotechnology (Washington, DC: OTA, 1987).

US Department of Health, Education and Welfare (DHEW), 'Protection of Human Subjects, Policies and Procedures', 16 November 1973, 38 *Federal Register* 31738.
'Protection of Human Subjects: Fetuses, Pregnant Women and In Vitro Fertilization', 8 August 1975, 40 *Federal Register* 33526.
NIH, 'Recombinant DNA Research: Guidelines', 7 July 1976, 41 *Federal Register* 27902.
US DHHS, Public Health Service, 'Draft Public Health Service (PHS) Guideline on Infectious Disease Issues in Xenotransplantation', 23 September 1996, 61 *Federal Register* 49920.
Guidance for Industry – Public Health Issues Posed by the Use of Nonhuman Primate Xenografts in Humans (1999) (at: www.fda.gov/downloads/Biologics BloodVaccines/GuidanceComplianceRegulatoryInformation/Guidances/ Xenotransplantation/ucm092866.pdf, accessed 23/3/11).
'New Initiatives to Protect Participants in Gene Therapy Trials' (2000) (at: http://archive.hhs.gov/news/press/2000pres/20000307A.html, accessed 25/03/11).
US DHHS, Food and Drug Administration (FDA), 'Application of Current Statutory Authorities to Human Somatic Cell Therapy Products and Gene Therapy Products', 14 October 1993, 58 *Federal Register* 53248.
PHS Guideline on Infectious Disease Issues in Xenotransplantation (2001) (at: www.fda.gov/downloads/BiologicsBloodVaccines/GuidanceCompliance RegulatoryInformation/Guidances/Xenotransplantation/UCM092858.pdf, accessed 16/03/11).
Center for Biologics Evaluation and Research (CBER), *Guidance for Industry: Guidance for Human Somatic Cell Therapy and Gene Therapy* (1998) (at: www.fda.gov/downloads/BiologicsBloodVaccines/GuidanceCompliance RegulatoryInformation/Guidances/CellularandGeneTherapy/ ucm081670.pdf, accessed 25/03/11).
Guidance for Industry: Precautionary Measures to Reduce the Possible Risk of Transmission of Zoonoses by Blood and Blood Products from Xenotransplantation Product Recipients and Their intimate Contacts – Draft Guidance (2002) (at: www.fda.gov/downloads/BiologicsBloodVaccines/Guidance ComplianceRegulatoryInformation/Guidances/Blood/ucm080375.pdf, accessed 23/3/11).
Guidance for Industry: Source Animal, Product, Preclinical and Clinical Issues Concerning the Use of Xenotransplantation Products in Humans – Final Guidance (2003) (at: www.fda.gov/downloads/BiologicsBlood Vaccines/GuidanceComplianceRegulatoryInformation/Guidances/ Xenotransplantation/ucm092707.pdf, accessed 16/03/11).
US DHHS, National Institutes of Health (NIH), 'Notice of Establishment', 26 August 1999, 64 *Federal Register* 46697.
US DHHS, Office of Biotechnology Activities (OBA), 'Recombinant DNA Research: Actions Under the NIH Guidelines' 19 November 2001, 66 *Federal Register* 57970.
US DHHS, Secretary's Advisory Committee on Xenotransplantation (SACX), *Informed Consent in Clinical Research Involving Xenotransplantation – Draft*

(2004) (at: www.scribd.com/doc/1111353/National-Institutes-of-Health-IC-draft-030905, accessed 22/03/11).
  Report on the State of the Science in Xenotransplantation (2004) (at: www.nelsonerlick.com/PDF/NIH%20Report%20on%20State%20of%20Xenotransplantation%202005.pdf, accessed 25/03/11).
US House of Representatives, *Hearings on Human Genetic Engineering Before the Subcommittee on Investigations and Oversight of the Committee on Science and Technology*, 97th Congress 2nd session, No. 170 (Washington, DC: Government Printing Office, 1982).
van Zwanenberg, P. and Millstone, E. *BSE: Risk, Science, and Governance* (Oxford University Press, 2005).
von Hirsch, A. 'Extending the Harm Principle: "Remote" Harms and Fair Imputation', in A.P. Simester and A.T.H. Smith (eds.), *Harm and Culpability* (Oxford: Clarendon Press, 1996), p. 259.
Valdés-González, R.A., Dorantes, L.M., Nayely Garibay, G., Bracho-Blanchet, E., Mendez, A.J., Dávila-Pérez, R., Elliott, R.B., Terán, L. and White, D.J.G. 'Xenotransplantation of Porcine Neonatal Islets of Langerhans and Sertoli Cells: A 4-Year Study' (2005) 153 *European Journal of Endocrinology* 419.
Vanderpool, H.Y. 'Critical Ethical Issues in Clinical Trials with Xenotransplants' (1998) 351 *The Lancet* 1347.
  'Informed Consent in Clinical Research' (2007) 14 *Xenotransplantation* 353.
  'The International Xenotransplantation Association Consensus Statement on Conditions for Undertaking Clinical Trials of Porcine Islet products in Type 1 Diabetes – Chapter 7: Informed Consent and Xeno-transplantation Clinical Trials' (2009) 16 *Xenotransplantation* 255.
Waring, D.R. and Lemmens, T. 'Integrating Values in Risk Analysis of Biomedical Research: The Case for Regulatory and Law Reform', in Law Commission of Canada (ed.), *Law and Risk* (Vancouver: UBC Press, 2005).
Lord Warner, Hansard, HL Written Statements, vol. 687, col. WS181 12 December 2006 (at: www.publications.parliament.uk/pa/ld200607/ldhansrd/text/61212-wms0001.htm, accessed 22/03/11).
Watson, J.D. 'Moving Toward the Clonal Man' (1971) 227 *Atlantic Monthly* 50.
Weeramantry, C.G. *Xenotransplantation: The Ethical and Legal Concerns* (Sri Lanka: Weeramantry International Centre for Peace Education and Research, 2007).
Weinberg, A.M. 'Science and Trans-science' (1972) 10 *Minerva* 209.
Weiss, R.A. 'Xenografts and Retroviruses' (1999) 285 *Science* 1221.
Welin, S. 'Starting Clinical Trials of Xenotransplantation – Reflections on the Ethics of the Early Phase' (2006) 26 *Journal of Medical Ethics* 231.
Welin, S. and Sandrin, M.S. 'Some Ethical Problems in Xenotransplantation: Introductory Remarks at Ethics Workshop' (2006) 13 *Xenotransplantation* 500.
Wellcome Trust, *What Do People Think About Gene Therapy?* (London: Wellcome Trust, 2005).
  Information and Attitudes: Consulting the Public About Biomedical Science (London: Wellcome Trust, 2005).

Welsh, I. and Evans, R. 'Xenotransplantation, Risk, Regulation and Surveillance: Social and Technological Dimensions of Change' (1999) 18 *New Genetics and Society* 197.

Wendler, D. and Grady, C. 'What Should Research Participants Understand to Understand that They Are Participants in Research?' (2008) 22 *Bioethics* 203.

Wertz, D.C. 'Embryo and Stem Cell Research in the United States: History and Politics' (2002) 9 *Gene Therapy* 674.

Wheatley, S. 'Human Rights and Human Dignity in the Resolution of Certain Ethical Questions in Biomedicine' (2001) *European Human Rights Law Review* 312.

Williamson, L., Fox, M. and McLean, S. 'The Regulation of Xeno-transplantation in the United Kingdom After UKXIRA: Legal and Ethical Issues' (2007) 34 *Journal of Law and Society* 441.

Wilsdon, J. and Willis, R. *See-Through Science: Why Public Engagement Needs to Move Upstream* (London: Demos, 2004).

Wilsdon, J., Wynne, B. and Stilgoe, J. *The Public Value of Science: Or How to Ensure that Science Really Matters* (London: Demos, 2005).

Wilson, C.A. 'Porcine Endogenous Retroviruses and Xenotransplantation' (2008) 65 *Cellular and Molecular Life Sciences* 3399.

Winston, R. 'Britain squanders pioneer work on organ transplants', *Sunday Times*, 7 September 2008.

Working Group on Xenotransplantation, *Xenotransplantation: Medical Use of Live Cells, Tissues and Organs from Animals* (Oslo: Ministry of Health, 2001) NOU 2001, 18.

Working Party of Council for Science and Society, *Human Procreation: Ethical Aspects of the New Techniques* (Oxford University Press, 1984).

World Council of Churches, Subunit on Church and Society, *Manipulating Life: Ethical Issues in Genetic Engineering* (Geneva: the Council, 1982).

World Council of Churches, Subunit on Church and Society, *Biotechnology: Its Challenges to the Churches and the World* (Geneva: the Council, 1989).

World Health Association (WHA), *Human Organ and Tissue Transplantation* 22 May 2004, WHA57.18.

World Health Organization (WHO), *Xenotransplantation: Guidance on Infectious Disease Prevention and Management* (1998) WHO/EMC/ZOO/98.1 (at: http://whqlibdoc.who.int/hq/1998/WHO_EMC_ZOO_98.1.pdf, accessed 23/03/11).

Report of WHO Consultation on Xenotransplantation, Geneva, Switzerland, 28–30 October 1997 (1998) WHO/EMC/ZOO/98.2 (at: www.who.int/emc-documents/zoonoses/whoemczoo982c.html, accessed 23/3/11).

Electromagnetic Fields and Public Health Cautionary Policies (2000) (at: www.who.int/docstore/peh-emf/publications/facts_press/EMF-Precaution.htm, accessed 16/03/11).

Operational Guidelines for Ethics Committees that Review Biomedical Research (Geneva: WHO, 2000) TDR/PRD/ETHICS/2000.1.

Ethics, Access and Safety in Tissue and Organ Transplantation: Issues of Global Concern – Madrid, Spain, 6–9 October 2003 – Report (Madrid: WHO, 2003).

International Health Regulations (2005) (2nd edn, Geneva: WHO, 2008), as amended in 2008.

Statement from the Xenotransplantation Advisory Consultation, Xenotransplantation: Hopes and Concerns, Geneva, 18–20 April 2005.

World Medical Association (WMA), *Declaration of Helsinki, Recommendations Guiding Physicians in Biomedical Research in Biomedical Research Involving Human Subjects*, adopted by the 18th WMA, Helsinki, Finland, June 1964, as amended in 1996.

WMA Statement on Genetic Counseling and Genetic Engineering, adopted by the 39th World Medical Assembly Madrid, Spain, October 1987, rescinded at the WMA General Assembly, Santiago 2005.

World Medical Association Statement on Human Organ Donation and Transplantation, adopted by the 52nd WMA on General Assembly in Edinburgh, Scotland during October 2000 and revised by the WMA General Assembly, Pilanesberg, South Africa, October 2006.

Declaration of Helsinki, Ethical Principles for Medical Research Involving Human Subjects, adopted by the 18th WMA, Helsinki, Finland, June 1964, as amended in 2008.

Index

2004 Regulations *see* clinical trials, 2004 Regulations

acute rejection 17
AIDS *see* HIV/AIDS
allotransplants
  acute rejection management 17
  chronic rejection management 17
  consent issues, xenotransplantation compared 175
  and doctors' dual role 161
  emerging infectious diseases 21
  as experimental procedure 66
  HAR management 16
  microbiological risk of infection 18–19
  outline consent to surveillance while on waiting list for 218–219
  parallel research with xenotransplantation 119
  reasons why xenotransplantation preferable 3, 14
  recipients with no other hope 89, 92
  risk of infection, xenotransplantation compared 133–134
archiving of samples, surveillance of procedures 193–197
assisted reproductive technologies (ARTs) regulation 105–106
Australia
  assisted reproductive technologies (ARTs) regulation 107, 117–118
  consent guidance 160–161
  counselling guidance 182
  definition of xenotransplantation 2
  ethical review of experimental procedures 77
  gene therapy regulation 112, 113–114, 114–115
  health tourism guidance 139–140
  information disclosure guidance 171, 175
  IVF guidelines 108

  NGOs' guidelines and reports 123, 124
  patient advocate, role of 181
  public consultation 53–54
  surveillance guidance 208
  vulnerable patients treatment guidance 96–97
  xenotransplant regulation 132–134, 144
Austria, gene therapy regulation 115

Baby Fae case 92, 119
Beck, Ulrich, risk society concept 14
benefit, definition of 69
Better Regulation Task Force
  guidance on xenotransplant regulation 146
  and harm principle 39
Blood, Diane, health tourism case 139–140
blood donations by recipients, surveillance of 200–201
British Medical Association (BMA)
  consent guidance 170
  consent working party 162
  IVF working group 109
BSE crisis
  media's role in 34–35
  and precautionary principle 39
  risk communication during 29–35
  as trans-scientific policy question 32–34

Canada
  assisted reproductive technologies (ARTs) regulation 107–108
  counselling guidance 182
  definition of xenotransplantation 2
  ethical review of experimental procedures 77
  gene therapy regulation 114–115
  human rights guidance 229
  information disclosure guidance 175–176
  public consultation 52
  public health statutes, effectiveness for xenotransplantation regulation 223

281

Canada (*cont.*)
 recipient selection guidance 99
 surveillance guidance
  close contacts 195, 201–202
  consent and compliance 212–213
  donations of blood, organs, etc. 200–201
  health workers 196, 202–203
  human rights 229
  local level generally 192–193
  national level 203
  post-mortems 201
  recipients 193, 197–198
  recipients' sexual activity 198–200
  third parties 214
 xenotransplant regulation 121–122, 134
capacity, statutory test 154–155
chapter summaries 5–12
China, health tourism 139–140
chronic rejection 17
CJD (Creutzfeldt–Jakob disease)
 continuing loss of life 35
 as cross-species infection 20
 PPS as treatment, legality of providing 67–69, 70–73
 risk communication 29–35
clinical governance committees (CGCs)
 approval from 73–74, 79, 93, 174
 information disclosure guidance 174–175
clinical trials
 2004 Regulations
  and Declaration of Helsinki 82–83
  definition of medicinal product 84–85
  research not under *see* research not under 2004 Regulations
 authorisation 80, 83–84
 consent 98, 153, 155–157, 179
 experimental procedures distinguished 62
 information disclosure requirements 173–174
 as legal process for xenotransplantation 83–84, 131, 173–174
 offers of treatment 94–95
 statutory regime 62
close contacts, surveillance of 195–196, 201–202
Clothier Committee on gene therapy 113–114
commercial sector
 health tourism by 140
 problems with regulation 141–143
competency for giving consent 150–151, 154–159 *see also* recipients, with no other hope

compliance
 consent procedures 211–217
 effect of measures, level of discussion 211–212
 methods 217–228
 specific legislation, need for 217
confidence, public *see* public involvement
consent
 ability to give or obtain 150–151
 adequacy of 150
 allotransplantation issues, xenotransplantation compared 175
 appropriateness of 149–150
 capacity, statutory test 154–155
 changes in procedure 179–183
 competency 150–151, 154–159
  see also recipients, with no other hope
 and compliance 212–214, 217–228, 241
 contract law consent to surveillance 218–220
 counselling 182–183
 effect of measures, level of discussion 211–212
 existing procedures, challenges to 9–10
 importance 148
 independent person, role of 181
 individual's right to give, balance with public safety 151–154
 informed decision-making 166–179
  see also information disclosure
 legal framework 150–154
 main issues 150
 patient advocate, role of 181–182
 permissibility of 149
 requirements for valid consent 154–179
 summary of issues 185–188
 to surveillance 206–207, 211–217, 218–220
 third parties *see* third-party consent
 voluntariness
  dual role of doctor 160
  issues affecting 159–160
  process of obtaining consent 160
  withdrawal of 216–217
contacts *see* close contacts
contract law
 compliance via 218–220
 'Ulysses Contract' 219
cost–benefit analysis, use of 36–37
Council for International Organisations of Medical Sciences (CIOMS)
 experimental procedures guidance 76
 guidance on risk evaluation 82
 information disclosure guidance 169

Index

vulnerable patients treatment guidance 93, 95–96
Council of Europe
  compliance guidance 232
  consent guidance 154
  counselling guidance 182
  definition of xenotransplantation 2, 66
  gene therapy regulation 115–116
  human rights guidance 229
  information disclosure guidance 175, 187
  and precautionary principle 40–41
  recipient selection guidance 93–94
  recommendations on xenotransplantation outside research 77, 83–84
  surveillance guidance 209, 213, 214, 215
  third-party consent guidance 184
  vulnerable patients treatment guidance 98
  xenotransplant guidance 126–127
Council of Science and Society, IVF report 109
criminal law, compliance via 223

decision-making process
  see also information disclosure
  decision-making categories 23–24, 36
  doctors' role 155–156
  importance 148
  precautionary principle 48–49, 58
  public involvement in 47–57
Declaration of Helsinki
  compliance with 80, 148
  consent guidance 153, 155, 181
  doctors' role, guidance on 160
  enactment into law 82–83, 142
  experimental procedures guidance 76
  information disclosure guidance 168–169
  principles for medical research combined with medical care 81–82
  recipient selection guidance 97
  requirement for informed consent 93
  vulnerable patients treatment guidance 95
Department of Health (DH)
  committee on biotechnology 120
  consent guidance 148
  definition of medicinal product 84, 85
  disregard of guidance from 87
  information disclosure guidance 169, 172, 179
  public consultation 51–52
  UKXIRA abolition 129–130

vulnerable patients treatment guidance 98
xenotransplant guidance 79, 83, 86, 131
disclosure of information *see* information disclosure
doctors *see also* health workers
  aim in using experimental procedure 63–64
  discretion to offer procedure 62–63, 75, 77, 79, 92–93, 100–102
    see also recipients,
  doctor–patient relationship
    and compliance 217
    and contract law 219
    in medical research 64–65
    obtaining consent 163–166
    patients with no other hope 155–157
  dual role 97, 101, 160
  duty to provide information 187
  information disclosure by 167–168
  informed decision-making, role in 155–156
  option to comply with regulatory scheme 78
  and patient advocates 181–182
  perception of risk, contrast with recipient 26
  surveillance and monitoring role 197–198, 201
donor organs *see* organ donations

Ebola, as cross-species infection 20
enforcement
  issue of 190–191, 199–200, 206–207
  level of discussion as to effect 211–212
  powers in new legislation 228
  of surveillance contract 219–220
ethical guidance
  experimental procedures 76–77
  medical research 81–83
  offers of experimental procedures 93
  offers of medical research 95–97
ethical norms
  challenges to, main issues 150
  as theme of book 9–10
European Centre for Disease Prevention and Control
  role of 210
  website 210
European Commission, and precautionary principle 39
European Convention on Human Rights (ECHR)
  individual's rights to health 44
  public health powers compliance 43–44
  and surveillance regimes 229–232

284   Index

European Convention on Human Rights
    and Biomedicine, information
    disclosure guidance 168
European Union
    assisted reproductive technologies
        (ARTs) regulation 110
    definition of medicinal product 84
    gene therapy regulation 115–116
experimental procedures
    allotransplants classified as 66
    clinical trials distinguished 62
    doctors' aim in using 63–64
    doctors' decision to offer 75, 77, 79,
        92–93, 100–102 see also recipients,
        selection procedures
    ethical guidance 76–77
    focus on individual patient 62–64
    information disclosure requirements
        174
    interests involved 61
    law as to 70–75
    legal definitions as to 62–64
    as legal process for xenotransplantation
        79, 83–84, 131, 174
    and medical research, distinction 64–65,
        70–73
    offers of see offers of experimental
        procedures
    'one-off' procedures, legality 70–73
    outside clinical trials framework, legality
        73–74
    regulatory schemes 70–79
    review 73–74, 77
    and xenotransplantation 78–79
Expert Scientific Group, review of
    TGN1412 drug trial 186

Feinberg, Joel, notions of harm 40
first-party consent see consent
France
    assisted reproductive technologies
        (ARTs) regulation 107
    definition of xenotransplantation 2
    gene therapy regulation 113–114,
        115
    information disclosure guidance
        175
    xenotransplant regulation 121,
        135

gene therapy
    public involvement in decisions as
        to 51
    regulation
        emerging themes 117–119

    government committee
        recommendations 113–114
    international regulation 115–116
    NGOs' guidelines and reports
        114–115
    post-clinical 1990–2000 113–115
    pre-clinical 111–113
    statutory regulation 115
Gene Therapy Advisory Committee
    (GTAC)
    consent guidance, compliance with
        173–174
    counselling guidance 182
    establishment 113–114
    ethical review by 83–84, 86
    information disclosure guidance 173,
        187
    rejection of proposed procedure 174
General Medical Council (GMC)
    consent guidance 153, 165–166,
        169–170
    definition of medicinal product 85
    experimental procedures guidance 77
    information disclosure guidance 179
    vulnerable patients treatment guidance
        96
genetically engineered solid organ
    xenotransplants, legal definitions
    65–70
Germany
    gene therapy regulation 112, 115
    xenotransplant regulation 121, 136
global issues
    global regulation 143
    global risks as theme of book 10–11
    problems with regulation 138–140
Glover Report on new reproductive
    technologies 112
GM crops
    public involvement in decisions as to
        49–50
    public suspicion of 29

harm principle
    application of 39–40, 45, 235, 238
    Feinberg's notions of harm 40
    and precautionary principle 15, 39,
        57–58, 185, 231
    prevention of harm, issue of 4–5
    public health measures and 43–44
    and risk 23
    and xenotransplantation 40–42
health tourism
    discussions on 209
    problems with regulation 138–140

Index

health workers *see also* doctors
  occupational health service (OHS), access to 196–197
  surveillance of 196–197, 202–203
HIV/AIDS
  as cross-species infection 20
  deliberate infection with, criminal law sanctions 223
  latent effect 18
  retroviral action 20
Hong Kong, SARS epidemic 34
Human Fertilisation and Embryology Authority, establishment 107
human rights *see also* individual, rights of
  compliance of new legislation with 226
  consideration of 191
  limitation of 240–241
  Siracusa Principles, applicability of 232
  and surveillance 228
  as theme of book 11–12
Human T cell Lymphotropic Virus, as cross-species infection 20
hyperacute rejection (HAR) 16

ICH guidelines
  experimental procedures guidance 82
  information disclosure guidance 169
  vulnerable patients treatment guidance 96
immunological barriers 16–17
India, health tourism 139–140
individual patient *see also* recipients
  consent *see* consent
  focus of experimental procedures on 62–64
  and harm principle 39–40, 41–42
  imposition of risks on other persons, permissibility 90
  perception of risk
    changes in 26
    contrast with health professionals 26
  rights of
    infringement of, prohibition of xenotransplantation as 46–47
    interaction with public health 4–5, 6, 9, 15, 44, 151–154, 238
    see also surveillance and monitoring
    prioritisation of 238–239
    respect for 11–12
  relationship with doctor *see* doctors
infections
  control methods 189
  from pig organs *see* PERVs; pig organs
  risk, allotransplants and xenotransplants compared 133–134
  transmission of
    across species, examples 20
    potential for 21–23
    risk evaluation 19–21
influenza
  as cross-species infection 20
  speed of response to epidemics 210–211
information disclosure
  content of disclosure 168–172
  decision to disclose 167–168
  information overload, problem of 178–179
  plain English, use of 166
  to recipients 172–177
  standards for 166–179
informed consent *see* consent; decision-making process
innovative practice, legal definitions of 62–64
International Conference on Harmonisation of Technical Requirements for Registration of Pharmaceuticals for Human Use (ICH) *see* ICH guidelines
International Covenant on Civil and Political Rights, departure from 232
International Society for Heart and Lung Transplantation, xenotransplantation recommendations 123–124
International Xenotransplantation Association (IXA)
  on importance of public involvement 54
  surveillance guidance 213
  on withdrawal of consent 217
  on xenotransplantation monitoring 23
investigator, doctors' dual role 97, 101, 160
Ireland, 'significant risk' defined in case law 167
Italy, IVF code of practice 109
IVF, regulation of
  consent schemes, statutory regulation 187
  emerging themes 117–119
  government committee recommendations 107–108
  international regulation 110
  NGOs' guidelines and reports 108–109
  post-clinical 1978–1988 107–110
  pre-clinical 104–106
  recommendations by World Congress 110
  statutory regulation 109

Index

Japan, gene therapy regulation 114–115

known infections, transmission of, risk evaluation 19–21

legal definitions as to medical research 62–70
legal norms
  challenges to, main issues 150
  as theme of book 9–10
legislation *see* regulation
Louise Brown, birth of, regulatory response 106, 107–108

media
  and BSE crisis 34–35
  risk communication 26–28
  and SARS epidemic 34
medical research *see also* clinical trials; experimental procedures
  doctor–patient relationship 64–65
  ethical guidance 81–83
  and experimental procedures, distinction 64–65, 70–73
  form of statutory regime 62
  interests involved 61
  law as to 80
  legal definitions as to 62–70
  offers of *see* offers of medical research
  regulatory schemes 80–87
  and xenotransplantation 83–87
Medical Research Council (MRC)
  ethical review of experimental procedures 105
  IVF working group 105, 108
medicinal product, legal definitions 84–86
Medicines and Healthcare Products Regulation Agency (MHRA)
  authorisation of clinical trials 80, 83–84
  definition of medicinal product 85
Mexico, health tourism 139–140
microbiological barriers 18–19
Mill, John Stuart *see* harm principle
monitoring *see* surveillance and monitoring

National Expert Panel on New and Emerging Infections (NEPNEI), and xeno-tourism issue 209
National Institute for Health and Clinical Excellence (NICE)
  effectiveness of guidance 102
  experimental procedures guidance 93
  information disclosure guidance 170, 174
  notification to 174
  review of experimental procedures 73–74
National Research Ethics Service (NRES)
  consent guidance, compliance with 173–174
  information disclosure guidance 169, 187
  rejection of proposed procedure 174
  review by 83–84
Netherlands
  assisted reproductive technologies (ARTs) regulation 107
  gene therapy regulation 112, 113–114, 115
  information disclosure guidance 175
  IVF regulation 109
  surveillance guidance 198, 215
  third-party consent guidance 184–185
  xenotransplant regulation 121, 135–136
new variant CJD *see* CJD
New Zealand
  consent, independent person's role in procedure 181
  definition of xenotransplantation 2
  ethical review of experimental procedures 77
  information disclosure guidance 171, 175, 187
  innovative practice, definition 63–64
  NGOs' guidelines and reports 123
  review of experimental procedures 74
  surveillance guidance 208–209
  vulnerable patients treatment guidance 97
  xenotransplant regulation 122, 125, 134–135
Nipah virus, potential for infection 21
Norway
  IVF regulation 109
  surveillance guidance 208
  xenotransplant regulation 120–121
Nuffield Council on Bioethics
  consultation on xenotransplantation 123
  definition of xenotransplantation 65–66
  disregard of guidance from 87
  guidance on treatment of patients with no other hope 91
  human rights guidance 235
  information disclosure report 177, 178
  and precautionary principle 41
  public consultation 51
  risk management guidance 36

occupational health service (OHS), access to 196–197

Index

offers of experimental procedures
  ethical guidance 93
  law as to 92
  regulation of 92–94
  xenotransplantation 93–94
offers of medical research
  ethical guidance 95–97
  law as to 94–95
  regulation of 94–99
  and xenotransplantation 98–99
'one-off' procedures, legality of 70–73
organ donations
  pig organs *see* pig organs
  by recipients, surveillance of 200–201
  shortage of, xenotransplantation as viable solution 5, 14
organ rejection, types of 16
Organization for Economic Co-operation and Development (OECD)
  surveillance guidance 205, 210, 213
  'Ulysses contract' 219
  xenotransplant guidance 125–126

patient *see* individual patient
patient advocate, role of 181–182
pentosan polysulphate (PPS), legality of providing 67–69, 70–73
PERVs
  action of 19–20
  effects of 20
  infection from 19–21
  listing as notifiable disease 210
  potential for infection 21–23
physiological barriers 17–18
pig organs
  infection from *see also* PERVs
    microbiological risks 18–19
    unknown viruses 21
  physiological differences to human organs 17–18
  rejection 16–19
  as source of xeno-organs 16
Plain English Campaign, role in drafting patient information 166
Pontifical Academy for Life, recommendations on xenotransplantation 123
porcine endogenous retroviruses *see* PERVs
post-mortems of recipients, surveillance regimes 200–201
precautionary principle
  application of 37–39, 238
  clinical trials 57
  and decision-making 48–49, 58
  and harm principle 15, 39, 57–58, 185, 231
  SARS epidemic 232
  and xenotransplantation 40–42, 154, 231, 232
prohibition of developing technology
  as infringement of recipients' autonomy 46–47
  precedent for 45–46
public health issues
  aspects relevant to xenotransplantation 15
  characteristics of public health measures 43–44
  developments in approach to 43–45
  interaction with individual patient's rights 4–5, 6, 9, 15, 44, 151–154
  prioritisation of needs 238–239
  as theme of book 10–11
  and xenotransplantation 45–47
public health law, compliance via 220–223
public health measures
  and harm principle 43–44
  justificatory conditions 190
public involvement
  BSE crisis 29–35
  in consultation on xenotransplantation 51–54
  in decision-making process 47–57
  gap between expert and public perceptions of risk 26
  GM crops 29
  increase in consultation 7
  and individual's right to give consent 151–154
  need for consultation 6–7, 239–240
  and risk communication 25–26
  as theme of book 6–7
  trust and confidence issues as to risk 28–29
  understanding of science issues, need for 14
  'Xeno Nation' debate 55–56
  in xenotransplant decisions 54–57

recipients *see also* individual patient
  close contacts, surveillance of 195–196, 201–202
  consent, obtaining *see* consent
  existing protection, whether sufficient 4–5
  information disclosure to 172–177
  infringement of autonomy of 46–47
  perception of risk, contrast with health professionals 26

recipients (*cont.*)
  with no other hope
    allotransplants 89, 92
    benefit to, definition of 69
    competency for giving consent
      155–157, 166, 177–178
    competency status 157–159
    ethical guidance as to 93, 96–97
    health status 75, 77
    obtaining consent from, approach to
      180–181, 241
    selection of 61–62, 88–92, 97, 98–99
    vulnerable patients, definition of 93
  selection procedures
    regulation generally 87–92
    xenotransplantation 90–92
  surveillance of
    donations of blood, organs, etc. 200–201
    post-mortems 200–201
    sample storage 200–201
    sampling 193–195
    sexual activity 198–200
  vulnerable patients, definition of 93
regulation *see also* compliance;
    enforcement; legal norms;
    surveillance and monitoring
  approaches to devising 117–119, 243–246
  of consent *see* consent
  doctors' option to follow 78
  existing protection, whether sufficient
    4–5
  forms of 61
  gene therapy *see* gene therapy
  global issues *see* global issues
  and human rights *see* human rights
  IVF *see* IVF, regulation of
  legal definitions as to medical research
    62–70
  main issues 61–62, 103–104
  new legislation, introduction 226–228
  of offers of experimental procedures
    92–94
  of offers of medical research 94–99
  problems with regulation 103–104,
    138–143
  regulatory schemes 70–87
  review and recommendations for reform
    80
  of selection procedures 87–92
  strengthening of 242–243
  summary of issues 99–102, 144–147
  as theme of book 7–8
  xenotransplantation
    compliance via introduction of specific
      legislation 226–228

    development of regulation 119–127
    government committee
      recommendations 120–122
    implementation legislation 135–137
    implementation of recommendations
      127–138
    international implementing legislation
      137–138
    international regulation 125–127
    national committees 128–135
    NGOs' guidelines and reports 123–124
    pre-clinical 119–125
    statutory regulation 124–125
rejection of organs *see* organ rejection
reproductive cloning, prohibition of 45–46
research ethics committees (RECs)
  approval from 76, 79, 80, 81, 82, 94, 97
  consent guidance 164
  problems with 87
  review by 73, 77, 81, 83–84, 86, 96,
    98–99, 100
  role of 130–131
research not under 2004 Regulations
  consent 179
  information disclosure requirements 174
  as legal process for xenotransplantation
    83–84, 131, 174
retroviruses *see* PERVs
risk *see also* global issues
  assessment 19–42
  balance with benefits 14, 45, 66–69
  communication
    complexity of issues 24–25
    gap between expert and public
      perceptions 26
    by media 26–28
    public understanding of 25–26
  concept of 23–24
  decision-making categories 23–24, 36
  evaluation 19–23
  and harm 23
  main issues 14–16
  management 35–42, 238–240
    see also cost–benefit analysis;
      harm principle; precautionary
      principle
  management principles 35–36
  manufactured risk, xenotransplantation
    as 24
  need to address 237–238, 245
  perception of *see* individual patient
  and public health issues 43–47
  and public involvement 47–57
  regulation of, xenotransplantation as
    example of 4

Index

risk society concept (Beck) 14
significant risk, definition 167
summary of issues 57–60
technological risks, characteristics of 24
as theme of book 5–6
trust and confidence issues 28–29
Royal College of Obstetricians and Gynaecologists (RCOG), IVF guidelines 109
Royal College of Physicians (RCP)
  ethical review of experimental procedures 77
  information disclosure guidance 169, 170
  innovative practice guidance 64
  vulnerable patients treatment guidance 96

samples
  storage, surveillance of procedures 193–197
  taking of, surveillance of procedures 200–201
SARS epidemic
  ability to monitor 189–190
  media–government relationship 34
  and precautionary principle 232
  responses to 228
  speed of response 210–211
selection of recipients *see* recipients
Sense About Science
  establishment of 26
  report on presentation of treatment claims 157
sexual activity of recipients, surveillance of 198–200
significant risk, definition 167
Siracusa Principles, applicability 232
Spain
  assisted reproductive technologies (ARTs) regulation 107
  IVF regulation 109
  xenotransplant regulation 121, 128
Strategy Unit, risk management principles 35–36
surveillance and monitoring
  see also enforcement
  of archiving procedures 193–197
  of close contacts 195–196, 201–202
  compliance methods 217–228
  consent to 206–207, 211–217, 218–220
  doctors' role 197–198, 201, 217

and ECHR 229–232
effectiveness 205–208
of health workers 196–197, 202–203
and human rights 228
international collaboration, need for 190–191
international level 204–205
local level 192–203
main issues 189–191
national level 203–204
need for 189
post-2000 regimes 208–211
pre-2000 proposed regimes 191–205
publication of guidance 41, 191–192
of recipients 193–195, 197–201
  see also recipients
of sampling procedures 193–197
strengthening of 241–242
summary of issues 233–236
surveillance contract, enforcement 219–220
Sweden
  consent, independent person's role in procedure 181
  definition of xenotransplantation 2
  gene therapy regulation 113–114
  information disclosure guidance 175
  IVF regulation 109
  public consultation 53
  vulnerable patients treatment guidance 99
  xenotransplant regulation 120–121
swine flu
  as cross-species infection 20
  as pandemic 154
swine hepatitis E virus, potential for infection 21
Switzerland
  definition of xenotransplantation 2
  direct democracy 47
  IVF regulation 109
  xenotransplant regulation 121, 136–137

technological imperative 4, 12–13, 44–45
TGN1412 drug trial, suspension of 186
therapeutic research, definition of 65–66
third-party consent
  compliance 214–216
  need for 150
  procedure 183–185

transmission of infections
  potential for 21–23
  risk evaluation 19–21
transplant activity in UK 2
Transplantation Society, Ethics Committee guidelines 123, 124
trust, public *see* public involvement

'Ulysses contract' 219
UNESCO, declaration on the human genome 116
United Kingdom Xenotransplantation Interim Regulatory Authority (UKXIRA)
  abolition 87, 100, 129–130, 173, 192
  consent guidance 151, 165
  definition of therapeutic research 93–94
  establishment 41, 144–145
  guidance on xenotransplantation outside research 79
  human rights guidance 230
  information disclosure guidance 172–173
  patient advocate, role of 181
  publication of report 228–229
  purpose 86
  recipient selection guidance 98–99
  surveillance guidance
    close contacts 195–196, 201–202, 207
    consent and compliance 212–213
    donations of blood, organs, etc. 200–201
    effectiveness 205
    health workers 196, 202–203
    human rights 230
    local level generally 192–193
    national level 203–204
    post-mortems 201
    publication 41, 192
    recipients 193–194, 197–198, 209
    recipients' sexual activity 198–200
    third parties 215, 216
    tissue storage 201
    withdrawal of consent 216–217
  validity of guidance post-abolition 192
  vulnerable patients treatment guidance 98
  work 128–130
  and xeno-tourism issue 209
United States
  assisted reproductive technologies (ARTs) regulation 105–106
  Baby Fae case 92, 119
  concerns as to research 105
  counselling guidance 182
  definition of xenotransplantation 2
  experimental procedures, guidance 70, 100
  gene therapy regulation 111–113, 115
  guidance on treatment of patients with no other hope 90
  health tourism guidance 139–140
  human rights guidance 229
  industry guidance 141
  information disclosure guidance 170–171, 176–177, 178
  IVF guidelines 109
  IVF regulation 109
  Model State Emergency Health Plan Act 227
  NGOs' guidelines and reports 123
  patient advocate, role of 181
  public consultation 55
  public health statutes, effectiveness for xenotransplantation regulation 223
  surveillance guidance
    close contacts 195, 201–202
    consent and compliance 212–213
    donations of blood, organs, etc. 200–201
    health workers 196–197, 202–203
    human rights 229
    local level generally 192–193
    national level 203
    post-mortems 201
    publication 192
    recipients 194–195, 197–198
    recipients' sexual activity 198–200
    third parties 214, 215
  vulnerable patients treatment guidance 99
  xenotransplant regulation 124–125, 131–132
unknown infections, transmission of, risk evaluation 21

vCJD *see* CJD
vulnerable patients, definition 93
  see also recipients with no other hope

Warnock Committee, report 107
websites
  European Centre for Disease Prevention and Control 210
  WHO xenotransplantation inventory 209
World Congress on IVF, recommendations 110

Index

World Health Assembly (WHA), xenotransplant guidance 125–126
World Health Organization (WHO)
  counselling guidance 182
  definition of xenotransplantation 2
  experimental procedures guidance 66, 76, 100
  guidance on risk evaluation 82
  human rights guidance 229
  information disclosure guidance 169
  International Health Regulations 211
  principles on xenotransplants, UK compliance with 83–84
  surveillance guidance 205, 206, 210, 242
  'Ulysses contract' 219
  vulnerable patients treatment guidance 93, 95–96, 98
  xenotransplant guidance 125–126, 137–138
  xenotransplantation inventory website 209

'Xeno Nation' debate 55–56
xeno-recipients *see* recipients
xeno-tourism
  discussions on 209
  problems with regulation 138–140

xenotransplantation
  barriers to successful transplant 3–4, 16–19
  consent *see* consent
  definitions 1–2
  and ethical norms *see* ethical norms
  focus on 4–5
  and human rights *see* human rights
  and individual rights *see* individual, rights of
  legal methods for performing 83–84, 173–175
  and legal norms *see* legal norms
  potential benefits 3
  process of 1–4
  public health issues *see* public health issues
  public involvement *see* public involvement
  purpose of book 1, 12–13
  recipients *see* recipients
  regulation of *see* regulation
  results to date 15
  risks from *see* global issues; risk
  science of 16–19
  summary of issues 237–246
  technological imperative 4, 12–13
  themes of book 5–12
  as viable solution to donor shortage 5